ESSEX
'full of profitable thinges'

Colonel Sir John Ruggles-Brise, Bt., C.B., O.B.E., D.Univ., T.D., J.P.
(Chelmsford Borough Council)

ESSEX
'full of profitable thinges'

Essays presented to
SIR JOHN RUGGLES-BRISE
*as a tribute to his life of service to
the people and County of Essex*

Edited by
Kenneth Neale

LEOPARD'S HEAD PRESS
1996

First published in 1996 by
Leopard's Head Press Limited
1–5 Broad Street, Oxford OX1 3AW

© Kenneth Neale 1996

ISBN 0 904920 36 4

Illustration on title-page:
Crest of the armorial bearings of Ruggles-Brise.
The Patent blazons the crest 'for the Crest of
Brise . . . A demi-crocodile Sable and for the
Crest of Ruggles . . . In front of twelve Arrows in
Saltire proper heads outwards a Tower Or
inflamed proper'. The Motto is 'Struggle'.

Typeset by Denham House, Yapton, West Sussex
and printed in Great Britain by
Progressive Printing (UK) Limited, Leigh-on-Sea, Essex

Contents

List of Illustrations, Maps and Tabulations

List of Subscribers

Abbott, Mrs J. I., 5 Colvin Close, Colchester, Essex.
Aberdour, Mrs J. R., The Old Rectory, Wickham Bishops, Witham, Essex.
Acres, Dr D. I., C.B.E., J.P., D.L., Thundersley Lodge, Runnymede Chase,
    Thundersley, Benfleet, Essex.
Acton, Mrs D. M., 26 Holmwood Avenue, Shenfield, Brentwood, Essex.
Adams, P., Pightle Cottage, Finchingfield, Braintree, Essex.
Adelaide, University of, Barr Smith Library, Adelaide, South Australia 5005,
    Australia.
Allnutt, Dr A. J., Woodside, Old Perry Street, Chislehurst, Kent.
Appleby, J. S., F.R.Hist.S., Little Pitchbury, Brick Kiln Lane,
    Great Horkesley, Colchester, Essex.
Arthur, A. J. V., M.B.E., D.L., Mount Maskell, Boreham, Chelmsford,
    Essex.
Astor, M. D., 8 Banyard Way, Rochford, Essex.

Baker, Mr and Mrs A., Range House, 57 Victoria Drive, Great Wakering,
    Southend-on-Sea, Essex.
Bamberger, P. A. L., 3 Parsonage Street, Halstead, Essex.
Bankes-Jones, Mrs R. J., The Old Rose, Littlebury Green, Saffron Walden,
    Essex.
Banks, Mrs E. L., Cobblers Croft, Great Sampford, Saffron Walden, Essex.
Barker, Miss A. E., 26 Swanage Road, Southend-on-Sea, Essex.
Barker, A. P., c/o Department of Government, University of Essex,
    Colchester, Essex.
Barking and District Historical Society, c/o Mrs T. Runchman,
    83 Clyde Way, Romford, Essex.
Barking and Dagenham, London Borough of, Central Library, Barking,
    Essex.
Barraclough, Lt. Col. M. C., M.C., O.B.E., Ivy Cottage, Mill Green,
    Ingatestone, Essex.
Bascombe, Dr K. N., M.A., D.Phil., 25 Monkswood Avenue,
    Waltham Abbey, Essex.
Baxendale, A. S., 164 Tolmers Road, Cuffley, Hertfordshire.
Beale, Mr and Mrs J. E. M., The Laurels, The Street, Great Waltham,
    Chelmsford, Essex.

Beer, N. F., 13 Nelson Road, Rayleigh, Essex.
Bekker, Mrs K. A., The Wing Brakeys, Mowden Hall Lane,
    Hatfield Peverel, Chelmsford, Essex.
Bell, Ms., E.
Belverstone, A. W. G., 61 Malford Grove, South Woodford, London.
Bendall, Dr A. S., Merton College, Oxford.
Berry, Mrs M., 10 Blackheath, Colchester, Essex.
Bettley, J., The Old Vicarage, Great Totham, Maldon, Essex.
Bigmore, Mr and Mrs T. J., Hilltop, Bardfield Road, Finchingfield,
    Braintree, Essex.
Binder, F. G., Rosecroft, Moreton, Ongar, Essex.
Bircher, D. E., 52 St. Andrews Road, Boreham, Chelmsford, Essex.
Bond, R. H., 88 Sandford Road, Chelmsford, Essex.
Boorer, Miss J. F., 8 Regency Close, Chelmsford, Essex.
Booty, S. C. H., St. Marks Apartments (B), St. Marks Street, Peterborough.
Bostock, A. J., 8 Avocet Drive, Swanlow, Winsford, Cheshire.
Bostridge, P. J., The Diary, Melton Park, Melton Constable, Norfolk.
Braybrooke, The Rt. Hon. Lord, Abbey House, Audley End,
    Saffron Walden, Essex.
Brentwood, The Rt. Revd. The Bishop of, McMahon, The Rt. Revd. T.,
    Bishop's House, Stock, Ingatestone, Essex.
Brentwood School, c/o The Bursar, Ingrave Road, Brentwood, Essex.
Bretton, J., 4 Lincoln Park, Amersham, Buckinghamshire.
Brodie, Mrs E. E., 1 Sir William Petre Almshouses, High Street,
    Ingatestone, Essex.
Brooker, A. B., J.P., D.L., Plowlands, Laundry Lane, Little Easton,
    Dunmow, Essex.
Broughton, Mrs U. A., Farthings, Layer Breton, Colchester, Essex.
Brown, A. J. F., 182 Lexden Road, Colchester, Essex.
Brown, I. A., 56 Overton Drive, Wanstead, London E11.
Brown, N. R., 14 The Chase, Boreham, Chelmsford, Essex.
Buchan, Mrs I. V. R.
Buggey, R. F. W., B.Sc.(Econ.), F.G.S., Oak Lodge, Denmark Street,
    Diss, Norfolk.
Burrow, J. H., C.B.E., Chief Constable's Office, Police Headquarters,
    P.O. Box 2, Springfield, Chelmsford, Essex.
Burton, B., 56 Daiglen Drive, South Ockendon, Essex.
Burton, J. T. A., 5 Quendon Drive, Waltham Abbey, Essex.
Butler, D. B., 52 Clacton Road, St. Osyth, Essex.
Butler, P. M., Little Silvers, 7 Mendoza Close, Hornchurch, Essex.
Butler, R., 14 Marlowe Way, Lexden, Colchester, Essex.
Buxton, The Rt. Hon. Lord, M.C., D.L., Old Hall Farm, Stiffkey, Norfolk.
Byrne, B. L., 108 Elmore Drive, Acton, Ontario, Canada.

Caldecourt, Mrs F. M., Haddon Close, Northop Road, Clwyd.

Cardwell, Mrs C. M. I., Street Farm, Rumburgh, Halesworth, Suffolk.

Carpenter, Dr P. K., 24 Windsor Road, Bristol, Avon.

Cassidy, R. J., B.A., L.R.A.M., A.R.C.M., L.T.C.L., A.C.P., Fernside, Copthall Green, Upshire, Waltham Abbey, Essex.

Chalmers, Mr and Mrs J. R., 4 Janmead, Hutton, Brentwood, Essex.

Charlton, R. T. S., 4 Nesta Road, Woodford Green, Essex.

Cheesman, Mrs R. S., c/o 4 Truro Path, Toothill, Swindon, Wiltshire.

Chelmsford Cathedral Library, Guy Harlings, New Street, Chelmsford, Essex.

Chelmsford, The Rt. Revd. The Lord Bishop of, Waine, The Rt. Revd. J., B.A., Bishopscourt, Main Road, Margaretting, Ingatestone, Essex.

Chichester Institute of Higher Education, Bishop Otter Campus, College Lane, Chichester, West Sussex.

Chigwell School, c/o The Librarian, Chigwell, Essex.

Chissell, P. J., Oaktree House, 96 Candlemas Lane, Beaconsfield, Buckinghamshire.

Chittenden, Mrs B. F., 69 Victoria Road, Maldon, Essex.

Chown, C. H. I., Uplands, Tomkyns Lane, Upminster Common, Essex.

Clark, H. L., Timbers, Lower Howe Street, Finchingfield, Braintree, Essex.

Clark, J., Cranleigh, Debden Green, Saffron Walden, Essex.

Clark, Dr M., M.P., Rochford Hall, Hall Road, Rochford, Essex.

Clark, M. W., C.B.E., D.L., Braxted Park, Witham, Essex.

Clarke, D. T.-D., M.A., F.M.A., F.S.A., F.R.N.S., 1 Orchard Close, Combe, Witney, Oxfordshire.

Clarke, Mrs J. D., Belbyne, Howe Street, Finchingfield, Braintree, Essex.

Clements, Mr and Mrs G. J., Dripping Pan Cottage, 20 Second Avenue, Chelmsford, Essex.

Clifford, Mrs F. M. P., Hydon House, Little Edge, Eyam, Sheffield.

Clough, Mr and Mrs D. I., 12 Wellstead Gardens, Westcliff-on-Sea, Essex.

Cluney, Mr and Mrs M., 109 Essex Road, Barking, Essex.

Coales, J., F.S.A., The Mount, Parsonage Hill, Somerton, Somerset.

Coe, S. R. E., 15A Horace Road, Billericay, Essex.

Coker, Miss B. A., B.Ed., 46 St. Bartholomew's Road, East Ham, London.

Colchester Archaeological Group, c/o A. J. Fawn, 2 Silvanus Close, Colchester, Essex.

Cole, Mr and Mrs W., Beddalls, Vicarage Road, Finchingfield, Braintree, Essex.

Collins, G. R., 51 Southview Drive, South Woodford, London E18.

Collis, J. R., Start Farm, Magdalen Laver, Ongar, Essex.

Condliffe, Mrs J., Coppingers, Maldon Road, Latchingdon, Chelmsford, Essex.

Cook, Mr and Mrs K. A., 38 Victoria Road, Maldon, Essex.

Cook, S. G., 20 Cautley Close, Quainton, Aylesbury, Buckinghamshire.

Cooper, A., Hill Farm, Gestingthorpe, Halstead, Essex.

Cooper, Mrs J., 24 Pelham Road, Clavering, Saffron Walden, Essex.

Cooper, Dr J. M., M.A., Ph.D., F.S.A., F.R.Hist.S., c/o Victoria County History of Essex, 70 Duke Street, Chelmsford, Essex.

Cooper, Mrs W. B., M.B.E., 5 Church Street, Harwich, Essex.

Copeland, J. W. J., 20 The Vale, Brentwood, Essex.

Corder-Birch, A., F.Inst.L.Ex., M.I.C.M., The Maltings, North End Road, Little Yeldham, Halstead, Essex.

Corder-Birch, Mrs P., The Maltings, North End Road, Little Yeldham, Halstead, Essex.

Courtauld, G., Knights Farm, Colne Engaine, Earls Colne, Essex.

Cox, Miss E. M. T., 91 Old Road, Harlow, Essex.

Crellin, M. S., Elm House, Rookery Road, Monewden, Woodbridge, Suffolk.

Cross, Mr and Mrs M. R., Monks Cottage, Great Sampford, Saffron Walden, Essex.

Culham, Mr and Mrs C., 58 Howard Agne Close, Bovingdon, Hertfordshire.

Curnock, Major P. L., The Red House, 11 South Entrance, Saxmundham, Suffolk.

Cuthbert, G. W. C., 6 Finchingfield Road, Steeple Bumpstead, Haverhill, Suffolk.

Daniels, Ms B., 34 Rayfield Close, Barnston, Dunmow, Essex.

Dare, E. H., 21 Ibbetson Path, Loughton, Essex.

Davies, Mrs C. H., Castle View Villas, 29 Castle Road, Colchester, Essex.

Davies, Mrs E. H., 15 Wennington Road, Southport, Merseyside.

Delderfield, R. B., 1 Marlin Close, Daws Heath, Benfleet, Essex.

Denney, P. S., 247 Old Heath Road, Colchester, Essex.

Dennison, Mrs M. J.

Devonish, L. A., 118 Dugdale Hill Lane, Potters Bar, Hertfordshire.

Dickinson, H. O., 25A Lindsey Street, Epping, Essex.

Dodd, R., 35 Gravel Hill Terrace, Boxmoor, Hemel Hempstead, Hertfordshire.

Doe, Mrs J. L., Woodham Mortimer Hall, Maldon Road, Woodham Mortimer, Maldon, Essex.

Doye, P. F., 22 Monkhams Drive, Woodford Green, Essex.

Dryhurst, Mrs J., 80 Kelvedon Close, Chelmsford, Essex.

Duffin, Dr G. F., Chandlers, Station Road, Chipping Campden, Gloucestershire.

Dunmow and District Historical and Literary Society, c/o Mrs S. E. Fletcher, The Old Vicarage, Lindsell, Dunmow, Essex.

Durgan, Mrs S., c/o Victoria County History of Essex, 70 Duke Street, Chelmsford, Essex.

Eaton, Mrs M. E., 10017 11th Avenue N.W., Seattle, Washington 206782, U.S.A.

Eckert, Ms M.-S., 12 Rue Massenet, F67000, Strasbourg, France.

Edkins, Mrs C., 15 Alwyne Avenue, Shenfield, Essex.

Edwards, D. A. W., Mardens, Little Sampford, Essex.

Edwards, Mrs D. M., 6 More Road, Godalming, Surrey.

Edwards, Mrs N. R., M.A., F.S.A., 43 Maltese Road, Chelmsford, Essex.

Elphick, D. J., Saint Alphege, Exton, Exeter, Devon.

Emery, D. J., 18 Gilmore Way, Great Baddow, Chelmsford, Essex.

Emery, M. A.

Enticknap, Dr J. B., 37 Bridewell Street, Clare, Sudbury, Suffolk.

Epping Forest District Museum, 39–41 Sun Street, Waltham Abbey, Essex.

Essex County Council, Chelmsford Area Library, P.O. Box 882, Market Road, Chelmsford, Essex.

Essex County Council, Colchester Area, Colchester Library, Trinity Square, Colchester, Essex.

Essex County Council, Epping Forest Area, Loughton Library, Traps Hill, Loughton, Essex.

Essex County Council, Greenstead Library, Hawthorn Avenue, Colchester, Essex.

Essex County Council, Harlow Area, Harlow Central Library, The High, Harlow, Essex.

Essex County Council, Tendring Area, Clacton Library, Station Road, Clacton-on-Sea, Essex.

Essex County Council, Wickford Library, Market Road, Wickford, Essex.

Essex County Council, Witham Area Library, 18 Newland Street, Witham, Essex.

Essex County Council, Planning Department, County Hall, Chelmsford, Essex.

Evans, D. W. R., D.L., Ridley Hall, Terling, Chelmsford, Essex.

Evans, Mrs M. E. D., Homeland, Bunbury Heath, Tarporley, Cheshire.

Eve, Mrs M. M., Carters, Station Road, Wickham Bishops, Witham, Essex.

Fairhurst, M. D., 46 Gaysham Avenue, Gants Hill, Ilford, Essex.

Fawn, A. J., 2 Silvanus Close, Colchester, Essex.

Fawcett, Mrs C. E., 8 Langton Close, Barton-on-Sea, New Milton, Hampshire.

Flaxman, C., F.R.S.A., Yeoman's, Hempstead, Essex.

Fletcher, Mr and Mrs K. W. R., The Old Vicarage, Lindsell, Dunmow, Essex.

Foley, P., 104 Cobham Road, Seven Kings, Ilford, Essex.

Fordham, Miss D. C., The Ferns, 163 Southwood Lane, London N6.

Fossick, W. G., The Grange, Greenstead Green, Halstead, Essex.

Fox, Dr A. W., 45 Cranham Gardens, Cranham, Upminster, Essex.

Francis, L. A. W., 81 Warren Road, Wanstead, London E11.
Freeman, C. P., Oron, 11 Avenue Road, Chelmsford, Essex.
Freeman, Miss E., B.A.(Cantab.), Wren House, 77 Ballingdon Street,
    Sudbury Suffolk.
French, Dr C. C. J., 303 Upper Shoreham Road, Shoreham-by-Sea, West Sussex.
Froom, A. J., Lindfield, 84 Fambridge Road, Maldon, Essex.
Frost, K. A., 3 Balmoral Road, Romford, Essex.
Fuller, D. W., Manor House Barn, Quendon, Saffron Walden, Essex.
Fuller, R. H., Tewes Farm, Little Sampford, Saffron Walden, Essex.
Fuller, R. H., 12 Field Road, Aveley, South Ockendon, Essex.
Fullerton, D., 33 Woodcroft Avenue, Mill Hill, London NW7.

Gallifant, D. W., Phaeton House, 8A High Street, West Mersea, Colchester,
    Essex.
Gentry, E., 11A Linkside Road, Bishops Stortford, Hertfordshire.
George, Mr and Mrs B. F. H., 9 Knighton Lane, Buckhurst Hill, Essex.
Gepp, T. C., T.D., D.L., M.A., Lane House, 2 Maberly Court, Castle Hill,
    Saffron Walden, Essex.
Gervers, Dr M., c/o Deeds Project, University of Toronto, Room 14290,
    Robarts Library, 130 St. George Street, Toronto, Ontario, Canada.
Gibbs, G. A., 18 Nairn House, Cameron Close, Brentwood, Essex.
Giles, S. C., Flat 3, 51 Waterloo Street, Hove, East Sussex.
Giles, P. A., 23 The Paddocks, Witham, Essex.
Gilham, Mrs D., Pentlow Hall, Cavendish, Sudbury, Suffolk.
Girling, Mrs S. J., 49 St. Peter's Road, Stowmarket, Suffolk.
Gonsa, Dr H., Troststrasse 98/3/20, A-1100 Vienna, Austria.
Green, Mrs G., 24 Henry's Walk, Hainault, Ilford, Essex.
Grey, W. P. C., Kemerton, Walcot Road, Ufford, Stamford, Lincolnshire.
Gowlett, Captain G. P., Green Corner, The Downs, Great Dunmow, Essex.
Great Bardfield Historical Society, c/o Halfhide, G. B., Old White Hart,
    Brook Street, Great Bardfield, Braintree, Essex.
Gregory, Mr and Mrs A., New Place, Bardfield Road, Finchingfield,
    Braintree, Essex.
Griffin, C. D. C., 31 Tunstall Avenue, Hainault, Ilford, Essex.
Griggs, C. L., 20 The Close, Clayton, Doncaster, South Yorkshire.
Griggs, D. F., 41 Wadeville Avenue, Chadwell Heath, Romford, Essex.
Grosvenor, W. J., Serendipity, Brent Mill Drive, Brent Eleigh, Suffolk.
Gunby, A. N., 31 Falmouth Gardens, Redbridge, Ilford, Essex.
Gunning, G. D., B.A.(Hons.), F.R.T.P.I., 2A Mill Lane, Broomfield,
    Chelmsford, Essex.

Hall, Revd. B. G., Harvard Cottage, Swan Lane, Stock, Ingatestone, Essex.
Hall, K., B.A.(Hons.), D.A.A., The Cottage, Sparepenny Lane,
    Great Sampford, Saffron Walden, Essex.

Hall, R., 2 High Tenterfell, Kendal, Cumbria.

Hammond, Mr and Mrs G. R., 4 Church Lane, Springfield, Chelmsford, Essex.

Hance, Mrs E. L., M.B.E., J.P., 384 Baddow Road, Chelmsford, Essex.

Harcombe, Mr and Mrs N., 76 Western Road, Romford, Essex.

Hardy, Mr and Mrs C., Vespers, Bardfield Road, Finchingfield, Braintree, Essex.

Harris, Mrs J. M., Barfields, Barling Road, Barling Magna, Southend-on-Sea, Essex.

Harrold, C., M.A., C.Chem., F.R.S.C., 6 Bradleigh Avenue, Grays Thurrock, Essex.

Harvey, G. W., 22 Meadowfield, Bradford-on-Avon, Wiltshire.

Havering, London Borough of, Central Library, St. Edward's Way, Romford, Essex.

Hawker, M. O., 2 Daen Ingas, Danbury, Essex.

Hawkes, P. E., Greenfields, Felsted, Dunmow, Essex.

Haylock, D. A., Hill Farm, Hempstead, Saffron Walden, Essex.

Hayward, Mrs L. S., 39 Acaster Lane, Bishopsthorpe, York.

Hazell, Mrs O. W. G., 118 Braiswick, Colchester, Essex.

Heal, Mrs P. F., Beards Farm, Herstmonceux, Hailsham, East Sussex.

Hearn, W. S., 35 Glenthorne Gardens, Ilford, Essex.

Hearsum, Mrs M. C., 36 Avenue Road, Harold Wood, Essex.

Hellen, Mrs J., Rumbolds, Frimley, Camberley, Surrey.

Henrys, R. E., 56 The Paddocks, Ingatestone, Essex.

Herrmann, F., F.S.A., West Bowers Hall, Woodham Walter, Maldon, Essex.

Hessayon, Dr D. G., Sloe House, Halstead, Essex.

Hilliar, Miss K. M., 42A Moulsham Drive, Chelmsford, Essex.

Hollings, Mr and Mrs J. A., Leycam, Finchingfield Road, Great Sampford, Saffron Walden, Essex.

Hopper, Col. P. D. L., D.L., Rose Lodge, Tea Kettle Lane, Stetchworth, Newmarket, Suffolk.

Horne, Mrs I. C., 3 Rye Close, Hatfield Peverel, Chelmsford, Essex.

Horne, S. D., Tewes, Little Sampford, Saffron Walden, Essex.

Houghton, G. A., 31 Aldeburgh Way, Springfield, Chelmsford, Essex.

Howes, Mr and Mrs J. W., 97 Staples Road, Loughton, Essex.

Hoy, Mr and Mrs D. L., 7 Park Crescent, Enfield, Middlesex.

Hudd, Dr N. P., 13 Elmfield, Tenterden, Kent.

Huddlestone, Mr and Mrs R., 1 Homebridge, Great Sampford, Saffron Walden, Essex.

Hughes, Miss B. M., 2 Freshwell Street, Saffron Walden, Essex.

Hughes, Mrs P. T., Great Clerkes Farm, Little Sampford, Saffron Walden, Essex.

Hume, C. J., 28 Howard Road, Ilford, Essex.

Hurrell, D. J., 241 Main Road, Broomfield, Chelmsford, Essex.

Imbush, Revd. B., 14 Martyns Grove, Westcliff-on-Sea, Essex.
Imbush, K., 50A Selwyn Avenue, Highams Park, London E4.
Ives, Miss J. and Miss M., 5 Parsonage Terrace, Vicarage Road, Finchingfield, Braintree, Essex.

Jarratt, Sir A. A., C.B., D.L., Barn Mead, Fryerning, Essex.
Jarvis, L. D., J.P., A.R.Hist.Soc., Middlesex Cottage, 86 Mill Road, Stock, Ingatestone, Essex.
Jarvis, R. L., 29 Grantley Close, Shalford, Surrey.
Jarvis, Mrs V. E. M., Risbygate, Carlton Road, Manby, Louth, Lincolnshire.
Jeff, Mr and Mrs F. A., Brick House Farm, South Fambridge, Rochford, Essex.
Jemmett, R., 9 High Street, Saffron Walden, Essex.
Jenkins, G., 17 Manor Road, Stanford-le-Hope, Essex.
Johnson, H. E. A., Saling Hall, Great Saling, Braintree, Essex.
Jones, A. D., 7 Cotswold Drive, Long Melford, Sudbury, Suffolk.
Jones, C. R., 4 Scott Drive, Lexden, Colchester, Essex.
Jones, Mrs J., Weir Bank Lodge, Monkey Island Lane, Bray, Maidenhead, Berkshire.
Jones-Baker, Dr D. W., M.A., Ph.D., F.S.A., F.R.S.A., Lamb Cottage, Whitwell, Hitchin, Hertfordshire.

Keary, Miss E. M. H., 8 Queen's Road, Brentwood, Essex.
Keeling, D. F., 4 Wigram Road, Wanstead, London E11.
Kerr, Mrs A. C., Rook Hall, Finchingfield, Braintree, Essex.
Kingston, D. A. L., Dunkery, 21 St. James Gardens, Westcliff-on-Sea, Essex.
Kirby, Prof. and Mrs D. P., Manoravon, Llanon, Ceredigion, Wales.
Knight, M. H., 11 Russell Kerr Close, Chiswick, London W4.

Lamb, Mrs E., 3 Garwoods, Norton Mandeville, Ingatestone, Essex.
Langstaff, R. D., The Plow, The Street, High Roding, Dunmow, Essex.
Laurie, Col. R. P., O.B.E., J.P., D.L., Heatley's, Ingrave, Brentwood, Essex.
Law, A. D., A.M.A., Clydfan, Tegryn, Llanfyrnach, Dyfed.
Lawrence, P., 273 St. Barnabas Road, Woodford Green, Essex.
Lawes, E. K., 22 Geddington Road, Grafton Underwood, Northamptonshire.
Leadbetter, Ms G., 9 Higham Station Avenue, Chingford, London E4.
Lee, R. J. H., White House Farm, Little Sampford, Saffron Walden, Essex.
Leslie, D. A., 57 Washington Road, Maldon, Essex.
Lewis, Lady, 39 West Street, Harwich, Essex.
Lewis, Mrs L., M.A., F.S.A., 38 Whitelands House, Cheltenham Terrace, London SW3.
Lloyd, R. J., 1 Eastacre, Chater's Hill, Saffron Walden, Essex.
Lockwood, Mr and Mrs H. H., 10 Alloa Road, Goodmayes, Ilford, Essex.

London, Corporation of, Bibliographical Services Section, City of London Libraries, Guildhall Library, London EC2.

Long, P., 38 Park Road, Wivenhoe, Colchester, Essex.

Lyster, A. St. G., Clay Hill Cottage, Great Henny, Sudbury, Suffolk.

Lyster, P. H., Little Chishill Manor, Royston, Hertfordshire.

Macdonald-Milne, Revd. B. J., M.A., The Rectory, Walden Road, Radwinter, Saffron Walden, Essex.

Macallan, Mrs M., 22 Lexden Road, Colchester, Essex.

McLaren, Mr and Mrs D. J., Hill Farm, Great Sampford, Saffron Walden, Essex.

Mackley, Dr A. L., 1 Angel Lane, Blythburgh, Halesworth, Suffolk.

Maldon Archaeological Group, Unit 2, Brickhouse Farm Community Centre, Marlowe Close, Maldon, Essex.

Males, R. M., 27 Sandton Road, Sentosa, Harare, Zimbabwe.

Mallinson, Mrs A. M. B., 28 Albion Street, London W2.

Manning-Press, Lt. Col. C. B., D.L., 14 The Avenue, Colchester, Essex.

Marson, G. L., M.A., F.R.G.S., Dip.Ed., 31 Westmoreland Avenue, Hornchurch, Essex.

Mascall, A. L., 50 Moorside Road, West Cross, Swansea.

Mason, Dr A. S., M.A., M.D., F.R.C.P., Pelham, 61A Main Road, Gidea Park, Essex.

Matthew, L. R., 191 Clockhouse Lane, Collier Row, Romford, Essex.

Matthews, Mr and Mrs J., White House, Howe Street, Finchingfield, Braintree, Essex.

Matthews, Miss V. J., 90 Bradleigh Avenue, Grays Thurrock, Essex.

Matthews, Dr R. M. S., M.B., A.R.Hist.S., 2 Repton Avenue, Gidea Park, Essex.

Mendelsson, W., 57 Leeside Crescent, Golders Green, London.

Millidge, Miss M. P., M.B.E., 27 Feering Hill, Feering, Colchester, Essex.

Monk, Mrs P. M., Eleys Farm, Roxwell, Chelmsford, Essex.

Moore, P. J., The Old Granary, Justice Wood, Polstead, Suffolk.

Moses, The Very Revd. Dr J. H., B.A., Ph.D., c/o The Cathedral Office, Guy Harlings, 53 New Street, Chelmsford, Essex.

Musson, J. L., 41 Moss Bank, Meesons Lane, Grays Thurrock, Essex.

Neale, Mr and Mrs K. J., Honeysuckle Cottage, Great Sampford, Saffron Walden, Essex.

Newens, A. S., M.E.P., The Leys, 18 Park Hill, Harlow, Essex.

Newman, R. G., D.L., Panfield Hall, Panfield, Braintree, Essex.

Newton, Mr and Mrs B., 32 Lavender Hill, Enfield, Middlesex.

Nicholson, Mrs V. F., The Old Rectory, Birdbrook, Halstead, Essex.

Nixon, G. M. B., Snowdrop Cottage, Great Sampford, Saffron Walden, Essex.

Norris, J. H. M., C.B.E., D.L., Mountnessing Hall, Brentwood, Essex.
Nugent, Miss M. C. R., 27 Courtlands, Patching Hall Lane, Chelmsford,
    Essex.

Oliver, Mrs R. J.
Osgood, Ms L., 48 King George's Field, Stow-on-the-Wold, Cheltenham,
    Gloucestershire.
Oxley, M. R., 2 The Downs, Great Dunmow, Essex.

Paget, Mrs V. A., Templewood Gate House, Northrepps, Cromer, Norfolk.
Pankhurst, C. J., 750 Foxhall Road, Ipswich, Suffolk.
Pamplin, Miss M. E. A., 43 Mill Road, Lode, Cambridgeshire.
Parsons, J. F., 15 Strouden Avenue, Bournemouth.
Patient, J. A., 4 Ingrebourne Gardens, Upminster, Essex.
Paul, W. N., 32 Watermans, Junction Road, Romford, Essex.
Pennington, Mrs J. V., Penfold Lodge, 17A High Street, Steyning, West Sussex.
Petre, The Rt. Hon. Lord, Writtle Park, Highwood, Chelmsford, Essex.
Pewsey, S., c/o 1112 Green Lane, Dagenham, Essex.
Pitcher, Mrs J. R., 26 Trent Close Stevenage, Hertfordshire.
Pittman, Mrs S., 27 Old Chapel Road, Crockenhill, Swanley, Kent.
Playfair, R. D., Woodhouse Farm, Pattiswick, Braintree, Essex.
Poynter, D. A. H., Martins Cottage, Matching Green, Harlow, Essex.
Pond, Dr C. C., M.A.(Cantab.), Forest Villa, Staples Road, Loughton, Essex.
Potts, Mrs P. E., 12 Keene Way, Galleywood, Chelmsford, Essex.
Prowse, M. J., Craiglea, 30 Abercromby Road, Castle, Douglas, Isle of Man.
Pryor, Miss J. E., 69 West Drayton Road, Hillingdon, Uxbridge, Middlesex.

Ramsay, Mrs M., 35 Newbiggen Street, Thaxted, Essex.
Rawlingson, K. A., 18 Twyford Avenue, Great Wakering, Southend-on-Sea,
    Essex.
Redbridge Libraries, London Borough of.
Reed, Major J. L., North Farm, Theydon Mount, Epping, Essex.
Reeve, Ms M.
Robinson, Dr D. B., c/o Surrey Record Office, County Hall,
    Kingston-upon-Thames, Surrey.
Richards, Dr P. R., 19B Queen Street, King's Lynn, Norfolk.
Richardson, Mr and Mrs J. C., Crest Lodge, Spains Hall Farm, Finchingfield,
    Braintree, Essex.
Rider, Ms M., 4 Vernon Avenue, Hooton, South Wirral.
Ridgewell, Mrs J., 15 Kempe Road, Finchingfield, Braintree, Essex.
Rippon, P. T., J.P., D.L., Little Orchards, Broomfield, Chelmsford, Essex.
Robertson, I. G., M.A., F.M.A., c/o The National Army Museum,
    Royal Hospital Road, Chelsea, London.
Robertson, Miss P., 5 Holly Close, Burnham-on-Crouch, Essex.

Robson, W. D., The Woods, Hatfield Broad Oak, Bishops Stortford, Hertfordshire.
Roche, N., 135 Auckland Road, Ilford, Essex.
Rochford Hundred Historical Society, Rochford, Essex.
Rodwell, Dr W. J., M.A., D.Phil., D.L.C., F.S.A., F.S.A.Scot.,
    The Old Vicarage, Stockhill Road, Downside, Chilcompton, Somerset.
Rose, M. T., c/o Elm Grove House, Elm Grove, Saffron Walden, Essex.
Round, Lt. Col. J. G., O.B.E., J.P., D.L., Bailey Meadow House, Birch,
    Colchester, Essex.
Rowland, A. C., 20 Shalbourne Rise, Camberley, Surrey.
Ruffle, Ms M., 9 Robletts Villas, Great Sampford, Saffron Walden, Essex.
Ruggles-Brise, Col. Sir John A., Bt., C.B., O.B.E., D.Univ., T.D., J.P.,
    Spains Hall, Finchingfield, Braintree, Essex.
Ruggles-Brise, Mr and Mrs T. E., Spains Hall Farmhouse, Finchingfield,
    Braintree, Essex.
Russell, R. C., 11 Priestgate, Barton-on-Humber, South Humberside.

Sainsbury, F., B.E.M., A.L.A., A.R.Hist.S., 16 Crownfield Avenue,
    Newbury Park, Ilford, Essex.
St. Pier, D. M., 20 Elmshurst Gardens, Tonbridge, Kent.
Sampfords Society, The, c/o Mrs M. Edwards, Mill Thatch,
    Great Sampford, Saffron Walden, Essex.
Sanders, P. B., The Old Post Office, High Street, Widdington,
    Saffron Walden, Essex.
Sanders-Hewett, Mr and Mrs G. S., 16 Alwyne Avenue, Shenfield,
    Brentwood, Essex.
Sansom, C. D., 76 Church Street, Coggeshall, Colchester, Essex.
Sargeant, P. C., J.P., Oakapples, East Side, Boxted, Colchester, Essex.
Saunders, M. J., B.A.(Hons.), 28 Cheelson Road, South Ockendon, Essex.
Scarborough, Mrs S. J., 12 Springfield Place, Springfield Green, Chelmsford,
    Essex.
Scarlett, H. E., Lauriston, 45 Dukes Avenue, New Malden, Surrey.
Schürer, Dr K., c/o Department of History, University of Essex,
    Colchester, Essex.
Scott, D. A., 30 St. Helena Road, Colchester, Essex.
Sellers, Mrs E. E., 1 Chignall Road, Chelmsford, Essex.
Shaw, Dr G. W., Cobblers, 8 Broadway, Grantchester, Cambridgeshire.
Shaw, Mr and Mrs M., Springmede, Finchingfield, Braintree, Essex.
Sheppard, P. R., 20 Bawtree Way, Colchester, Essex.
Sherwood, N. E. C., Easthorpe Hall, Easthorpe, Kelvedon, Essex.
Simpson, Mr and Mrs M., 11 Cottesmore Court, Stanford Road, London W8.
Slack, C. C., 27 Parsonage Downs, Dunmow, Essex.
Sloman, Sir A. E., C.B.E., 19 Inglis Road, Colchester, Essex.
Smale, J. R., D.M.S., F.C.I.O.B., Millers Croft, Little Orchard Lane,
    Broomfield, Chelmsford, Essex.

Smeeth, Mrs M. M., Clock House, Locks Lane, Leavenheath, Colchester, Essex.

Smith, Mrs M., 25 Glastonbury Close, Stafford.

Smith, M. C., 29 Hay Street, Leichhardt, New South Wales 2040, Australia.

Smith, Mrs P., The Mill, Roxwell, Chelmsford, Essex.

Smith, R. B., Wethersfield Hall, Wethersfield, Braintree, Essex.

Smith, Revd. W. J. T., 7 Trelawn, Church Road, Boreham, Chelmsford, Essex.

Society of Antiquaries of London, Burlington House, Piccadilly, London W1.

Sparrow, A. C., Q.C., D.L., Croyde Lodge, Whites Hill, Stock, Ingatestone, Essex.

Staines, Ms B., Glebe Cottage, Manor Road, Little Easton, Dunmow, Essex.

Stanton, A. H., Brakeys, Hatfield Peverel, Chelmsford, Essex.

Stark, Lady R. H. O., Fambridge Hall, White Notley, Witham, Essex.

Starling, Mr and Mrs B., Hazeldene, The Street, Shalford, Essex.

Starr, Mr and Mrs C. R., 63 Abbey Gardens, London W8.

Stewart-Smith, C. D., C.B.E., S.M., M.A., Stanley Hall, Halstead, Essex.

Stiles, Mrs L. B., 376B Hardy Street, Nelson, New Zealand.

Stitchbury, Mrs J. M., 15 Crosslands, Stantonbury, Milton Keynes, Buckinghamshire.

Stokes, Mrs D. M., 41 Tey Road, Earls Colne, Colchester, Essex.

Street, Mr and Mrs P., 18 Jubilee Court, Dunmow, Essex.

Streeter, P. T., Watermans End Cottage, Matching Green, Harlow, Essex.

Strugnell, I., 22 Hatfields, Loughton, Essex.

Stuchfield, H. M., Lowe Hill House, Stratford St. Mary, Suffolk.

Sullivan, Mrs H., P.O. Box 5623, Maroochydore South, Queensland 4558, Australia.

Sunnocks, J. H. G., East Mersea Hall, Colchester, Essex.

Sunnucks, W. D'U., East Gores Farm, Salmons Lane, Coggeshall, Colchester, Essex.

Sutton, Ms J., Pond Cottage, Fir Tree Lane, Haughley Green, Stowmarket, Suffolk.

Swire, Sir John A., C.B.E., Luton House, Selling, Faversham, Kent.

Tait, C. G., 6 Fambridge Road, Maldon, Essex.

Tann, P. L., Town Place, Belmont, Faversham, Kent.

Tarbin, B. J., 2 Wood Lane Cottages, Lanes End, Darenth, Dartford, Kent.

Taylor, A. J., 51 The Drive, Loughton, Essex.

Taylor, J. E., Wayside, Great Sampford, Saffron Walden, Essex.

Taylor, S., Little Linton, Linton, Cambridgeshire.

Thomas, Mrs B., April Cottage, Danesway, Oxshott, Surrey.

Thomas, Mrs P., Hill House, Brent Hall Road, Finchingfield, Braintree, Essex.

Thompson, R. H., 107 Fairview Road, South Tottenham, London N15.

Thornton, Ms G. B., 4732 Talleybrook Drive, Kennesaw, California 30152, U.S.A.
Threlfall, J. B., 5518 Barton Road, Madison, Wisconsin 53711, U.S.A.
Thurrock Local History Society, c/o 13 Rosedale Road, Little Thurrock, Grays, Essex.
Todd, K., Little Willow, Parsonage Downs, Dunmow, Essex.
Travers, M. D., 27 Jubilee Court, Dunmow, Essex.
Turner, Miss A. C., 1 Robin Close, Great Bentley, Colchester, Essex.
Turner, A. W., 21 Joydon Drive, Romford, Essex.

Vincent, B. W., Gwendra, 37 Ridgeway, Hutton Mount, Brentwood, Essex.
Vincent, Mrs M. J., 14 Skene Street, Broughty Ferry, Dundee.
Vincent, Mrs V. J., Shardeloes, Vines Cross, Heathfield, East Sussex.

Wager, R. J., Reddens, Doddinghurst Road, Canterbury Tye, Brentwood, Essex.
Waite, C., Capricorn, Victoria Gardens, Saffron Walden, Essex.
Walford, D. M., 18A West Coast Road, #03-02 Greenacres, Singapore.
Walker, Mrs J. E., 69 Hawes Lane, West Wickham, Kent.
Waller, Mrs A. M., Rose Cottage, 9 Pye Corner, Castle Hedingham, Essex.
Wallis, J. G., 9 Temple Avenue, Dagenham, Essex.
Wallis, Miss P. M., 37 Suffolk Road, Maldon, Essex.
Ward, Dr J. C., M.A., Ph.D., F.R.Hist.S., Unsted, 51 Hartswood Road, Brentwood, Essex.
Warner, Sir Henry, Bt., M.A.(Oxon.), The Grove, Southend Road, Chelmsford, Essex.
Warren, Mrs J. C., Southdene, Arundel Road, Worthing, West Sussex.
Watson, Mrs M. G. C., Bromptons, Colne Engaine, Colchester, Essex.
Weaver, N. D. W., O.B.E., Walsingham House, Castle Street, Saffron Walden, Essex.
Webb, Mr and Mrs J. B., 10 Woodview, Grays Thurrock, Essex.
Webb, L. D., 31 Quebec Avenue, Southend-on-Sea, Essex.
Welch, Mr and Mrs R., Barnston House Moat, High Roding, Dunmow, Essex.
Welchman, Mrs R. W., The Old Rectory, Little Sampford, Saffron Walden, Essex.
West, W. M., 82 Ashdell Road, Sheffield.
Whalley, Mr and Mrs D., Church Cottage, The Street,, Matlaske, Norwich, Norfolk.
Whitmore, Ellis Lady, 155 Beehive Lane, Chelmsford, Essex.
Wilby, Mr and Mrs A. R., 17 Roxburgh Garden Court, Plymouth Road, Penarth, South Glamorgan.
Wilce, Miss R. M. A., B.Sc., 2 Hastingwood Court, Pembroke Road, Walthamstow, London E17.

Wilde, M. R., 47 Eastwood Crescent, Broomhill, Bristol.

Wilford, W., M.B.E., B.A., 6 Brook Road, Brentwood, Essex.

Wilkinson, D., 18 Richmond Court, High Road, Loughton, Essex.

Wilkinson, P. M., Holly House, West Ashling, Chichester, West Sussex.

Willesden, R., 3 Grey Towers Avenue, Hornchurch, Essex.

Wilson, Miss L., 15 The Causeway, Finchingfield, Braintree, Essex.

Wilson, Miss R. J., Hart Croft, 14 Pear Tree Close, Chipping Campden, Gloucestershire.

Wombwell, S. A., 7 Tarragon Close, Earley, Reading, Berkshire.

Wood, D., The Red Lion, Great Sampford, Saffron Walden, Essex.

Wood, R. G. E., B.A., 51 Longstomps Avenue, Chelmsford, Essex.

Woolford, Miss I. E., 43 Vicarage Road, Chelmsford, Essex.

Wormell, P. R., Langenhoe Hall, Abberton, Colchester, Essex.

Wright, P. J., 174 Aldborough Road South, Seven Kings, Ilford, Essex.

Writtle, Baroness Platt of, C.B.E., D.L., F.Eng., Greenbury House, 46 The Green, Writtle, Chelmsford, Essex.

Young, D. A., Brook Cottage, 112 Whitehall Road, Chingford, London E4.

List of Financial Contributors

Financial support towards the cost of this publication has been gratefully received from:

Augustine Courtauld Trust

Aurelius Charitable Trust

Barking and District Historical Society

Essex Archaeological and Historical Congress

Essex Heritage Trust

Essex Society for Archaeology and History

Marc Fitch Fund

Friends of Historic Essex

Intercity Print Financial PLC

Sampfords Society

Thurrock Local History Society

Walthamstow Historical Society

Editorial Note

THIS BOOK COMPLETES a trilogy of commemorative volumes presented by the Essex Archaeological and Historical Congress to three people, Frederick Emmison, William Addison and John Ruggles-Brise. Between them they have enriched the traditions and heritage of Essex in various ways with which numerous people, in all walks of county life, can readily identify. All who have worked in support of this project have done so with a keen sense of gratitude to the recipient of this tribute, our former Lord Lieutenant, John Ruggles-Brise.

The main themes of the book are historical but, as readers will discover, the essays have other dimensions, literary and cultural. When I was young I was introduced to the works of G. M. Trevelyan and inspired by those in a life-long devotion to British history, especially in its local aspects. In an annual lecture to the National Book League in London in 1945, at which John Masefield the then Poet Laureate took the chair, Lord Macaulay's scholarly descendant discussed the elusive boundaries of science and art in the work of historians. The relative influence of these two disciplines in the writing of history has changed significantly since Macaulay wrote his compelling historical narratives. In his London lecture Professor Trevelyan's approach rested on the proposition that the discovery of historical facts (his word not mine) was a matter for scientific method. But that the exposition 'partook of the nature of art, the art of the written words commonly called literature'. History, he opined, should not be the rival of the classics or of modern literature but 'rather the house in which they all dwell'. I hope that this book reflects that aphorism.

As Editor, I have the sad duty to record the death of Derick Emmison, one of the essayists, in November 1995. A major contributor to Essex history, he developed the Essex Record Office to its acknowledged standards of excellence. His lively personality and scholarship ensure that he will be remembered with gratitude by all those who value Essex and its history as he did.

It is with sincerity that I record my gratitude to the essayists for their admirable work and to many other people who have contributed their skills and energies. I hesitate, if only for a moment, for it can be invidious to mention names. However, there have to be exceptions. The editor benefits from the Project Group's guidance and authority. That this group, led by John Webb, Congress President, and Mark Davies, Congress Chairman, has worked so comfortably together is due to their wise and supportive counsel. The special experience and skills of Martin Stuchfield, the Business Manager and Dorothy Lockwood our

Secretary, have made the editorial burdens not merely tolerable but rewarding and congenial. For the index, essential in a work of this kind, I and the users of the book are indebted to the expertise and industry of Wyndham Woodward. Valuable help with typing was also given by Nicola Thomas.

Once again the unique experience and professional knowledge of Roy Stephens of the Leopard's Head Press has been at our disposal. His contribution is hidden in the pages of this book but has not escaped the notice of those of us who worked closely with him. As previously, we came to rely on his special expertise and friendly co-operation. Essex history, in this and so many other ways, has much to thank him for.

My friendship with and admiration for John Ruggles-Brise and our shared devotion to Essex extends over many more years than either of us can remember. I am grateful, therefore, to have been invited to edit this volume of essays in his honour. The task has been for me, and for those with whom I have worked, a privilege and a pleasure. John Ruggles-Brise, needless to say, has been of great help in numerous ways in ensuring the progress of the project. So to him, and colleagues in this enterprise, I extend my thanks for all their kindly help and co-operation. It would not have been possible without that. They, and I, have now the satisfaction of seeing it fructify in this new book of Essex.

Great Sampford,
July, 1996

Kenneth Neale

Biographical Notes

Michael Beale, M.A.

Educated at Brentwood School and was a Scholar of Jesus College, Cambridge, where he read history. Growing up in Essex during the war years, he spent much of his time cycling round Essex villages and visiting their churches — then usually open. After a career in the Civil Service he has returned to Essex history as Hon. Secretary of the Friends of Historic Essex from 1987 and Editor of the *Essex Journal* from 1990.

John H. Boyes, A.R.Hist.S.

Retired Civil Servant. Rolt Memorial Fellow, Bath University; Past President, Essex Archaeological and Historical Congress; Bulletin Editor, the Newcomen Society for the Study of the History of Engineering and Technology; Joint author, *The Canals of Eastern England*, (1977); Member, V.C.H. Essex Editorial Committee; Member, Wind and Watermill Section Committee of S.A.P.B.; President, Lee and Stort Rivers Society; Lecturer for, *inter alia*, the National Trust and the Inland Waterways Association.

Janet Cooper, M.A., Ph.D., F.S.A., F.R.Hist.S.

Became Editor of the Victoria History of the County of Essex in 1986 after many years as Assistant Editor of the Victoria History of Oxfordshire. She edited and contributed to the *V.C.H. Essex* volume IX, on the borough of Colchester (1994). She has also published articles on Oxfordshire and Essex history and a calendar of *The Oxfordshire Eyre of 1241* (1989) for the Oxfordshire Record Society, and edited *The Battle of Maldon: Fiction and Fact* (1993), the proceedings of the Battle of Maldon Millennium Conference which she helped to organize.

Adrian Corder-Birch, F.Inst.L.Ex., M.I.C.M.

A native of Essex where he was educated and has lived and worked all his life. Chairman of Halstead and District Local History Society since 1983 and Vice-Chairman of Essex Archaeological and Historical Congress from 1993, Committee member of the Friends of Historic Essex, 1988–93, and of the Essex History Fair Group, 1984–95. Member of the British Archaeological Association, Essex Society for Archaeology and History, Essex Society for Family History and British Brick Society being its Hon. Auditor since 1988. Author of *A History of Little Yeldham* (1981), *A Centenary History of Halstead Hospital* (1984), *A Pictorial History of Sible Hedingham* (1988), *A History of Great Yeldham* (1994), and other articles on local history.

G. Mark R. Davies, M.A., F.S.A., F.M.A.

Read Classics at Trinity College, Dublin, followed by a post-graduate diploma in Archaeology at London University, Institute of Archaeology. After three years at the Grosvenor Museum, Chester, he was appointed Assistant Curator of Colchester Museum in 1970, becoming Curatorial Services Manager in 1993. He has served as Secretary of the Society of Museum Archaeologists, 1980–86 and Chairman 1991–94; Chairman of the Colchester Archaeological Group, 1975–78 and 1991–94; Chairman of the Essex Archaeological and Historical Congress, 1993–96; Hon. Secretary of its Research Committee, 1972–86, and since then as the Chairman. He has been a part-time lecturer in Archaeology since 1967. His published work includes *Roman Colchester* (1980) with David T.-D. Clarke and *Prehistoric and Roman Colchester in the Colchester Area*, Supplement to the *Archaeological Journal*, 149 (1992).

F. G. Emmison, M.B.E., D.U.(Essex), F.S.A., F.R.Hist.S.

County Archivist of Essex, 1938–69; Past President, Essex Societies for Archaeology and History, and for Family History; Past Deputy President, Historical Association and Medlicott Medallist; Vice-President, British Records Association, British Records Society, Society of Archivists, and Essex Victoria History; compiler or editor of numerous H.A., B.R.S. and E.R.O. publications; author, *Tudor Secretary: Sir William Petre at Court and Home* (1961), *Archives and Local History* (1966), *Elizabethan Life* (5 vols., 1970–76), *Essex Wills, 1558–1603* (10 vols., 1982–95); editor, *Feet of Fines for Essex, 1547–80 (1991) and 1581–1603* (1993).He died on 9 November, 1995.

Edith Freeman, B.A.(Cantab.)

G.P.D.S.T. Scholar; Scholar of Girton College, Cambridge; Honours degree in History; Lecturer for the W.E.A., and the Cambridge University Extra-mural Board; freelance journalist contributing to a wide variety of East Anglian and national newspapers and magazines; author of many publications, especially on local history, including four on the Ruggles-Brise family.

Victor Gray, M.A., D.Univ.

County Archivist of Essex from 1978–93 after nine years working in county record offices in Devon and Suffolk. He is a past Chairman of both the Association of County Archivists and the Society of Archivists. Currently Chairman of the National Council on Archives. He was awarded an Honorary Doctorate of the University of Essex in 1993.

Donald William Grimes, F.I.M.

Born in Shoeburyness, Essex in 1925 he remains an Essex chauvinist despite considerable travel around the world; married Yvonne in 1953 and both enjoy searching out ancestors and Essex history. Vice-Chairman of the Essex Society for Family History since 1994.

Ken Hall, B.A.(Hons.), D.A.A.

A native of Liverpool, Ken Hall arrived in Essex in 1993 when he was appointed County and Honorary Diocesan Archivist. He is also responsible for Cressing Temple as Project Co-ordinator. His career in archives began in West Suffolk and he was successively County Archivist of Durham and County Archivist of Lancashire. He is a past Secretary and past Chairman of the Society of Archivists and was, until 1995, a member of the Executive Committee of the International Council on Archives and President of its Section of Professional Associations. He is currently Director of the International Archival Survey for Climate History, and a member of the International Institute for Archival Studies.

Frank Herrmann, F.S.A.

Author of *The English as Collectors, Sotheby's: Portrait of an Auction House* and a series of children's books, collectively entitled *All About the Giant Alexander* which have been immensely popular. He spent 30 years in publishing, then became director of overseas operations at Sotheby's. In 1983 he founded the auction house, Bloomsbury Book Auctions, which specializes in the sale of books and prints. He was for many years Chairman of the Friends of the Thomas Plume Library and did much fund-raising for them. He is also a Plume Trustee and gave the Plume Lecture in 1991.

John Hunter, M.A., F.S.A., A.A.dip., A.A.dip.P.

Read Architecture at Gonville and Caius, Cambridge and at the Architectural Association. Worked at the L.C.C. and R.M.J.M. Became strongly involved in conservation issues in north London and studied planning in order to be better armed. Joined Essex County Council Planning Department in 1971 and in 1979 became the Assistant County Planner responsible for the Environmental Services Branch. Particular interest in landscape history. Author of *Land into Landscape* (1985) and various papers, some published in *Essex Archaeology and History*.

Alan Jones, A.L.C.D., L.Th., Dip.Th.

After curacies in Ipswich and Southend-on-Sea the Reverend Alan Jones held an incumbency in Leytonstone and subsequently the parishes of Hatfield Broad Oak, Theydon Bois and Finchingfield (where Sir John Ruggles-Brise was Churchwarden and valued friend). Born and educated in Norwich and at London University, his interest in Essex history commenced whilst serving in the county Regiment. He has researched, written and lectured on his various parishes and is particularly interested in the social history of the East Anglian village. Now retired he lives at Long Melford in Suffolk and very much enjoys assisting at Melford's magnificent church and in the surrounding villages. From the advantage of this peripatetic ministry he is convinced that English village life is alive and well.

Herbert Hope Lockwood, B.A.(Hons.), A.K.C.

University of London, King's College; former Lecturer in History and Social Studies at Tottenham College of Technology; Vice-Chairman, Essex Archaeological and Historical Congress, 1987–92, President, 1992; contributor to *V.C.H., Essex*, V (1966); author, *Sources and Development of Local Historical Studies in Barking and Ilford* (1969), *Where was the First Barking Abbey?* (1986), contributor, *An Essex Tribute* (1987) and *Essex Heritage* (1992), author, *Barking 100 Years Ago* (1990), editor and co-author, *Long Ago and Not So Far Away* (1991).

A. Stuart Mason, M.A., M.D., F.R.C.P.

Retired consultant physician who specialized in endocrinology and has lived in Essex since 1943. As founding editor of the Journal of the Royal College of Physicians he developed a continuing interest in the history of the College. In 1993 he published a biography of George Edwards, the eighteenth century ornithologist and artist, who was born in Essex and served the College as beadle. After retiring from medicine he indulged his delight in Essex cartography by studying the estate maps and their makers, publishing *Essex on the Map* in 1990. He is now engaged on a similar study of early maps.

Geoffrey H. Martin, C.B.E., M.A., D.Phil., D.Univ., F.S.A., F.R.Hist.S.

Research Professor of History, University of Essex, and Fellow of Merton College, Oxford since 1990; born in Colchester and educated at Colchester Royal Grammar School, Merton College, Oxford, and the University of Manchester. From 1952 he lectured in history at the University of Leicester where he was Professor of History, 1972–82 and Pro-Vice Chancellor, 1979–82. Keeper of Public Records, 1982–88. He is the author of several studies of urban history, including a history of Colchester published in 1959, and a Vice-President of the Essex Society for Archaeology and History (formerly the Essex Archaeological Society).

John Moses, B.A., Ph.D.

The Very Reverend Dr John Moses was educated at Ealing Grammar School, Nottingham University, Trinity Hall, Cambridge, and Lincoln Theological College. He was a Visiting Fellow of Wolfson College, Cambridge in 1987. He was ordained in 1964 and his ministry included a curacy in Bedford and an incumbency in Coventry prior to his coming to Essex as Archdeacon of Southend in 1977 and to the Cathedral as Provost of Chelmsford in 1982. His work in Essex in recent years has included his appointment as Chairman of the Council for the Study of Theology at Essex University and as Rector of the Anglia Polytechnic University. He is a member of General Synod and a Church Commissioner. His publications include a study of atonement theology, *The Sacrifice of God* (1992), and church-state relations, *A Broad and Living Way* (1995).

Kenneth Neale, O.B.E., F.S.A.

Author, lecturer, consultant (international penology) to Council of Europe and Open University working especially in Europe, Russia and America; served in Royal Navy, Civil Service, Colonial Service and Diplomatic Service. Chairman of the Essex Archaeological and Historical Congress, 1984–87, President, 1987–90; Chairman, Friends of Historic Essex since 1986. Published books include, *Discovering Essex in London* (1969), *Victorian Horsham* (1975), *Essex in History* (1977), now under revision, *Her Majesty's Commissioners 1878–1978* (1978); editor and contributor, *An Essex Tribute* (1987) and *Essex Heritage* (1992); contributor, *Imprisonment: European Perspectives* (Open University, 1991); has also published studies and articles on local history, natural history and penology.

John, Lord Petre, M.A., D.L.

The great-great-great-great-great grandson of the subject of his essay, he continues to manage the family estate, now, thanks to the depredations of taxation and economic reverse, barely 5 per cent of its extent in his ancestor's day. Educated at Eton and Trinity College, Oxford, he has, apart from a brief period working in London, lived in Essex all his life. Having shamefully and unexpectedly failed History O-level, he can claim no qualification as an historian but is closely involved with a number of history orientated organizations in the County *vis.* Committee member of the Friends of Historic Essex and the Essex Heritage Trust, Chairman of the Victoria History of the County of Essex, President of the Essex History Fair and Trustee of the Thomas Phillips-Price (Marks Hall) Trust.

Andrew Phillips, B.A., Dip.Ed.

Head of School of Humanities at the Colchester Institute. President of the Essex Society for Archaeology and History (formerly the Essex

Archaeological Society), 1984–86. He has published many articles on Colchester and Essex and is the author of *Ten Men and Colchester: Public Good and Private Profit in a Victorian Town* (1985).

Ian G. Robertson, M.A., F.M.A.

Read Modern History at The Queen's College, Oxford; Museums Diploma with Archaeology Option; Assistant Curator, Chelmsford and Essex Museum, 1965–67; Curator, Passmore Edwards Museum, 1967–88; President of the Society for Post-Medieval Archaeology, 1982–85; Member of the Statutory Ancient Monuments Advisory Committee of English Heritage, 1984–90; President, Museums Association, 1986–88; Director, National Army Museum since 1988.

John R. Smith, M.Phil.

Educated at Cooper's Company School, Bow and at Leicester University. He joined the Essex Record Office in 1965 and his career included the setting up of the Southend-on-Sea branch office in 1974. He is the author of a number of works in the field of English local, medical and urban history including *The Speckled Monster* (1978).

Michael John Sommerlad, M.A., D.Phil.

Born 1932, Brighton. Educated at City of Oxford High School and St. Catherine's College, Oxford. Graduate Assistant at the Bodleian Library, principally in the Department of Printed Books but with occasional secondment to the Department of Western Manuscripts. Sub-Librarian in charge of acquisitions at the Albert Sloman Library, University of Essex, 1964–96. Public Orator, 1990–95. Has published on Scottish bookbinding styles and on aspects of the antiquarian movement in the seventeenth and early eighteenth centuries.

David Stenning, Dip.Arch.

Born in Worthing, Sussex and educated at Worthing High School for Boys and Brighton College of Arts and Crafts. He is a Registered Architect and has worked as a Conservation Officer in Essex since 1968. A member of the Vernacular Architecture Group with a particular interest in timber-framed buildings, he has had a number of articles published in learned journals including *Essex Archaeology and History*.

Jennifer C. Ward, M.A., Ph.D., F.R.Hist.S.

Senior Lecturer in History at Goldsmiths College, University of London. She has published articles on the Clare baronial family and on Essex history, has edited *The Medieval Essex Community — The Lay Subsidy of 1327* for the

Essex Record Office Series, *Essex Historical Documents*, and is author of *The Essex Gentry and the County Community in the Fourteenth Century* for the series, *Studies in Essex History*, published by the Essex Record Office in collaboration with the Local History Centre, University of Essex. Her book on *English Noblewomen in the Later Middle Ages* was published in 1992 and *Women of the English Nobility and Gentry, 1066–1500*, a source book, in 1995.

Iris Woodward, B.A., Dip.Ed., J.P.

She gained a degree in Fine Art and History of Art at Durham University; has lectured for Nottingham and Cambridge Universities and for the W.E.A., giving courses at over 40 towns and villages in Essex and East Anglia since 1973. She has studied particularly English, Dutch, Flemish, French and Italian art, the Pre-Raphaelites and East Anglian art extensively. Author of a history of Wem, Shropshire, published in 1952 (Third edition, 1994).

Foreword
by
LORD BRAYBROOKE

IT IS A GREAT HONOUR to be allowed to serve as the Queen's Lieutenant in Essex. The office, in which John Ruggles-Brise served for twenty years, involves the holder closely in numerous aspects of the life of the county. John Ruggles-Brise's Lieutenancy was one of distinction and his personal commitment added lustre to all of the varied duties that came his way. It was, as the biographical essay in this book shows, the highlight of his life of service to the people of Essex.

The Essex Archaeological and Historical Congress has played an important part in encouraging interest and support for the study and practice of history and archaeology in the county. This book is a notable symbol of the co-operation and hard work that has characterized the role of the Congress in promoting the county's historic traditions. How fitting it is, therefore, that the editor and his team of authors should have devoted their scholarship to the literary tribute which the Congress has decided to dedicate to its Patron's life and work. I know in how much honour and affection John Ruggles-Brise is held by all those who have enjoyed his friendship, support and encouragement. He, I am sure, just as the county in general, will be grateful to the contributors and appreciate the academic standards they have brought to their work.

John Ruggles-Brise's pride in the county has been manifest throughout his life. Now, with the publication of this book, there has been an appropriate opportunity to show how proud the county is of him. We all hope and believe that he will enjoy the book along with its numerous readers and that it will be a permanent reminder of what is owed to him by the people of Essex.

Braybrooke

Lord Lieutenant of Essex

Audley End, Saffron Walden
June, 1996

John Ruggles-Brise: Patriot and Patron

KENNETH NEALE

PATRIOTIC LOYALTY to the Crown and to Britain, alongside a benevolent patronage of the causes and institutions in which he believes, have been the hallmarks of the life of John Ruggles-Brise. He has, over the decades, dedicated himself to upholding the values of our national traditions and heritage. At the heart of his commitment has been his devotion to Essex in almost every aspect of the county's life and inheritance.

Spains Hall, c.1900.

Those who labour in the fields of Essex history and archaeology have enjoyed his consistent and sincere support for what they have tried to do to nourish the county's pride and interest in its past. The decision of the Essex Archaeological and Historical Congress, which represents the societies and institutions working in those fields, to promote this book in honour of John Ruggles-Brise and as a tribute to his services to the county, reflects the admiration, respect and affection in which he, as its Patron, is held. His association with Essex history, of which he is now a part, I shall return to later in this biographical essay. First, it will be appropriate briefly to trace his family background and to adumbrate the principal phases and features of his own life.

1

Spains and its people

Most of our Patron's life has been centred on his ancestral home at Spains Hall alongside the charming Essex village of Finchingfield. He was, however, born on 13 June 1908, at the nearby Brent Hall, eldest son of Sir Edward and Lady Ruggles-Brise, a Gurney of Keswick Hall at Norwich, and thus into a family with an authentic Essex and East Anglian lineage. Brent Hall is a pleasant building with

Brent Hall.

(Photograph by Edith Freeman)

early timber-framing, eighteenth century facings and extensions, a familiar formula for country houses in the arable lands of rural Essex. In the sixteenth century Brent Hall was owned by the Bendelowes family one of whom was the eminent lawyer, William, who became Judge of the Assize, Serjeant-at-Law, Governor of Lincoln's Inn and first Recorder of Thaxted. His father, Christopher Benlowes (or Bendelowes) came from Yorkshire to Great Bardfield where he purchased Place Farm about the year 1500.[1] He prospered and among several other properties he acquired in the vicinity was Brent Hall at Finchingfield. The date of William's birth at Place House is uncertain; he died in 1584 and is remembered, apart from his legal eminence, as a generous local benefactor. Another interesting association of Brent Hall is with the religious poet Francis Quarles who wrote many of his *Emblems* at the house when staying there with Edward Bendelowes, his friend. Nevertheless, John's birthplace, although it still enjoys his affections and pleasant associations, was modest compared with the Tudor elegance of Spains, as it is usually known among those who admire and enjoy this fine building.

Spains came into the family in 1760 when it was purchased by Samuel Ruggles of Bocking, where he was one of the leading textiles merchants in a trade that then flourished in that part of the county. Its acquisition by the industrious and astute Samuel marked the arrival of the family into the squirearchy. Spains itself had a much longer tradition having derived its eponymous name from the Ispania or d'Espagne family who were beneficiaries of the land grants and tenurial preferments that flowed from the rewards of the Norman Conquest. A moated medieval house on the site was partly demolished and then developed in the sixteenth century by its then residents, the Kempe family, from whom it eventually passed to Samuel Ruggles. At the heart of the present house, over which only three families, the d'Espagnes, Kempes and Ruggles-Brises, have presided since the eleventh century, is the great hall, a fine room that evokes a sense of dignity and is embellished with treasured items of relevance to family history. The charming dining room in which some very attractive portraits of the family are displayed, the panelled library with its Adam mantlepiece and the Tapestry Room are the other principal features of the interior. The exterior elevations are replete with authentic Tudor idioms, gabled roof lines, period brickwork and elegant mullioned square-headed windows. All is set in lovely grounds, in which Humphry Repton's ideas were engaged with flower gardens, a kitchen garden, handsome trees, driveways, a moat and ponds which seem to have early origins that associate them with the original buildings.

At the time the Ruggles family entered into this estate the landed gentry, in effect the squirearchy, enjoyed a monopoly of wealth and thus influence, even power, in the English countryside. Parliament was dominated by the squires, as was the Bench, and it was they and their relations who fashioned the social framework of life in the rural reaches of Georgian England. They were often arbitrary in the exercise of their official functions at a time when family background and affluence were more definitive than formal status or responsibility. Historians and contemporary authors have given us an ambivalent profile of the squires among whom, by the latter part of the eighteenth century, the Ruggles family were to be counted. P. H. Ditchfield, an interesting but hardly rigorous antiquarian historian, wrote of the old English country squires in 1912:[2] 'England owes much to the race of country gentlemen, denominated squires, who have left their mark upon English social life, and tried to do their duty . . . A strong sturdy race was that of the squires.' Their opponents, the rising rich middle class which thrived on the proceeds of their enterprise in exploiting the opportunities offered by the Industrial Revolution, the dissenting

COACHMAN'S HAT   JR-B

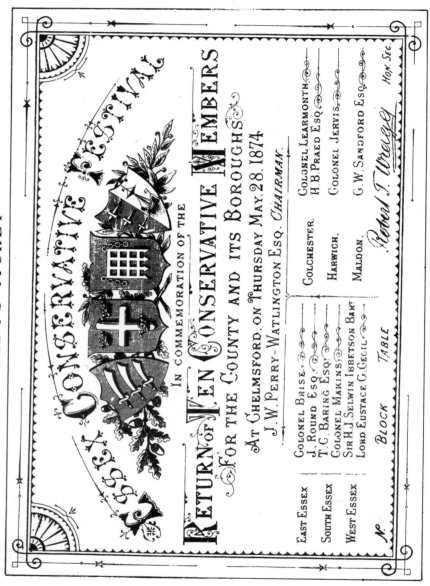

LADY'S TICKET

ESSEX CONSERVATIVE FESTIVAL

IN COMMEMORATION OF THE

RETURN OF TEN CONSERVATIVE MEMBERS

FOR THE COUNTY AND ITS BOROUGHS

AT CHELMSFORD, ON THURSDAY MAY 28. 1874

J. W. PERRY-WATLINGTON ESQ. *CHAIRMAN.*

EAST ESSEX
COLONEL BRISE.
J. ROUND ESQ.
T. C. BARING ESQ.
COLONEL MAKINS.
SIR H. J. SELWIN IBBETSON BART.
LORD EUSTACE G. CECIL.

SOUTH ESSEX

WEST ESSEX

COLCHESTER.
COLONEL LEARMONTH.
H. B. PRAED ESQ.

HARWICH,
COLONEL JERVIS.

MALDON,
G. W. SANDFORD ESQ.

Robert T. Wright
Hon. Sec.

№

BLOCK

TABLE

Essex Conservative Celebration, 1874.

religious sects, some eighteenth and nineteenth century novelists and radical activists like William Cobbett were less generous in their comments. That was only to be expected. In his preface to Cobbett's essentially practical and useful *Cottage Economy*[3] G. K. Chesterton described the author as 'the noblest example of the noble calling of the agitator'. Quite so, but he did not pretend to utter carefully balanced opinions as historians should try to do. The truth is that a commendable record of public service by many of the squires was mirrored by the authoritarian posturing of others. What we may be sure of is that the Ruggles family were part of all that; and that we, who have been privileged to know the present John and of his roles in Essex, are quite comfortable with Ditchfield's image.

The Ruggles family had a Suffolk background, particularly in Sudbury, but also at Glemsford, Boxted and Lavenham in the wool and textiles trades for several centuries before settling in Bocking.[4] The Brise connection came through the marriage of Thomas Ruggles to the wealthy heiress, Ann Brise, in 1736. The cognomen was adopted in 1827 by John Ruggles-Brise who was married to Catherine Harrison of Copford Hall near Colchester, some time after the acquisition of Spains which, as we have seen, dated from 1760. He was High Sheriff of Suffolk, and did much to improve the scenic qualities of the mansion being particularly enthusiastic for the extensive planting of trees. He was succeeded by Colonel Samuel Ruggles-Brise who, educated at Eton, commanded the West Essex Militia from 1854 to 1889 and was one of the Conservative Members of Parliament for Colchester and later for East Essex. We have an interesting glimpse of county politics in a celebration 'Festival' held at Chelmsford on 28 May 1874 to commemorate the victory of the Essex Conservatives in winning all ten seats in Essex. The name of Colonel Brise heads the list. As a consequence of parliamentary reform under the Act of 1867, Essex lost two of its ancient and corrupt 'pocket' borough seats, one each at Harwich and Maldon and was left with two for each of the county divisions, East, South and West, two for Colchester and one each for the Harwich and Maldon divisions. The Ballot Act of 1872 introduced the secret vote for the first time and by then the electorate had grown as the franchise was extended. At the election in 1874 Gladstone was defeated and Benjamin Disraeli took office. The Conservatives made a 'clean sweep' in Essex — hence the celebration at which Colonel Ruggles-Brise, who reputedly enjoyed a vigorous social round of dining, balls, tea parties and other public occasions, was a prominent figure as the member for one of the divisional seats. He was followed at Spains by Archibald Ruggles-Brise, a barrister and soldier in the Royal Suffolk Hussars, the family connections with the East Anglian county still persisting. Next came John's father,

ℛ-ℬ

LEATHER
CARTRIDGE BAG.

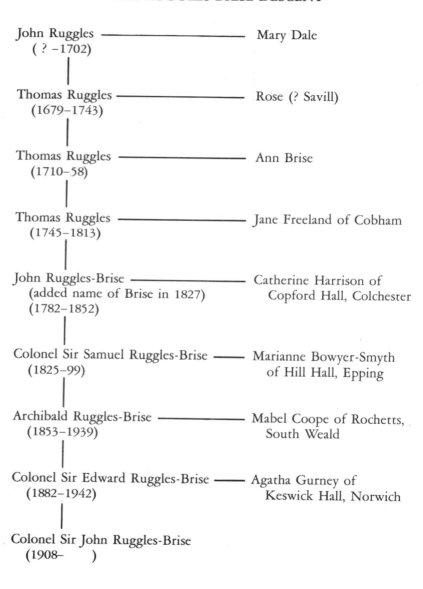

THE RUGGLES-BRISE DESCENT

John Ruggles ————————————— Mary Dale
(? –1702)

Thomas Ruggles ————————————— Rose (? Savill)
(1679–1743)

Thomas Ruggles ————————————— Ann Brise
(1710–58)

Thomas Ruggles ————————————— Jane Freeland of Cobham
(1745–1813)

John Ruggles-Brise ————————————— Catherine Harrison of
(added name of Brise in 1827)   Copford Hall, Colchester
(1782–1852)

Colonel Sir Samuel Ruggles-Brise ——— Marianne Bowyer-Smyth
(1825–99)   of Hill Hall, Epping

Archibald Ruggles-Brise ————————— Mabel Coope of Rochetts,
(1853–1939)   South Weald

Colonel Sir Edward Ruggles-Brise ——— Agatha Gurney of
(1882–1942)   Keswick Hall, Norwich

Colonel Sir John Ruggles-Brise
(1908–   )

Colonel Sir Edward Ruggles-Brise who was created a Baronet in 1935. It was James I who, in 1611, instituted this order of chivalry, candidates for which were required to be 'men of quality and good reputation' though the king's own motives were not wholly idealistic. At first the eldest son became a knight bachelor on reaching the age of majority, then twenty-one. But under royal warrant in 1827 this provision was revoked and since then the title of Sir has descended to the eldest son only on the death of his father.[5] This was the case in 1942 when John succeeded to the Ruggles-Brise baronetcy.

Sir Edward, following the family traditions, had been the Member for Maldon, Commanding Officer of the Essex Yeomanry and in the second World War of the Essex Home Guard. After his father's death, now more than half a century ago, John Ruggles-Brise entered into his inheritance of this fine Essex property. It was not without its problems. He restored Spains and modernized it. John had also to struggle with the economics of estate management, but his business experience and acumen enabled him to cope with the inevitable problems that arise in our contemporary circumstances.

'WOODCOCK'
SCOLOPAX RUSTICOLA
R-B

'Not all beer and skittles'

In 1917 the nine year old boy and heir to Spains went to St. David's school at Reigate in Surrey. He was there until 1921 and left as Captain of the school having enjoyed his cricket and football as a member of the school 'elevens'. From Reigate, as had become a family tradition, he went to England's premier public school, Eton College. He was placed in M. D. Hill's House, was Captain and a member of 'Pop' the Eton Society and played cricket for the college II 'eleven'. But life at Eton and the young scholar's subsequent varied experience was, he discovered, 'not all beer and skittles'. Eton was no doubt, at least in this respect, like Rugby, about which 'An Old Boy' wrote the famous Victorian novel in 1857[6] from which this quip is derived. This rigorous schooling and discipline, as well as the responsibilities that went with them were to stand him in good stead for the demanding roles that were to come his way later in life and from which he never shrank. He left Eton in 1927, not for Cambridge, as family precedent might have suggested, but for Alberta in Canada to stay with his uncle and aunt, Guy and Octavia Pym.

Still in his late 'teens' he did what many young people do with advantage today. He had a glimpse of the wider world before progressing to other things. Not quite, perhaps, the 'Grand Tour' of the cultural centres of Europe, the essential, if speculative, and even hazardous, experience for the scions of the noble families in an earlier age who invested a great deal of wealth and ambition in it. But it was a valuable experience for John and enabled him to see something of the beauty and awesome immensity of the dominion of Canada and to benefit from a spell of work on his uncle's ranch at Mirror in Alberta before he returned home enjoying brief visits to Vancouver Island and New York on the way. Life in the real world had, for John Ruggles-Brise, begun and he made the most of it.

The world of insurance in the City of London was the scene for the next stage in his career. He joined the Employers' Liability Assurance Company at the modest salary of a pound a week in March 1928. After a spell in the company's West End offices in St. James' Square he was appointed as an Inspector in 1930 and later promoted, in 1935, to Assistant Branch Manager and ultimately Branch Manager in 1937. He found the work satisfying and rewarding in the sense of business experience, but his personality demanded wider horizons.

His sporting life which he always enjoyed was, at the time, centred on squash racquets which he played for the Bachelors and Junior Carlton Clubs. It was all stimulating and enjoyable; life was not all that bad then. But in Europe the shadows were lengthening. The threat to the peace and stability of Europe posed by the Nazi regime in a re-vitalized and re-armed Germany was an all too obvious menace. Britain began to prepare itself for what many saw as an inevitable renewal of the hostilities that had, ostensibly, ended at Versailles in 1919. In that climate, one of anxiety and determination to defend our country and the freedom in which we believed, John enrolled like many others of his generation, in 1938, in the Territorial Army as a Gunner in the 54th Anti-Aircraft Regiment at Putney. The Munich crisis, which subsided into a brief postponement of the coming conflict, led to the mustering of the Territorial Army units like the militias of his forefathers. John found himself manning a gun battery which was part of the defences of London then being deployed as a precautionary measure. He was commissioned in November 1938 and called up in August 1939 when war with Germany was inevitable and imminent. He served with the gunners until the end of the war in 1945. During the bombardment of London by the Luftwaffe in what was called 'the Blitz' he commanded anti-aircraft batteries which were defending the capital, including one of the first mixed batteries on the sites at Wormwood Scrubs and in Gunnersbury Park. His promotion in October 1942 to command the 180th (mixed) Heavy Anti-Aircraft Regiment took him to Scotland at Dumbarton and thence to Edinburgh and Aberdeen. The regiment returned south to Plymouth as part of the 'D-Day' deployment in May 1944 to defend the seaport which had a key role in the operation. When the regiment was disbanded at the end of 1944 he was posted to command the 1st Anti-Aircraft Demonstration and User Trial Regiment at Minster on the Isle of Sheppey in Kent. He left the army in September 1945 having been awarded the

O.B.E.(Mil) in May of that year. After the war, still devoted to his professional calling as a gunner, he commanded the 599th Heavy Anti-Aircraft Regiment, Royal Artillery (Essex) in the Territorial Army at Chingford from 1947–50 and subsequently became its honorary Colonel. For his long and meritorious service with the Territorial Army he received the Territorial Decoration.

His military career had been a challenging and arduous experience but one in which his qualities of leadership had been proven and honed, his technical and management skills enhanced. He was to need all of these personal resources. As I have already briefly mentioned, it fell to John to take up the burden of rescuing Spains and the estate from the wreck — his own word — it had become as a result of neglect in the inter-war period and the ravages of the war years. Low pre-war rents from the farms that belonged to Spains, the burden of maintaining derelict thatched buildings and general decay had impoverished his inheritance. With purposeful management and financial discipline he succeeded in modernizing the agricultural estate to ensure its efficiency and viability. The old Tudor mansion was preserved for future generations of his family. With the help of a grant from official sources, but mainly by his own endeavours, it was all, fortunately, restored and developed to a state worthy of the representative functions of the Lieutenancy. John's personal qualities and his now versatile and mature experience were soon to be called upon for the duties of that office. These, as I shall describe, were highly compatible with his patriotic instincts and appetite for roles that required him to accept the sometimes onerous but always eagerly sought responsibilities.

Her Majesty's Lieutenant

When John Ruggles-Brise was appointed as Her Majesty's Lieutenant in Essex, his high sense of loyalty to the Crown and pride in the county were thereby dedicated to an office of great antiquity and an honourable tradition in British public life. He succeeded the previous Lord Lieutenant, Colonel Sir Francis Whitmore, under whom he had happily worked as a Deputy Lieutenant from 1944 and as Vice-Lieutenant since 1947, in August 1958. He was to serve the Queen and the county in that office for twenty years, after which, in August 1978 his duties passed to the late Admiral Sir Andrew Lewis. The appellation Lord Lieutenant arose as a courtesy soon after the institution of this office because many of those appointed were from the nobility or peerage. However, formally, the incumbent of the office is Her Majesty's Lieutenant and the wording of the commision has always used that terminology. Nowadays, the formal and ceremonial roles of the Lieutenancy along with the numerous social obligations and semi-official duties that arise are extremely demanding of time and energy. The Deputies share the routine roles of the office but the Lord Lieutenant, who is normally also Custos Rotulorum and thus, by the exercise of that responsibility, the Chief Magistrate of the county, naturally carries the major

Spains Hall, 1979.

burdens. It is he, or she, who must represent the sovereign, or manifest by personal attendance, at a wide variety of functions and occasions in county life, the importance attached to them by the public at large for whom the Lord Lieutenant is the figure-head in the county hierarchy. The presence of the Lord Lieutenant at such events thus confers a status on the activity or the organization concerned and encourages support for it, albeit in an intangible sense, that cannot obviously be attained in any other way. Moreover, free of formal party affiliations, the Lord Lieutenant, except when the occasion has an obvious political purpose or flavour, is a more acceptable representative of public approbation.

The history and traditions of the Lieutenancy in Britain are of intrinsic interest and important to an understanding of the ways in which the authority and influence of the Crown have been sustained and promoted in areas of public life remote from the immediate proximity of the Court. I digress here, therefore, to offer a brief historical background of the public role that the Queen bestowed on John Ruggles-Brise in 1958. The post of Lieutenant of a county was given permanent status under an Act of 1662. This transferred control over the county militias from the sheriffs although, curiously, the precedence of the Lieutenants was not formally established until King Edward VII decided in their favour in 1905. The origins of the appointment, although clearly related to military organization and arrangements for national defence, date however, from at least a century earlier. The office was in fact given legal status by statute in 1549 and, under the Tudors, the incumbents assumed supreme military authority in the counties to which they were appointed. This included the power to muster forces to resist invasion, oppose any internal threat to public order or to the sovereign and to enforce martial law.[7] They were commissioned from among people of proven loyalty and with local influence and authority and could be supported by Deputies then appointed by the Lieutenants themselves. Nowadays the appointments of Deputies are subject to the approval of the Crown and, of course, the duties no longer have a primarily military purpose. In the early days of the office there could be a plurality in a particular county and the commissions could be issued for short periods and at infrequent and irregular intervals. After 1585 the commissions of appointment were made on an indefinite basis. The Lord Lieutenant's responsibilities extended to the raising, maintenance and training of mounted troops and infantry, equipment, magazines, beacons and coastal defences.[8] The tensions that arose from the confrontation between the Crown and Parliament in the seventeenth century led to some anomolous situations. The right of the Crown to commission Lieutenants was challenged and under the Commonwealth lapsed. This isolated, for a time, the function of Custos Rotulorum from the office of Lord Lieutenant. The role of Custos Rotulorum had originated about 1400 when every commission of the peace nominated a Keeper of the Rolls who, as such, became under a statute of 1545, Clerk of the Peace. He thus became responsible for the appointment of Justices of the Peace under the authority of the Lord Chancellor. At the

Restoration in 1660 the situation was stabilized and from that time the Lord
Lieutenancy and the post of Custos Rotulorum have usually been vested in the
same person. During the eighteenth century the military resources of Britain
were seriously stretched by successive foreign campaigns culminating in the
revolutionary struggle in Europe. This necessitated a reorganization of the
militia which was effected under George II in 1757. These changes extended and
defined the powers of the Lieutenants and of the Deputies to raise and organize
the volunteers into local militia units and sanctioned their use, in a regular
capacity, to release the line regiments for service abroad. At the end of the
eighteenth century, in the Napoleonic wars, these local militias, mustered and
controlled by the Lieutenants, were a valuable and stabilizing element in the
nation's defensive capacity.

Robert Burns, as he so often did, perhaps caught the popular spirit of the time
and of the volunteer forces, in the year before his death. In May of 1795 several
Scottish newspapers[9] published his defiant poem of which this is the first
verse:

'Does haughty Gaul invasion threat?
Then let the loons beware, Sir!
There's wooded walls upon our seas
And volunteers on shore, Sir!
The Nith shall run to Corsincon
And Criffel sink in Solway
Ere we permit a foreign foe
On British ground to rally!'

It continues in ringing cadences consistent with the unifying ethos of the
Lieutenancies in words that are relevant today:

'O, let us not, like snarling tykes,
In wrangling be divided,
. . . .
Be Britain still to Britain true,
Among oursels united!'[10]

Later, by the Regulation of the Forces Act of 1871 (34 and 35 Vic c186), the
direct control of the militia was taken from the Lieutenants but their right to
muster was not finally withdrawn until 1921. Nevertheless, it was the long tradition
of those functions that made it natural and appropriate for them to have close
associations with the Territorial Army and, when Britain was threatened with
invasion in 1940, the Home Guard. So far as the Lieutenancy records are
concerned the most informative are those that, for obvious reasons, relate to the
late eighteenth century and the period of the Napoleonic wars when pre
parations for opposing an invasion entailed the keeping of comprehensive

minutes, accounts and administrative data at parish and county level. For Essex, insights into the nature of the duties and multifarious roles of the Lieutenants are also to be found in the brilliantly edited volumes of the Maynard Lieutenancy Book of 1608 to 1639.[11]

This description of the evolution of the roles and formal responsibilities of the Lord Lieutenant inevitably emphasizes the definitive legal nature of the appointment. In practice, although of course, the Lord Lieutenant is bound to conform to his statutory obligations and the formalities demanded by his commission of appointment, the performance of his many functions will largely depend on the style and personality of an individual Lord Lieutenant. His interests and the priorities of public life in a particular community will determine the responses that he makes to the numerous requests that reach the Lord Lieutenant's office. John Ruggles-Brise certainly stamped his own personality on his Lieutenancy during the two decades over which he carried out those duties. Whether his presence was required on the occasion of a royal visit to the county, in the performance of a civic duty, lending his support to the many organizations of which he was Patron or attending a modest social event he consistently upheld the dignity of his office, his commitment to its duties and the engaging qualities of his personal style. The much respected and loved Lord Lieutenant was honoured on his retirement by numerous tokens of the gratitude of the county and its people. He was the recipient of illuminated addresses from the County Council, county boroughs, boroughs and district councils of the ancient county and of a wealth of personal tributes. Typical of the formal addresses was the citation in that from the County Council. It read:

> 'We, the Chairman and Councillors of the ESSEX COUNTY COUNCIL on behalf of all the people of the County of Essex offer our most sincere appreciation of the outstanding and devoted services that you have given to this County and its people over a period of TWENTY YEARS. We recall especially with gratitude and affection the unfailing and active interest that you have always shown in the many services for which the Council is responsible. It is our most earnest wish that you may long continue in health and happiness so as to enjoy a retirement so richly deserved.'

An association with his services to the county that he particularly values is the project that produced what are known as 'The Spains Hall Chairs'. The seats of the Chippendale chairs in the front hall at Spains were re-covered by the needleworkers of the Essex Handicrafts Association. The chosen theme was 'Essex'; each chair or stool now carries one of the arms or emblems of the fourteen Districts of Essex and the county shield all worked in the traditional heraldic colours. Visitors to Spains will enjoy this beautiful work and the other tokens of esteem in which Her Majesty's Lieutenant was held in the county and which exemplify his own respect and admiration for its people and traditions.

Noblesse Oblige

On 6 April 1967 John Ruggles-Brise was granted the Honorary Freedom of the Borough of Chelmsford, the county town. The origins of this distinction have been traced, if somewhat tenuously, to the status of the free citizens of Rome and, later, the feudal concept which distinguished subservience from freeman status. It was refined in practice over time to define those who enjoyed special privileges within the jurisdictions of cities and towns or under the regulations of the gilds and livery companies. Today, Honorary Freedoms, first recognized in law by the Honorary Freedom of Boroughs Act in 1885 and subsequently by local government legislation, are conferred on individuals as a mark of respect which honours their special distinction or exceptional services to the community. At the ceremony in Chelmsford in April 1967 John Ruggles-Brise was escorted by The Essex Yeomanry, the Councillors and Aldermen of the Borough. At the request of the Mayor, the Town Clerk read the Resolution of the Council, as was required by law, which sanctioned the admission of John Ruggles-Brise as an Honorary Freeman in 'deep appreciation of and gratitude for the eminent and devoted services which he has rendered over the many years both to the people of the County Town and of Essex as a whole'. In his formal reply the Lord Lieutenant declared 'I will preserve the common peace and tranquillity of the said Borough so far as in me lieth . . . and I will defend the customs and privileges of this Borough in every just and lawful cause'. Having signed the Roll he was con-gratulated by the Mayor and presented with the scroll recording his Honorary Freedom.

Thus in public and with appropriate dignity and ceremony Chelmsford honoured the Lord Lieutenant of Essex on behalf of the county. Certainly, it would hardly be possible, within the compass of this brief essay, to list all of the organizations to which John has devoted his patronage and practical endeavours. Over the last half-century he has been Patron, President, Commissioner, Chairman, officer or member of more than 50 national and county bodies in the fields of social work, the Church, sport, agriculture, military, magistracy and education thus touching virtually every aspect of community life. A few examples must serve to illustrate the range of these interests and thus to give some indication of the amount of time and the level of commitment demanded of him. In view of the unique work of his famous great-uncle, Sir Evelyn Ruggles-Brise, the founder of the Borstal system for the treatment of young offenders and his role as a prison administrator and reformer, it is very appropriate to mention John's chairmanship of the Essex Discharged Prisoners' Aid Society. The well-known story of Sir Evelyn's funeral at Finchingfield recorded by Shane Leslie, his biographer, bears repetition here, for John's own humanitarian instincts reflect those of his great-uncle. 'The flowers were considerable' wrote Shane Leslie, in his book. 'They included beside the official and family bouquets one inscribed — To the memory of a humane man, Sir Evelyn Ruggles-Brise, K.C.B. He saved me from the cat. Convict 2148.'[12] Elsewhere in the social field we find John involved, as Patron of the Essex Branch of the Red Cross Society and as President of the St. John's Ambulance Brigade in Essex and of the county branch of S.S.A.F.A.

His activities in the rural community are exemplified by his work with the Essex Agricultural Society of which he was, uniquely, twice the President. He was also President of the Country Landowners Association and co-founder of its Game Fair. He had been approached, as Chairman of its Executive Committee, as it had been difficult to find a sponsor. A reluctant committee, who feared a financial loss, was persuaded to go ahead with the proposal. In the end, under the patronage of the Duke of Gloucester, it was attended by more than 8,000 people at Stetchworth. In education there was his important role in the founding of the University of Essex to which I shall come. But, he was active too, as a school manager at Finchingfield and as a governor of Felsted School and Chigwell School, two well-known and historic Essex educational foundations. His associations with the military have already been mentioned but, after he left the army, he also devoted himself to the Territorial and Auxiliary Forces Association and the Royal Artillery Association in the county. He was Chairman of the Council of the Baronetage for five years from 1958 to 1963. In the village, among other things, he has been Vicar's Warden at St. John the Baptist, Finchingfield for many years and President of the local British Legion branch, cricket and football clubs. Nothing, it would seem, has been beyond his interest or sense of duty.

'PHEASANT'   R-B

I shall, however, dwell a little on his part in the foundation of the University for that was very important to the status of the county and the quality of its academic life. That story is, rightly, the subject of an essay in this book. The proposal for the establishment of the University of Essex was first put formally on the county agenda by a resolution of the Essex County Council in 1959. The following year a Promotions Committee was formed of which he was asked to be Chairman. He later became the first Chairman of the University Council and Pro-Chancellor. The site at Wivenhoe was acquired in 1961 and by 1964 the University had received its first students. John's pioneering support for and

To Sir John Ruggles-Brise, Baronet

Commander of the Most Honourable Order of the Bath, Officer of the Most Excellent Order of the British Empire, Holder of the Territorial Decoration, Her Majesty's immediate past Lieutenant and Custos Rotulorum in and for the County of ESSEX.

GREETINGS and WARM CONGRATULATIONS from the Officers and Members of the Essex Archaeological and Historical Congress on achieving the 80th year of your age. We recall that it was at a County meeting held at Chelmsford on the thirteenth day of June in the year Nineteen Hundred and Sixty Four with yourself presiding as Lord Lieutenant that the Congress was inaugurated with the object of bringing together for purposes of mutual interest and exchange of information the many archaeological and local history societies that have been formed in Essex since the end of the Second World War. Congress continues to prosper and we know how much of its strength is derived from your active patronage. But our greatest gratitude is for the many Red Letter occasions on which you have so courteously received us in your gracious home amid the rolling hills of North Essex and in your welcoming addresses that have given us renewed insight into the strength of your abiding love of Essex and your faith in the steadfast loyalty to Queen and Country of its people. It has been on these occasions that we have been most conscious of the privileges we have enjoyed in your generous sharing of so much of your long and distinguished life with us.

15th June 1988

Commemoration of Sir John's 80th birthday, presented by the Essex Congress.

continuing devotion to the University reflected the importance he attached to higher education in the county. He regards the establishment of the University as one of the high points of his term as Lord Lieutenant in Essex.

I and my colleagues in Essex history may, I hope, be forgiven for placing emphasis on John's involvement with us in the sphere of Essex archaeology and history. His interest in and enduring commitment to our work has been remarkable and he has never failed to respond to our enthusiasms which he always shared. Even in these recent years when he might, understandably, have preferred to enjoy the quiet pleasures of life in his lovely home and delightful gardens, rather than attend our annual general meetings, executive committees and the annual symposium organized by the Congress, he is regularly to be found in the front seats taking a deep interest in all we are trying to do. A telephone call is enough; there is no fuss, no prevarication but a cheerful response to every request. We have come to expect that he will be there on these occasions; but never failed to appreciate it and to enjoy his company. His personal support for The Friends of Historic Essex, the Essex Society for Archaeology and History and the other Essex historical societies with which he had personal connections has afforded much encouragement to them. He finds time to attend a village festival organized by the Sampfords Society or to spend a day at a Congress symposium; and he enjoys it.

When, in 1964, the Essex societies decided to form the Essex Archaeological and Historical Congress he presided over the founding meeting held at Chelmsford on 13 June which was, by a happy coincidence his birthday too. Since then the Congress has gone from strength to strength, having been responsible for the publication of the excellent *Essex Journal* (the successor to *Essex Review*), the books *Essex Tribute*, and *Essex Heritage*, as well as an overall promotion and coordination of Essex archaeological and historical activities. John has been a leading participant in all this work and contributes his experience and wisdom at the Executive Committees which are held regularly to guide and inspire the roles of the Congress and to facilitate liaison between the numerous societies and institutions that are members of it.[13] Nothing could be more appropriate than that John, as he is of other Essex organizations, should be Patron of the Congress and thereby acknowledge the value of its work in county history and archaeology.

The Kindly Squire

What manner of man is our Patron? It would be easy to conjure, in view of his obvious stature and experience, an image of distant dignity and a somewhat patrician style. Nothing could be further from the truth. There is dignity of course, but it is not distant and he has style which is charming and quite uncontrived. His kindly and gentlemanly sincerity has earned him the affection of those who have known him and worked with him. His unremitting labours for the county, his loyalty to his beliefs and the record of his life of service has resulted in the high respect and admiration in which he is held. He has often been described as a true English gentleman of the authentic tradition. Naturally, he is, in every sense of the word. The minor aberration can be forgiven although it overlooks his Scottish family background and his connections with that most beautiful part of Britain which he cherishes along with his devotion to England and its way of life.

He stands for and loves the things that we like to think of as defining Britain and all it has come to represent in the world of human endeavour and aspiration. I know from many rewarding discussions I have had with him at Spains, or travelling together, that for him these extend to the cultural areas of life, the countryside, gardens, history, books, family traditions, standards and the safety, integrity and prosperity of Britain. However, to express those higher aspects of life in such a prosaic way is to introduce a suggestion of pomposity and rigid formality which is no part of this man. When, some twenty years ago, I asked him to write the Foreword to *Essex in History*[14] he replied, promptly and crisply 'Bob's your uncle'. That, typically, was his kindly, friendly way of agreeing and I was grateful for it.

A brief quotation from what he wrote in that Foreword is, I think, pertinent and a useful summary of his philosophy and belief in the county and its people: 'The relevance of our national heritage to contemporary problems is too often overlooked, but Essex people have never failed to assert their pride when they have felt it to be threatened . . .'. It is clear that he, the kindly squire, has been inspired throughout his life by a deep sense of history and tradition, a love of his country, an enjoyment of people and pride in the county of Essex of which, as patriot and patron, he is the most distinguished personality of his generation.

REFERENCES

1 W. and B. Dunell, *A History of Great Bardfield*, 1986.
2 P. H. Ditchfield, *The Old English Country Squire*, Methuen, 1912.
3 W. Cobbett, *Cottage Economy*, Peter Davies, edition 1926.
4 Edith Freeman and J. Ruggles-Brise, *Sudbury's History through the Ruggles Records*, 1987.
5 Sir Ivan de la Bere, *The Queen's Orders of Chivalry*, Spring Books, 1964.
6 T. Hughes, *Tom Brown's Schooldays*, 1857.
7 D. M. Walker, ed., *The Oxford Companion to Law*, Clarendon Press, Oxford, 1980.
8 B. W. Quantrell, ed., *The Maynard Lieutenancy Book 1608–1639*, E.R.O., 1993.
9 Including *The Edinburgh Courant*, *The Dumfries Journal* and *The Caledonian Mercury*.
10 W. E. Henley and T. F. Henderson, eds., *The Poetry of Robert Burns*, Caxton Centenary Edition, vol. III, 1896.
11 B. W. Quantrell, ed., *The Maynard Lieutenancy Book 1608–1639*, E.R.O., 1993.
12 S. Leslie, *Sir Evelyn Ruggles-Brise*, John Murray, 1938.
13 For a more detailed description of the roles and development of the Essex Archaeological and Historical Congress see J. Boyes, *A Footprint in Time*, E.A.H.C., 1989.
14 K. Neale, *Essex in History*, Phillimore, 1977.

Acknowledgement: We are grateful to J. R. Ruggles-Brise for the line drawings of game birds and items of interest from Spains Hall in this essay. — Ed.

Colchester and its oldest record

MARK DAVIES

ALTHOUGH NOT THE COUNTY TOWN, Colchester is unquestionably the oldest town in Essex and as such is distinguished by a long and venerable history. Its late Iron Age origins and early Roman development — not to mention its destruction by insurgent British rebels — are reasonably well known, not least because of the famous historical personages associated with it, such as Cunobelin, the emperor Claudius and Queen Boudicca, to name but three. In spite of the special importance and varied fortunes of the town's history, or rather because of them, the story of Colchester also contains a number of popular mythological figures with such well known stories attached to them that, regardless of the factual basis of their true existence, ·they are often taken for real characters of British history in almost every traditional detail. These include Queen Boadicea, King Coel, Helena and from time to time King Arthur.

The suggestion that Arthur's Camelot is to be found at Colchester has something to commend it, as a plausible explanation for the myth, in that here was the archetypal Roman town in Britain, whose buildings survived in substantial ruins that strongly reflected the grandeur of a former age. Perhaps more significantly, Camulodunum provides an acceptable verbal form from which it might be argued, if so wished, that Camelot derived. Unfortunately, in terms of hard facts or real evidence, Camelot only occurs in literature for the first time in the late twelfth century, while by the time that Arthur was performing his heroic deeds in the late fifth century — that is if he really was a historical character — Colchester had already passed out of Romano-British hands.[1] Recent archaeological evidence has strikingly shown that Saxon settlers were already building their modest huts within the Roman town by about A.D. 450.

The name of Colchester itself is particularly fascinating for its association with the myth of King Coel, whose invention in the tenth or eleventh centuries gives a colourful explanation for its origin.[2] Geoffrey of Monmouth writing in the twelfth century described how Coel, duke of Kaelcolim, overthrew Asclepiodotus, king of Britain, during the time of Diocletian to become king himself. However, a near contemporary writer, Gaimar, tells the completely different story of how a Danish king Adlebrit conquered Kair Koel or Colchester.

19

Initial letter of the 1413 Charter depicting St. Helena and Constantine in contemporary medieval dress.

The traditional Colchester version of Coel's story, as set out in chronological detail in the fourteenth century Oath Book, links strongly with Colchester's still highly visible Roman remains, while his supposed daughter, Helena, was the real mother of the Roman emperor Constantine (A.D. 306–37).[3] Both of the latter are depicted on the illustrated initial letter of Henry V's charter of 1413, as are the Borough Arms that are still fairly much in evidence today. Colchester Castle was known to have been built upon King Coel's Palace (the Temple of Claudius), while the blocked or Balkerne Gate at the main Roman western entrance of the town was Colkyng's Castle. What is now understood to have been a gravel quarry at Lexden was called King Coel's Kitchen and at the top of the town in High Street, near North Hill, stood King Coel's Pump until its removal in about 1819. These last two references to Coel, who supposedly gave his name to the town, are more recent examples of a long-held medieval tradition of associating with Colchester's great Roman past, to which Helena as a genuine historical figure was meant to give greater credence.

This strong Roman connection provides what at first sight may seem an obvious context for understanding the etymological derivation of the name Colchester, although the first part is not so easy to define as might appear. The Revd. Philip Morant, who knew his classical texts, has some significant comments to make about Colchester's name and origins, arguing that 'from Colonia, both this Town and the river Colne running by it, took their names'.[4] The second part of the name, as he correctly observes, comes from the Saxon or Old English *ceaster*, which is derived from the Latin *castra* and gives the well-known ending of so many British towns and cities with Roman origins. However, for some scholars the combination of a reduced form of *colonia* with *ceaster* is too awkward. Reaney, in particular, specifically denies that 'modern *Colchester* is pleonastic, consisting of the addition of OE *ceaster* to a syncopated *colonia*'.[5]

Your most obedient humble Servant

Phil. Morant

Philip Morant, historian of Essex and Colchester (1700–70).

The earliest form of the name is *Cair Colun* of Nennius, dating to about A.D. 800. Ekwall says that Colchester is 'The Roman station on the R. Colne' and that this river 'is identical with *Colne* (Hertfordshire) and with *Clun*. It is of British origin and had the form *Colun* originally'.[6] Reaney agrees, firmly asserting that 'There can be no doubt . . . that the first element is the name of the river Colne'.[7] He goes on to observe that the river's name cannot be a back-formation because of the existence, further upstream, not far from Colchester, of four parishes named *Colne*. These are Earls

Colne, Wakes Colne, White Colne and Colne Engaine. Rivet and Smith are a little more cautious in that, although agreeing that the name of the various Colne rivers is British in origin, they consider that 'to assume that the Essex Colne is one of them, *ab initio*, and that Colchester took its first element from that is perverse'.[8] They observe that *Colonia* was used for naming the town in the Antonine Itinerary, which will be considered later, and that there are continental analogues, especially Cologne, as well as the particularly significant British parallel of Lincoln, which derives from *Lindum Colonia*.

Two other early forms of the name date from the tenth century. These are *Colneceastre* from the Anglo-Saxon Chronicle, dating to 921, and *Colenceaster*, which is to be found in a charter of 931. On balance, then, the river Colne is perhaps to be preferred as providing the first element of Colchester, although if this is right, quite how it came about cannot be determined for certain. In any case, to know for sure would merely qualify with more precise local information what is already clear from the second element, that Colchester is descriptive of a particular camp. While in one sense it would be academically satisfying to be able to prove the precise derivation of the town's name, in another sense this does not matter too much since a much more important achievement is to be able to understand, appreciate and value the historic origins and development of this, the most ancient town in Essex.

Considerable archaeological evidence has been gained about Colchester's early past since the First World War, and particularly during the last 30 years or so. This can all be interpreted against the more general background of historical events that are described by various classical authors. There is, therefore, a wide range of useful records relating to Colchester which survive as pieces of recorded evidence or information, or accounts of fact preserved in a permanent form, or which themselves represent documents or monuments preserving them. However, not content with mere archaeological and historical riches, Colchester, as anyone approaching the town by car knows from the signs that greet them at the old borough boundaries, claims to be 'Britain's oldest recorded town'.

For a lot of local people this phrase sums up Colchester's unquestionable antiquity, which can often be taken for granted, while for many the detailed evidence does not much matter. For others it is a conceit that must be challenged or contradicted, and thus it certainly is from time to time. The most obvious danger, though, is for the whole business to be taken far too seriously so that its message is inevitably misconstrued, while its real origins and meaning are totally overlooked. One writer, for whom the phrase unsurprisingly became a 'wearisome canard', went so far as to define the meaning of 'recorded' in precise historical terms and categorized the different types of settlement according to the Greek and Latin words used by ancient authors.[9] After considering the literary evidence he chose to conclude that the 'oldest, recorded town' in Britain is 'the promontory of Belerion', which is generally thought to be the Lands End peninsula. The friendliness of its inhabitants, who prepared tin and exported it to the island of Ictis, is described by Diodorus Siculus writing in the mid-first century B.C.

with reference to the explorations of Pytheas in about 330 B.C.[10] Unfortunately this conclusion is supported by no archaeological evidence, although it was once favoured by the *Guinness Book of Records*.[11]

Among the various other views expressed on the subject, there is the confident assertion that 'the phrase was coined as a tourist advertisement in the 1930's'.[12] This may well be so, and the most likely perpetrator seems to have been none other than Sir Gurney Benham, who was both a committed guardian and a serious, as well as jocular, interpreter of Colchester's historic past for many years. In Benham's *Guide to Colchester*, 18th edition, 1932, the following statement is revealed:

> 'There is no town in Great Britain that can compare with Colchester
> in the fact that it is the oldest recorded town that we know of at all in
> these realms.'

These words are attributed to Sir Henry Howorth, K.C.I.E., D.C.L., F.R.S., F.S.A., and they also appear on an undated pre-war map of Colchester which gives the date of the quotation as 1907. In July of that year the Royal Archaeological Institute of Great Britain and Ireland held its annual general meeting in Colchester under the presidency of the Rt. Hon. James Round, P.C. The proceedings, which extended over eight days and were reported in detail in the local newspaper, commenced with a civic reception in the Moot Hall on Tuesday 23 July at 12 noon, when the Mayor, Councillor W. B. Sparling, arriving in procession with members of the Council and other distinguished guests, greeted the assembled gathering.[13]

In his response, Sir Henry Howorth, the Society's president, made a felicitous speech containing the now famous and much vaunted reference to Colchester's antiquity, which had previously been mentioned merely in terms of 'the oldest town in England'.[14] His other observations also contained the view that 'archaeology itself has improved very greatly since the days when this society met here last. It has become more scientific, it has become more inductive — we are obliged to methodise our knowledge a good deal more, to make it more precise and accurate.'

The Royal Archaeological Institute's previous visit to Colchester in 1876 had done much to stimulate interest both in the Town's archaeological remains, which were then suffering from decay, and in the museum recently established in Colchester Castle, where a special loan exhibition was displayed. From the members' researches it was thought that 'they had traced out that the site of the British Town Camulodunum was in Lexden Park, and that Colchester is the Roman City; these two towns were connected together by what were now called ramparts'.[15] Our current state of knowledge on these themes is now much further advanced, but such sentiments reflect important researches which had continued to challenge the minds of those with antiquarian interests over many years.

The generally excellent Colchester volume of the *Victoria County History of Essex* states simply that 'The identity of Colchester with Camulodunum was finally established only in the nineteenth century', quoting references of Philip

Cartoon for Colchester Oyster Feast menu depicting historical and mythical personages connected with Colchester.

Morant, William Camden and British Library manuscripts.[16] In fact Camden claims that, 'Others wholly addicted in opinion to Leland affirmed it to be Colchester: when as ... it is called at this day, instead of Camalodunum, Maldon'.[17] Morant for his part rejects this view in favour of placing both Camulodunum and the Roman colony at Colchester; he assesses all the literary evidence, gives consideration to the 'Opinions of our most learned Antiquaries', and most significantly calls upon his own acute observations of the available archaeological evidence.[18]

A particularly interesting assessment of the coin evidence, added to historical knowledge from Dio Cassius that Camulodunum was the royal seat of Cunobelin,[19] leads him to say, 'Now, more of his Coins have been, and are daily found at Colchester, than in any other part of the kingdom, both in gold, silver and bronze ... And by their being found here in greater quantities than any where else in England, it is at least extremely probable, if not demonstrably certain, that this very spot was That Ancient Camulodunum'. From the lettering on Cunobelin's coins, Morant also correctly deduces that the right name is Camu- and not Cama-lodunum.

If one were looking to the coins for Colchester's oldest record, then they are not those of Cunobelin (*c.*A.D. 10–41), whom Suetonius writing in the second century calls 'King of the Britons'.[20] The earliest coins to bear the Camulodunum mint-mark and the name of a British king belong to Tasciovanus, who was king of the Catuvellauni, the western neighbours of our Trinovantes. There are two of his types with this combination from the early period of his reign: the gold stater numbered Mack 186 from Leyton[21] and a bronze type first recognized by a find at Great Canfield in 1980.[22] Both of these coin types are far less common than those from his capital mint at Verulamium and represent a very short period of Catuvellaunian control at Camulodunum around 10 B.C. In terms of the oldest mint name, therefore, Verulamium (St. Albans) can claim precedence over Camulodunum in this respect.

Although no archaeological evidence can yet be specifically associated with Tasciovanus at Colchester, the name of his mint clearly indicates that here already in the late first century B.C. was a fortified site connected with the worship of a Celtic deity. Camulodunum is the Romanized form of what would have been the Celtic Camulodunon. The first element *Camulos* means 'powerful' and was the name of a Celtic god whom the Romans equated with Mars, known principally as a god of war.[23] The second element, -*dunum*, from Celtic *dunon*, is found quite widely in place-names throughout Britain (over 16 examples) and Gaul, as well as occasionally further east. It means a fortified place or fortress, deriving originally from 'hill'. At Colchester the earliest defensive earthwork or fortification is the Heath Farm Dyke which serves to protect the Gosbecks site. Here, then, is thought to be the earliest 'fortress of Camulos', whose name Camulodunum was to extend in due course to the whole of the area encompassed by the dykes that Cunobelin mainly had constructed.[24]

The Gosbecks site continued in importance for the native population into the

Roman period. Its major archaeological characteristics are known partly from excavation, but mainly through the aerial photography of cropmarks and now increasingly by means of geophysical surveying methods. They include a large enclosure possibly once occupied by Cunobelin himself and his predecessors, a complex system of fields and trackways, a large Roman theatre within a trapezoidal enclosure next to the road leading to the *colonia*, a Romano-Celtic temple set inside a protective ditch and double portico, and a Roman auxiliary fort. On Monday, 7 August 1995, some 163 acres of farmland, containing almost all but the first and last of these features, were formally handed over to Colchester Borough Council with a dowry of £500,000 for the creation of an archaeological park.

In 1994 the theatre and temple were first marked out in plan with white lines on the ground, and programmes of resistivity surveying and the biological recording of flora and fauna commenced.[25] In recognition of the site's national importance, English Heritage agreed to fund a Gosbecks Education Officer for two years on the staff of Colchester Museum, commencing in January 1995. During the summer term of that year, after preliminary teacher-training sessions and the production of site labels and a temporary exhibition to be housed in a portacabin on site, the first school parties began to make pre-arranged study visits to the park. Members of the general public were also able to enjoy the special facilities provided, which included the opportunity to converse with archaeologists undertaking investigative work on the site of the temple. The purpose of this work was to locate and evaluate the surviving structural remains as part of a programme of assessment for the site's future interpretation and protection.[26]

Not only was valuable structural evidence obtained, including unusual white tessellated paving and part of a brick column drum which has important implications for understanding the temple's appearance and proportions, but

also one particular find has a potentially significant bearing on the temple's dedication. The discovery of an iron finger-ring bearing an intaglio with the finely engraved figure of the Roman god Mars, when considered in relation to a platter sherd inscribed MARTI which was discovered at the south-west angle of the double portico in 1842, enticingly suggests that here was the shrine not only of Mars but also of his Celtic counterpart, Camulos. In any case Gosbecks, whose outstanding archaeological resources are now being preserved for general public benefit and enjoyment, clearly represents the central focus of Camulodunum, the capture of which the emperor Claudius made his personal objective in the Roman invasion of A.D. 43.

Intaglio of Mars from Gosbecks

Colchester's early political and economic importance as the first capital of Britain is emphasised in Professor S. S. Frere's pertinent summary:

> 'It may be hard nowadays to picture Colchester as the capital of Britain; but it is a fact that for a hundred years either side of the beginning of our era developments at Colchester hold a crucial importance for any understanding of the history of our country at that period, and that all that we can learn of them by archaeological exploration must be eagerly pursued.'[27]

An account of Claudius's part in the capture of Camulodunum, the capital of Cunobelin, is given by Dio Cassius who records the emperor's journey from Rome, how he took over command of the army at the Thames, engaged and defeated the natives and was awarded a triumph by the Senate.[28] In stating that 'In the late twentieth century Colchester prided itself on being the oldest recorded town in Britain', the *V.C.H. Colchester* volume cites Dio Cassius's use of the name Camulodunum in relation to these events as being the earliest mention of it. While these historic events are, it is true, the earliest in which Camulodunum is recorded by name, the chronicler Dio Cassius (*c*.A.D. 160–230) was writing some 150 years later, so this reference will not do. Nor will that of the early second century writer Suetonius, whose fairly similar description of the conquest does not actually mention the capture of Camulodunum, since he prefers to concentrate rather on Claudius's celebration of his triumph at Rome which seems to have been the main point of the exercise.[29]

Some of the most vivid descriptions relating to Roman Colchester are furnished by the historian C. Cornelius Tacitus (*c*.A.D. 56–115+), even though his account of the first six years of the emperorship of Claudius sadly does not survive. In the *Annals* he tells how a colony was established by a strong group of ex-soldiers on captured land at Colchester (*colonia Camulodunum*), its mission being to give protection against revolt and to imbue the British allies with a sense of their legal obligations.[30] As the highest form of Roman self-governing community and the first town of this rank in Britain, the colony would have been established with all appropriate legal formalities including a charter, of which copies will have been kept both at Colchester and in Rome. These do not survive, nor have any relevant inscriptions yet been found at Colchester or elsewhere. Colchester would doubtless have been endowed with many civic and personal inscriptions in Roman times, but these have almost all completely disappeared or been recycled because of the dearth of good building stone in Essex. The colony's charter or any contemporary formal reference to it would have been the oldest proper record, so Colchester could still justifiably call itself 'the oldest chartered town in Britain'.

The name of this Roman colony founded at Colchester in A.D. 49 is not known, but is presumed to have been at least *colonia Claudia* on analogy with elsewhere and from the tombstone of Titus Statius Vitalis, a legionary soldier, who died while serving at Carnuntum on the Danube in the first century.[31] His origin is given as *Camuloduni* (of Camulodunum), while the use of the term *Cla* (short for Claudia) may be either an epithet of his voting tribe or an honorary epithet of the colony. In the Vatican Museum at Rome, however, there is an inscription, dating to the second century, which records military and civilian appointments in the early career of an equestrian officer called Gnaius Munatius Aurelius Bassus.[32] It was set up in his home town of Nomentum, which is in Latium 14 miles north-east of Rome, and among his other offices it states that, after serving as Prefect of the Second Cohort of Asturians (presumably in Britain where it is recorded), he was appointed *censitor civium Romanorum coloniae Victricensis quae est in Brittannia Camaloduni*. In other words he was 'census officer of the Roman citizens of *Colonia Victricensis* which is in Britain at Camulodunum'. Together with the references made by Tacitus, this inscription corroborates a clear distinction between the fortress of Camulodunum and the Roman town or *colonia*. A first century soldier of the Aquitanian Cohort, called Tarcho, who died at Salona near Split in Yugoslavia, may have come from Colchester, but interpreting his funerary inscription with *dom Camul* — his home being at Camulodunum — is not without some difficulty.[33]

Another inscription, from a Roman tombstone found in Holborn in March 1960 and subsequently presented to the British Museum, gives brief details of a legionary soldier called Gaius Pomponius Valens, who was serving in London with the special responsibilities of a *beneficiarius* at the time of his death.[34] Precisely when he died is not certain, but he is recorded as coming from *Victricensis*, which is generally considered to be the colony's new name. This title was given on its reconstruction after the victory achieved in putting down the Boudican Revolt, although Claudius's victory could just prove the cause. As is now well known from the archaeological evidence, the legionary fortress founded in A.D. 43 became the basis of the colony established at Camulodunum for retired soldiers in A.D. 49, whom Tacitus describes as *'in colonia Camulodunum recens deducti'*.[35]

Together with Dio Cassius's Account, the *Annals* of Tacitus provide a fascinating, although sometimes debatable, description of the causes and events of Boudicca's Revolt. According to his account, the statue of Victory at Camulodunum (*Camuloduni*) fell down without any apparent reason, while the *colonia* was protected by no defences.[36] He mentions how the Temple of Claudius (*templum divo Claudio constitutum*)[37] was regarded as a citadel of everlasting oppression, explaining graphically how the colonists were finally massacred there after a siege lasting two days.[38]

Although writing well after these events — the *Annals* were completed between A.D. 115 and 117 — Tacitus was able to draw on earlier accounts as well as the personal experiences of his famous father-in-law, Gnaius Julius Agricola, who was a junior officer at the time of the revolt and rose to become governor of the British province in A.D. 78. In his biography of Agricola published in A.D. 98, Tacitus gives unparalleled detail about Britain and its early Roman history. However, he only mentions Colchester twice by name, on both occasions merely referring to it as *colonia*.[39]

Geographical or cartographical works may be said to account for the few references to Colchester that still remain to be mentioned, among which is Ptolemy's *Geography*. Claudius Ptolemaeus was a mathematician and astronomer who worked in Alexandria towards the middle of the second century A.D.; he compiled his *Geography* in Greek between A.D. 140 and 150 with the help of other sources. In the second of his eight books which deals extensively with Britain he mentions 'the Trinovantes amongst whom is the city of Camulodunum'.[40] Near them he also records these two islands, Toliatis and Counnus, which are difficult to identify but are thought to be Thanet and Mersea or Foulness (or Sheppey).

Ptolemy's calculations and co-ordinates represent the highest scientific achievement of their kind in the ancient world, despite being based on Posidonius's slightly inaccurate calculation of the earth's circumference. They have attracted much attention from William Camden and other antiquarians in later times, but with regard to the question of Colchester's oldest record they need no further comment since the answer is clearly not to be found there.

On a more practical cartographic level is the Antonine Itinerary, a series of 225 routes which range across the Roman Empire giving distances in miles between each named stopping point. These are Iter V, which refers to *Colonia*, and Iter IX, which has *Camuloduno* (to Camulodunum). The distance between Colchester and London amounts to 52 miles in both cases, which Morant uses in his argument for placing both Camulodunum and the *colonia* at Colchester in preference to Maldon.[41] There are slight variations in individual measurements between routes, for example from Colchester to Caesaromagus (Chelmsford), but these and the use of 'colonia' in one, as against 'Camulodunum' in the other, merely suggest different sources and dates, while the existence of a town zone around the *colonia* is thought to have affected measurements relating to it.[42]

The Peutinger Table, which is a pictorial map with recorded distances apparently derived from a third century original, also includes *Camuloduno* among the 16 British towns named. On the other hand, the Ravenna Cosmography, dating from a little after A.D. 700, has the somewhat strange form of *Manuloduno colonia*, although the first name can quite easily be read as relating to Camulodunum.[43]

Lastly, an incidental reference to Colchester is made by Pliny the Elder (Gaius Plinius Secundus), who was born in A.D. 23 or 24 near Lake Como in northern Italy. He had an insatiable appetite for consuming facts and is principally famous for his great work on Natural History, which he completed in 37 books and dedicated to Titus in A.D. 77. In Book II, which deals with cosmology, astronomy, meteorology, geography and geology, consideration is given to the varying length of daylight in different parts of the then known world; it includes this comment:

'They even say it can be seen in Mona which is about 200 miles from Camulodunum, a town in Britain.'[44]

Cartoon by W. Gurney Benham for Colchester Oyster Feast, 1936.

Mona is the Isle of Anglesey in north Wales, where Suetonius Paulinus the governor of Britain had gone to suppress the Druids in A.D. 60 when the Boudican Revolt broke out.[45] Educated Romans might well have read or heard about these events, but if they had any knowledge at all of just one town in far-flung Britain, they would probably have known the name of Camulodunum, which Pliny uses here merely as a geographical reference point. This passing mention is the earliest dated literary reference made to a British town by name and thus turns out to be Colchester's oldest record.

It was left to Pliny the Younger to publish posthumously his uncle's monumental *Natural History*. While commanding the fleet at Misenum on the Bay of Naples in A.D. 79, Pliny the Elder, with his unquenchable thirst for scientific knowledge, had sailed across the bay to Stabiae to gain a close-up view of the fateful eruption of Mount Vesuvius. There on the beach he died, overcome by sulphurous fumes, having approached too close to the subject of his enquiry.[46]

The question of Colchester's oldest record, or of its being Britain's oldest recorded town, is perhaps more of a red herring than a volcanic eruption when viewed in terms of importance as a subject for serious study. It need not, therefore, be approached with too much serious expectation of itself. However, as a simple means of drawing popular attention to our incomparable heritage of Camulodunum and early Roman Colchester, such propositions can prove invaluable when treated in proper context. Colchester's historic beginnings may be sought both indirectly through its well-known mythological characters and directly by means of its many famous historical personalities and events, although to be properly understood these must all be viewed in the light of appropriate historical writings. Such a rich heritage of national and international importance represents the essential ingredient of Colchester's own special identity, but only through careful preservation, research and interpretation of its surviving archaeological remains can it be truly brought alive.

Acknowledgements

All illustrations in this essay have been reproduced by courtesy of the Colchester and Essex Museum.

REFERENCES

1   L. Alcock, *By South Cadbury is that Camelot . . .*, 1972, p.14.
2   Janet Cooper, ed., *The Victoria History of the County of Essex: The Borough of Colchester*, vol. IX, 1994, pp.19–20.
3   W. G. Benham, 'Legends of Coel and Helena' in *J.B.A.A.*, 1919, pp.229–44.
4   P. Morant, *The History of Colchester*, 1748, ch. II, pp.11–17.
5   P. H. Reaney, *The Place-Names of Essex*, English Place-Name Society, 1935, pp.368–9.

6   E. Ekwall, *The Concise Oxford Dictionary of English Place-Names*, 3rd ed., 1947.

7   P. Morant, *op. cit.*, pp.11–17.

8   A. L. F. Rivet and C. Smith, *The Place-Names of Roman Britain*, 1979, pp.312–3.

9   F. Roberts, 'Colchester Mythology' in *Essex Archaeological News*, winter 1978, pp.15–16. See also 'Colchester Myths — A Reply, *op. cit.*, summer 1979, pp.13–14.

10 Diodorus Siculus, *History V*, p.22.

11 See older editions. But the 1996 volume, edited by Peter Matthews, states: 'the oldest town in Great Britain is often cited as Colchester, the old British Camulodunum, headquarters of Belgic chiefs in the first century B.C. However, the name of the tin trading post Salakee, St. Mary's, Isles of Scilly, is derived from pre-Celtic roots and hence *ante* 550 B.C.'.

12 W. Rodwell, 'Colchester Mythology — A Comment' in *op. cit.*, spring 1979, pp.14–15. See also D. Clarke, 'Colchester — The Same Old Story' in *op. cit.*, spring 1979, p.15.

13 *Essex County Standard*, 27 July 1907, p.6. See also *Arch. J.*, LXIV, 1907, pp.172–202, and *Trans. Essex Arch. Soc.*, X, N.S., 1909, pp.279–80.

14 J. Breton Davies in Wright's *Colchester*, 1891, for example, commences his narrative with 'Colchester — sylvan Colchester — which is only about an hour's run by train from London, is the oldest and one of the most picturesque and flourishing towns in England'.

15 See Royal Archaeological Institute of Great Britain and Ireland: Colchester Meeting, 1 to 8 August, 1876 — Full Report of the Proceedings. Reprinted from the *Essex Standard*, 1876.

16 Janet Cooper, ed., *The Victoria History of the County of Essex: The Borough of Colchester*, vol. IX, 1994, p.1.

17 W. Camden, *Britannia*, 1610 edition. The original edition of 1586 was published in Latin.

18 P. Morant, *op. cit.*, pp.12–17.

19 Dio Cassius, *Historiae Romanae*, LX, 21.

20 Suetonius, *Gaius* 44.

21 R. P. Mack, *The Coinage of Ancient Britain*, 1953, p.66.

22 M. R. Eddy and M. Davies, 'Great Canfield' in *Essex Archaeol. Hist.*, 13, 1981, pp. 35–7.

23 For the latest explanation see M. Green, *The Gods of the Celts*, 1986.

24 A comprehensive discussion on Camulodunum, including its origin and the dykes, can be found in C. F. C. Hawkes and P. Crummy, *Colchester Archaeological Report 11: Camulodunum*, 2, 1995.

25 P. Crummy, 'Gosbecks Archaeological Park' in *The Colchester Archaeologist*, 8, 1995, pp.7–14. See also A. Mackenzie and S. Newell, 'The Beetles are coming' in *op. cit.*, pp.5–6.

26 P. Crummy, 'Visitors welcome!' in *The Colchester Archaeologist*, 9, 1996, pp.1–7.

27 S. S. Frere, Introduction in P. Crummy, *Not Only a Matter of Time*, 1975, p.3.

28 Dio Cassius, *Historiae Romanae*, LX, 21–22.

29 Suetonius, *Claudius*, 17.

30 Tacitus, *Annales*, XII, 32.

31 Corpus Inscriptionum Latinarum (C.I.L.), III, 11233. For this and other inscriptions relating to Colchester, see D. T.-D. Clarke and G. M. R. Davies, *Roman Colchester*, 1980, pp.49–50.

32 C.I.L., XIV, 3955.

33 C.I.L., III, 2053.

34 K. S. Painter, 'A Roman Tombstone from Holborn' in *Antiq. Journ.*, 43, 1963, pp.123–8.

35 Tacitus, *Annales*, XIV, 31.

36 Tacitus, *Annales*, XIV, 32.

37 The most comprehensive interpretation of this phrase is given in D. Fishwick, 'The Temple of Divus Claudius at Camulodunum' in *Britannia*, XXVI, 1995, pp.11–27.

38 Tacitus, *Annales*, XIV, 31.

39 Tacitus, *Agricola*, 14 and 16.

40 Ptolemy, *Geography*, II, 3, 2.

41 P. Morant, *op. cit.*, pp.15–16.

42 W. J. Rodwell, 'Milestones, Civic Territories and the Antonine Itinerary', in *Britannia*, VI, 1975, pp.76–101.

43 For a full discussion of the itineraries and the Ravenna Cosmography, see A. L. F. Rivet and C. Smith, *op. cit.*, pp.148–212.

44 Pliny the Elder, *Naturalis Historia*, II, 187; '... quidam vero et in Mona, quae distat a Camaloduno Britannia oppido circiter ducentis milibus, adfirmant'.

45 Tacitus, *Annales*, XIV, 29–30.

46 Pliny the Younger, *Epistulae*, VI, 16; VI, 20. In these two letters addressed to Tacitus, he gives a graphic description of the eruption and his uncle's demise.

Archbishop Samuel Harsnett, 1561–1631 and his Library at Colchester

G. H. MARTIN

SAMUEL HARSNETT, ARCHBISHOP OF YORK from 1629 to 1631, was born and baptized in Colchester in 1561, and was buried in Chigwell, to his own careful directions, in 1631. He has memorials in both places. He chose Chigwell for his resting-place because he had once held the vicarage there, and because his wife Thomasine and their only daughter were buried together in the church. Nineteenth-century enlargement and restoration have left only half of the church which Harsnett knew, but his imposing brass survives, and says even more of the man than its inscription conveys.

In Colchester Harsnett is most obviously commemorated in Harsnett Road, a residential street of stock-brick houses developed at the end of the nineteenth century on the site of the Napoleonic War barracks. It is an honour which he shares with King Stephen (1097–1154) and Philip Morant (1700–70), who are his immediate neighbours there on the edge of New Town.

Harsnett and Morant have each (and, indeed, together) a more distinctive part than King Stephen in the history of Colchester, but most of the inhabitants of the modern borough, a community now some 12 times larger than it was even in Morant's day, probably know no more of any of the three than their post-codes. However, Morant lives on in his histories of Colchester and of Essex, in which the king and the archbishop have each their place, and Harsnett bequeathed his library for the benefit of the clergy of the town who, if they wish it, have access to it still.[1]

Samuel Harsnett was the son of a baker, William Harsnett of St. Botolph's parish, and was baptized in the old priory church on 20 June 1561. His father spelled his name Halsenoth in his will, and there were other versions current in the town, all apparently of one kin. Samuel was most probably educated at the town school. There is at least no evidence of his being educated elsewhere, until he was admitted a sizar of King's College, Cambridge, in 1576. He was evidently a youth of some promise, for he had no notable connections to assist his career. His most likely patrons in Colchester, given his opinions and later affinities, would have been the Lucases,[2] but he rapidly made his mark in Cambridge. From King's he became a scholar of Pembroke Hall, and having graduated B.A. in 1581

Monumental brass commemorating Archbishop Samuel Harsnett at Chigwell.
(Photograph courtesy of Dr Malcolm W. Norris)

he was elected to a fellowship at Pembroke in 1583, and took holy orders, followed by his M.A., in 1584. His first public act outside the university was to preach a sermon at St. Paul's Cross on 27 October 1584, in which he attacked the doctrine of predestination professed by the followers of John Calvin. It was a declaration of faith that brought instant trouble.

When Harsnett was born the Elizabethan settlement of the church, the first stage of the great Anglican compromise, was itself only three years old.[3] After the progressively radical protestantism of Edward VI's reign, and the holocaust of the Marian reaction, Elizabeth I and her advisers had returned to a position close to Henry VIII's notions of a traditional orthodoxy without the pope, whilst accepting the milder developments of her brother's reign. The doctrine of transubstantiation had gone, the English prayer book was prescribed (though learned communities could use Latin prayers), the religious houses were not restored. There were, however, to be bishops, deans and chapters, archdeacons and rural deans, rectors, tithes, and patrons. There were also to be surplices, liturgical ceremony, including the sign of the Cross in baptism, kneeling at holy communion, and a conservative regard to the historic furnishings of churches. All those offices, devices, and assumptions were anathema to the radical protestants, who took their inspiration from John Calvin's *Institutes*, and a source of anxiety to many souls who either could discern no logical stopping-place on what seemed to be the steepening slope of Geneva, or who hoped, ingenuously, to buy a more peaceful life by conceding points to radical fanaticism.[4]

Even by English standards the notion of compromise might seem a strange one in religion, but the Elizabethan settlement would not have survived if it had not been acceptable to the greater part of the population. It satisfied a conservative regard for tradition, and especially for proprietorial rights, a matter of great consequence, but at the same time conceded the principle of individual access to the Scriptures for which the martyrs of Mary's reign had been seen to die. The English reformation would nevertheless have been a much bloodier affair if Mary had not married a Spanish husband, and then by her single-minded enthusiasm irrelevantly identified the old religion with alien rule. Not even the power of the pope, which had since the later Middle Ages been a matter of some ambivalence in England, mattered as much as the detested Spanish connection, a danger of which Mary's father-in-law, the Emperor Charles V, had repeatedly and vainly warned her.

There were nevertheless dangers enough for Elizabeth and her advisers. The bishops themselves were divided, some being unwilling and others reluctant to enforce a conformity without which their own order could not survive.[5] By the time that Harsnett went to Cambridge the first precarious years of the settlement were past, but there was a looming threat from Spain, which for some time was more apparent than real, and from 1568 to 1587 the troublesome presence of Mary, Queen of Scots. While she was alive Mary's French affiliations were the best protection that the country had against a Spanish invasion. Yet she was also a continuing focus of plots which howsoever disparate or impracticable were a threat to stability, as were many of the measures proposed to resolve the problem. There was therefore both before and after Mary's death and the great deliverance from the Armada in 1588 a climate of irritable excitement, in which it was more profitable to accuse an opponent of papistry than of an excessive zeal for the protestant religion.

It was correspondingly a hazardous time at which to attack the Calvinist doctrine of predestination, the assertion that only the elect would escape damnation, with a corollary that only the elect should be eligible to manage the affairs of this world. It was a creed that has the merit of making even the extremest views of most other sects seem warm and open-hearted, but it had a powerful appeal to those whose cast of mind or inner promptings told them that, without presuming to anticipate the ineluctable judgement of God, they either were or might well be of the elect. Harsnett chose to assail the doctrine, and did so in the most prominent pulpit in the kingdom. It was a bold gesture, even for a young man, and it produced an indignant response. He was denounced as a Romanist, an instrument of the pope, of Spain, and of Antichrist.

The archbishop of Canterbury, John Whitgift, summoned him and ordered him never to preach upon the issue again, an injunction which Harsnett obeyed. Whitgift was peculiarly vexed because he accepted the logic of Calvin's views on divine grace without subscribing to the Genevan theory and practice of government. His great object was to secure uniformity in the Anglican church by the use of the book of common prayer, a burden then as later to those who preferred spontaneous effusion to measured prose, and subscription to the 39 Articles, a statement of faith better taken whole than chewed.

It was not a light matter to cross the archbishop, but Whitgift had a regard for talent, and there were others in the church who had more sympathy with Harsnett's opinions. He found no immediate preferment, but in March 1587 he was appointed master of the free grammar school in Colchester, which had been re-established under royal letters patent in 1585. The statutes prepared for the school by the bishop of London and the dean of St. Paul's required the master to teach his pupils Latin and Greek, and to be of sound religion devoid of papistry. Harsnett's fitness was attested by letters from Pembroke which were signed amongst others by his colleague Lancelot Andrewes, later bishop of Winchester and one of the most distinguished theologians of the time. A year's experience, however, convinced Harsnett that he was not apt to teach, and that he would be better employed in theological studies. He therefore resigned and returned to Cambridge, urging the corporation of Colchester to appoint his friend Mark Sadlington of Peterhouse in his place. The corporation preferred William Bentley of Clare Hall, and so moved Harsnett to ask to be reimbursed for his expenses about the schoolhouse and its orchard, which otherwise, he said, he would have borne in silence.[6] Sadlington went on to become master of St. Olave's school in Southwark, and died vicar of Sunbury.

Harsnett remained in Cambridge for a decade, though he did not formally complete his studies for the doctorate. He was junior proctor in 1592, and he evidently enhanced his scholarly reputation. In 1596 he was again involved in controversy when with Andrewes, then master of Pembroke, and John Overall, the regius professor of divinity, he took the side of Peter Baro, the Lady Margaret professor of divinity, who had laid himself open to accusations of heretical tolerance.

The opinions which Baro had aired were of the kind later known as Arminian, from the Latinized form of the name of the Dutch theologian Jakob Hermansen.[7] Arminianism came to be a generic term for the high church Anglicanism of the early seventeenth century, covering views as various as those of Andrewes and Harsnett on the one hand and Archbishop Laud on the other. Hermansen's own position was undogmatic and humane, disposed to see merits in other professions of faith, and convinced of a need for toleration to preserve the amenities of civil society. The views and experience of Baro, a refugee from religious intolerance in France, were very similar, and the positions taken by Baro's supporters were substantially those of the dominant party in the Anglican church before the Civil War. However, Archbishop Whitgift had promulgated articles at Lambeth in 1595 which were framed to accommodate Calvinist dogma within the Anglican church, and he did not wish to see his careful construct assailed. In the event Baro withdrew from Cambridge, but his friends remained unscathed despite the local strength of Calvinist and broadly puritanical feeling.

Harsnett was the youngest and the least well established of the three theologians who had refused to condemn Baro. That Baro also enjoyed the support of Lord Burleigh as chancellor of the university was a reassurance, but Harsnett's defiance was probably decisive in earning him the approval of Richard Bancroft, bishop of London. Bancroft had had some sympathies with puritans in his youth, but they had vanished with time. He made Harsnett one of his chaplains, and shortly afterwards instituted him to the vicarage of Chigwell, and to the prebend of Mapesbury at St. Paul's in 1598. He also put Harsnett on to a commission which examined and condemned John Darrell, a busy but careless exorcist who had told his accomplices what they should say, but not that they should conceal the instructions which they had received. Harsnett's attitude to such abuses of credulity and the accusations of witch-craft that went with them was exemplary for its time.[8]

Soon afterwards Harsnett was himself betrayed by a former friendship. John Hayward, also of Pembroke College, wrote a history of the deposition of Richard II and the first year of Henry IV's reign. The theme was one to which Elizabeth was sensitive, and the work bore a dedication to the earl of Essex, who was about to take up the deputyship in Ireland that led on to his rebellion and ruin. Hayward was flattered by the interest which Essex had shown in his work, and the dedication may have been inserted after the text came to Harsnett as the bishop's commisary. It was Harsnett's duty to license works for the press, and when Hayward's text reached him, through the hands of another member of Bancroft's household, with a request that he approve it, he did so without studying it.

It seems likely that Hayward acted naïvely rather than treasonably, and

St. Mary the Virgin, Chigwell.
(Photograph courtesy of Essex Record Office)

St. Mary the Virgin, Shenfield.
(Photograph courtesy of Essex Record Office)

All Saints, Hutton.

(Photograph courtesy of Essex Record Office)

All Saints, Stisted.

(Photograph courtesy of Essex Record Office)

Harsnett acted carelessly. There is little to be said in favour either of writing or endorsing seditious works by inadvertence, and even if Essex himself had had a stronger instinct of self-preservation Hayward would probably have been in trouble. As it was he was examined in the Star Chamber, and spent the whole time of Essex's eclipse, rebellion, trial, and execution in the Tower. Harsnett feared imprisonment and worse, and had to exculpate himself by humble submissions to Coke, the attorney general. Hayward too survived, after a longer term of anxiety, pursued historical research undeterred by his experiences, and lived to be knighted by James I, to whom he expressed a warm regard for the divine right of kings.

Harsnett's own return to grace was marked early in 1603 by his appointment as archdeacon of Essex. In the same year he renewed his attack on pretended exorcisms, this time by Jesuits, in a work published at the behest of the privy council.[9] It is a curiosity of the episode that Shakespeare seems to have drawn on Harsnett's text for the tally of spirits recited by Edgar in *King Lear*.[10] In 1605, when a second edition of the tract was printed, he returned to Pembroke, being elected master upon the resignation of Lancelot Andrewes, who had become bishop of Chichester.

In the event, Harsnett's time as master was not a happy one. That there was friction with some of the fellows was not remarkable. Harsnett's high church views were not universally popular, and heads of houses are not always and continuously in accord with their colleagues. He had, however, many distractions. He became vice-chancellor of the university in 1607, and then in 1609 was elected to the see of Chichester, again following Lancelot Andrewes, who had been translated to Ely. In that year he exchanged and surrendered some of his benefices. He had resigned Chigwell in 1605, but was presented to the vicarage of Hutton in 1606. Before his election to Chichester in 1609 he resigned his prebend at St. Paul's to Bishop Bancroft's nephew, John Bancroft, who had been Robert Burton's tutor at Christ Church and later became master of University College and bishop of Oxford. He received the rectory of Stisted, a valuable living, on that occasion, and was allowed to retain it when he became bishop of Chichester, though he resigned it on his further promotion in 1619.

In 1614 Harsnett again became vice-chancellor, and received James I and Prince Charles on the king's first visit to Cambridge in the following year. The vice-chancellor took pains over the event, and the king was pleased by the results. Harsnett's standing was now high at court, but his college was no better contented with him. He had expressed a wish to resign in 1612, but in 1616 the fellows petitioned the king with a tale of 57 grievances against him. His supposed affection for popery ranked first, but his absences were a cause of discontent, and he was accused of misusing college funds, as well as many lesser delicts of a kind readily remembered when a community devotes itself to denunciation. A leading figure in the movement against him was the young Matthew Wren, later bishop of Ely, father of Christopher. Wren's public career brought him much the same disapprobation as Harsnett endured, but he showed a lively interest in the administration both of Pembroke and of Peterhouse, where he was master from 1625 to 1635, and he was a notable benefactor of Pembroke after his long imprisonment during the Civil War and Interregnum.

There was nothing to be done about the doctrinal rift between Harsnett and his colleagues; his views were unambiguous and consistent. He was conservative, comfortable with and comforted by what was familiar; devout, with a scholarly interest in the traditions of the church. He had no patience with radicalism, and he probably did not judge individuals well if he suspected their motives, or conversely, if their declarations were reassuring. Much of his trouble in college seems to have arisen not simply from his absence but from the fact that he appointed unsatisfactory presidents in his place. Yet he was not wholly preoccupied by university and public affairs, and although he was fitful in his attention to the accounts he made a valuable lease of land on Pembroke Street, and found the funds to build the northern wing of the Inner Court.

The fellows persisted in their campaign, appealing to Bishop Andrewes at Ely and to the chancellor of the university, the earl of Suffolk. Opposition almost certainly made Harsnett less willing to leave, but there was no prospect of peace for either party until he did. He resigned on 18 February 1616, and was succeeded by Nicholas Felton, who later became bishop of Bristol in 1617, and of Ely in 1619, when Lancelot Andrewes was translated to Winchester.

In 1619 John Overall died only a year after he had been translated from Lichfield to Norwich, and Harsnett was appointed to succeed him.[11] Norwich was a large and populous see. In the later Middle Ages the wealth of the region had filled its churches with many tokens of personal piety, and the abundance of woodwork, sculpture, and painted glass which remains even today shows that the reformers' zeal had not succeeded in purging them bare.[12] Much of the piety had, nevertheless, turned to puritan feeling, which was rife all over East Anglia. The spiritual state of the diocese therefore offered an irresistible challenge to a devout bishop of 'great learning, strong parts, and stout character', as Fuller described him.

Harsnett applied himself to the good order of the church in his diocese, enforcing discipline and the maintenance of church buildings as well as the performance of the prescribed liturgy. Almost everything that he did of that sort was offensive to the puritan conscience, whilst his own undeniable piety left his opponents with little to denounce but his opinions, and what Prynne called his domineering outrage in expressing them.[13] He was not always at odds with his flock, and worked closely with the authorities in Norwich in maintaining the interests of the refugee Walloon church which was accommodated in the bishop's chapel there.[14] There were other susceptibilities, however, and the citizens raised a petition against him in parliament in 1624, which was presented to the Lords with some embellishment from Sir Edward Coke, who was busy at the time with popular causes. The petition alleged that he had set up images of various kinds in churches, that he enforced ceremonial, had taken extortionate fees, but neglected to register institutions. Their chief grievance, however, was that he had suppressed the Sunday lecturers whom the corporation had appointed, and whom the petitioners rejoiced to hear.

Lecturers were preachers appointed by corporations and other bodies of trustees. They could be seen as supplementing or enhancing the work of the parochial clergy, or as subverting the role of the clergy, their patrons, and for good measure the hierarchy, in the interest of some sectarian group. They were commonly though not invariably associated with puritan feeling, but corporate pride and other sensibilities were also involved.[15] Harsnett defended himself in the Lords without difficulty, refuting the allegations, and pointing out that he had sought only to ensure that the lecturers' godly exercises were held at hours that would not conflict with ordinary services. He had some similar exchanges with the corporation of Great Yarmouth, commending the magistrates over the suppression of anabaptism in the town, but watching them closely in their appointment of preachers. At Yarmouth, where there was a long history of dissent, the farm of the rectory was used to endow what might be termed a civic clergy, but there were everywhere as many nuances at large as there were congregations.[16]

Harsnett maintained some state in the palace at Norwich, 'keeping residence and hospitality all the time it was fit for his place and degree', and paying a keeper to watch the buildings and grounds. He spent more than £2,000 there and at the palace at Ludham in the Broadlands, where he built a chapel.[17]

In 1628 Harsnett was appointed archbishop of York, in succession to George Montaigne, who had once been chaplain to the earl of Essex, and who had realized a long ambition in attaining the see only to die within a few months of his election. Harsnett's own tenure, as it happened, was of less than three years. He was elected on 26 November 1628, and was sworn of the privy council a year later. On that occasion he received congratulations not only from the university of Cambridge but also from his former colleagues at Pembroke, who may have felt that they had judged him too readily. In 1629 he endowed a school at Chigwell to mark his ascent from the vicarage there to the dignity of the archbishopric. It was a double foundation, with an English and a Latin school on the same premises. The English school provided a general education and the first rudiments of Latin to all the boys of Chigwell, with four places for two boys from each of Loughton, Woodford, and Lambourne, whilst the Latin school offered a classical education to 12 Chigwell boys, with six other places reserved for the neighbouring parishes. Harsnett stipulated that the master, who was to use the best ancient authors in his teaching and to punish his pupils only with moderation, was to be neither a tippler nor a smoker. He built a gallery in the church to accommodate the school at services, which remained in use until the restoration of 1886.[18]

Harsnett had little time in which to make an impression in his new diocese, though he gave every sign of continuing the work which he had started in Norwich. He built a chapel at Armley, to serve the expanding population of Leeds, which was finished in 1630 though it was not formally consecrated until 1670. He is said to have been greatly taken with the church of All Saints, North Street, in York, to which he presented a silver cup and cover in 1630. He may, with his interest in the antiquities of the church, have been impressed by the array of medieval glass in All Saints, which is remarkable even by the high standards of the city of York.[19]

In the first year of his time in York, Harsnett was engaged in drafting 'Considerations for the better settling of church government' which William Laud, then bishop of London, laid before the king in December 1629. He fell ill in 1630, and spent some time at Bath in the following winter. After a brief remission in the spring he died at Moreton-in-the-Marsh on 25 May 1631, and was buried at Chigwell on 7 June. He wanted no pomp at his funeral beyond 'a sober civil banquet' for those parishioners who chose to attend it, but he specified the design of the great brass which was placed over his tomb, and which shows him in mitre, cope, and rochet, holding a book and his pastoral staff.

Harsnett's memorial is an eloquent statement of his beliefs and values. The very form of the brass, with the figure set between shields and enclosed with an inscribed border, looks back consciously to medieval effigies, and away from the engraved plates which were characteristic of the sixteenth century. Harsnett's life, scholarly and devout, was imbued with tradition, but with tradition as a lively source of inspiration. His library in turn reflected his life, and it was natural that he should think of preserving it for the use of posterity. In making his provisions for it, however, he was undoubtedly influenced by the example of Tobias Mathew, his predecessor but one in the see of York (1606–28), whose books became the foundation of Bristol City Library.[20]

Harsnett bequeathed his books to the bailiffs and corporation of Colchester, upon condition only that they provided a suitable room for them, and that the clergy of the town and other readers should have free access to them. The corporation accepted the legacy, and housed the books, which numbered nearly a thousand, in a room at the east end of the Red Row, the old cloth hall which stood at the top of the town, on the site of the later Essex and Suffolk Fire Office. In 1635 the town appointed a keeper of the library, and later ordered a catalogue to be made. The books remained there until the room was let for other purposes in 1663, when they were transferred to the free school in Culver Street. In the meantime they had been mortgaged for a time in 1654 to the chamberlain.[21] They had probably always been an object of indifference if not of suspicion to Colchester's radical protestants, and there was evidently no great press of readers. They were rescued from neglect and decay by Philip Morant in the eighteenth century, and housed in the Castle in the rooms which had been restored by Charles Gray. There they remained, together with the collection, begun by Gray, known as the Castle Library, until the first municipal library was opened in West Stockwell Street in 1894. In the meantime, however, under the promptings of J. H. Round, the corporation commissioned a catalogue by Gordon Goodwin, which was printed in 1888. The catalogue, completed only a few years before R. G. C. Proctor revolutionized the classification of early printed books,[22] is a highly competent piece of work, and essential to any study of the collection.[23]

The title-page, with the signature of John Foxe, of Juan de Torquemada's Questiones spiritualis convivii delitias preferentes, *printed in Paris by François Regnault, 1510, and bound in London by John Reynes, c.1525 (Harsnett Lib. K.d.4).*

In 1939 Harsnett's books and the most valuable material from the Castle Library were removed for safety to a country house in Herefordshire, where they suffered some damage from damp.[24] On their return to Colchester in 1946 they were treated and restored by the library staff, and the stench of the fumigant paste which was applied to the bindings is still vividly remembered by those who can recall the time. In 1947 they were installed in a specially fitted room in the new public library in Shewell Street. They are now housed in a controlled atmosphere in Colchester Central Library in Trinity Square.

A private library is a very expressive document; books have something to say about their owners as well as about those who wrote them. The message may be muted by time and circumstances, and a library which has survived the vicissitudes of more than three hundred years may not have survived in precisely the form that its original owner intended, though its tale may well be the richer for that.

There are now some 875 books in the Harsnett collection, though that figure includes at least a score of later accretions. The original size of Harsnett's own library is probably now impossible to ascertain, but it was clearly larger than what remains. There have certainly been some losses in the past, but a small number of volumes may have strayed in from the Castle collection, though none seems to have moved in the opposite direction. It is also difficult, however, to take a precise account of what remains. There are a number of apparent duplicates, which may be distinct editions, and works printed and ostensibly issued together but separately paginated. Some of the volumes contain, after the manner of medieval manuscripts, subsidiary works bound in which might or might not be regarded as separate titles. There are also some inconsistencies and a small number of breaks in the sequence of shelf marks. The arithmetic of editions, imprints, and places is likely always to have some rough edges.

Harsnett wrote his name in his books often but not invariably, and he more frequently noted a press-mark. There are, however, volumes enough which either have lost those marks or never bore them. The library was reclassified at some later date, not apparently by Morant but probably before it was lodged in the Castle. A figure of some 900 works is, however, a reasonable one for the collection as it now stands.

The library is a working theologian's library, and not the accumulation of a collector or connoisseur. It contains some remarkable antiquities and some fine pieces of printing, but there is probably nothing that Harsnett acquired and kept for the sake of its appearance alone. Associations are another matter, for there are many works which came to him from friends, though again they were books which were chosen chiefly for use. It seems too that Harsnett did not bind his books in any systematic way. He was an unostentatious man, and he appears to have favoured plain bindings when he did not preserve the volume as it came to him. The books stamped with Whitgift's arms, or bearing Bancroft's initials, were kept as they were for their associations. A substantial number of books came to him from his college friend John Field, who was elected to a fellowship at Pembroke in 1593. There is nothing to show how or when they did so, but the annotations and marks of earlier ownership suggest that Field may have been a more conscious collector of titles than Harsnett himself.

The heart of the library is a collection of 120 Bibles and biblical texts, including the five volumes of Plantin's polyglot Bible, in Hebrew, Syriac, Greek, and Latin, printed at Antwerp between 1569 and 1571.[25] There is also a fine polyglot edition of the psalms, in Hebrew, Greek, Arabic, and Syriac, with Latin glosses, printed at Genoa in 1516. The oldest of the biblical texts dates from 1500, printed at Lyons, and the latest from Cologne, the *Book of Numbers* with a commentary printed in 1623. There is only one English Bible, the version of the Genevan text known as the Breeches Bible because Genesis 3:7 speaks of breeches of fig-leaves, printed in London in 1589, and bound with a battered copy of the *Book of Common Prayer*.[26] Harsnett must have had copies of the Authorized Version, but they were either not kept with his working books or were removed before or after the books came to Colchester. His chapels at Norwich and York, and in his other residences, were surely so provided.

What is striking about the biblical texts is that, with their much larger supporting apparatus of commentaries and patristic writings, they continue the medieval tradition of scriptural studies. Like the collected editions of the fathers of the church,[27] the multi-lingual editions were a product of the previous century of scholarship, and they gave to those able to use them an opportunity to consider and reflect upon the making of the Vulgate itself. The famous lectures which Colet gave at Oxford in 1498 on St. Paul's epistle to the Corinthians had opened the Bible to study as an historical and literary text, but the traditional emphases on the harmony of the Old and New Testaments continued. The intensive scholastic commentaries on individual passages and books known as postils were still studied, and medieval writers such as Nicholas de Lira, represented here in an edition of 1502, from Basle, and the Dominican Nicholas Gorran as published in Paris in 1531,[28] were still read for their own sake. The use and comprehensive nature of printed texts would be surprising to a medieval student, but the syllabus of study would be more than broadly familiar.

The older works plainly came to Harsnett through other hands, but it is not clear how he acquired those which were not bequests. The largest number of titles, nearly 200, dating from a single decade fall between 1581 and 1590, whereas there are only 50 between 1570 and 1580, and 60 between 1590 and 1600. The numbers then decline quite sharply, with 41 from the first decade of the seventeenth century, 15 from 1611–20, and only four printed after 1620. It is not surprising that he should have acquired fewer books in that time than during his years of study and teaching in Cambridge, though he might then have received presentations from colleagues and aspirants. Archbishop Abbott's *A Treatise of the Perpetuall Visibilitie, and Succession of the True Church in All Ages*, London, 1624, would fall into that category.[29] Harsnett certainly added a volume to his extensive collection of the works of and commentaries on St. Thomas Aquinas in or after 1622.[30] Those last years are the only time at which we can be sure that current titles came into his possession. It is also quite possible that the very earliest works, which include some fine printing, came to him in the later years of his life.

Those older works stretch back into the fifteenth century. The year 1500 had no particular significance for the printing trade, but it is conventionally accepted as marking off the time when printing was in its swaddling clothes or infancy. In fact the principal innovation that differentiated the printed book from the manuscript, the title page, was introduced before 1500, though it established itself quite slowly even after that date, whilst the full alphabetical index of contents, which was one of the most important advances in the management of information, was still something of a novelty until the later years of the century. There are at least 13 works from the late fifteenth century in the Harsnett Library, besides one or two incomplete texts. The oldest of them was printed at Strasbourg in 1483, a collection of meditations on the life of Christ by Ludolph of Saxony, prior of the Charterhouse there.[31] Other titles from the 1480s are from Cologne (1486), two from Nuremburg (1489), and a *summa* or Pantheologia by Rainer de Pisis in two handsome volumes with illuminated initials, printed in Venice by Herman Lichtenstein of Cologne.[32] There is one other title from Strasbourg, two from Rouen (1495), a *Destructorium viciorum* of 1496 from Nuremburg, and one title each from Basle (1498), Freibourg (1493),[33] Paris (1495), besides a fine copy of Bernhardt von Breydenbach's *Journey to Jerusalem*, illustrated with folded woodcuts, printed at Speyer in 1490.

There are then 15 works from the decade 1511–20, and another six from 1521–30, including titles from the Paris master printers Jean Petit and the family of Estienne. One of the finest of the early sixteenth century works is the three volumes of the *Questiones* of Marsilius de Ingen on the Sentences of Peter Lombard, printed by Martin Flach the younger at Strasbourg in 1501.[34] There are also two copies of Francis Regnault's edition of the *Questiones* of Juan de Torquemada (1388–1468) printed in 1510, a commentary on the Gospel lectionary, the first with Henry VIII's arms on the cover, and containing the signature of John Foxe, and the second in the characteristic binding of Whitgift's library.

Of the many centres of printing represented in the library the first is London, though its predominance is not as great as might be expected. Harsnett's interests and tastes made his books a genuinely European collection. There are some 150 London imprints, but that number is substantially increased by the 24 forms of prayer, beginning with a Litany of 1559, issued on various occasions in Elizabeth's reign and now bound together.[35] There is also a small number of titles from Oxford and Cambridge, largely commemorative pieces. Pietro Martire Vermigli's tractate and debate upon the Eucharist, the occasion of a major debate and some disturbance in Oxford in 1549, was printed in that year in London, as its nature warranted.[36]

The next city after London is Basle, with more than 100 titles, with Paris close behind at 90. There are then some 75 from Antwerp, and more than 60 each from Zurich and Cologne. There are fewer than 50 from Venice and Geneva, 40

PASCHA.
಄

T O M V S. P R I M V S.

P A R I S I I S, m
Apud Iacobum Dupuys, ſub Samaritana in vico
D. Ioannis Lateranenſis.

1 5 5 3

The device of Jacques Dupuys (Christ at the well with the Samaritan woman), at the end of vol. I of
Johan von Eck's Homiliarum, *Paris, 1553 (Harsnett Lib. I.A.9.).*

from Frankfurt-am-Main, and 20 from Mainz. Three late works from Venice are the *Flagellum Demonum* of Girolamo Menghi, a work on exorcism published in 1597 and again in 1599, and a volume of adjurations called *Fuga Demonum*, 1596,[37] which are texts which Harsnett asembled for his continuing study of the subject. There are only a handful of titles from Amsterdam, a significant centre of printing during the period, but of less immediate consequence to Harsnett and his colleagues than Douai or Louvain, where the recusant presses produced works of exegesis and controversy that commanded their attention. The same is true of Italy, where Rome, Florence, and Milan are quite thinly represented.

In the same way the collection at large contains no literature other than classical literature, and almost no history but ancient history. Of science there is a work on alchemy, *Artis auriferae*, Basle, 1593, but no sign of William Gilbert's *De Magnete*, London, 1600, the work of a distinguished fellow Colcestrian. There are, however, some geographical books, including Peter Martyrus Anglerius, *De Rebus Oceanicis*, printed at Cologne in 1574, and an incomplete Gerard Mercator *Atlas sive Cosmographice Meditationes* revised at Amsterdam in 1613. Given the general cast of the collection, however, the presence of Andrew Maunsell's *The First Part of the Catalogue of English Printed Books*, a monument of English bibliography printed in London in 1595, and extensively annotated by Harsnett, can be taken at least as an earnest of good intentions.

Harsnett had predominantly a Latin library, and he used Latin freely. There are comparatively few Greek texts amongst his books, though they include an annotated Euclid,[38] and a Horologium, containing the canonical hours of the Greek Orthodox church, printed at Venice in 1581.[39] He probably read French, and possibly German, though the currency of Latin throughout the European churches made those accomplishments of the less consequence to the scholars of the day. He seems to have laboured at Hebrew, having a Plantin Old Testament in four volumes printed at Antwerp in 1566, and several grammars, one of which had belonged to Whitgift.[40]

There is still much to be won from the contents of Harsnett's library. His preference for keeping books in their original bindings has preserved specimens of English work dating from the early years of the sixteenth century,[41] examples of Oxford and Cambridge bindings over several decades,[42] and a wide conspectus of taste throughout the century. The range of the works which he accumulated is a commentary both upon his own education and career and upon the religious, scholarly, public, and social issues of his time. He sought to make some return to the town and county of his birth by his bequests, and the briefest view of his labours will show that his bounty is by no means exhausted.

REFERENCES

1   See G. Goodwin, *A Catalogue of the Harsnett Library at Colchester*, London, 1888. I am glad to express my thanks to Mr Peter Henderson, Principal Area Librarian (Operations), at Colchester Central Library, for enabling me to consult Harsnett's books, to Dr A. V. Grimstone, of Pembroke College, Cambridge, for friendly assistance, and to my colleague Dr Michael Sommerlad for the use of his valuable notes on the bindings in the collection.

2   He was presented to the rectory of Shenfield by Sir Thomas Lucas in 1604. On the religious climate in Colchester, see further the D.Phil. thesis by M. S. Byford, 'The price of Protestantism: assessing the impact of religious change on Elizabethan Essex: The cases of Heydon and Colchester, 1558–94', Oxford, 1988.

3   For the general posture of affairs, and especially the interplay of politics and doctrine, see P. Williams, *The Later Tudors: England 1547–1603*, Oxford, 1995, pp.454–96.

4   For the phenomenon and phenomenology of puritanism, see P. Collinson, *The English Puritan Movement*, London, 1967. There is a sharply focused and valuable acount of the ideological contest for control of the church in T. C. Porter, *Reformation and Reaction in Tudor Cambridge*, Cambridge, 1958.

5   For a sympathetic account of a reformer in office, see P. Collinson, *Archbishop Grindal, 1518–93: The Struggle for a Reformed Church*, London, 1979.

6   G. Goodwin, *Catalogue*, pp.vi–viii.

7   See further N. Tyacke, *The Anti-Calvinists: The Rise of English Arminianism, 1596–1640*, Oxford, 1987.

8   See Harsnett's account, *A Discoverie of the fraudulent practises of John Darrell, bacheler of artes, detecting in some sort the deceitfull trade in these latter days of casting out devils*, London, 1599; and Morant's comments in *History of Colchester*, 1768, p.122.

9   *A declaration of egregious Popish impostures under the pretence of casting out devils, practised by Edmunds, alias Weston. a Jesuit*, London, 1603.

10 Act iii, scene iv; Act iv, scene i.

11 On Harsnett's mastership, see Pembroke College, Cambridge; S. C. Roberts, ed., *A short history by Aubrey Attwater*, Cambridge, 1936, pp.58–70. See also G. Goodwin, *Catalogue*, p.xiv and n.

12 See, e.g., the fine roodscreen and the painted rood at Ludham, where the bishops had a palace. The painted tympanum was preserved by the simple and interesting expedient of reversing it and painting the royal arms on the back: H. M. Cautley, *Norfolk Churches*, Ipswich, 1949, p.218.

13 W. Prynne, *The Antipathie of the English Lordly Prelacie*, London, 1641, pp.241–2. Prynne, who had suffered much from bishops, also called Harsnett a furious Hildebrand, which is at least a better model for a prelate than a Borgia would be.

14 See *V.C.H. Norfolk*, ii, pp.279–80. It is interesting that some of the churches in Norwich were regularly dressed with holly and ivy at Christmas, which suggests a fund of conservative feeling: *ibid.*, p.281.

15 See Morant's delicate account of the General Preachers or Lecturers of Colchester in *The History of Colchester*, 2nd edition, 1768, p.100.

16 See further H. Swinden, *The History and Antiquities of Great Yarmouth*, Norwich, 1772, pp.816–43.

17 See R. S. Rait, ed., *English Episcopal Palaces, Province of Canterbury*, London, 1910, pp.235–6.

18 He had earlier built a gallery at the west end of the church, perhaps when raising a memorial to his wife: *V.C.H. Essex*, iv, p.34.

19 See *V.C.H. Yorks: City of York*, p.370.

20 See N. Mathews, *Early Printed Books and Manuscripts in the City Reference Library, Bristol*, Bristol, 1899, pp.7–8. Archbishop Mathew's collection, though richer in early printed works, was much smaller than Harsnett's.

21 G. Goodwin, *Catalogue*, p.xxv.

22 See further R. G. C. Proctor, *Index of Early Printed Books from the Invention of Printing to the Year MD*, London, 1898.

23 See above n.1. The catalogue was printed but not published, the 250 copies being held and distributed by the corporation. For a recent notice of the collection in the light of other private libraries, see D. Pearson, 'The libraries of English bishops', *The Library*, xiv, 1992, pp.221–57, at p.242.

24 See Borough of Colchester, *52nd Annual Report of the Public Library Committee, 1945–6*, p.8.

25 K. h. 2–6.

26 I. g. 13.

27 See the three sets of St. Augustine's works, in 23 volumes printed between 1529 and 1543: *Catalogue*, pp.12–13; and the 26 volumes of the works of St. Thomas Aquinas, ranging from 1500 (on Aristotle's Ethics, H. g. 35 (2); and on the Gospel lectionary for Sundays and Lent, H. g. 35 (3), both printed at Venice) to 1622 (Francisco Suarez on three sections of the *Summa*, H. h. 17, printed at Mainz).

28 H. c. 27–31; and K. f. 28.

29 Printed by Humfrey Lownes for Robert Milbourn: K. d. 37.

30 Commentaries and disputations by Francisco Suarez: see above, n.27. An earlier volume of Suarez's commentaries had come to him from Whitgift: H. h. 18, printed at Mainz in 1600.

31 K. h. 7.

32 H. c. 15–16.

33 The works from Basle (K. f. 11) and Freibourg (H. b. 18) are editions of the *Sententiae* of Peter Lombard, bishop of Paris, 1159–60, which was the principal text for speculative theology from his day to the seventeenth century.

34 H. b. 11–13. Each part bears the signature of Thomas Cranmer (1489–1556) and of John, Lord Lumley (1534–1609), a collector, most of whose books were bought for Henry, prince of Wales, and so entered the royal library.

35 I. f. 11; G. Goodwin, *Catalogue*, pp.99–103.

36 K. d. 29.

37 I. b. 24 and 27; and I. c. 5.

38 *Euclidis Elementarum Libri XV*, Paris, 1558, conceivably an undergraduate text: I. g.20.

39 I. g. 20. There are, in comparison, only five works of the Roman liturgy, as distinct from biblical and theological texts. They include a Sarum processional, printed in Rouen in 1555: K. e. 51.

40 H. a. 32–5; Nicolas Clenard, *Tabula in grammaticen Hebream*, Paris, 1550, H. d. 14.

41 See, e.g., Torquemada's *Questiones*, K. d. 4; and Bercheur, *Dictionarius*, K. g. 13–15, an early Cambridge binding.

42 See, e.g., the border stamps of Nicholas Spierinck (1507–15) on Antoninus *Summa Theologica*, Florence, 1506: K. f. 30; and above n.41.

The Religious Census of Essex, 1851[1]

MICHAEL BEALE

IN 1851 — AND THEREAFTER NEVER AGAIN — it was decided to include, as part of the normal decennial national census, an additional section about churches and other places of worship. Britain then still saw itself as a Christian country, and hence Government and people had a proper public concern in assuring themselves that sufficient seating was available in places of worship of all denominations to ensure that no part of the community was deprived of the opportunity — indeed of fulfilling the duty — of worshipping in the church of their choice. The implicit assumption was that in a free and wealthy society men of goodwill, having been alerted that these gaps existed in the provision of a necessary service, would exert themselves to ensure that the shortfall was met. And the great number of churches of all denominations built in the decades immediately before and after 1851, even by the impoverished and unpopular Roman Catholic community, showed that this assumption was nearly correct.

This decision having been taken, other associated questions offered themselves for inclusion. Many of these were inspired, to a greater or lesser extent, by the politics of the day. It would be helpful to know something of the time-span within which these new places of worship had been built. The endowments of the Anglican church[2] had much the same appeal to the Nonconformists (and it was then a Liberal government, much dependent on the Nonconformist vote) as the monastic endowments had to Henry VIII, and it would be helpful to quantify them. Above all, the Nonconformists reckoned that their numbers and influence were being under-estimated, and that a head-count would prove their point. So a question about church attendance on the Sunday of the census was also included, partly perhaps for disinterested information, but probably more as a gesture to the Free Churches. It was certainly not to meet Anglican wishes — they were either opposed on principle, apprehensive of what would emerge, or both.

For whatever reason this was included, it was not thought through. The other questions were factual matters which the respondent could answer in his own time. But the more thought one gave to the census of church attendance, the greater the practical problems it set. Horace Mann, the young barrister charged with administering the whole religious census, inevitably had no precedents to

The interior of Great Waltham church at about the period: a watercolour, probably the work of Miss Augusta Tufnell (1842–1918). (By permission of the Incumbent and Churchwardens)

work from. It is not surprising that we can say, with the benefit of hindsight, that it was not very well done. But we must remember that, whilst now the census of church attendance is much the most interesting part of the religious census, it was at the time no more than a secondary aspect.

The local units for the administration of the census were the Poor Law Unions: in Essex there were 17 of these, together with numerous parishes which fell within Poor Law Unions centred in neighbouring counties. In each Union a substantial local figure, often a professional man, was appointed registrar. He might well use the services of subordinate registrars. But all had to work in accordance with the edicts of, and under the distant supervision of, Mann's superior, the Registrar-General in London.

The census form, as sent to Anglican churches, is shown in Figures 1a and 1b. The attached Notes are of considerable interest, at least as much for what they failed to deal with as for what they say: having no doubt been printed fairly early on, they left untouched many problems that Mann was grappling with as the census day loomed closer. A form omitting Question V, but otherwise broadly similar, was sent to all other denominations other than the Society of Friends, but including the Roman Catholics. The form sent to the Quakers was much shorter, and included little more than the floor space in square feet and the numbers actually attending on census day.

Sunday, 30 March was not a good choice of day for the religious census. Easter was very late that year and the census day was the fourth Sunday in Lent, that is, Mothering Sunday or Refreshment Sunday. The tradition that apprentices, indentured servants and others had that day free to return to their own homes remained strong in some parts of the country and had not been allowed for. It was a busy time of year for the farming community and particularly, as respondents from such places as Brightlingsea pointed out, for fishermen — though this would no doubt have been said of any day chosen.

Finally, and most important, though hardly within the Government's control or prevision, it proved to be a very wet day throughout the country. This, as many returns pointed out, undoubtedly reduced attendance.

The Churches of England

In his Report on the Religious Census[3] Mann devoted many pages to a review of the theological position of the various denominations. His example is not one to be followed, but there are some general points which require to be made, as well as others more specifically applicable to Essex which are mentioned later.

In 1851 full religious toleration was still a very new thing, and membership of the Church of England still had some formal, and many less tangible, advantages. Though for generations Protestant nonconformists had enjoyed effective freedom of worship, the Test and Corporation Acts had only lately been removed from the statute book. The old universities were still closed to them.

State money had only recently ceased to be used for the building of Anglican churches and nonconformists resented that some was still being used for the building of church schools. Tithe was still payable by nonconformist farmers. The power of a Vestry to levy a Church Rate on all parishioners was still being argued at length in the famous Braintree Church Rate case. Any acceptance of Roman Catholic worship was still newer and more precarious, and just at that time prejudice was stirred again by the furore about the creation of the English Roman Catholic diocesan hierarchy in 1850.

The Church of England was very sensitive about this erosion of its status and authority. Its prevailing ethos was that it was specifically the church of the English nation, and on this sentiment the divergent schools of thought, the old-type high churchmen, the newer style high churchmen influenced by the Oxford Movement, the evangelicals and even the Whig Erastians and latitudinarians could all unite. The Ecclesiastical Commission, dominated by the remarkable Bishop Blomfield of London, had substantially completed its great work of eliminating the evils of plurality, non-residence and gross disparity of incomes which had disfigured the church for so long. The prevailing respect for the rights of property in a benefice meant that these evils could not be dealt with at a blow, but where they survived they were no more than personal perquisites enjoyed by ageing beneficiaries just for their lifetimes.[4]

The 'young Turks' among the bishops and senior clergy, of whom Bishop Samuel Wilberforce of Oxford was the leader, fought hard against the ecclesiastical census. They saw it as the thin end of a wedge of governmental intervention which could well lead to the partial disendowment already suffered by the Church of Ireland, and perhaps yet further. The stricter high churchmen saw any state intervention, even in matters of no great significance, as objectionable on grounds of principle. But they failed to influence the Government into either cancelling it or reducing its scope. It was however acknowledged that a clergyman was not breaking the law by refusing to answer, so this was the course of action recommended by Wilberforce and his colleagues. But they were in the minority — the Archbishops and most of the senior clergy either recommended compliance with the census or stayed discreetly silent.

The chief dividing line among the free churches was that between the 'old dissent' of the Independents, now coming to be called Congregationalists, and the Baptists, and the 'new dissent' of the various Methodist groups. Mann treated Independent and Congregationalist as synonymous, but one may suspect that some of the small and long-established 'Independent' rural congregations in such counties as Essex had very tenuous links — if any at all —with the Congregational Union in London.

The Baptists were still less homogeneous. Centralism had no place in the Baptist tradition. Their chief internal disagreements were on two theological issues. 'Particular' Baptists were Calvinists who believed that salvation was restricted to the predestined: 'General' Baptists did not share this theology. 'Strict' Baptists believed that only those who had received Believer's Baptism could be full members of the congregation: others were less rigid about membership. Hence congregations tended to divide into 'General Baptists' or 'Strict and Particular Baptists'. But this division was not invariable: not all that were 'Particular' were 'Strict', whilst some were 'Strict' but not 'Particular'.

The Methodists had entered into an era of fission. The census showed that, over the country as a whole, but not in Essex, the Wesleyan Methodists (Original Connection) were far and away the biggest religious body after the Church of England, but many other Methodist splinter groups had formed. Of these the Primitive Methodists, (often, and not always contemptuously, called 'Ranters') were undoubtedly already the largest. 1840 to 1860 was the period of their most vigorous growth, and the year of the census was therefore just the time when their missionary work, principally among the poor in many parts of the country, was at its height. Census returns point to not a few newly-formed congregations, often meeting in private houses, but no doubt there were other similar groups which the local registrars missed.

There was a multiplicity of other smaller denominations but, the Roman Catholics and the Society of Friends apart — and by comparison with those mentioned these were small in numbers — they were not of national significance.

Problems of the Attendance Census

The recalcitrance of a part of the Anglican clergy, which I have mentioned above and to which I shall return later, was by no means the only problem which Mann and his registrars had to grapple with. Some of the leaders of nonconformist congregations were men of little book learning, occasionally unable even to sign their own names, and they cannot have found it easy to complete correctly the form sent them.

One of the gravest defects of Mann's planning was that the wording of the questions on the census form, as shown in Figure 1a, made it almost inevitable that there would be double counting of many church and chapel attenders. In the first place, and probably inescapably, those who attended twice or three times on census Sunday must be counted twice or thrice. Recognizing this, the Report scrupulously spoke of 'acts of worship' not of 'worshippers', and offered the reader no excuse for believing that gross totals of worshippers for the day were to be identified with the number of church- or chapel-goers in the community. Had any made this mistake, they would have recognized their error when they saw that, in the very devout county of Bedfordshire, the total number of 'acts of worship' represented 104.6 per cent of the population.

In practice, the problem about the counting of Sunday scholars was perhaps a more serious aspect of double counting. The numbers of Sunday scholars was large — at All Saints, West Ham there were 558 on the return sent in, and at

Saffron Walden parish church, 600. These numbers were returned separately on
the form, but, then as now, many Sunday schools spent part of the time in the
church or chapel with the adult congregation. How they should be counted was a
fruitful source of uncertainty, and Mann's advice did little, if anything, to reduce
the risk of double counting.

The published Report to Parliament gives, county by county and within each
county Union by Union, the number of places of worship of each denomination
and the total number of worshippers at morning, afternoon and evening
services. The figures for Essex are summarized in Table 1 of this essay. In the
Report a note is appended giving the number of places of worship, and their
denomination, though not their names, which had failed to supply respectively
details of their seating capacity or of the numbers attending. For obvious
reasons, if no figures were supplied, none could be included in the totals. But we
shall find that, at least in Essex, it is not only these which are omitted. Mann
claimed in his report that 'he had checked the number of places of worship of
the Established Church against the clergy list' but quite a few seem to have been
completely overlooked.

There also seems to have been no consistent practice on the inclusion of
places of worship in hospitals, workhouses, residential schools and other
institutions.

When the results of the census were published its Anglican critics drew attention
to these and other methodological shortcomings as making its conclusions of little
or no value. This was of course largely a ploy to minimize both the shock and the
potential political embarrassment of finding the nonconformist share of the
population so much larger than they had thought. The critics were also rather
disingenuous, because widespread Anglican non-co-operation was a major cause
of the figures' shortcomings. But Mann's failure to see the practical problems in
sufficient time, and the rough-and-ready expedients to which he had to resort,
gave the Anglican criticisms a little more legitimacy than the usual loser's
complaint against the system.

There is another unquantifiable matter on which the census figures shed no
light. There is quite a lot of anecdotal evidence from diaries and the like that
some people had double loyalties, perhaps going to church in the morning and
chapel in the afternoon. In particular in the early days of Methodism this practice
was widespread, and indeed commended, and Methodist meeting times were
often chosen with this in mind. The census figures give no guidance as to the
survival of the practice, and whether it was a further significant source of
double counting.

The National Figures

For the reasons I have given these figures are not a trustworthy guide to either
the actual or (except perhaps in the broadest sense) the comparative strength of

the various denominations. Strictly understood, they tell us no more than the number of attendances in church or chapel on 30 March 1851, and even that with something less than full accuracy or completeness.

They indicate that the total of attendances, after, it is stated, allowances were made for defective returns, amounted to 60.8 per cent of the population of England and Wales (25.9 per cent in the morning, 17.8 per cent in the afternoon and 17.1 per cent in the evening). The figures for Anglican worship were 29.5 per cent (morning 14.2 per cent, afternoon 10.5 per cent, evening 4.8 per cent). Hence the total number of acts of Anglican worship was just marginally under half the total. In view of the substantial, but unquantifiable, amount of double counting it would not be legitimate to assume that the number of individual worshippers divided in the same proportion.

The broad geographical pattern was on the whole predictable. In general the lowland counties of the south-east from Lincolnshire to Devon were chiefly Anglican and fairly observant in religion: the towns less so than the countryside in both respects. Wales was overwhelmingly nonconformist, with a remarkably high level of observance. The northern counties of England were less observant than the south or than Wales, but the proportion of chapel-goers was appreciably higher than the number of church-going Anglicans.

In two respects these figures, when they were published, were a considerable shock to the Victorians. The first was the discovery that at least 40 per cent, and probably appreciably more, had not attended any place of worship, and this was a blow to their self-assurance that they were a religious society. This realization spurred the churches on to greater effort, but there is no reason to think that the total proportion of those who did attend public worship ever went significantly above the 1851 level.

The second is that the apparent virtual equality in size between the Anglicans and the free churchmen came as a surprise to almost all, on both sides of the divide. The realization that the Nonconformist constituency, and as successive Reform Acts were passed, the nonconformist vote, was so large had a great impact on Victorian politics. Even so, a closer look somewhat modified the picture. In all English counties except Cornwall and Durham, the Church of England remained the largest denomination. In 25 out of the 40 English counties over half of the acts of worship were in Anglican churches. The next largest denomination, the Wesleyan Methodists (Original Connection), with about 25 per cent of the acts of worship, was not more than half the size of the Church of England, and in some counties, of which Essex happened to be one, its allegiance was of no great size.

Looking at the Essex Returns

The figures in Table 1, being extracted from the Report to Parliament, have the qualities and the inadequacies noted in this essay. The tables in the Report relating to Essex, however, give only the statistics for the parishes forming part of the 17 Poor Law Unions wholly within the county. Nearly 40 parishes then forming part of the county were included in Unions chiefly within the neighbouring counties of Cambridgeshire, Hertfordshire and Suffolk. For the sake of completeness I have appended the figures for these parishes, taken from the actual returns for these parishes, to Table 1.

The figures of the returns, parish by parish, are inevitably very miscellaneous; they reflect, at least to some extent, purely local factors such as the personality of the parson or the minister. There may be other more general factors. For example it may be that much would be learned from a comparison between the comparative size of the Anglican and free church congregations in 'closed' communities — those dominated by a single landowner — and those in 'open' communities, where it was much more difficult to pressurize tenants and tradespeople into conformity. But this will have to await further research.

One point which readily, if roughly, emerges from the figures in Table 1 is that the proportion of the population which attended church or chapel increased the further one was away from London. The only Unions where the number of 'acts of worship' represented less than half of the population were West Ham, Romford and (dubiously) Orsett. In Colchester and north Essex generally the proportion was far higher, rising in the strongly nonconformist Union of Braintree to virtually 100 per cent.

Another point which emerges at least as powerfully, particularly looking from the vantage point of nearly 150 years on, is the remarkable size of the village church- and chapel-going communities. I have made no effort to compare church attendances with the total population of the parish in question as shown by the contemporary census figures because, then as now, for a multitude of reasons of personal convenience and preference, many would choose to go to a place of worship outside their parish. But to take two parishes almost at random, it is surprising that Castle Hedingham, with a population of 1,343[5] should have had 400 at its best attended church service, 798 at its best attended chapel service — and other services at both. Or that Stock, with a population of 605[6] should have had figures of 375 and 250 for its comparable services. Such figures suggest that in the rural community attendance at Sunday worship was still a prevailing part of the social pattern. The villager may or may not have been truly devout, but at least in the villages the dissociation of the working class from organized religion had not yet begun.

It is also worthy of note how frequently churches and chapels were reported as filled to, or nearly to, capacity. Sometimes, of course, this may have been wilful inflation of numbers by the signatory of the report, though those who have worked on the census believe that the returns were seldom wilfully dishonest.

In the case of Anglican churches, this puts Victorian church extensions into a different light. So often present-day incumbents and churchwardens criticize their Victorian predecessors for new building projects which, they say, were never needed and inspired only by *folie de grandeur*. But this criticism fails to appreciate the position in 1851, the year of the Great Exhibition. English agriculture was then at its highest level of prosperity for many years, villages were prosperous and well-nigh self-contained, and we have noted the size of the church and chapel attendances. It was natural to expect this state to be maintained and enhanced. Conscientous clergy, patrons and landowners would plan ahead accordingly and see themselves as far-sighted. They were unlikely to foresee either the agricultural depression, the decay of the village or the decline of church-going. Furthermore the church's most influential leaders of thought, the ecclesiologists, were pressing for the destruction of galleries and the opening up of the view to the altar: this necessitated a much larger church to accommodate the same size of congregation.

Essex — the individual denominations

The fact that Essex was so close to London did not greatly impact on its being an agricultural southern, and therefore church-going, county. There was already a modest overspill from London which had brought the population of West Ham up to 8,200[7] and Stratford to 10,600. Even so, it had no substantial town except Colchester, and this was, as it happened, of all the 60 larger English towns individually noted in the religious census, the one with the largest number of acts of worship proportionate to its population.

The figures show that 57.5 per cent of the total attendances at places of worship in the county were Anglican — the vast majority at parish churches, but some few at chapels-of-ease and daughter churches or at the few workhouse and other institutional chapels which submitted returns. The indications are that the established church in Essex was in a fairly healthy state. One may speculate that this was in no small part due to the efforts of Charles James Blomfield, briefly from 1822 to 1824 Archdeacon of Colchester, and then Bishop of London from 1828, who was much the most effective reforming bishop of the day. In 1845, as part of the reforms for which he had been working, he handed over responsibility for the whole of Essex, apart from nine parishes of the then Barking deanery, to George Murray, Bishop of (of all places) Rochester. Murray's new residence was at Danbury and he became in effect bishop of Essex with a bit of Kent and Hertfordshire tacked on. Anomalous as this arrangement was, it did at least mean that Essex had more nearly a bishop of its own than hitherto.

Methodism in Essex was weak. There were some Primitive Methodist congregations, but the majority were Wesleyan Methodists of the Original Connection. It had in all 22,799 acts of worship on the census day — many fewer than the Independents and just slightly more than the Baptists. Also, divided as this number was between 90 places of worship, their average size of congregation was considerably smaller than was that of the other leading denominations. This was perhaps in part because in many of the towns Wesleyan Methodist and

Primitive Methodist places of worship duplicated one another. Tendring hundred was exceptional in having a substantial number of Methodist village chapels. There were 20 Wesleyan and five Primitive places of worship in that Union, out of the 90 in the whole of Essex. Here the pattern of most of England replicated itself in that the Methodists were the strongest competitors with the established church.

But in the rest of Essex it was the Independents — as the Congregationalists in Essex seem for the most part still to have called themselves — who had that position. As Table 1 shows, they had 134 places of worship in the county and a total of 61,160 acts of worship on census day, that is, just under 23 per cent of the total number — seemingly a higher proportion than in any other county of England. They had chapels in all the towns and most of the larger villages throughout the county, and in their strongest areas in not a few of the smaller villages too. It seems reasonable to assume that much of this strength had been retained from Puritan times, and much of their geography would corroborate this. Their chief areas of strength were in north Essex. In Braintree Union there were more Independent than Anglican acts of worship, and villages like Castle Hedingham and White Colne had notably large Independent congregations. Perhaps the extreme case was that of Ridgewell, which on census day had 148 attendances at church and 615 at chapel.

Baptists, more usually Particular (that is, strict Calvinist) Baptists, had a not inconsiderable following spread widely throughout the county.

For the Society of Friends the glory was departed. Throughout England the meeting house accommodation for Quaker worshippers vastly exceeded their very modest attendances, and north Essex, with its powerful Quaker traditions, was an extreme case. The 16 active Meeting Houses there (Felsted was closed) had capacity to hold about 5,000, but in all 627 attended in the morning and 342 in the afternoon. The total attendance at Stebbing was six and at Witham fourteen — all credit to them for their honesty in reporting such pathetic figures. Their figures were improved a little by the relatively well-attended Meetings at Chelmsford and Plaistow. Most of those submitting returns for the Society declined on principle to give their names, but the signatory at Plaistow was a Gurney Buxton, and at the small Meeting at Theydon Garnon it was the eminent naturalist Henry Doubleday.

The position of the Roman Catholics was very different. The Petre family had sustained small groups throughout the penal period at their residences, Thorndon and Ingatestone. More recently other wealthy families like the Leschers and Taskers had established themselves around Brentwood, and doubtless some less affluent too. Another modest nucleus of worship had developed around the chapel and convent of the Canonesses of the Holy Sepulchre, who had settled at New Hall, Boreham, in 1798. But by 1851 these groups had been much surpassed in size, and would soon be swamped, by the immigrants arriving from Ireland, and their descendents. Principally to serve these incomers, by 1851 six churches had fairly recently been built, at Stratford and Walthamstow, and the four largest towns along the main road, Brentwood, Chelmsford, Witham and Colchester.

Essex was not particularly a home for the smaller religious sects. The Peculiar People did not separately identify themselves, but the groups at Rochford and other nearby places calling themselves 'Protestant Dissenters' whose returns are signed by J. Banyard and others of their leaders can be identified. It would seem that the zeal which later was to lead to the formation of the Pentecostalist groups was then sufficiently catered for by the mainstream dissenting bodies, especially the Baptists and the Primitive Methodists.

The Mormons had two congregations, at Colchester and at Barking. The Irvingite Catholic Apostolic church also had two, and the Swedenborgian New Church four, mostly in the Colchester area. Of all these, only the Mormon church at Colchester was at all well-attended. One surprising phenomenon was the 'Freethinkers' Chapel' at Great Chesterford: it would be interesting to speculate on their form of worship. There were no Presbyterian or Unitarian places of worship in the county, and no Jewish congregations.

The Reliability of the Census in Essex

The religious census contained several different questions and these had different objectives. Most of them are by now dead and irrelevant issues. But the attendance figures remain of value as the most nearly objective snapshot available of one of the most important aspects of Victorian life. Whilst mere figures cannot probe into peoples' hearts, they show in a way no other existing records can the extent of the outward profession of the Christian faith, and where the populace at large stood in the 'church v. chapel' issue, which became so important in Victorian political and social life. Hence an assessment of the reliability of these figures has continuing importance.

Anglicans suggested at the time that the free churches did a 'round-up' of their less active members to maximize their figures for the day. A few were bitter partisans enough to suggest that the ministers and deacons reporting the figures then inflated them further. Conclusive proof here is impossible, but there is no evidence or good circumstantial grounds to suggest that there was more than, at the most, occasional petty rounding-up of the figures.

Yet, even if this is conceded, a further important question remains. All that the figures in the Report to Parliament can do with full claim to credibility is to record the numbers of those who on 30 March 1851 attended those places of worship which submitted returns which were duly totted up. But what present-day students would wish to be able to gain from the figures is information that is trustworthy in the wider sense of being as nearly as is reasonably possible the complete picture. Both the attendant circumstances of the census and Mann's own statements, Union by Union, of places of worship whose attendance figures remained unrecorded leave no doubt that the omissions were mainly Anglican.

Hence closer scrutiny of the Anglican returns is necessary if one is to establish whether or not these omissions affect the wider credibility of the census.

It seems clear that the local registrars were allowed — or at least took upon themselves — a very substantial amount of discretion in how they undertook their task. This applied particularly in cases where the census forms were not returned, or returned with questions left unanswered. These could have been expected to have been mainly Anglican, and a glance through the returns confirms this. Registrars were instructed to do what they could to obtain the desired information. When clergy were unhelpful they sometimes sought the assistance of the church's lay officers — for example, the Churchwarden at St. John's, Harlow expressly said that he was making the return in view of the Vicar's refusal. In some Unions — for example, in quite a number of churches in the Colchester area — the registrar or his assistant submitted their own estimates under their own signature, without any source being named. More often than not these returns were incorporated into the Union figures, and hence ultimately into the national figures. But in other Unions such estimates were not made.

The number of Anglican parishes throughout the county which were unwilling to complete the original form was enough for Mann, at a late stage in his follow-up work, to authorize the use of a shorter form containing only the seating and attendance figures. Even so, a not insignificant number never did submit figures.

The various different Anglican responses in Essex are summarized in Table 2. It will be seen that in 17.6 per cent of the parishes which undoubtedly received returns to complete, the parishes themselves never returned their attendance figures. An appreciably higher proportion of these unhelpful parishes were urban ones. One might speculate that it was they who felt more challenged by the nonconformist churches, and were therefore the more inclined to follow the Wilberforce line. Some clergy gave reasons for their refusal to answer the questions on attendance. For example, the Vicar of Coggeshall 'declined to estimate the attendance at so large a church, nor would the attendance on one day fairly represent the general congregation'.

Furthermore there were a certain number of churches which, despite Mann's scouring of the clergy list, seem to have been left out altogether. Seemingly no returns were received from these churches (we do not know whether they were ever sent returns to complete); they do not figure in the totals in the Report to Parliament, nor, as a consequence of this are they included in Table 1. The numbers of those I have noted are given in the final column of Table 2, but there may well be others which I have missed. They are mainly in Billericay and Orsett Unions, and they include the Anglican churches of such significant places as Billericay, Brentwood, Grays Thurrock and Halstead. It is just not credible that, for example, Cornelius Butler,[8] the registrar for the Billericay Union, should have merely overlooked the first two of these. Why he — and seemingly others — did nothing about these absent returns cannot now be answered. There is of course another possibility — that they were completed and despatched, but went astray in the General Register Office.

My by no means thorough checks on the figuring of the Union totals as given in Table 1 also suggest that there is considerable variation between Unions in how the figures were totted up. Whilst most have totalled all the figures supplied, including averages, registrars' estimates etc., a few seem to have confined themselves to totalling figures supplied by the church authorities as the actuals for the day. In the extreme case of Chelmsford Union I estimate that if these less definite figures had been included in the total, the figure of Anglican attendances would have risen from 8,889 to something of the order of 12,500.

Very few returns indeed were made in Essex in respect of services conducted on census Sunday at workhouses, schools, hospitals and other residential institutions. It would seem that ordinarily forms were not supplied by the registrar. One of the few such returns made, that for Romford Union chapel (the workhouse, now Oldchurch Hospital) was for a morning attendance of 192 and an afternoon attendance of 193. Since nearly all such services would have been in the Anglican form, whatever the personal views of those willingly or reluctantly attending, this points to a further under-recording of the nominally Anglican numbers. And the Romford figures would indicate that they were not negligible.

The work I have done suggests that, therefore, the totals as reported to Parliament, though strictly true as representing the sum of the returns received, are an under-estimate of the Anglican attendance on census Sunday. This arises from:

a. the inevitable lack of figures relating to places of worship from which no returns, or blank returns, were received. (For their numbers in Essex, see Table 2.)

b. the omission in certain Unions of estimated figures of attendance from the gross totals as submitted to Parliament.

c. the virtual absence of returns from chapels of institutions.

There is no indication from my work, nor so far as I know has it been suggested elsewhere, that there are anything like comparable deviations in the free church figures. Though it is inevitable that some small religious meetings were missed, these are unlikely to have been statistically significant.

My very tentative view therefore would be that if the religious census were to be regarded as a correct account of attendance at places of religious worship on the census Sunday, the Anglican figure would need to be increased by a figure of not less than 5 per cent, and perhaps as much as 10 per cent.

If in this Essex is representative, the religious picture of England as drawn from the religious census of 1851 would require quite a substantial amendment. But the Anglicans would have no right to complain that their strength was under-estimated in this way: it was their fault in seeking to frustrate the census.

Had they co-operated, their position would have been appreciably stronger in the religious and educational wrangles over the ensuing decades: as it was, they shot themselves in the foot.

Conclusion

The foregoing is no more than a tentative and introductory essay on the Essex census. Much more work is needed, and my tentative conclusions may well prove to be wrong.

It poses many interesting questions for local historians and others to pursue. For one example, why is the history of nonconformity in Tendring hundred so different from that of the rest of Essex?

But perhaps the foremost conclusion is that the religious census, in shedding a bright light on just one day of Victorian England, thereby illuminates the rest, even if more faintly. For one moment we see the Victorian families, the great majority of them on foot,[9] trudging through the rain to church or chapel. That those wet Victorians went that day to their place of worship, undeterred by the heavy rain, in such large numbers says something important that the local historian or the social historian studying the period forgets at his peril.

Acknowledgements

My most particular thanks are due to Mrs Avril Powell, on whose very reliable transcript of the Essex returns (ERO T/A4701–4) I have principally, though of course not exclusively, relied.

I am also most grateful to the PRO, Kew, for the sight of their photocopy of the original returns, to the Record Offices of Cambridgeshire, Essex and Hertfordshire, and to Dr Janet Cooper, of the Victoria County History of Essex, for their assistance and the opportunity to refer to documents held by them.

Among numerous colleagues I have consulted I should like especially to thank Mr Adrian Corder-Birch for his help in relation to Halstead.

REFERENCES

1   The Report on the Ecclesiastical Census, 1851, was published as *Parliamentary Papers (1852–3)*, lxxxix. The returns are held in the P.R.O., Kew, class no. HO 129.

2   I readily confess to purists that the term Anglican for the period in question is something of an anachronism as it was not then common parlance. It was however already so used (e.g. by Gladstone) and is both correct and convenient.

3   See reference 1 above.

4 A good (in both senses) and long-lived example of such a beneficiary was Charles Almeric Belli (1791–1886), Vicar of South Weald: *cf.* W. Wilford, *Essex Journal*, vol. 21.1, p.9, 1986.

5 W. White, *History, Gazetteer and Directory of the County of Essex*, 1848.

6 *Idem.*

7 Census Report, 1851, (*Parliamentary Papers (1852–3)*, lxxxi).

8 For Cornelius Butler, F.R.C.S., (1789–1871), surgeon and poetaster of Brentwood, see J. Larkin, *More Fireside Talks about Brentwood*, 1921, (unpublished typescript in E.R.O. library), p.97 and G. Ward, *Essex Journal*, vol. 2.1, p.12, 1967.

9 Many of the 'carriage folk' too, would probably not, as a matter of principle, have used their carriages on the Sabbath.

Figure 1a.

FORM A.

CENSUS OF GREAT BRITAIN, 1851.
(13 & 14 Victoriæ, Cap. 53.)

A RETURN of the several Particulars to be inquired into respecting the under-mentioned Church or Chapel in England, belonging to the United Church of England and Ireland.

[A similar Return (*mutatis mutandis*) will be obtained with respect to Churches belonging to the Established Church in Scotland, and the Episcopal Church there, and also from Roman Catholic Priests, and from the Ministers of every other Religious Denomination throughout Great Britain, with respect to their Places of Worship.]

I.	NAME AND DESCRIPTION OF CHURCH OR CHAPEL.			
II.	WHERE SITUATED.	Parish, Ecclesiastical Division or District, Township, or Place.	Superintendent Registrar's District.	County and Diocese.
III.	WHEN CONSECRATED OR LICENSED.	UNDER WHAT CIRCUMSTANCES CONSECRATED OR LICENSED.		

IV.	IN THE CASE OF A CHURCH OR CHAPEL CONSECRATED OR LICENSED SINCE THE 1st JANUARY 1800: STATE	
	HOW OR BY WHOM ERECTED.	COST, HOW DEFRAYED.
		By Parliamentary Grant - - - Parochial Rate - - - Private Benefaction or Subscription, or from other Sources - } Total Cost - - £

V.		VI.
HOW ENDOWED.		SPACE AVAILABLE FOR PUBLIC WORSHIP.
Land - - - £ Tithe - - - Glebe - - - Other Permanent En- } dowment - }	Pew Rents - - £ Fees - - - Dues - - - Easter Offerings - Other Sources - -	Free Sittings - - - £ Other Sittings - - - Total Sittings -

VII.	ESTIMATED NUMBER OF PERSONS ATTENDING DIVINE SERVICE ON SUNDAY, MARCH 30, 1851.				AVERAGE NUMBER OF ATTENDANTS during Months next preceding March 30, 1851. (See Instruction VII.)			
		Morning.	Afternoon.	Evening.		Morning.	Afternoon.	Evening.
	General Congregation - } Sunday Scholars -				General Congregation - } Sunday Scholars -			
	Total -				Total -			

VIII.	REMARKS.

I certify the foregoing to be a true and correct Return to the best of my belief.
Witness my hand this_____day of_____1851.
IX. (*Signature*) _____
    (*Official Character*) _____ of the above-named.
    (*Address by Post*) _____

Figure 1b.

CENSUS OF GREAT BRITAIN, 1851.

INSTRUCTIONS FOR FILLING UP THE SCHEDULE ON THE ADJOINING PAGE.

(*Prepared under the direction of one of Her Majesty's Principal Secretaries of State.*)

I.—*Name and Description of Church or Chapel.*—In the column thus headed insert—1st. The Name given to the Church on its Consecration, or the Name by which it is commonly known, if only licensed for Public Worship by the Bishop of the Diocese:—2ndly. Its Description,—(that is to say) Whether it be an ancient Parish Church, or the Church of an ancient Chapelry, the Church of a distinct and separate Parish, District Parish, District Chapelry or Consolidated District, or of a new Parish under the provisions of 6 & 7 Vict. c. 37. (Sir R. Peel's Act,) or of a District under the provisions of 1 & 2 W. 4. c. 38. (the Private Patronage Act), or a Chapel of Ease, or a Church or Chapel built under the authority of a local or private Act of Parliament; and if such information can be given, state the year, reign, and chapter of such Act.

II.—*Where situated.*—Describe accurately in the proper columns,—
The Parish, Ecclesiastical Division or District, Township, or Place, in which the Church is situated; and if it be in a Town, the Name of the Street or other locality.
The Superintendent Registrar's District or Poor Law Union.
The County and Diocese.

III.—*When consecrated or licensed.*—State in this Column whether the Church was consecrated, or only licensed by the Bishop of the Diocese. This will be sufficiently done by writing the word "Consecrated," or "Licensed," as the case may require. And if the Consecration or License was *before the 1st January* 1800, write after "Consecrated" or "Licensed" as follows,—"Before 1800." But if it took place *on or after the 1st January* 1800,'insert, as nearly as can be, the *precise date* of such Consecration or License.
Under what circumstances Consecrated or Licensed.—If the Consecration or License was *before* the 1st January 1800, this column *may be left blank*; but, if it was on or after that date, state under this heading whether the Church, if consecrated, was consecrated as an additional Church, or in lieu of an old or previously existing one.

IV.—*How or by whom erected.*—If the Church was consecrated *before* the year 1800, the column thus headed, and also the column headed "Cost, how defrayed," *are to be left blank.* If the Church was consecrated or licensed *since* the 1st January 1800, and as an additional Church, *but not else,*—insert under this heading the words "By Parliamentary Grant,"—"By Parochial Rate,"—"By Private Benefaction or Subscription," —or the Name of the individual at whose expense the Church was built, or such other words as will briefly express the facts of the case.
Cost.—And, in the same circumstances, *but not else.*—state in the column headed "Cost, how defrayed," as nearly as may be known, the total cost of the Building. And if it was erected partly by Parliamentary Grant and partly by Private Subscription, or from other sources, state also the respective proportions contributed.

V.—*How endowed.*—Insert under this heading in what manner it is endowed,—whether by land, tithe, glebe, or other permanent endowment; by pew rents, fees, dues, Easter-offerings, or now otherwise, and the aggregate annual amount of such endowment.

VII.—*Estimated Number of Attendants on March 30, 1851.*—
If—as is sometimes the case in Wales and elsewhere—two or more Congregations successively assemble in the Building during the same part of the day.—and also in all cases where two or more distinct services are performed in the morning, afternoon, or evening, either by the same Minister, or by different Ministers,—denote the fact by drawing a line immediately *under* the gross number of attendants during that part of the day, thus | 750 |—in order to show that it expresses the aggregate of persons attending at *all* such distinct services. Make a × under each portion of the day—if there be any—during which *no* service is performed.
Average Number.—
If from any cause the figures in the first three columns of Division VII. should not truly represent the numbers *usually* in attendance, the person making the Return is at liberty to add in the fourth, fifth, and sixth columns of the same Division, the estimated *average* number of attendants on Sunday during the 12 calendar months next preceding March 30, 1851, or during such portion of that period as the Building has been open for Public Worship, stating in the heading over the numbers so inserted the exact number of months for which the additional Return is made.
And if, in consequence of repairs, or from any other temporary cause, the Building should not be open for Public Worship on March 30, 1851, write across the first three columns the words "No Service," and insert in the remaining columns the average number who are supposed to have attended at each Sunday during twelve months next preceding the Sunday on which Divine Service was last performed.

VIII.—*Remarks.*—Any observations in explanation of the Return may be inserted in this column; or—if the space provided for the purpose be insufficient—they may be written on a separate paper and appended to the Return.

IX.—*Signature. &c.*—The Return is to be made and signed by the Minister, or by a Church or Chapel Warden, or other recognized and competent officer; and the person signing will have the goodness to state in what capacity he signs, by writing immediately below his name the word "Minister," "Churchwarden," &c., as the case may be. He will also add his *Address by the Post*, in order that, if necessary, he may be communicated with direct from the Census Office in London, on the subject of the Return.

Approved,   GEORGE GRAHAM,
                                                     Registrar General.

Whitehall,   } G. GREY.
28th Jan. 1851. }

N.B.—The Return must not relate to more than ONE *Church or Chapel. Clergymen having the charge of two or more Churches will be furnished with a separate Form for each. And any Minister, Warden, or other person requiring an additional supply of Forms, may obtain them, free of postage or other charge, on application by letter (the postage of which may be left unpaid), addressed to "Horace Mann, Esq., Census Office, Craig's Court, London."*

Table 1 — Summary of Essex Returns.

Poor Law Union	Total population	Total		C. of E.		Cong./Ind.		Other Prot.		R.C.	
		a	b	a	b	a	b	a	b	a	b
West Ham	34395	36	14798	16	10084	9	2365	9	1399	2	950
Epping	15631	33	10351	21	7111	7	1300	4	1940		
Ongar	11855	33	6874	27	5929	5	688	1	257		
Romford	24607	37	11115	17	6888	6	1498	13	2707		
Orsett	10642	25	4949	15	3496	4	883	6	566		
Billericay	13787	29	8803	18	4400	6	2596	3	1354	2	453
Chelmsford	32272	62	18747	34	8889	15	7047	9	2067	3	652
Rochford	15838	48	14334	28	9194	9	2081	11	3059		
Maldon	22137	42	16679	32	10288	8	3918	11	2374		
Tendring	27710	64	22958	31	12207	2	1009	31	9742		
Colchester	19443	34	17404	16	8451	6	4419	10	4244	1	140
Lexden	21666	62	18942	34	10779	9	4534	19	3629		
Witham	16099	34	13540	18	8804	6	3386	9	1300	1	50
Halstead	19273	36	18356	17	8144	8	5934	11	4278		
Braintree	17561	26	17540	14	6533	8	8327	4	2680		
Dunmow	20498	41	17104	25	9875	10	6187	6	1042		
Saffron Walden	20716	50	19489	25	11121	7	2983	17	5365		
Poor Law Unions in											
Cambridgeshire		1	301	1	301						
Hertfordshire		29	8383	19	6261	3	1130	7	992		
Suffolk		24	6943	21	6068	3	875				

a — Number of places of worship.
b — Total number of worshippers throughout the day.

The figures in the above table are (apart from those in other counties' Poor Law Unions, which I have myself extracted from those counties' returns) extracted from the tables in the official Report on the Census (Parliamentary Papers (1852–53) lxxxix) and share their qualities as discussed in my essay. In particular it should be noted that:

1 — Attendances at morning, afternoon and evening services are totted up. Therefore those who attended twice are double-counted, and three times, triple-counted.

2 — Sunday scholars are included, and perhaps in some cases double-counted.

3 — Churches in respect of which no figures were submitted are of course omitted and (it would seem from spot checks) some or all estimated returns have in some Unions been likewise excluded.

A very few — and in almost all cases sparsely-attended — places of worship of smaller and undefinable sects such as the Mormons are excluded from the denominational breakdown above.

Table 2 — Response to Census from Anglican Places of Worship.

Poor Law Union	No. of Places of worship reporting	Full or sufficient return signed by ordained man	Full or sufficient return signed by lay person or unsigned	Return by church with insufficient figures	Return made blank or without relevant figures	Estimate made by or for Registrar	Parish church with no return traced
	2	3	4	5	6	7	8
West Ham	14	2	—	—	2	—	—
Epping	21	9	3	2	—	7	—
Ongar	27	19	2	6	—	—	—
Romford	15	13	1	1	—	—	—
Orsett	15	14	—	—	1	—	4
Billericay	18	16	—	—	1	1	7
Chelmsford	35	21	3	3	7	1	—
Rochford	28	24	1	1	—	2	—
Maldon	32	26	—	—	1	5	—
Tendring	30	18	1	3	3	5	—
Colchester	16	6	3	—	1	6	—
Lexden	34	28	3	—	1	2	—
Witham	18	10	4	3	1	—	—
Halstead	17	14	2	1	—	—	1
Braintree	14	13	—	1	—	—	1
Dunmow	25	24	—	—	—	1	—
Saffron Walden	26	22	2	2	—	—	—
Parts of Cambridgeshire	1	1	—	—	—	—	—
Parts of Hertfordshire	18	17	—	—	—	1	—
Parts of Suffolk	21	18	—	—	—	3	1
TOTAL	425	325	25	23	18	34	14
% of those reporting	100	76.5	5.9	5.4	4.2	8.0	—

In columns 3 to 7 of this table, the relevant criterion is the sufficiency or otherwise of the attendance figures included in the return.

Robert Edward, 9th Lord Petre
Common-sense, virtue, religion and loyalty

THE LORD PETRE

The Right Honble
RobertEdwardL^{d.}Petre
Thorndon in Eſſex.

ROBERT EDWARD PETRE, the son and heir of the 8th Lord Petre, was born in the Spring of 1742. It had been more than 200 years since the execution of Sir Thomas More and Bishop John Fisher had ushered in the period that English Roman Catholics refer to as the Penal Times. During this period, a wide assortment of laws had been put in place which either forbade Roman Catholics the practice of their religion or deprived them of their rights and freedoms. Between the accession of Elizabeth I and the early years of the reign of George I, thirty separate statutes of this kind had been enacted and, such was the scope and severity of the strictures they imposed, it would be easy to suppose that, by the middle of the eighteenth century, there would not have remained a single English Roman Catholic who had not been driven either into penury or into the arms of the Church of England.

It is therefore surprising to find that, although his family had resisted apostasy throughout the Penal Times, Robert was born to an inheritance of exceptional

75

Robert Edward, 9th Lord Petre: portrait by George Romney.

wealth and influence. The claim that he was one of the dozen richest men in the Kingdom is probably fanciful but his estates were certainly extensive. His ancestor, Sir William Petre, had acquired some 45,000 acres, chiefly in Essex and the West Country. To this Sir William's son, John, added a further 14,500 acres. Furthermore, his grandfather, the 7th Lord, had married Catherine Walmesley, who had inherited the whole of her family's large estates in Lancashire and Surrey which, at the time of her marriage, were reputed to be worth £7,000 per annum.

How it was that at least some 'treacherous' Roman Catholics were left relatively unmolested by the draconian legislation laid against them cannot be considered in detail here but the Petre family was not unique in this respect. Many did defect, of course, but, at the time of the first Relief Act (1778), there were still eight peers, nineteen baronets and 150 gentlemen of substantial property who remained Roman Catholics. Even among the common people, loyalty to Rome was not entirely extinct; a national census of 1767 identifies, out of a total population of seven to eight million, 67,916 Roman Catholics and there is good reason to suppose that this was a considerable under-estimate. Indeed, in some places under the patronage of Roman Catholic gentry, there had been an increase in the number of their co-religionists; in the 27 parishes between Brentwood and Chelmsford which were under the aegis of the Petre and the Roman Catholic Wrights of Kelvedon Hall, the population of Roman Catholics rose from 106 in 1625 to 202 in 1706.

Mark Bence-Jones, in his recent book, *The Catholic Families*, even goes so far as to suggest that the effects of the Penal Laws were not entirely disadvantageous to Roman Catholic gentry. Barred as they were from all public office, they were at least spared the risks associated with such ambitions — the heavy cost of 'electioneering expenses' (or, bluntly, bribes) and the dire consequences of a fall from favour — and could concentrate their energies on the management of their estates which accordingly prospered. The principal factor, however, which, over the years, helped to protect some Roman Catholic families from the worst effects of the legislation was the simple matter of the personal loyalty and support extended to them by their local community, even by those who might particularly have been expected to point an accusing finger. Thus, in 1766, Thomas Newman, the Vicar of West Horndon, in whose parish the Petre mansion, Thorndon Hall, lay, was required by the Bishop of London to respond to a questionnaire on the number of Roman Catholics in his parish. He reported, 'From the best Advice I can collect there are about Fifty Persons who are reputed to be Papists; Ld. Petre is supposed to be of that Persuasion'. The truth of the matter was that the old Thorndon Hall contained a private chapel consecrated by Robert's cousin, Bishop Benjamin Petre in 1739, and the Visitation of Essex conducted by the Roman Catholic Bishop Richard Challoner in 1754 discovered a congregation of 260 there: indeed, in that year alone, 41 had received the sacrament of Confirmation.

Within a few months of Robert's birth, his father died of smallpox at the age of 29 and so Robert succeeded as the 9th Lord Petre. As a minor, he remained, of

Sir William Petre (1505?–72): founder of the family's fortune.

course, under the guardianship of his mother and it was only as a result of her death in 1760 that he was permitted to take over his estates at the age of eighteen. There is, in the Petre family archive, a disappointing lack of personal writings and correspondence and so it is difficult to form a rounded impression of the man; legend has it that, in later life, he himself destroyed many of his personal papers. They bore witness to the acrimonious disputes which he was to have with the Roman Catholic hierarchy and which, in retrospect, he came deeply to regret. It is fairly clear he was no great intellect; one now anonymous commentator is particularly unkind: 'His literary equipment fell short even of the moderate standard then expected of a nobleman and his generous patronage of men of letters and art seems to have been dictated by other considerations than intellectual sympathy'. On the other hand, as Charles Butler, lawyer and Secretary of the Catholic Committee of which Robert was Chairman, wrote in his obituary, 'All his actions were distinguished by rectitude, openness and dignity'. Indeed, from the events of his life emerges a picture of a man of great energy, determination and perseverance with a keen sense of patriotism and duty.

Robert's dogged resolve may well have sprung from a stoicism in face of adversity learnt from those under whose tutelage he was brought up, if it is not too extravagant so to characterize an environment as privileged as his. As we have seen, his mother had lost her husband only months after Robert's birth but both her father and her uncle, executed for their parts in the Jacobite Uprisings of 1715 and 1745 respectively, and also her brother, killed in a riding accident, had died prematurely. Robert's grandmother, the redoubtable Catherine Walmesley, was also no stranger to tragedy. Both her parents had died by the time she was four and, during the following nine years, her brother and her two sisters also succumbed. She had married the 7th Lord Petre but, a year later, he too died of smallpox and she was left, at the age of barely 15, a widow with an infant son. She subsequently married Lord Stourton but, when he died in 1753, she became a widow for the second time.

There remained too the fact of the Penal Laws. It is true that, by now, the emphasis had changed; Roman Catholics could at least adhere to their beliefs and even worship discreetly without undue risk to their life or liberty but the legislation, particularly to exclude them from any public office or profession, was still in place. Roman Catholics remained, effectively, second class citizens. As late as 1771, Bishop James Talbot appeared in the dock at the Old Bailey charged with 'exercising the functions of a Popish bishop' (although the authorities regarded the trial as something of an embarrassment). Even if, in practice, the laws were no more than an inconvenience, they were a source of great distress and frustration to one with Robert's sense of patriotic duty.

Accordingly, restoring to Roman Catholics their rights and liberties as citizens became Robert's mission. There were very real obstacles to overcome. The continued existence of the Penal Laws was not just a result of bigotry and intolerance. It was years since any supposed heresy or blasphemy in Roman Catholic dogma or liturgy had been an issue but the question of the nature and

Thorndon Hall: engraving.

extent of the allegiance that Roman Catholics owed to the Pope and his temporal 'power over princes' was quite another matter. There were a number of venerable constitutional precedents to suggest that the English throne did indeed lie within the gift of the Pope — King John had 'ransomed' his crown from the Holy See for one thousand marks — and, even if that were not the case, it was widely perceived that, such was the moral authority of the Pope over his flock, that, if he was to command them to dethrone a heretic ruler, they would be obliged to obey. Moreover, any promise a Roman Catholic might make to the contrary would be null and void since it was no sin to break faith with an heretic. Such a perception was perfectly justified for it was in those very terms that Pius V had issued his Bull of Excommunication against Elizabeth I, declaring that she was

> 'to be deprived of her pretended title to the kingdom aforesaid, and of all dominion, dignity and privilege whatsoever; and also the nobility, subjects and people of the said kingdom, and all others which have in any sort sworn unto her to be for ever absolved from any such oath.'

The Vatican had slightly modified but never withdrawn this Bull.

The task of Robert and his fellow Roman Catholics was, therefore, to find a way of persuading their sceptical compatriots that they did not recognize the authority of the Pope in temporal matters and that, whatever Rome might say, their allegiance to King George was unequivocal. It was for that reason that, in 1771, Robert became a Freemason. Not only did this give him access to many influential figures in the Protestant Establishment but it was, in itself, a snub to the authority of Rome. As recently as 1738, Pope Clement XII had issued a Bull excommunicating Catholics who took part in Freemasonry, a judgement reiterated by his successor, Benedict XIV, in 1751. By a quirk of Canon Law, Robert's apparent defiance of these rulings was only a gesture; since there was then no official Roman Catholic hierarchy in England, the Bulls could not be formally proclaimed and were not therefore binding. Nevertheless, it was a gesture that was evidently much appreciated; only a year after joining the brotherhood, he was elected Grand Master, a position which he held until 1777.

Nevertheless, the most practical contribution that Robert made to the cause of Catholic Emancipation was his chairmanship of the two successive committees of Roman Catholic laymen formed to lobby government and negotiate means by which the disabilities enshrined in the Penal Laws might be swept away. It fell to Robert to take the role of senior Roman Catholic layman in this way since of the two Roman Catholic noblemen who outranked him, the 10th Duke of Norfolk was a scholarly recluse who rarely left his garden at Greystoke Castle in Cumberland and the 14th Earl of Shrewsbury also had no taste for public life – even though two of the four Apostolic Vicars who administered the Roman Catholic Church of England were his brothers.

In promoting the abolition of the Penal Laws, Robert's committee was in large part pushing at an open door as far as Parliament was concerned. The Whig opposition was very much in favour of Catholic Emancipation — Burke vociferously so — but the Tory administrations of Lord North and, later, Pitt were also guardedly sympathetic, albeit for entirely pragmatic reasons; they saw measures favouring the Roman Catholics both as a means of stemming massive emigration from Ireland and also as an encouragement to the overwhelmingly Roman Catholic Scottish Highlanders to enlist in the Army. The Press also largely supported the Committee's objectives and, indeed, when, eventually, legislation came before both Houses of Parliament, it was passed speedily and without opposition.

It is a convincing token of the acceptance that the State was now beginning to extend to Roman Catholics that, in 1778, George III chose to lodge at Thorndon for two days in order to carry out a review of the troops at Warley barracks. This was an event of considerable significance since it was the first occasion on which the monarch had visited a Roman Catholic household since the Reformation. The visit was a great success if not an entirely unalloyed pleasure for Robert. The bill for the two days amounted to £1,001 7s. 2d. and, as Robert's journal of the occasion makes clear, the tumultuous activity which accompanied it threatened to descend into farce. It is only on 22 September that Robert learns that His Majesty's visit is to take place on 5 October. In spite of the shortness of notice, Robert is determined to impress the royal visitors and resolves to redecorate four of the main rooms entirely in time for the visit. Within a week, Thorndon is a hive of activity with more than a hundred extra staff and workmen brought in to help with the preparations including not only several coachloads of French cooks and confectioners from London and staff recruited locally to assist them but an army of upholsterers, gilders, japanners, cabinet-makers and painters to carry out the redecorations. Extra tableware would also be required for the royal retinue and so

> 'Davy went out with the proper carriage to collect all the plate, which consisted of the Duke of Norfolk's, of Mr. Conyer's, Lord Waldegrave's, Lady Mildmay's, all that I could hire in London'.

Then, only three days before that appointed, a message arrives to say that His Majesty's visit is delayed a fortnight. All the extra cooks are sent back to London and Robert, with rather bad grace, holds a series of dinner parties to eat up the food that would otherwise go to waste. 'Very good things', he observes sourly in his journal. Finally, on 19 October 1778, the great day dawns.

> 'At Ten minutes after Three behold in the Avenue the finest sight of the kind I ever saw. The sun bright out, the Army Drawn up on each side, innumerable people, & the King & Queen appearing with their Equipages, Horse Guards & attendants and numberless Horsemen who had been at my desire to meet them, having my tenants with my

steward at their Head & every Body Els he could collect. The Park of Artillery saluting all the time, the Echo of the woods, the shouts of the people, Rapidity with which the King's chaise run the lawn in an instand, covered with Horse men, the Horses panting, made the whole resemble an enchantment for I verily believe from the time of the Royal chaise appearing at the top of the Avenue a mile and half full from the House to their majestys coming up to the door did not exceed five minutes.'

Robert and his Committee may have had little difficulty in enlisting the sympathy and support of the Government in their cause but there were two very real obstacles to overcome. In the first place, mistrust and intolerance of Roman Catholics was still widespread among at least some sections of the populace at large. Some commentators have claimed that the frenzy of unrest that was fomented by Lord George Gordon in response to the very modest First Relief Act in 1778 was the most serious episode of public disorder ever seen in this country.

The Gordon Riots: from a contemporary print.

To what extent it was a manifestation of genuine opposition to Roman Catholicism rather than an expression of general dissent is open to question — as Daniel Defoe wrote, 'There are 40,000 stout fellows ready to fight to the death popery without knowing whether popery is a man or a horse' — but it was undoubtedly serious. The rioters burnt down Robert's new house in Park Lane and a mob of three thousand marching on Thorndon were only diverted by the military at the last moment. The Government was understandably nervous about granting concessions to the Roman Catholics which might further inflame the mob.

The Committee had also to overcome considerable opposition and obstruction from their own clergy. Some, like the mild and gentle Bishop Walmesley, Vicar Apostolic of the Western District, had been so horrified by the ferocity of the Gordon Riots that they wanted their fellow Catholics to give up their demands rather than risk more violent persecution. Many other senior clergy, however, were opposed to the overtures that the Committee were making simply because they would brook no compromise over the Pope's authority in all matters including affairs of state. No doubt this Ultramontane faction (so-called because they saw authority residing exclusively in Rome, 'beyond the mountains') accounted themselves sincere in this belief but it is hard to avoid the suspicion that it was equally their own authority to govern the lives of their flock which they saw at risk. At any rate, their quarrelsome and often inconsistent opposition came close to sabotaging the progress the Committee was making and exchanges between the two factions became increasingly acrimonious. The Bishops condemned the Committee for their 'unwillingness to abandon any one of their own fond deceits'; the Committee responded that the Bishops' statements were 'impudent, arbitrary & unjust'.

It is not possible here to recount in detail the twists and turns of this debate. The Committee never managed to win the argument conclusively — even as recently as 1955, the Roman Catholic historian, David Mathew, condemns the Committee as 'a closed corporation of the polite unenthusiastic Catholicism of the Thames Valley' but they were able to reassure Parliament sufficiently to permit the process of dismantling the Penal Laws to get under way. In 1778, the First Relief Act passed through both Houses of Parliament without a Division. It was a modest measure which essentially only reversed the 1700 Act for Further Preventing the Growth of Popery but it did put an end to the persecution of Roman Catholic clergy and removed the restrictions on Roman Catholics holding land. The Second Relief Act (1791) was more substantial; Roman Catholic schools were permitted, and chapels too — so long as they had neither steeple nor bell — but Roman Catholics continued to be barred from Parliament, the Bench or a Commission in the Army or Navy.

Robert Petre's other great enterprise was the building of the new Thorndon Hall. His father, who was a distinguished plant collector, had embarked on an ambitious scheme to reconstruct the old fifteenth century house and its park but his untimely death in 1742 brought the unfinished work to a halt. During Robert's long minority, the house and park fell into neglect. In 1757, the house had been badly damaged by fire as a newspaper report of 16 August bears witness, 'Great Part of Lady Peters's House near Brentwood in Essex was burnt by the Lightning on Monday Night, which did a great deal of other Damage in that Neighbourhood, and was so violent that it greatly terrified several Persons on the Road'. The nurseries established by Robert's father contained, at his death,

219,925 plants. When the botanist, Peter Collinson, visited in 1762, he found a scene of desolation: the house was falling down, the nurseries overgrown and the stoves empty, apart from two date palms, a cactus and a few sickly shrubs. Fashion, too had moved on; in 1754, Horace Walpole, on a visit to see 'the famous plantations and buildings of the last Lord Petre', found the unfinished house 'execrable', the avenue of elms 'outrageous', the clumps of trees 'gigantic and ill-placed' and the whole 'the Brobdingnag of bad taste'.

In view of this, Robert's plan to build an entirely new house and to remodel the park seems reasonable enough but its realization owed much to a *folie de grandeur* which was to place a severe financial strain on succeeding generations. Robert engaged Lancelot *Capability* Brown to remodel the park and the house was designed by James Paine. He was a favourite architect of the Roman Catholic community and had designed Wardour Castle for Lord Arundell and Worksop Manor for the 9th Duke of Norfolk, which, had it been finished, would have been one of the largest private houses in the land.

In 1764, with the family temporarily ensconced at their other principal residence, Ingatestone Hall, work began on the vast palladian mansion, using materials salvaged from the old house. A central block, dominated by a hall, 42 feet square and lined by 18 columns, leading, via a grand staircase, to a lofty salon measuring 60 feet by 30 feet, contained most of the reception rooms and bedrooms including the 'State Rooms' and 'Cardinal's Room', His Lordship's study, Her Ladyship's boudoir, two drawing-rooms, the dining-room, the ballroom, the billiard room, the nurseries, the library, the strong room, the armoury and a theatre (a programme for a performance of *The Rivals*, given in 1792, survives). At each end of this main block stood an outlying wing, connected thereto by a quadrant gallery. The East wing contained the kitchens, laundry and chapel while the West wing accommodated the extensive coach-houses and stables.

Building continued for six years at a cost which has been estimated at £250,000 but, as the house was nearing completion, Robert further commissioned James Paine to design a house in Park Lane to replace the family's existing London residence in Curzon Street. This was the house that was subsequently burnt down by the Gordon Rioters. Its design is included in James Paine's publication, *Plans, Elevations & Sections of Noblemen's & Gentlemen's Houses 1767–1783*.

The bare cost of building these houses was, of course, only part of the story. The expense of running such large establishments in a manner appropriate to their opulence was stupendous. Unfortunately, the only detailed household accounts which have survived date from the period just before the new houses were completed but a detailed study of these accounts made by Bishop B. C. Foley reveals that, in 1760, Robert employed, in the Thorndon Hall household alone, 35 servants. In spite of the modest salaries involved (which ranged from £2 per annum for Elizabeth Summers, the under-nurserymaid, to £40 per annum for Mr Montier, the chef), the wage bill for the year amounted to the tidy sum of £473 18s. 0d. Moreover, it is likely that, once the new Thorndon Hall was

The Gatehouse at Ingatestone Hall.

complete, the roster of household staff would have been significantly increased; there are but three housemaids on the 1760 list, not enough for a house the size of the new Hall.

Although any attempt to translate olden-day sums of money into modern values is always a perilous game, it may be instructive, given the host of figures quoted above, to refer to a study by Robert Twigger of the House of Commons Library which, drawing on a number of sources, constructs an index of the purchasing power of the pound between 1750 and 1993. This suggests that, in 1773, one pound had the purchasing power of something over £70 today.

Robert also brought an energetic enthusiasm to his family life. He married well. His first wife was Anne Howard, niece of the 9th Duke of Norfolk, who brought a respectable dowry of lands in Yorkshire and Norfolk. Having borne him three children, including a male heir (also named Robert), Anne died in 1787 but, within a year, he married again. His second wife was Juliana Howard, a distant cousin of his first wife and sister of the future 12th Duke of Norfolk. Juliana was 19 years old, 27 years younger than Robert, and, indeed, Robert's son had himself married her older sister two years previously.

As a matter of curiosity, there is, in addition, a suggestion of an extra-marital affair. An American family who go by the name of Rumball-Petre claim to be descendants of an illegitimate liaison between Robert and an unnamed lady of quality. Thomas, the offspring of this union, was fostered, so the story goes, with George Rumball, one of Robert's tenants, and his descendants subsequently emigrated to America. There is some circumstantial evidence to substantiate the tale. A family called Rumball did indeed occupy Begrum's Farm on the Petre estate at Mountnessing, Brentwood in the eighteenth century and the supposed portrait of Thomas as a boy, which is in the possession of the Rumball-Petres, shows him far too richly costumed to be the son of a humble tenant farmer. Their prize exhibit is, however, a journal allegedly kept by the boy's mother. Unfortunately, this now survives only as a printed and obviously heavily edited version and so it is impossible to determine its authenticity; in particular, for reasons of supposed delicacy, all names referred to in the text have been excised. As a result, although the father of the lady's child is referred to as 'the Baron', there is little to identify him with Robert Petre, apart from the fact that one of the philosophical reflections in the journal is entitled *Sans Dieu Rien*, the Petre family motto. Indeed, it is only too likely that the whole thing is a flight of Victorian fancy; the lady herself is described as lodging in the household of 'the Old Earl' somewhere near Epping. As far as can be ascertained, there were no old Earls anywhere near Epping in the eighteenth century.

Robert also devoted himself to a number of other enterprises. He made annual charitable donations of £500, chiefly to Roman Catholic priests and religious orders both here and on the Continent. He was the first Chairman of the Chelmer and Blackwater Navigation which was responsible for building the canal connecting Chelmsford to the sea near Maldon and, in the early 1790s, with the French Wars looming, he raised and equipped the Ingatestone and

Brentwood Volunteers, a militia of 250 men. It was his dearest wish that his son should take command of the company but the King refused to waive the ban on Roman Catholics receiving commissions and so young Robert was obliged to enlist as a private.

Robert died on 2 July 1801. He departed this life as he had lived — in grand style. The *Chelmsford Chronicle* reported that the funeral procession which escorted his body from Thorndon to Ingatestone Church for interment was over a mile long. Accompanying the hearse were three divisions of the Ingatestone and Brentwood Volunteers, two companies of Pioneers, two artillery field pieces and the band of the Royal Buckinghamshire Regiment together with 30 mutes and cloak men, Robert's tenants, two by two, the post-chaise and two carriages from the Thorndon stables, seven mourning coaches, each drawn by six horses, carrying members of the family, clergy and household and a host of outriders, grooms and other mourners. As the cortege left Thorndon and again as it came within a mile of Ingatestone Church, two field pieces fired at minute intervals in salute.

For the Petre family, at any rate, Robert's death marked the end of an era. His lifetime had been the apogee of the family fortunes and they were never again to aspire to such affluence. In a more general sense, too, his passing was a watershed. The gathering pace of the Industrial Revolution and the emergence of an enfranchised middle class signalled the end of the comfortable paternalism of the squirearchy as focus, patron and protector of the community. This was particularly the case for Roman Catholics; it had been a feature of the Penal Times that ordinary Roman Catholics had clustered in communities where they could enjoy the patronage and protection of Roman Catholic gentry but, now that the process of emancipation had begun, such patronage and protection was of less consequence and the Roman Catholic gentry lost much of their influence.

It would nevertheless have been a disappointment to Robert that he did not live to see more far-reaching emancipation for Roman Catholics. The trend towards it had become irreversible but it was still a long time coming. It was over a quarter of a century later that the Emancipation Act of 1829 removed the bulk of the restrictions which continued to beset Roman Catholics. Even then, some survived. It was only in 1974 that it was formally enacted that a Roman Catholic may hold the office of Lord Chancellor and, to this day, it is only Roman Catholics who are barred, on religious grounds, from ascending the Throne.

Chelmsford Cathedral

'A great county should have a great cathedral as its heart'

JOHN MOSES

The Foundation of the Town

CHELMSFORD TAKES its name from Ceolmar, one of the early Germanic settlers after the Roman evacuation of Britain in the early fifth century. Ceolmar's ford was one of a number of crossing places over the rivers that ran throughout the extensive woodland region which became the kingdom of the East Saxons. The name survived, and the hundred of Celmeresforda gave way over the centuries to Chelmersford, Chelmesford, Chemsford, and finally Chelmsford.

The manor of Chelmsford, a sparsely populated manor of some six hundred acres, passed into the possession of the bishops of London in the years immediately preceding the Norman Conquest. The area around the ford was uninhabited. It was a wasteland, marshy, and at times of flooding, impassable. The bishop's hall — together with the manor buildings, the watermill, the cultivated fields and the dwellings of the villeins — were located on higher ground half a mile away to the north of the ford.

The evolution of Chelmsford as a market town in the later middle ages owed much to the patronage of successive Norman bishops of London. It was probably Bishop Maurice (1085–1107) who built the bridge over the Great River, the river Can. It is possible that he also built two other bridges over the river Chelmer; but it was his bridging the Great River which provided the beginnings of a main thoroughfare, by-passing Writtle and ensuring that the two hamlets of Chelmsford and Moulsham were ultimately joined together.

It was, however, Bishop William of Sainte-Mère-Église (1199–1221) who secured from King John a succession of charters which, taken together, constituted for all practical purposes the foundation of the town. These charters conferred the right to hold a market within the bishop's manor (1199), the right to confer the status of freeholder upon all men who received from the bishop houses or plots of land for building (1200), and the right to hold an annual fair (1201).

There is no evidence of any church in the manor of Chelmsford prior to the twelfth century, but certainly by the beginning of the thirteenth century there was a church on the bishop's manor on the site where the cathedral now stands.

View of Chelmsford Cathedral from the south-east.

(Photograph courtesy of Pitkin Pictorials Limited)

Archaeological excavations at the time of the re-ordering of the cathedral in 1983 revealed the remains of the flint rubble walls and the foundations of this earlier building. It is clear that the church, which was not significantly smaller than its fifteenth century successor, consisted of a chancel, a nave and a west tower. The church was dedicated to St. Mary. It stood for over two hundred years.

The names of the earliest rectors of Chelmsford are not known. Lists of incumbents in the medieval period are notoriously unreliable, but there is certainly reference from 1220 to a priest called Roger, who was styled the dean of Chelmsford, and who may or may not have been the rector of the parish. Richard de Gorges, who was presented to the living in 1242, is the first priest who can be positively identified as the incumbent. The advowson of the living, endowed with glebe land near bishop's hall, remained in the gift of the bishops as the lords of the manor until the sixteenth century.

The new market town, established by Bishop William, was able to take full advantage of its central geographical position and secure its place in Essex in a remarkably short space of time. The bishop's officers and court had long since been located in the manor, and by the middle years of the thirteenth century Chelmsford had become the place normally appointed in Essex for the transaction of the king's business and the administration of justice. It was already beginning to emerge as the county town.

Chelmsford continued as a relatively small community throughout this period. It was essentially a market town, and one that was geared in large part to the needs of travellers. Its traders and craftsmen and innkeepers could meet the basic needs of its inhabitants and of the ever-increasing number of people for whom Chelmsford, located on the road from London to Colchester and Harwich and Ipswich, was becoming a great thoroughfare.

The parish church's close relationship with the bishops of London, together with its relatively handsome size, enabled it to be used for ordinations and for local church courts. It is recorded that the Bishop of London held an ordination service in the church in 1223, when the most violent storm caused great consternation to those assembled for the occasion, an event which was interpreted by one chronicler as a sign of divine displeasure at the worldly motives of those who were presenting themselves for ordination. By the late fourteenth century, candidates presented for ordination at services in the parish church numbered as many in a single day as 121 in 1368, 165 in 1370, and 126 in 1373.

There is inevitably a good deal of uncertainty concerning the diligence with which rectors of Chelmsford pursued their pastoral responsibilities at this time. There is little record of the mid-fourteenth century rectors of Chelmsford, and it may be — but this can only be a matter of speculation — that they were pre-occupied elsewhere with more remunerative and prestigious preferments. Certainly the rapid succession of priests in the second half of the fifteenth century — quite apart from any pattern of non-residence — raises some intriguing questions concerning the responsibility for the re-building of the parish church during that period.

A small cottage on the west side of the churchyard was described early in the fifteenth century as the house of the rector or the *presteshows*. But it may well be that this house was more frequently inhabited by the priests who served as chaplains either to the parish church or the chantry chapel.

A chantry chapel, the chapel of the Blessed Virgin Mary, had been built in the churchyard by the Mounteney family in the fourteenth century. The Fraternity of the Holy Trinity, open to men and women, had been founded around 1368 by the generosity of the townspeople of Chelmsford. Three additional fraternities or guilds — dedicated in the names of Corpus Christi, of the Blessed Virgin Mary, and of St. John the Baptist — were endowed at different times in the fourteenth and fifteenth centuries, to provide for priests to sing mass in the church and to assist in the pastoral care of the parishioners.

The guilds were presided over by their wardens and trustees. They owned a good deal of property in the town, and it is apparent that they met important needs — maintaining the liturgical life of the church and its pastoral ministrations through the work of their chaplains; contributing to the needs of the poorest members of the community; and possibly managing the Chelmsford players, who continued to perform religious plays and ceremonies in and around Chelmsford as late as the 1570s.

The Rebuilding of the Parish Church

Nothing is known of the circumstances in which the parish church was re-built in the course of the fifteenth and the early sixteenth centuries. It may well have been that Chelmsford, in common with many market towns in East Anglia, had flourished in the later middles ages and that its citizens required a church of greater size and dignity. But the floor plan of the new church was not significantly greater, and it is clear that some stones from the earlier building were used in the reconstruction.

A precise dating of the re-building has proved to be impossible, but it seems likely that the work commenced with the two guild chapels of Corpus Christi and of Our Lady, standing on the south and the north sides of the chancel respectively. It is reckoned that the oldest features of the new church are the arcade which separates the chancel from the chapel on the south side; the graceful double fan arch which separates the chancel from the chapel on the north side; the western arches of both the south and the north chapels; and the south chapel itself, including the piscina in the south wall.

It is probable that the later years of the fifteenth century saw the building of the chancel arch, the north and south arcades of the nave, the clerestory, the north and south aisles, the massive west tower, and the south porch. It is known, however, that bequests for the building of a new steeple were made only in the early years of the sixteenth century, and that monies for the decoration of the south porch and the building of a south aisle were received only in the 1520s and 1530s.

The church consisted of the chancel, the north and south chapels, the nave with its clerestory, the north and south aisles, the south porch, and the west tower. Flint rubble intermixed with blocks of stone were used in the building of the new church. Stone and flint were both used in an elaborate inlay pattern in the decoration of the south porch, which was completed by a panelled and pinnacled parapet. The parapet at the west tower was also embattled and pinnacled. The tower was capped by a lantern which supported a slender spire.

Documentary evidence from the early years of the eighteenth century suggests that there was what must originally have been a chapel on the outside of the north wall of the church. The excavations of 1983 revealed beneath the floor of the outer north aisle that had been built in 1873 the flint rubble and medieval brick foundations of this small building which had been previously attached to the north wall of the north aisle. It seems probable that this had been the chantry chapel of the guild of St. John the Baptist.

Little expense was spared in decorating the interior of the church. The gallery at the west end almost certainly housed the great organ. The glory of the building was judged by some to be the four-light east window depicting scenes from the life of Our Lord. But it was the roof or ceiling of the nave which would undoubtedly have captured the imagination of later generations if it had been allowed to survive the destruction of images at the hands of the puritans in the 1640s. It appeared to rest on the heads of the carved wooden figures of angels which ran the whole length of the nave on both the north and south sides just beneath the roof, while the inside of the roof was adorned with a large number of angels, also carved in wood, with wings outstretched.

There have been significant changes to the appearance of the church — externally and internally — in the course of the last five hundred years; but it is this perpendicular church, dating in large part from the fifteenth century, but standing on the site — indeed, on the foundations — of its thirteenth century predecessor, which is known today as Chelmsford Cathedral. It has been throughout much of its history the parish church of Chelmsford, and its vastly extended role since the early years of the twentieth century as the cathedral church of one of the largest dioceses in the Church of England, does not sit uncomfortably with the inherent simplicity of its design and the quiet dignity of its architecture.

The re-building of the parish church and its refurbishment undoubtedly reflected the increasing prosperity of Chelmsford as a market town and its growing significance as the shire town. It had become by the end of the fifteenth century a busy, bustling place with large numbers of visitors and travellers; but it could still be described a century later as 'one ancient goodlye manor scituate in the harte of the countye of Essex . . . convenientlie and well housed and well builte for timber and tile . . . with moe than three hundred habitacions, divers of them seemelye for gentlemen, manie fayre inns, and the residue of the same habitacions for victuallers and artificers of cytie like buildings.'

But the intervening years had witnessed one change of profound importance within the developing life of the town. The manor of bishop's hall in Chelmsford

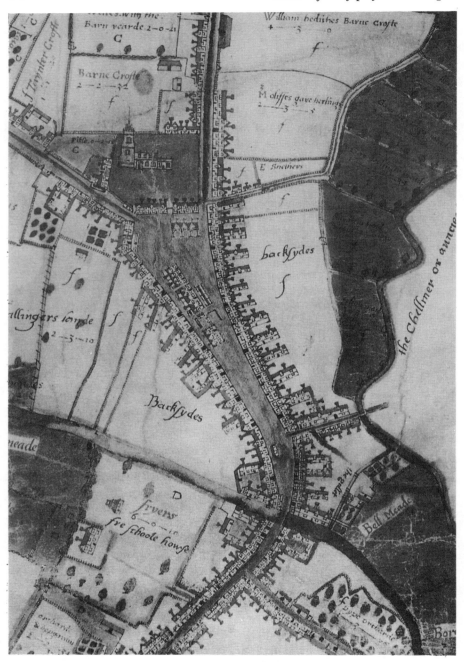

Chelmsford Town mapped by John Walker in 1591.

and the advowson of the rectory, which passed from the bishops of London to the crown in 1545, were purchased eighteen years later by Thomas Mildmay.

The Mildmay family had been established in Chelmsford since the first decade of the sixteenth century. The early prosperity of the family had derived from their trade as mercers in the town. Thomas, who succeeded eventually in purchasing the lordship of the manor, had made his career not in trade but in government employment, serving over many years as an auditor of the crown's land revenues. He had benefited greatly from the suppression of the guilds and the compulsory sale of chantry property in Chelmsford at the time of the reformation. He had previously acquired the lordship of the manor of Moulsham, and his newly built manor house — Moulsham Hall — was judged by many to be 'the greatest esquire's building' in Essex. The story of Chelmsford was to be inseparable from the story of the Mildmays for over three hundred years.

The emergence of the Mildmay family symbolized the growing importance of the leading citizens in the general affairs of the town. The tradition of non-residence on the part of successive rectors persisted. The parish and the parish church were served in large measure by curates; but civil duties, especially in relation to the Poor Law, had been imposed upon churchwardens by Tudor legislation, and the management of the affairs of the parish appears to have been left in the hands of the churchwardens and other prominent parishioners.

Chelmsford Parish Church was described in 1591 as 'goodlye, seemely and large . . . meete for the receipte of two thousand people or more . . . situate in one faire church yarde . . . furnished with many goodlye pues, one goodlye steeple ymbattled . . . and a convenient ring of foure belles'. But the evidence from the middle years of the sixteenth century suggests several grounds for concern over a period of two or three generations.

The long period of reconstruction and refurbishment continued as repairs to the fabric of the building and some re-ordering of the internal arrangements were carried out even at a time when the parish was burdened by debt. There were repeated attempts to secure the dignity of the churchyard and to stem the incursions of neighbouring properties and the abuse of the churchyard by the disposal of household refuse. The building of private pews led to disputes concerning sittings in the church and the right of access to certain pews. Absentees from church were necessarily pursued by the churchwardens. There was unquestionably evidence of pastoral neglect in the early years of the seventeenth century. There were disputes between the rector and the parishioners regarding the election of churchwardens. Indeed, there was a deeply divisive and long-running dispute regarding the presentation of one incumbent.

Reformation

Chelmsford — the town and the church — appears to have suffered less than many places in all the turmoil of reformation and counter reformation. The townspeople were clearly divided in their allegiances. Some undoubtedly preferred the old ways and were zealous for the conversion or persecution of heretics. Some rejoiced in the liberation that was offered through the translation of the scriptures and found the test of truth in the protestant affirmation of justification by faith in the atoning death of Christ. Parishioners endured the inevitable changes in public liturgy and in the adornment of the church; but the men and women of Chelmsford, although they were well aware of the transport of many facing trial for their faith, witnessed far less than their counterparts in other towns of the brutalities of public execution.

The reformation became associated in the minds of many with the tradition of godly learning. The suppression of the chantries had ensured that their endowments were applied in Chelmsford to the appointment of a stipendiary curate and the establishment of a free grammar school. The activities of a growing number of puritans demanded that scrupulous attention should be paid to the relationship between the plain teaching of scripture and the rites and ceremonies of the church. It was in the spirit of this tradition of biblical teaching and godly learning that Thomas Williamson endowed the Chelmsford lectureship at his death in 1614. He was mindful of the large numbers of people who came into Chelmsford and passed through, and he was concerned 'to make a begyning of this godly exercise of preaching in this place'.

One of the most redoubtable men associated with Chelmsford throughout its long history was Thomas Hooker, a puritan divine, who came as the Town Lecturer in the 1620s. There was already ample evidence of a spirit of laxity and indiscipline in the town — non-attendance at the parish church; rowdy behaviour on the sabbath; a deriding of the authority of the churchwardens and the church courts. Hooker came to Chelmsford with a reputation as a powerful and a popular preacher.

He spoke fearlessly about the sovereignty of God, freedom of worship, the power of the state over the church and of the church over conscience. It was, perhaps, inevitable that he would fall foul of the crown and of the Bishop of London. He was disciplined and subsequently removed from office, and became in the early 1630s the leader of a large group of people who fled to New England to establish a new life in which Christian faith and respect for all people might be the foundation of political liberty and religious freedom. His heroic trek through swamp and river forest to the Connecticut River in 1636 has long since become part of the story of a man who has been judged by history to be not merely the founder of the state of Connecticut but one of the early fathers of American democracy.

Hooker had touched a raw nerve in the religious life of the town. A small group of religious zealots continued to be active and vocal after his departure; and early attempts to enforce Archbishop Laud's requirements concerning church furnishings and ceremonial were stoutly resisted. Politics and religion could not be disentangled from each other, and Chelmsford as a town was caught up in the deep divisions and the destructiveness of the civil war.

Extremists in the town were not satisfied with the removal of some of the images from the east window of the parish church in 1641, and a rabble with poles and staves destroyed what remained of the coloured glass. Dr John Michaelson, the rector, condemned from the pulpit this 'popular tumultuous Reformation'; but he was personally abused in church, suffered the repeated indignity of interruptions during divine service, and was finally compelled to flee the town. The parliamentary ordinance of 1643 for the demolition of all images in churches brought to a conclusion the undoing of so much that had been achieved in the rebuilding and beautifying of the parish church. The removal of the cross from the church spire and the wanton destruction of the carved wooden angels that had decorated the roof of the nave symbolized what would prove to be the short-lived triumph of puritan zeal.

The limited evidence that has survived suggests that the parish church recovered slowly from the traumas of these years. The restoration of the monarchy in 1660 ensured the restoration of episcopacy and of the ecclesiastical settlement that had been established at the beginning of the reign of Elizabeth I. But it is recorded that only 17 parishioners received the sacrament of Holy Communion in Chelmsford on Christmas Day in 1662, and few more than 30 on Easter Day in 1663. The fabric of the church was giving great cause for concern 20 years later, and disturbances in church continued to be an unhappy feature of religious life in Chelmsford.

The Town and the Church

Chelmsford continued to be the main seat of justice and administration in the county. The Assizes, the General Quarter Sessions for the Peace, the Petty Sessions and the County Courts were held there. The County Gaol had been transferred from Colchester to Chelmsford in the 1660s. The Commissioners for the Land and Window Tax sat in Chelmsford whenever they were required to meet. The election of the knights of the shire took place in the county town.

Chelmsford continued to draw large numbers of people into the town, and Daniel Defoe commented in the early 1720s on 'the excessive multitudes of carriers and passengers who are constantly passing this way to London'. But Chelmsford presented a pleasing aspect, and one unknown visitor, writing just two years after Defoe's visit to the town, found its situation 'charming, for it lies in a beautiful plain, with a little river running through it. The inns are very good, and so many Gentlemen's seats round it, that a Stranger may pleasantly pass a week here.'

The eighteenth century saw a transformation in the fortunes of the parish church. The long and distinguished incumbencies of Oliver Pocklington (1706–39), John Tindall (1739–74) and John Morgan (1774–1817) served the town well and call in question the caricatures of worldliness and indolence with which the parochial clergy of the Church of England in the eighteenth century have been so

Chelmsford Parish Church, 1800 (Engraved by J.-Z. Mazell).

often identified. By the later years of the century appreciative comments were received from visitors concerning the dignity of the church and the openness and tidiness of the churchyard. The population of the town continued to grow, and significant improvements to the church — the erection of galleries and pews at the west end, the building of a new organ, and the hanging of a new peal of eight bells — speak also of the town's increasing prosperity.

The tragedy that overtook the parish church late during the evening of the 17 January 1800 when the columns of the south arcade collapsed, bringing down the roof of the nave, the south aisle and part of the north aisle, and destroying the pews and the west gallery, led to its re-building in a relatively short time and gave to the building some of the distinctive architectural features which it has retained to this present time.

It is probable that the foundations of the piers had been disturbed by careless workmen who had been opening a vault in the course of the preceding day. The *Chelmsford Chronicle* spoke of 'this stupendous ruin' and described 'a scene of awful and magnificent grandeur'. A public meeting held on the following day took the necessary decisions to make the building safe; to seek the professional advice of John Johnson, the architect who had built the Shire Hall only a decade earlier; and to request a licence to hold services in the Shire Hall.

Parliament was petitioned for the necessary powers to raise the monies required for restoration. The Act for Repairing Chelmsford Parish Church empowered trustees to borrow up to the sum of £5,000 on the security of the church rate, and to raise rates not exceeding four shillings in the pound, in order to restore the church, to erect galleries, to repair the organ, and to provide a salary for the organist.

It had been agreed from the outset that the restoration of the building should keep faith with the original design. Coade's artificial stone was used to supplement the original stone to re-build the piers of the arcade. Portland stone was used as a cladding stone on the south walls and clerestory, while the north aisles were merely faced with white brick. The roof of the nave was plastered in what was subsequently described as 'a prettily, coved Tudor ceiling'. Plaster figures, reminiscent of the carved wooden angels that had supported the ceiling prior to their destruction in 1643, stood between the clerestory windows on the north and south sides of the nave. The organ and the monuments were restored. The Table of Commandments and the Table of Benefactions were re-painted and re-mounted.

Provision was also made in the Act of Parliament to erect galleries on the north and south sides of the nave, and these, together with other improvements to the interior of the church — including the hanging of two additional bells and the commissioning of a new four-light east window depicting the four evangelists — followed in the course of the first two decades of the nineteenth century.

Successive members of the Mildmay family had been diligent and generous in exercising their responsibilities as lords of the manor and patrons of the parish church. The long association of the family with both the town and the church

Collapse of the roof of Chelmsford Parish Church, 1800.

was brought to a conclusion in the long incumbency of Carew Anthony St. John Mildmay as rector of Chelmsford from 1826–78. Mildmay's distinguished tenure of his office coincided with significant changes: the removal from the churchwardens of their responsibilities for the care of the poor; the confrontation with the non-conformists over the payment of church rates; the building of a daughter church in Moulsham; the coming of the railway; and the eventual handing over of the powers of the town's paving and lighting commissioners to a statutory and elected board of health.

His incumbency also witnessed significant changes in the parish church — the removal of the high-backed family pews (1842); the commissioning of the present five-light Gothic east window (1858); the removal of the west gallery and the organ (1867); the removal of the north and south galleries and the building of the outer north aisle and the north transept to accommodate the organ and the vestry (1873); and the restoration of the chancel and the provision of its clerestory (1878).

But Mildmay's energies extended far beyond the parish church and the church school. He enjoyed a primacy of honour within the town, embodying not only the place of the parish church and the office of rector but also the long-standing connection of his family. At the time of his death in 1878, the *Essex Weekly News* acknowledged that any account of his work in Chelmsford would be 'almost to write the history of the progress and improvement of the town for the last half century'. His death created a vacancy in the social hierarchy of the town, and the *Chelmsford (Essex) Chronicle* observed that, 'The want of a recognised head of the town was seriously felt'.

The Incorporation of the Borough

The provision of a recognized head was to come within a decade of his death through the incorporation of the borough of Chelmsford and the election of its first mayor. The idea of incorporation was raised in various places throughout the early and mid-1880s. A public meeting and a public petition, followed in due course by a Commission of Inquiry, prepared the way for this new transition in the government and leadership of the town.

The manor of Chelmsford, which had been established as a market town in the middle ages through the patronage of the bishops of London, had passed in due course to the Mildmay family who had secured a position of substantial wealth and pre-eminence in the town by the middle years of the sixteenth century. But Chelmsford had become by the mid-1880s the only county town in the country — with the exception of Oakham in Rutland — which had not already secured incorporation. What was now being sought was the incorporation of the town under the Municipal Corporation Acts of 1835 and 1882, providing the citizens with an elected council which would replace the local board of health.

It was argued by the protagonists that incorporation would be good for business

Interior of Chelmsford Parish Church, 1850.

and would enable new initiatives to bring industry into Chelmsford. The actual process of debate, petition, enquiry and submission was remarkably brief, and the town was finally incorporated on 7 September 1888 as 'One body politic and corporate by the name of the Mayor, Aldermen, and Burgesses of the Borough of Chelmsford'

The Creation of the Diocese

The place of the parish church within the life of the town continued unchanged, but developments were already taking place which would lead within a relatively short time to the creation of a diocese for the county of Essex and the designation of Chelmsford Parish Church as Chelmsford Cathedral.

The long-standing ecclesiastical connection between Essex and London had been broken in 1846 when the whole of the county, with the exception of nine metropolitan parishes in Barking, was united with the diocese of Rochester, which was required for 30 years to straddle both sides of the Thames. The Barking parishes followed the rest of the county in 1867, but the whole of Essex was transferred from Rochester in 1877 to join the neighbouring county of Hertfordshire in creating the newly formed diocese of St. Albans. Another 37 years were to pass before the division of St. Albans could be achieved and the diocese actually came into being.

The impetus for the creation of a diocese for the county of Essex came from the urgent need to make adequate provision for the rapidly escalating population in the area that was identified at an early stage as 'London in Essex' or 'London over the Border'. The movement of people out of London into Essex had commenced in the second half of the eighteenth century, and the population of this south-western corner of the county continued to grow remorselessly throughout the nineteenth century, increasing from 14,000 inhabitants in 1801 to 97,000 in 1867 and some 700,000 by 1903.

There were repeated attempts in the middle years of the nineteenth century to raise significant sums of money in order to extend the church's work, but the response to these initiatives could not keep pace with the scale of the increase in population. Eleven new churches were built in London over the Border between 1891 and 1901, but the population grew by more than a quarter of a million during those ten years alone.

It was this phenomenon — the unprecedented growth of population — that led Bishop Edgar Jacob, the third bishop of St. Albans, to identify the needs of London over the Border as 'the great problem' within weeks of his enthronement in 1903. He worked tirelessly over the years that followed for the creation of a new diocese. He never wavered in the conviction that the mission of the Church of England in the east end of London could not be advanced by a bishop who resided in St. Albans and who carried responsibilities for Hertfordshire as well as Essex. He has been rightly identified as the father of the diocese.

Early negotiations led to the setting up of the Essex and Hertfordshire Bishopric Fund towards the end of 1905. Much energy went into raising in less than two years the sum of £45,000 for the endowment of a new bishopric. But local considerations and demands were then brutally overtaken as parliament, and especially the House of Commons, refused to countenance the general legislation which would have permitted the creation of new dioceses with comparative ease.

The Bishoprics Bill, which was introduced into the House of Lords in March 1909, attempted to secure for the whole church a simplification of the process whereby the creation of new dioceses or the establishment of cathedral foundations or the revision of diocesan boundaries might be achieved through Orders in Council. But the Bill encountered opposition, prevarication and the delays that were inevitably caused by the other demands upon parliamentary time. In the event, it proved expedient to abandon the general enabling bill four years later in March 1913 and to proceed instead by a special bill, acting in concert with the Sheffield and Suffolk Bishoprics Committees. The passage of this new bill required a good deal of negotiation behind the scenes — and not least of all with the Nonconformists in the House of Commons who demanded concessions where charity bills in which they had an interest were concerned — but the bill eventually passed all its stages and received the Royal Assent on 15 August 1913 as the 'Bishoprics of Sheffield, Chelmsford, and for the County of Suffolk Act 1913'.

Decisions concerning the designation of the see town and the establishment of the cathedral had long since preceded the passage of the bill. There had been seven claimants — Barking, Chelmsford, Colchester, Thaxted, Waltham Abbey, West Ham and Woodford. The Chelmsford Borough Council had established a 'Cathedral City Committee' as early as November 1906. The Mayor of Chelmsford, Frederick Chancellor, a distinguished local architect, who had been closely identified with both the town and the parish church over many years, served as the chairman. He acknowledged the claims that might properly be made by London over the Border, but he was also certain that unless the cathedral and the bishop's residence were located in Chelmsford 'the county districts will hardly realise that it is an Essex diocese'.

The decision to recommend Chelmsford as the 'Essex See Cathedral City' was determined in large measure by the voting that had taken place on the part of the parishes.

	1st place	2nd place	3rd place
Chelmsford	191	66	34
Colchester	101	77	38
West Ham	63	91	47
Woodford	13	28	31
Barking	8	25	53
Waltham	6	7	21
Thaxted	1	4	19

Bishop Jacob was surprised by the result, but he was aware of 'a prevalent feeling that if the Cathedral were in London over the Border the county would be entirely absorbed in the metropolis'. But the needs of London in Essex remained paramount and, even before the outcome of the voting was known, he had ruled out any possibility of spending 'large sums of money upon a cathedral church, whatever town is ultimately chosen. Our pressing need will be to care for souls, and buildings that are not absolutely necessary must wait.'

Bishop Jacob had undoubtedly envisaged a subsequent division of the county — north and south — into two dioceses. Indeed, his comments upon the selection of Chelmsford in the *Diocesan Gazette* for April 1908 carried the rider that a collegiate church might also be established in London over the Border in order to assist work in the metropolitan area as a whole. It may well be that the selection of Chelmsford, bearing in mind its central geographical location, actually prevented the polarization that could so easily have followed if either Colchester or any place in the metropolitan area had been chosen as the see town.

A second decision that had preceded the passage of the bill establishing the diocese related to the location of the bishop's residence. Bishop Frank Johnson, the bishop suffragan of Colchester, who had purchased Guy Harlings on his appointment as rector of Chelmsford in 1880, hoped that the Chelmsford Rectory, which occupied a large site on the west side of Rectory Lane, might be purchased for the bishop, enabling Guy Harlings to be offered for sale to the benefice. No thought appears to have been given at this stage to the possibility that the rector of Chelmsford might be designated the dean or provost of the cathedral church. There are references only to the benefice and the rector.

The Bishopric Committee moved in a different direction, however, from the one that had been espoused by Bishop Johnson. It was Guy Harlings that was purchased from the executors of his estate in the hope that the house and its extensive grounds might accommodate both the rector and the bishop. It was assumed that the rector would continue to live in Guy Harlings, and preliminary drawings proposed a new house with eighteen bedrooms for the bishop. But differing perceptions of the offices of the rector, albeit one with responsibility for a cathedral, and the bishop in the early years of the twentieth century were neatly encapsulated in the suggestion that a small stable might be provided for the rector and a 'motor shed' for the bishop.

In the event, these proposals were abandoned. The rector continued to occupy Guy Harlings, renting the house from what was to become the St. Albans and Chelmsford Church Trust until 1951, while the acquisition of another property for the bishop — 'Redgates' in the Colchester (or Springfield) Road — was not finally made until after the appointment of the first bishop in 1914.

The Priorities of Diocesan Life

It was the size and the complexity of the diocese that confronted Bishop John Watts-Ditchfield on his appointment as the first bishop of Chelmsford in 1914.

DIOCESE OF CHELMSFORD

Harwich
Walton-on-the-Naze
Clacton-on-Sea
Merséa Island
St. Peter ad Murum, Bradwell
Colchester
R Stour
R Colne
Halstead
Burnham-on-Crouch
Southend-on-Sea
R Blackwater
R Chelmer
CHELMSFORD
Saffron Walden
Thaxted
Stansted
Brentwood
Basildon
Tilbury
Harlow
Greensted
Romford
Barking.
R Stort
R Roding
Waltham Abbey
Newham
R Lea
R Thames

Map of the Diocese of Chelmsford.

The primary statistics of community and church life can be easily presented. It had a population of 1,355,000 with 463 benefices and over 700 clergy. But the diocese has been from the time of its creation an area of great diversity and strong local identities. The early judgement that 'anything like cohesion seemed well-nigh impossible' has remained to challenge those who have wrestled over the years with the tasks of episcopal leadership, diocesan administration, and the promotion of a common sense of identity.

Watts-Ditchfield brought to his appointment his fierce evangelical zeal. 'A bishop ought to be the *biggest soul-winner in his diocese*'. But he brought also a different perception from Edgar Jacob concerning the unity of the diocese. He set his face from the beginning against any division. He was totally persuaded that the church in London over the Border required 'the help of the rest of Essex', and that the rural areas, if they were deprived of all the problems associated with the metropolitan area, would lose 'a stimulus and a broadened outlook which is often difficult to preserve in the tiny parishes'.

The early years were overshadowed by the First World War, but by 1919 Watts-Ditchfield was able to turn with new resolve to the problems that must be addressed. The needs of London over the Border alone required the completion of 13 unfinished churches, the replacement of 26 temporary church buildings, the provision of new parsonage houses, and the augmentation of clergy stipends. But there were significant new housing areas in other parts of Essex, and not least of all at Southend, and the entirely different needs of the church in the more remote rural areas also required attention.

An important acknowledgement of the story of Christianity in Essex was secured through the rededication of St. Peter's Chapel at Bradwell-on-Sea in June 1920. It was here that St. Cedd had come *c*.653 to evangelize the East Saxons, and the fortified site at Bradwell had been one of the early centres from which the mission of the church had been taken forward in this part of England.

The chapel had fallen into disuse as a barn in later centuries, but the cathedral chapter had already expressed the hope that 'this interesting relic of the past' might be restored. The chapel and the surrounding land had been duly conveyed by the Parker family to trustees with the intention that they should be vested in the cathedral chapter once it was properly constituted. Annual diocesan visits or pilgrimages to the chapel commenced in 1921 and these gatherings, enlarged in more recent years through the participation of other churches, have enabled many to appreciate not merely the continuing significance of the Celtic tradition of spirituality but also to see St. Peter's Chapel as being in some small way the proto-cathedral of the diocese.

Watts-Ditchfield acknowledged the scant attention that had been paid to the cathedral both before and immediately after the creation of the diocese. Plans were drawn up by Charles Nicholson in 1920 for a major enlargement which would have had the effect of acknowledging and bringing under one roof the dual roles of the building as a cathedral and a parish church. What was envisaged was the creation of a new and substantial nave and quire and sanctuary on the north side, but going far beyond the east end of the present building, together with a second tower at the west end. The cathedral, duly and magnificently enlarged, would have been able to seat two thousand people. But in the absence of any constituted authority for the government and leadership of the cathedral, it was inevitable that such a scheme would be abandoned and the energies of the diocese turned almost exclusively, in the direction of London over the Border.

In 1924 the Church Assembly appointed a Commission 'to make enquiries and report on the properties and revenues of cathedrals and to consider the best means of promoting the greater efficiency of cathedral chapters as centres of learning'. One of the Commission's seven area sub-committees visited Chelmsford in June 1926. Its report, printed in the *Diocesan Chronicle* in 1927, noted with some surprise that the Act for the creation of the see 'set up no chapter, merely allowing the bishop to appoint twenty-four (honorary) canons . . . (that) . . . the powers of the bishop over the cathedral were neither less nor more than those which he exercises over any other parish church', and that the legal status of the incumbent was still only that of the rector of Chelmsford.

The report could not fail to draw attention to the fact that the Cathedral was 'quite unendowed for its special function'. It found no desire on the part of 'the bishop or anyone else, that residentiary stalls should be endowed, even with diocesan obligations attached to them'; and it concluded that 'this hard-pressed diocese is wise to move slowly in the development of its cathedral; and that, because of the problems with which London over the Border is faced, the cathedral deserves the practical and intelligent sympathy of the church at large'.

The rector had become sub-dean of the Cathedral in 1924. But it was only in 1935 — 21 years after the creation of the diocese — that an Order in Council provided the Cathedral with a constitution and statutes for the first time, the rector and sub-dean thereupon becoming provost, together with the establishment of the chapter and of the cathedral council as the governing body of the institution. It was only in 1957 — 43 years after the creation of the diocese — that the first residentiary canon was appointed.

This protracted development of the cathedral as an institution was matched by the piecemeal approach that was necessarily adopted with regard to the building. A two-bay extension of the chancel was built in the late 1920s as a memorial to the first bishop. The extension accommodated the bishop's throne and the statue of Watts-Ditchfield and made provision for the canons' stalls. It was, however, at the suggestion of Bishop Guy Warman, the second bishop, that the extension beyond the north transept took place in accordance with the designs of Charles Nicholson, providing vestries and the original chapter room.

Chelmsford has been from the beginning a parish church cathedral. It stands at the heart of the county town. Its congregations, although they were drawn from all over the town, took seriously their parochial responsibilities. This parish church dimension was certainly judged by the first two bishops to be an important ingredient at the heart of the diocese's life. The cathedral continued to have, in spite of the modest extensions to the chancel and to the north transept, the appearance of a parish church; and although there is ample evidence during these early years of the cathedral providing hospitality — and more than hospitality — to a wide variety of diocesan and county activities, the work of the cathedral — like its architecture — remained essentially parochial and domestic.

The services that marked the 21st and the 25th anniversaries of the diocese in 1935 and 1939 saw the cathedral enter more fully into one of its proper roles as the diocesan centre for liturgy and celebration. The modest foundations were also laid during this period for other aspects of its work through the generosity of Mrs Lavinia Clarissa Keene in making donations to the cathedral in memory of her late husband, Mr John Henry Keene. The cathedral has never been greatly endowed, but these benefactions enabled it to make some provision both for the maintenance and development of cathedral music and for the establishment of annual lectures which addressed social and economic questions and what was termed 'practical religion'.

The perennial problems of diocesan leadership and diocesan priorities remained. It was the judgement of Bishop Henry Wilson, the third bishop, writing in the mid-1930s, that 'had Bishop Watts-Ditchfield been given ten normal years to administer the diocese the whole situation would have been different . . . but its life has been one of struggle and anxiety from its birth'.

The most notable feature throughout the whole history of the diocese has been the expansion and movement of its population. Many have come from outside, but some of the underlying threads of continuity have been provided by those who have moved from London over the Border into south and mid Essex as a result of increasing prosperity, the development of improved communications by rail and road, great social mobility, and extensive new housing developments. There was as a consequence of all these things the experience of living with continuous change. The constant need to provide new churches for new communities in new development areas meant that the diocese moved inexorably from one major commitment to another.

Sooner or later the point was bound to be made that a diocese as large and diverse as Chelmsford could accommodate more than one set of priorities at any one time. The parish church tradition continued to loom large in the thinking of the cathedral, and the chairmanship of the cathedral council by the diocesan bishop during its first 30 years ensured that the cathedral was unlikely to find its own integrity and creative independence. It was not without significance that Bishop Wilson's recollections of the untimely death of Provost Waller in 1951 included the approving words, — 'More than once he declared to me that the work of the parish would never be displaced by the claims of the cathedral'.

A Vision for the Cathedral

It was, however, the claims of the cathedral that were advanced resolutely by Provost Eric Gordon throughout the 1950s and the early 1960s. Thought had already been given by the cathedral's new consultant architect, Stephen Dykes Bower, to further improvements — new choir stalls, a large chapel in the outer north aisle, a further extension of the sanctuary. Gordon set his heart on 'a much finer, worthier cathedral'. His address to the Diocesan Conference on 'The Place of the Cathedral in the Life of the Diocese' in October 1953 challenged the assumption that choices must constantly be made to the disadvantage of the cathedral. 'Our aim should be to provide *both* for the housing areas *and* for the cathedral, and not to keep saying, "*Either* the housing areas *or* the cathedral". Surely in the end we can do both.' Gordon's vision was unambiguous — 'A great county should have a great cathedral as its heart'.

Provost Gordon's address was welcomed by the Essex Churchman as 'inaugurating a new stage in the thinking and feeling of the diocese towards the cathedral'. Something of the early story of the church in Essex was picked up at the end of the celebrations to mark the 40th anniversary of the diocese in 1954 when Bishop Falkner Allison, the fourth bishop, extended the dedication of the cathedral to include St. Mary the Virgin, St. Peter and St. Cedd. The refurbishment of the cathedral was given a high priority — the transformation of the south porch (1953), the renovation of the south and the north chapels (1955 and 1961), the rich colouring of the roof beams in the chancel (1957), the painting of the nave ceiling (1961), the renewal of the stonework of the tower and the porch (1961).

The vision for the cathedral went beyond the refurbishment and beautifying of the building, and there were serious attempts during these years to develop the cathedral's role as a centre for learning and as a focus for the celebration of the arts. The Keene benefactions enabled the cathedral to host the Keene Lectures on various aspects of Christian faith and social witness, while the Cathedral Festival Week, commencing in 1954, established a tradition of music and drama for church and community which would also be taken up again in later years.

The most significant development in the life of the cathedral during the middle years of the century was the appointment of the first three residentiary canons in 1957, 1964 and 1970. Diocesan responsibilities were attached to these appointments in every case — for religious education, post-ordination training, and social concern — but they represented an acknowledgement by successive bishops and provosts alike that the cathedral had an appropriate contribution to make to the wider life of the diocese. The establishment of a residentiary chapter, even though it had no executive power as a corporate body, would become over the years the launch-pad for a fuller development of the work of the cathedral.

English cathedrals have been associated at various times in peoples' minds with traditions of excellence and experiment. Provost Connop Price, writing about the task of the cathedral in 1971, emphasized its role as 'a centre of experiment' for the diocese, both in worship and in 'exploring more effective ways of communicating with people today, and of expressing mission to present-day society'.

This perception of what a young cathedral might be was taken up in a distinctive fashion from the early 1970s by Canon (subsequently Provost) Richard Herrick through the work of the Cathedral Centre for Research and Training. The Centre, which was informed in part by the disciplines of the behavioural sciences, offered to the diocese and the parishes over a period of some ten years a consultancy service which influenced diocesan structures, patterns of training, and the self-understanding with which clergy developed their ministries. It played a vital part during that time in all areas of training for clergy and laity.

The Re-ordering of the Cathedral

One of the recurring themes in the story of the cathedral has been the need or the desire to maintain and re-order and beautify the building. Bishop John Trillo, the sixth bishop, while acknowledging the limitations imposed upon the work of the cathedral by its size, remained grateful for the fact that 'grandiose extensions in mock Gothic' had not been added. A far-reaching re-ordering of the nave was discussed in the 1970s, but these early plans were necessarily abandoned because of the need to carry out extensive repairs to the roof and the external walls.

Preliminary thoughts concerning the re-ordering of the nave addressed the need to provide a new heating system, to lay a new floor, and to create the flexible space which would enable the cathedral to develop its work more easily. In the event, it fell to a new provost to preside over a public appeal for £400,000 and to carry through a comprehensive scheme of re-ordering and refurnishing in the early 1980s.

Four principles were held on to as plans developed in discussion with the cathedral's new consultant architect, Robert Potter — first, that the building should be seen in its entirety; secondly, that the opportunity should be taken to commission new items of furnishing from significant but relatively unknown artists; thirdly, that the flexible space that was judged to be so important should be secured; and, fourthly, that nothing should be done that would compromise the fundamental character of the building as a place of worship and prayer.

The removal of the pews and of all other fixed items of furnishing, together with the use of French limestone for the new floor, created a sense of light and space. It was as though the building had been set free, allowing the simplicity and the sensitivity of the architecture to be fully appreciated. Work by Guisseppe Lund (the ambos and the grilles enclosing the new chapels), Alan Evans (the support for the font), Petra Clare (the ambo crosses), Beryl Dean (the patchwork hanging at the east end and the designs for the hassocks), Georg Ehrlich (the statue of the Bombed Child and the bronze relief of Christ the Healer) and John Skelton (the cathedra) brought new and significant items of furnishing into the cathedral.

The re-ordered cathedral was to become the primary resource as attempts were made to take forward the work of the cathedral on various fronts. The

Nave view of the Cathedal facing east.
(Photograph courtesy of Pitkin Pictorials Limited)

inherent qualities of the architecture — its dignity and its intimacy — enabled the building to provide the setting for public worship and private prayer, for music, for drama, for lectures, for schools of prayers, for synods, for graduation ceremonies, for training days, for consultations. The oft-repeated words of welcome — 'This is *your* cathedral' - spoke of the conviction that ultimately the cathedral had no *raison d'être* unless it was seen to be at the service of the diocese and the wider community.

Relatively young parish church cathedrals invariably lack the ancillary buildings which can be so important in the development of their work. The cathedral had played an important part in the development of the Guy Harlings complex in the mid-1970s, and the scheme for the renovation of the old house and the provision of new diocesan offices had included the building of the Cathedral Centre (1977–78). The way in which the Centre is used has changed and will continue to change over the years, but it accommodates today the Cathedral Office, the Cathedral Festival Office, the Cathedral Library, and Seminar Rooms which are frequently used by cathedral and diocese alike, and not least of all for training programmes.

A comprehensive scheme of mixed development at the west end of the cathedral churchyard in the late 1980s enabled the cathedral to make provision for the building of the Chapter House (1989–90). The circumstances of the development were such that private fund raising in the order of £100,000 ensured that the cathedral could make the required contribution to the costs of the new building. The Chapter House, which incorporates the Chapter Room on the second floor, provides facilities which are extensively used throughout the year by the cathedral, the diocese and the community at large.

The Work of the Cathedral

The cathedral has continued to enjoy over the years the wholehearted support of its congregations in all the work it has undertaken in its role as the cathedral. It is inevitable, however, that the primary responsibility for the development of its work will rest with the residentiary chapter and the permanent staff of the cathedral. The way in which the chapter and the staff of a cathedral develops cannot be planned in advance, because so much will turn upon personalities and opportunities and the vision to which men and women are prepared to work.

The primary commitment — for Chelmsford as for all cathedrals — is the offering of worship. The English cathedral tradition of worship, in which the choir plays a tremendously important part, is one in which the congregation is invited to participate through quiet and joyful contemplation. The establishment of a daily tradition of choral worship at Chelmsford is one that is still being actively pursued, but the cathedral has been able to take important steps forward through the successful appeal for £1.4 million (1991–95) for the building of the nave and chancel organs and for the endowment of a choral foundation.

The Cathedral Chapter House, 1990.
(Photograph courtesy of Malcolm Crowthers)

The choral foundation requires a developing relationship with three schools — the Cathedral School, St. Cedd's School, and the King Edward VI Grammar School — together with the newly established Anglia Polytechnic University. This network of relationships with institutions that do not necessarily have a formal relationship with the church is judged to be important and may yet prove to be a model for other younger cathedrals to follow.

The hope that the cathedral might take up and interpret in new ways the ancient tradition of cathedrals as centres of learning is one that has persisted. The cathedral's work throughout the year — the Keene Lectures, the Theological Society, the Schools of Prayer — is important, but the entering into new and potentially significant relationships with Essex University and with the Anglia Polytechnic University has been properly seen as creative work in the field of adult education and applied theology.

The Centre for the Study of Theology at Essex University was established in 1987 through the sponsorship of the cathedral chapter and the Anglican chaplaincy at the University. It has been concerned from the beginning to work on the boundaries of academic life in the area of theology and society. Its work — in research, teaching and publication — has owed much to the Directors of Studies of the Centre; but the Centre has continued to be supported by the cathedral chapter — in finance and personnel — and has attempted to secure a place for theology in one of the primary centres of higher education in the county.

The establishment of a master's degree in Liturgical Music (at the Anglia Polytechnic University from October 1994) and the projected establishment of master's degrees in Pastoral Theology (at the Anglia Polytechnic University from October 1997) and in Theology and Society (at Essex University from October 1997) are further instances of ways in which cathedrals, using creatively their independence and the resources they possess, are able to serve both church and community.

The parish church dimension, which had been so dominant in earlier years, has now been properly subsumed within the wider ministry of the cathedral. Every service is a cathedral service. Every activity is a cathedral activity, even though it might relate directly to the spiritual or educational or pastoral needs of the congregations. The pastoral care of the cathedral parish, the Cathedral School and the cathedral congregations continues to remain a high priority; but the primary focus is the relation of the cathedral *as a cathedral* to the bishop, the diocese and the wider community.

Chelmsford Cathedral is never able to forget that it has been Chelmsford Parish Church throughout much of its long history. It serves as the town church and the county church — as well as the diocesan church — and welcomes greatly the links that have been established over the years with local government, schools and universities, the law, the emergency services. The cathedral parish, which encompasses the heart of the county town, brings into close physical proximity with the cathedral several institutions whose work relates directly to the life of the county and the borough. It is against this background that

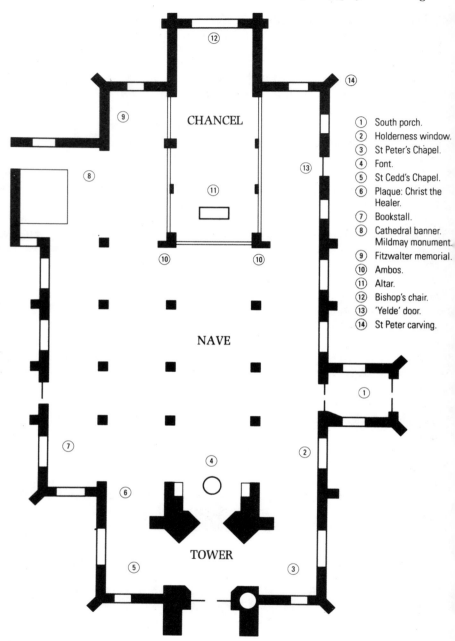

① South porch.
② Holderness window.
③ St Peter's Chapel.
④ Font.
⑤ St Cedd's Chapel.
⑥ Plaque: Christ the Healer.
⑦ Bookstall.
⑧ Cathedral banner. Mildmay monument.
⑨ Fitzwalter memorial.
⑩ Ambos.
⑪ Altar.
⑫ Bishop's chair.
⑬ 'Yelde' door.
⑭ St Peter carving.

CHANCEL

NAVE

TOWER

Plan of the Cathedral.

industrial chaplaincy has been initiated and maintained by the cathedral over a period of more than 30 years, and continues today to have important links with County Hall, the Crown Court, the County Fire and Rescue Service, and the G.E.C. Marconi companies.

The relationship between the church and the arts — between the Christian faith and the arts — has always been intimate and pervasive. English cathedrals have shown that they are well able — even in the second half of the twentieth century — to be patrons of the arts. They have worked with artists and craftsmen in finding news ways of expressing in sculpture, in painting, in tapestry, and in music something of the majesty of God, the drama of the human predicament, and the promptings of the human spirit.

Cathedrals are natural settings for celebrations of the arts, and the Chelmsford Cathedral Festival, which owes much to the vision and the commitment of the cathedral's Master of the Music, was seen initially by some as a way of marking the re-ordering of the cathedral in 1984. But it has continued as an annual festival of music and the arts, drawing large numbers of people into the cathedral, Guy Harlings and its grounds, the Cathedral Centre and an ever-increasing number of locations throughout the town where the activities associated with the Festival Fringe are to be found. It has depended from its inception upon the goodwill and the financial support of local authorities, of industry and commerce, and of the large numbers of people who as concert-goers ensure that the Festival remains a celebration for church and community.

The Vision and the Task

The work of the cathedral in recent years has taken up and interpreted — albeit in new ways — many of the aspirations that have been held over the years by those who have cared for the cathedral and its developing life. Those who serve the cathedral today as members of the residentiary chapter and its permanent staff have attempted to encapsulate something of what is being sought in public statements which set out simply the vision and the task to which the cathedral is committed.

The vision statement asks that the cathedral might be 'a place where people can find God; a place where people can pray; a place where people can make music; a place where the large issues can be thought through and argued out; a place where people can meet to look again at their hopes; their goals; their values.' The statement regarding the task of the cathedral acknowledges that the cathedral is by definition the seat of the Bishop of Chelmsford, and asks that it might 'develop to the full its life and work as a centre for worship and prayer, theology, celebration and mission, both for the bishop and for the wider community'.

The relation of a cathedral to the bishop and, therefore, to the diocese matters tremendously. Cathedrals have their own integrity and independence, but the

Seal of the Provost and Chapter of Chelmsford Cathedral, 1990.
(Photograph courtesy of Malcolm Crowthers)

cathedral serves within the life of the diocese as one of the symbols of the unity of the church which is ultimately focused in the office of the bishop.

Earlier thoughts concerning the division of the diocese have given way to a pattern of episcopal oversight through an area scheme which ensures a good deal of devolution and day by day pastoral care of clergy and their congregations, while enabling the Bishop of Chelmsford to preside over the diocese as a whole. But the scale of the task confronting the church in the diocese is daunting. The diocese encompasses large inner city areas, new towns, established urban communities, small villages, large areas of farmland and an extensive coastal strip. Its population continues to grow and current projections suggest that it will be a little over 2,650,000 by the beginning of the 21st century.

A young, large and disparate diocese like Chelmsford requires symbols — living, working symbols — of its unity. The cathedral may not impinge greatly day by day upon the parishes of the diocese, but it remains a community of worship and prayer — a living, working symbol — at the heart of the diocese, sharing fully in all the responsibilities and opportunities of diocesan life.

Cathedrals are diocesan churches but they are not only diocesan churches. Some are large and ancient foundations that are well established within the life of the nation. Some are unpretentious parish church cathedrals that are struggling to establish a local identity. Some possess buildings of incomparable beauty. Some have relatively modest buildings that are handsome but undistinguished. But for all cathedrals — young and old — the expectations and the possibilities are enormous. There is a rich and distinctive pattern of worship which continues to speak to the needs and aspirations of many people. There are traditions of scholarship, of artistic endeavour, of ministerial resource, and critical enquiry. There is invariably a vast network of local interests and associations in which cathedrals are required to work out their roles.

Chelmsford takes it place within this tradition of cathedral life. It is mindful of its origins, inextricably bound up with the story of the town; but it is mindful also of the unique position in which it finds itself today as the cathedral of a vast diocese. A great diocese — like a great county — requires a great cathedral as its heart.

The Prettiest Village?

Finchingfield: the making of an icon

VICTOR GRAY

THE RAMBLER did not last long. Born amid great hopes in May 1897, it was dead within two years. 'A penny weekly newspaper devoted to outdoor life', it was aimed at the burgeoning army of weekend cyclists. Among the advertisements for Osoezi cycle saddles and Griffiths' Puncture-Stop, it ran features to tempt them to new and little explored corners of the country, among them an eight-week series on 'The prettiest village in England', in which England's 'greatest and best-known men and women' were invited to write in with their opinion. On 12 February 1898, it was the turn of Sir Walter Gilbey of Elsenham Hall, near Bishop's Stortford, a President of the Royal Agricultural Society and well known in the livestock world.[1] How long he pondered over his answer we shall never know, but when it came, it was straightforward and unequivocal:

> 'In reply to your letter, if you asked me the finest city in the United Kingdom I should say Edinburgh; and if you asked me the prettiest village in the eastern counties I would say Finchingfield, but beyond this I cannot go.'

And there, given *The Rambler's* limited circulation, it might have ended. But, somehow, Gilbey's terse accolade was to take on a life of its own, echoing across the next century, colouring attitudes and leaving many a thumbprint on the raw clay of events. Its impact is there still on every summer weekend in Finchingfield.

It was probably in the pages of the *Essex County Chronicle*, which eagerly copied Gilbey's words to fill a column inch (his was in fact the only nomination of an Essex village in the whole series), that Archibald Weyland Ruggles-Brise spotted it.[2] It obviously stuck in his memory. Three years later, in a letter to the *Chronicle* defending the reputation of Finchingfield as a healthy, happy place in which to live, he used the Gilbey Accolade to endorse his own view of the current state of the village:

> 'The people that remain have never been better off or I may say in happier circumstances than they are today. Sir Walter Gilbey called our village the prettiest in Essex and I think you will allow that he is a good judge.'[3]

121

Even a quarter of a century after their first utterance, journalists were still
remembering Gilbey's words as in this picture of the 1924 Rogation Service on
the Green:

> 'A beautiful scene was presented by this gathering on the green, in all
> its verdant beauty, with the river running through and with its
> delightful surroundings. The whole was lighted up by the slanting
> rays of the setting sun and viewing it, one could well understand the
> late Sir Walter Gilbey's eulogy of Finchingfield as "the prettiest
> village in Essex".'

'No village seems to pose more charmingly for its portrait': a turn of the century postcard of Finchingfield.

By now Finchingfield's pre-eminence as the jewel of Essex villages was fixed in
the communal mind. To A. K. Wickham, writing *The villages of England* in 1932,
it was 'the model, homely village of two centuries ago'. Humphrey Pakington,
President of the Architectural Association, refers, in *English villages and hamlets*,
1936, to:

> 'a charming group of West Essex villages, of which Finchingfield is
> the undisputed queen . . . This loveliest of villages, whose houses
> build up to the grey tower of the church at the top of the hill with a
> sense of composition which the greatest artist could not better. No
> village seems to pose more charmingly for its portrait — to arrange
> its garments, so to speak — yet none looks less conscious of pose than
> does Finchingfield.'

For Clifford Bax in *Highways and Byways in Essex*, 1939, it was 'an almost perfect type of the English village'.

'An almost perfect type of the English village':
Finchingfield drawn by S. R. Badmin in Clifford Bax's Highways and Byways in Essex, *1939.*

By this time, the origin of the Accolade had been long forgotten, but, now fully matured, it needed a father no longer.

> 'A village which, by reason of its undulating ground, its green, and the happy grouping of the houses about the green, is usually acclaimed as the most picturesque in Essex.'

is how Phoebe Gage's Essex volume in the *Vision of England* series re-staked the claim in the post-War world of 1949 and W. Blythin was not, I am sure, alone in taking Gilbey's claim and inflating it geographically: 'one of the prettiest villages in Britain . . . a veritable mecca for artists and others in search of beauty', he claimed in *Essex, county of contrasts, a pictorial study,* 1968. And so the chorus runs on down to the present.

It is worth following this pedigree of praise across the years in order to demonstrate the mysterious osmosis by which one man's opinion, perhaps hastily given (who can say?), becomes transmuted into received wisdom, until in the public mind it triggers an almost automatic mental response. Finchingfield? Why, the Prettiest Village in Essex, of course!

It is tempting to argue that Gilbey was simply voicing an unarguable, objective truth; that the very setting and composition of the village, as you overlook the

Green towards the church, cannot fail but raise an aesthetic response. Listen to Humphrey Pakington re-painting the village in words and in so doing attempting to analyse the elements of the composition:

> 'It is better to approach Finchingfield from the west or south —from the direction of Saffron Walden or of Dunmow — for you may then see with what noble sweeps the roads fall into the cup of the village green, and how they are gathered into one to pass over the little brick bridge and so up the winding street of the village. And you should not only approach from the west or south, but you should go to Finchingfield in the evening light, and pause before you cross the bridge, to see the sunlit plastered fronts of the little houses on the hill reflected between the duck-weed on the pool. The pool is guarded by a white-post railing — most English of methods — and the white posts make a steady rhythm in the water among the tangled reflections of the cottages.'

But beauty is neither objective nor unchanging in the collective mind. Half a century before Pakington wrote, many if not most of the elements in his picture passed entirely unnoticed. It had taken a particular moment in history to create the sensitivity which had then been distilled and bottled in the Gilbey Accolade. You will search in vain for a word of appreciation of the Green and its setting among the giants of Essex topography. Holman, Morant or Wright, for example had no eye for this kind of detail. By 1861, D. W. Coller in *The People's History of Essex* was conceding that 'the church stands on a fine eminence' — but that is it, no more, no less, for Finchingfield as a beauty spot. The tourists for whom Edward Walford produced his *Tourist's Guide to Essex* in 1882 were allowed only a moment of cold, almost geometric topography, before being rushed away, like all their antecedents, to view the monuments in the church:

> 'Finchingfield, 3 miles south east [of Little Sampford] is built on an acclivity which slopes towards an affluent of the Blackwater . . . The church . . . stands on rising ground.'

Among a whole cluster of guide-book writers who swarmed across Essex in these last decades of the nineteenth century, only one small voice is raised, only one soul stirred to print by the sight of the Green, the Church and the Pond. Whoever it was that revised *Kelly's Directory* in preparation for the 1890 edition slipped in almost surreptitiously one small sentence between the by now stale repetition, edition on edition, of the seating capacity of the Congregational Church and the dates of the village charities: 'In the centre of the village is Finchingfield Green, a very picturesque spot'. What had happened to him there upon the Green to give rise to this momentary but — by the standards of Kelly — almost rhapsodic outburst among the cold tombstones of fact?

Perhaps he was an admirer of Ruskin whose vision of a rural revival, a quasi-idyllic resurgence, based on craftsmanship, honest labour and mutual support had been gaining ground since his *Fors Clavigera* first appeared in 1871. Perhaps he took his lead from William Morris's anti-industrialism or from Edward Carpenter's socialistic interpretation of Ruskin. For there was undoubtedly developing a new interest in the countryside and the 'older truths' which, it was now suggested, were, if you only looked and listened hard enough, still embodied in it. Novels like Thomas Hardy's were 'recreating' an older, simpler and more attractive way of life in the country and the works of people like Richard Jefferies were re-exploring rural crafts and skills. An interest had developed too in older English domestic building. The Society for the Protection of Ancient Buildings had been formed in 1877 and the new interest in the qualities of smaller rural buildings blended with the folksy nostalgia of Hardy in the cottage paintings of Helen Allingham, with granny at the gate and roses round the door, which were first exhibited in 1886 and found a wider and wider audience over the next quarter of a century. Other rural interests were finding an institutional footing: the National Footpaths Preservation Society was formed in 1884, the National Trust in 1894, and the first published fruits of the revival of interest in folk song were fresh on the bookshelves alongside Kelly's 1890 *Directory of Essex*.[4] The whisper of the word 'picturesque' which barely stirs the staid air of Kelly's pages was about to turn into a gusting breeze of ruralism.

> 'A series of sharp turns and we find ourselves again among houses, clustered irregularly round a wide green hollow, and enter an inn-yard surrounded by stables and outbuildings. Close above us appears the church, and the moon near it, now clear of the mist, shining brightly over the whole scene.':

thus Reginald Beckett of Finchingfield in the tellingly named *Romantic Essex* in 1901. And in 1905 in R. H. Ernest Hill's *Picturesque Essex* with sketches by Duncan Moul, the purpose of which was 'to call attention to the less known and more obscure beauties of Essex' we hear how:

> 'the church overlooks the quaint old houses all round it [note the adjectives, which in less than twenty years have come to express charm rather than condescension], the latter standing at irregular angles with each other and the street, and making a delightful subject for a sketch.'

And sketch they did, for Finchingfield had now been discovered by the artistic community. In 1904, the 25-year-old Alfred Munnings was invited by a fellow artist to join a Summer School of Animal Painting which was being run in a remote Essex village by Frank Calderon, Founder and Principal of the School of Animal Painting in Kensington. Though he had never heard of Finchingfield, Munnings, already exhibiting at the Royal Academy and earning his keep with portraits of horses at £10 a time, went along. He found:

> 'An Arcadian scene, . . . all around at easels, standing or sitting, was a bevy of damsels and one or two men who didn't count. Many of these

A study of cottages in Finchingfield by Alfred Munnings, 1905.

fair creatures belonged to what is known as The County. In studious gracious attitudes, they looked most wonderful to me.'

Munnings' eye was not just for the girls; he left behind at least one Finchingfield study, of cottages, completed on his second visit in 1905.[5]

The Gilbey Accolade had found just the right moment. Ten years before, the question 'Which is the prettiest village in England?' would not have been asked, for those economically depressed groupings of decaying cottages which littered the country would not have been deemed worthy of the epithet. Ten years later, and Gilbey's opinion would not have mattered, for the world and his wife had discovered the picturesque, had probably read about it and might even have painted it. The secret of the Accolade's survival was that it provided a ready-made testimonial from a respected source just at the moment when the world began to thirst for the pretty and the picturesque.

It is as well to pause at this point and take stock of the reality of the Finchingfield which Gilbey saw, but did not perhaps know. It was, in 1899, a village of some 1,400 souls with a parish and a Congregational church, two schools, a Post Office, a windmill, four inns and two beer retailers, three grocers, four bakers, a butcher, a plumber, a shoemaker, two drapers and a clothier, two dressmakers and a hairdresser, a watchmaker, an ironmonger, a harnessmaker and a blacksmith. Its 8,417 acres were farmed by some 20 farmers of whom four were regarded as significant landowners.[6] It was self-sufficient to a degree impossible now to imagine and part of the reason for that self-containedness was that Finchingfield 'doubtless owes some of its rural charm to the long miles that at present separate it from the nearest market town or train' as Eliza Vaughan, daughter of a sometime vicar of the parish and a lifelong enthusiast for the village, put it in 1903.[7] But isolation meant no kind of refuge from the depression in agriculture which had hung over the fields for three decades, depressing land values and causing what seemed to be an unstaunchable haemorrhage of young people seeping away inexorably into the more prosperous towns. A. R. Hope Moncrieff, while extolling the aesthetics of the village in *Essex* in 1909 had to point out that 'in the last generation Finchingfield has lost nearly a third of its inhabitants'. John Vaughan, Eliza's father, had bemoaned it poetically in 1893:

> 'The old families are gone. New names fill the parish registers
> . . . Boards are nailed over the windows of the empty cottages on the
> green. Poverty is stamped on the face of the village. Change and
> decay is everywhere apparent. Only the church bells ring out merrily
> from the Norman tower, and the stream flows silently on.'[8]

Even the squire, Sir Samuel Ruggles-Brise, speaking on the joyful occasion of a village celebration of his golden wedding in 1897, could not help turning an old man's wistful eye on the village in which he had lived for half a century. When he had come, there had been no school, or if any a very small one. They had built their schools and restored the Church . . . The population had been double its present level. There had been a very successful straw-plaiting industry. In those days, they could not get the population to go away from Finchingfield. Then the straw-plaiting came to an end. Nowadays, people were better off because of education. But now the children left as soon as possible to chance perils in service.[9]

He was not exaggerating about the population. In 1801 it had stood at 1,606 and by 1851 had risen to 2,594. But thereafter it slid, decade on decade, until in 1901 there were just 1,333 people left. Nothing seemed to be able to halt the slide. And the decline was to continue. By 1961 the figure was down to 1,130.

There was little to keep anyone. Housing, picturesque perhaps to Munnings' 'bevy of damsels' at the easel, was, in some measure at least, quaint precisely because of its decaying and overcrowded condition. The most basic of basics, the water supply, was deficient. In 1891 the local Medical Officer of Health had taken a number of samples from the Howe Street Well, north of the village centre. All were polluted. In May 1901, four children fell ill at a farmhouse on the edge of the parish. Two of them died, their death attributed to enteric fever, caused by drinking the water of a stagnant pond at the back of their farmhouse.[10]

It was the press report of this incident which led Archibald Weyland Ruggles-Brise to leap to the defence of the village in the pages of the *Essex County Chronicle*, pulling out of his hat the Gilbey Accolade as incontestable proof of his arguments.

> 'In our village proper there is a very good supply of water from four pumps, besides private ones and we can thankfully say we have had no outbreaks of illness from impure water for many years and that the health of our village is excellent and will compare favourably with any other. The decrease in population is largely in the outlying districts. The people that remain have never been better off or I may say in happier circumstances than they are today. Sir Walter Gilbey called our village "the prettiest in Essex" and I think you will allow that he is a good judge.'

This was the first of many occasions when the Gilbey Accolade was to be carried into battle, a standard around which the defenders could rally. And usually the scene of hostilities was the Village Green.

As many pointed out, the Green was — and is still — the meeting point of four roads, but none of them had ever carried any volume of traffic. Nine miles from Braintree and nine from Dunmow, it was beyond the easy reach of the weekend cottagers and rural explorers who, armed with books like W. R. Evans' *Rustic walking routes in the London vicinity*, 1887, were beginning to spread like invasive shoots from the stems of the railway network. To get to Finchingfield you had really to want to. Once a day the carrier's cart from Braintree could take you there, and some days there was a cart from Saffron Walden. But few had either need or wish.

But by 1916 the tell-tale harbingers of the motor invasion were beginning to show. In that year the Parish Council instructed the Clerk to write to the County Surveyor suggesting the cutting off of corners at Little London to reduce the danger now being caused by speeding vehicles.[11] Seven years later, it was no longer the isolated car which was giving cause for concern; the County Surveyor was asked to put up signs warning traffic of the dangerous approaches to the bridge on the green 'now that there is such an enormous increase in motor traffic in lorries and omnibuses'. It was the start of a decade of notice-boards. Four years later it was a School notice to be affixed to the signpost near the Congregational School. In 1930 a notice board was put up on the corner of the green demanding 'No thoroughfare for lorries', to prevent them using the path by Mrs Stock's house, and another went up near Brick House saying 'Footpath only'. The County Council was asked for another danger notice near the Green Man.

Strangely, it was not these intrusions that appear at the time to have offended the eye. Instead, a stern, reproachful gaze was fixed on the ground. It was the gaze of the redoubtable Eliza Vaughan, daughter of the former vicar, writer on the village's history and defender *par excellence* of the Legacy of the Prettiest Village. In June 1928, she wrote to the local press drawing the attention of 'all lovers of rural Essex' to the way in which 'our most picturesque spots are being spoilt by modern methods of road repairing. The introduction of the unsightly curb and the straightening out of our main roads in order to gratify the craving for speed have already left their mark on our countryside.' The occasion of her outburst was the laying of a 'deep curb' along the road across the green and on the other side of the bridge — 'an act of vandalism that nothing can excuse and one hopes that the pressure of public opinion may be brought to bear on the County Council'. 'Such places', she went on, her tone swelling with emotion 'are the heritage of Essex as a whole and indeed appeal to all who love, in these times of rush and din, the atmosphere of beauty and of charm. Let us see to it that such "haunts of ancient peace" are handed down unspoilt, as a priceless heritage, to the generations that are yet to come.' (To many who have come to regard the Heritage as a modern talisman, this earlier use of the word will come as a surprise.)

But the prosaic forces of bureaucracy, in the shape of Major Morgan, D.S.O., County Surveyor, stood their ground. The kerbing, he insisted, had been done at the request of the Parish Council to strengthen the road because of the extra traffic it was now carrying. Only 50 feet of kerbing at the corner of the Green was involved. Anything more comprehensive would, Major Morgan concurred, be wrong.

> 'It will be a long day, I think, before we should dream of doing such a thing. I am perfectly satisfied that the beauty of the village green has not been affected by the work.'

In the event the 'long day' turned out to be about 25 years; in the early 1950s the Parish Council urged the County to complete the kerbing of the roads across the green, since the verges were being eroded by heavy traffic and thoughtless parking. For the moment, however, Eliza, although ostensibly defeated on the specific, won, like many another campaigner, the compensatory victory of inducing in the opposition an abiding memory of the advantages of a quiet life. When in 1929 the Parish Council wanted the road near the pond to be made up, they were at pains to ask that it should be done without kerbing.

'The church overlooks the quaint old houses all around it':
a drawing by Duncan Moul for R. M. Ernest Hill's Picturesque Essex, *1905.*

But it was on another front, where the forces of cold reality met the defenders of the Prettiest Village, that the Gilbey Accolade was paraded most forcefully. Poor housing had long been identified as one of the problems which Finchingfield and villages like it had to address if they were to staunch the flow of depopulation. The first Council houses had made their appearance in the village in 1926, well tucked away on the Bardfield Road out of sight of the Green but evoking, nevertheless, a hostile reaction among the aesthetes for their 'bold scarlet faces and smart blue roofs of slate, fashionably trimmed with vermilion edging, this dual effect being enhanced in front by plastrons of rough-cast and on the hinder parts by the substitution of a more modest pink and brawn-like brick for the flamboyant splendours glaring at the road'.[12]

The addition of new housing on the periphery was one thing, but an assault upon the essence of Finchingfield's picturesqueness, its cottages, was another. Ironically it was an artist, Henry Reynolds, living in Wethersfield Road, who in 1928 first dared hint in the press at a shadow on the face of the village. Even here, in attacking the complacency which 'the prettiest village' epithet could bring, some nimble footwork brought him quickly behind the shield of the Gilbey Accolade.

> 'The village certainly maintains its claim to being the prettiest in the county, but in some of its cottages the elimination of dampness, a drawback to comfort in many pretty little dwellings, would stop the dry-rot that is eating the timbers and fast aiding in the destruction of the very structures that make the village so picturesque.'[13]

Though the Parish Council leapt to the defence of the village — 'a very clean bill of health, never any epidemics, the children are healthy and the majority of the inhabitants live to a good old age' — the problem was to rear its head again. In 1929 the Sanitary Inspector of Braintree Rural District Council produced a damning report on housing conditions in the village, so bad that the Council decided thereafter to receive his reports in private. In 1934, 21 houses were condemned, unless the owners carried out improvements. But it was in 1936 that the storm broke. In May of that year, the press reported that more than half the cottages in the village had been condemned by the R.D.C. on the advice of the Medical Officer of Health. Seventy-seven had been scheduled for clearance and 40 tenants were to be given 10 weeks notice to vacate once the order became operative. Nine tenants at Little London joined forces with an indignant parish council to demand a public inquiry under the terms of the Housing Acts.[14]

When, to a packed audience in the R.D.C. offices in July, Mr A. D. Hills, the Clerk to the Council, rose to open his case, his very first abaisance was to the Shade of Walter Gilbey:

> 'Finchingfield was famous as one of the most charming villages in England, and the people keenly felt what they supposed to be an attack upon it. He would assure them that the Council was not out to slaughter their delightful "Sweet Auburn". The Council was well aware of its duty to preserve the beautiful old cottages of England and no-one regretted more than the Council that "Sweet Auburn" had allowed some of her old cottages to wither and decay. But rambler roses around the door did not atone for the absence of a sink in a cottage, and trailing honeysuckle was not a substitute for a definite food store.'[15]

Had it not been for Finchingfield's scenic reputation, Mr A. D. Hills would almost certainly not have found himself facing the kind of forces now ranked against him. To begin with there was J. G. Covernton, C.I.E., M.A., Chairman of the Parish Council and scourge of the modernisers. 'Did they really wish to extirpate the beauty of one of England's fairest villages, and was root-and-branch destruction inevitable? . . . Were they fanatics enough to brave the odium that even yet dogs the steps of those who dispossess the widow, evict the old and helpless and grind the faces of the unresisting poor', he asked.[16] Then there were the expert witnesses for the defence. A local doctor of 30 years standing assured the hearing that he had seen much worse in his time. Three architects attested the quality of the vernacular architecture now under threat. The Council for the Protection of Rural England and the Society for the Protection of Ancient Buildings were present to attest to the homelike qualities, the character, the individuality, and the distinctive scenic value of the threatened cottages, contrasting them with the council houses which 'have no character, are not homelike and are an eyesore'. *The Times* reported the dispute, drawn to it by the fact that 'Finchingfield, Essex, has been described as one of the three finest villages in England'.[17]

'The white posts make a steady rhythm in the water among the tangled reflections of the cottages': the pond in Gilbey's day.

By chance, at this time, Marion Grierson and Evelyn Spice, prominent figures in the film documentary movement, were planning a film on change in village life. It was to Finchingfield, typical in its problems and with proven photogenic qualities, that they came. They walked into the middle of the great housing dispute, which so aptly suited their theme, the bitter-sweet mix of change and continuity. And so it was that two elderly Finchingfield characters found themselves and the village housing question cast large upon the nation's silver screens, their rather stagey dialogue outside the Fox framed within Benjamin Britten's folk-tune score.

> 'As soon as they pull 'em down, they'll never build n'more up same as the old cottages and therefore if we got in 'em we should never pay the rent. The house that I live in is 400 years old and I pays the squire three shillings a week and it suits me all right. I got a radio and a gramophone and I haven't got a bath, but I've got a river down the bottom of the garden, so I can have a good bath there when I want one.'[18]

By the time the film toured the cinemas in 1937 under the title *Around the Village Green*, the dispute itself had ground to a compromise. The number of condemned cottages had been drastically reduced to 26 amid showers of promises by landlords to improve their properties and commitments by the Council to increase the rate of Council House building.

The Gilbey Accolade was to play a part — and still plays a part — directly or indirectly, in many more battles to balance modernization — essential to the survival of the village — with the retention of its special quality and reputation. The tracing of all those steps would require a larger canvas than is available within this article. So too would a comparison between the fate of Finchingfield and that of other nearby villages which escaped the blessing and the burden of an Accolade and whose development took place away from the public spotlight. During the 1930s, when the rush to modernize was undertaken with less vigorous controls than later years were to bring, Finchingfield, because of its own belief in and insistence on a special quality, was sometimes able to fend off mistakes which compromised the landscape of other villages. In 1935, the East Anglian Electric Supply Co. was able to reach an agreement with the Parish and County Councils which allowed public and private money to subsidize the additional cost of providing electricity to the centre of the village by means of underground cables rather than overhead wires, a luxury afforded to few others.[19] The Village Hall, the Windmill, litter bins and parking places were all fought over with a degree of passion which arose from the sense of responsibility for preserving a singular reputation. And with each preservative step successfully taken, the gap widened between the 'unaffected old-world beauty' of Finchingfield and the increasingly changing face of other villages, a gap which served only to heighten the readiness with which still more protection was demanded and afforded, a cumulative phenomenon which planners might do well to study.

There is of course another side. Already, by 1969, Marcus Crouch, in the Essex volume of the Batsford County books, acknowledged Finchingfield as 'the only place in Essex which has been adopted by the tourists' and bemoaned the fact that it was now impossible to photograph the view across the Green to the church because of 'the cars which clog its streets and litter the banks of the pond'. Thirty years on, the impact of tourism remains a mixed blessing. Were the shade of Sir Walter to return one summer weekend to the Green, he might well be surprised to see how pride and care have retained the white-painted railings around the pond exactly as they were nearly a century ago. And in the pond the reflection would show him the same line of cottage roofs with the church tower behind as he saw the last time he visited. But if the gaudy fringe of cars which hugs each kerb and the snaking line of visitors which climbs the hill from the gift shop to the church are not quite what he might have expected, would he even remember, I wonder, that one day, almost exactly a century ago, among the hectic affairs of a businessman, agriculturalist and writer, he had paused momentarily to pen a single brisk sentence to the editor of *The Rambler* and, in so doing, had ensured that, for better or for worse — indeed, for better and for worse — Finchingfield would never be the same again.

Acknowledgements

All illustrations in this essay have been reproduced by courtesy of the Essex Record Office.

REFERENCES

1 Walter Gilbey, born 1831, died 1914. Son of a Bishop's Stortford coach proprietor. Set up as a wine merchant off Oxford Stret. Developed a keen interest in livestock and in particular horses. Reared Jerseys at Hargrave Park and bred at Elsenham Hall, where he built up a Shire Horse Stud. Built model cottages at Elsenham and laid down 100 acres of lavender, fruit and peppermint for jams and preserves. Instrumental in founding the Shire Horse Society, member of the Royal Agricultural Society from 1870, President 1895. Founded a Cambridge lectureship in the history and economics of agriculture. Barony 1893. Collector of Stubbs, Morland and other painters. Published on wines, livestock and horses.

2 Archibald Weyland Ruggles-Brise of Spains Hall, Finchingfield. Born 1853. Died 1939. Eldest son of Sir Samuel Ruggles-Brise. Called to the Bar 1877, J.P. 1875, Deputy Lieutenant 1886, Member of Essex County Council, 1903–30. President of the Saffron Walden Conservative Association for 27 years. Managing Director, Essex Agricultural Society for 15 years. Master of East Essex Foxhounds for four years. Founder of the Essex Game Guild.

3 *Essex County Chronicle*, 10 May 1901. This and all other texts from the local press quoted in this article can be found in the invaluable Cuttle Collection of newscuttings in the Essex Record Office, Chelmsford (E.R.O., T/P181/5/16).

4 For an excellent summary of the growth of ruralism, see Jan Marsh, *Back to the land: the pastoral impulse in Victorian England from 1880 to 1914*, 1982.

5 Munnings' visits to Finchingfield are referred to in Reginald Pound, *The Englishman: a biography of Sir Alfred Munnings*, 1962, p.37 *et seq.* and in *Alfred Munnings, 1878–1959*, the catalogue of an exhibition at the Athenaeum Gallery, Manchester, 1986–7, p.96.

6 *Kelly's Directory of Essex*, 1899.

7 Eliza Vaughan, 'William the Silent', in *Essex Review* XII, 1903.

8 John Vaughan, 'Twenty-five years of village life' in *Longman's Magazine*, 7 Jan. 1893. (I am grateful to Kenneth Neale for drawing this to my attention.)

9 *Essex County Chronicle*, 4 May 1897. Colonel Sir Samuel Ruggles-Brise. Born 1825. Died 1899. Lived at Spains Hall from 1853. President of Essex Agricultural Society 1856. Chairman of Central Chamber of Agriculture. M.P. for Eastern Division of Essex 1868–83. C.B. 1881. K.C.B. 1897. Chairman of Bardfield Bench. Member of Braintree Board of Guardians. Alderman on Essex County Council 1890–93.

10 Report of the Medical Officer of Health for Braintree Rural District, 1894; *Essex County Chronicle*, 3 May 1901.

11 References to developments in Finchingfield between the Wars are taken from the minutes of the Finchingfield Parish Council and the records of the Braintree Rural District Council, now in the Essex Record Office. (My thanks are due to the staff of E.R.O. for their help in making available to me these as yet uncatalogued records.)

12 J. G. Covernton, 'The Gods, some Goths and a village of the plain: the harrowing of Finchingfield' in *Essex Review*, XLVI, 1937.

13 *Essex County Chronicle*, 31 August 1928.

14 *Essex County Chronicle*, 22 and 29 May 1936.

15 *Essex County Chronicle*, 3 July 1936.

16 J. G. Covernton, *op. cit.*

17 *The Times*, 28 November 1936.

18 A copy of this film is preserved at the East Anglian Film Archive, University of East Anglia. (I am indebted to Jane Alvey of the Archive for her invaluable help in allowing me to see it.)

19 Parish Council minutes and letter from A. J. A. Symons to *The Times*, 13 May 1936.

A Royal Imposter in Elizabethan Essex

JANET COOPER

ELIZABETHAN ESSEX was often alive with rumours and prophecies, some of them seditious, but few of them were taken very seriously by the authorities, and those who spread them usually escaped with a spell in the pillory. In the late 1570s, however, one incident did alarm not only the Essex justices, but also the Privy Council: the claim made by Robert Blosse or Mantell that he was Edward VI.

Rumours that Edward was alive had circulated since the reign of Mary, and the boy king has been described as the most curious sleeping hero of the Tudor and Stuart period.[1] Edward, a passionate Protestant, died on 6 July 1553 at the age of 15 from an obscure illness and after a prolonged spell of ill health. The secrecy which surrounded his death, as the duke of Northumberland attempted to set aside Edward's sister, the Catholic Mary, and place his cousin Lady Jane Grey on the throne, fuelled rumours that the king had been poisoned. Northumberland's plans failed, and within a few days Mary had been proclaimed queen, but it was not until a month after his death that Edward's state funeral finally took place. Mary's policies, especially her marriage in October 1553 to Philip of Spain, aroused considerable opposition, and the first rumours of Edward's survival surfaced in London in November 1553.[2] They continued in 1554, as the government moved to re-establish Catholicism and started burning Protestants as heretics. By July 1555 the rumours had spread to Essex where two men were arrested for saying that King Edward was still alive.[3] A few days earlier Edward Fetherston, otherwise William Constable, a Londoner, was imprisoned in the Marshalsea for claiming that he was Edward VI. One of his supporters was committed to the Tower in January 1556 for having distributed seditious letters on his behalf, and another was removed from his minor government office and briefly imprisoned.[4]

That Protestants suffering persecution in Catholic Mary's reign should have dreamed of Edward's survival is not surprising. It is more remarkable that the rumour spread again after the restoration of Protestantism under Elizabeth. The Elizabethan settlement of religion was threatened, however, by the growth of extreme Protestantism, as well as by the survival of Catholicism; it was also endangered by uncertainties over the succession to the throne. By the late 1570s the chances of Elizabeth's marrying and producing children were remote, and the next heir, as some of those involved in the Essex rumours pointed out, was the Catholic Mary, Queen of Scots. The prospect of further upheavals in church and state if she succeeded to the throne, undoubtedly worried many people. A man from Wakes Colne who made his will in 1578 expressed doubts probably shared by many others. When he asked his wife to pay 'some godly preacher to preach the gospel of Jesus Christ truly' during her lifetime, he felt it necessary to add, 'if it please God to suffer the same in England so long'.[5] It was in that climate that the rumour of Edward's survival circulated in Elizabethan Essex, and in the dissemination of the rumour Robert Mantell played an important part.

Almost all that is known about Mantell before 1576 derives from his own interrogation and those of his followers, all made in 1579 or 1580. According to his own account Mantell was born Robert Blosse, the son of a London goldsmith, probably about 1520.[6] It is not clear when or why he changed his name to Mantell, but it is tempting to suggest that he had some connection, real or imagined, with the Mantell family of Heyford, Northamptonshire, and Horton Priory, Kent. They were a gentry family two of whose members, Sir Walter Mantell and his nephew Walter Mantell, were executed for their part in the Kentishman Thomas Wyatt's Protestant and anti-Spanish rebellion against Mary in 1554.[7] Robert Mantell had lived, or claimed to have lived, in both Kent (at Sandwich) and Northamptonshire (at Maxey).

Robert Mantell told his interrogators that he was educated at the White or Carmelite Friars in Ipswich under the 'learned man' John Bale, prior *c*.1533.[8] The association with Bale, who was at Ipswich for only about a year, having earlier spent two or three years at the Maldon friary, was undoubtedly significant for the development of Mantell's own religious views. During his time at Maldon and Ipswich, Bale was converted from conventional Catholicism to a 'hot-headed' Protestantism. Under Edward VI he became bishop of Ossory, and until his death in 1563 engaged in polemical anti-Catholic writing.[9] A follower of his might well have dreaded a restoration of Catholicism; he might even have found the Elizabethan settlement too moderate for his taste and longed for a restoration of the more extreme Protestantism of Edward VI's later years. Mantell's education suggests that he was designed for the church, and indeed he later claimed to have been ordained priest by Edmund Scambler, who was bishop of Peterborough 1561–85.[10] Nevertheless, he started his career at sea, becoming a gunner in the King's ships and learning to 'shoot off and discharge great ordnance'. It was presumably his seafaring which brought him to Sandwich where he married the town clerk's daughter, a marriage which did not work out. 'His wife and he not well agreeing' as Mantell's examination puts it, they parted and she removed to Cambridge. It was presumably also during his seafaring career that Mantell made the contacts in Maldon and Colchester which he used as an imposter. About 1555 Mantell heard the story of Edward VI's survival from a man called Walker 'a scholar of Oxford' who said the king was alive and living in Flanders, and was planning to return to his kingdom.[11] If Walker really was a member of Oxford University he was probably the Peter Walker who was rector of St. Leonard's, Colchester, from 1557 until *c.*1559, and who was one of only two Walkers who matriculated at Oxford in the 1540s or early 1550s.[12] That Peter Walker was sentenced to a spell in Colchester pillory in 1559 for 'lewd and untrue reports' of the queen. He disappears from Colchester thereafter, and nothing is known of him after he was deprived of the rectory of Tendring in 1562.[13] His opposition to Elizabeth, however, is more likely to have been inspired by Catholic than by Protestant views, and Mantell's Peter Walker, if he existed, was perhaps a wandering scholar whose connections with Oxford were tenuous. Whoever he was, Walker was presumably associated with the man called Fetherston or Constable who was then claiming to be Edward VI. Despite the failure of Constable's imposture, Mantell 'nourished in his mind that lewd and false matter [that Edward VI was alive] and reported it for a truth', but not sufficiently publicly to get himself into trouble until 1572. He may already have had a reputation as a malcontent and rumour-monger, for about 1566 he was told another seditious tale, this time by 'an old priest in Hampshire': that Elizabeth I had been secretly married *c.*1564 to her favourite, Robert Dudley, earl of Leicester, and had borne him four children. Variations of the story, which may have been partly wishful thinking in the desire for a Protestant heir to the throne, seem to have been widely known in Essex; one was perhaps among the 'slanderous reports of the queen' which a Colchester shearman was accused of spreading in 1563.[14] Mantell retailed the story of the queen's secret marriage as well as that of the survival of Edward VI. He was caught in October 1572 in a house near Aldersgate, London, in true cloak and dagger fashion when 'Norris the pursevant, standing behind a cloth, did hear him and thereupon did arrest him'. There was apparently some suspicion of unorthodox religious views, for Mantell was asked about his religion and replied that he had not heard Mass since the early Protestant, Anne Askew, was burnt in 1546. The otherwise strange answer may be further evidence of the influence of John Bale on Mantell's thinking, for Bale had supported Anne, and had published in 1546 and 1547 two accounts of her examination and trial.[15] Remarkably, Mantell seems to have got off with a short imprisonment. As, unlike Constable in 1555, he had not actually claimed to be Edward VI, his offence was deemed not to be treason; for spreading the rumour that the queen was married to the earl of Leicester he should have lost an ear, but because he had not been convicted within three months of the offence the penalty could not be exacted, and he was released.[16]

Mantell was in trouble again in August 1576 when he was bailed to appear at Essex Quarter Sessions. The names of his sureties confirm his connections with both Essex and London, and also demonstrate that his appeal was mainly to small traders and artisans: they were Thomas Luskin or Lufkin of Dedham, a surgeon, Stephen Kilden of Southwark, a tailor, and Elias Nichols of Maldon, a shoemaker.[17] Mantell cannot at this stage have posed a great threat to the stability of Elizabethan Essex. He may have failed to surrender to his bail, for in July and October 1577 the court was pursuing all three of his sureties to pay the

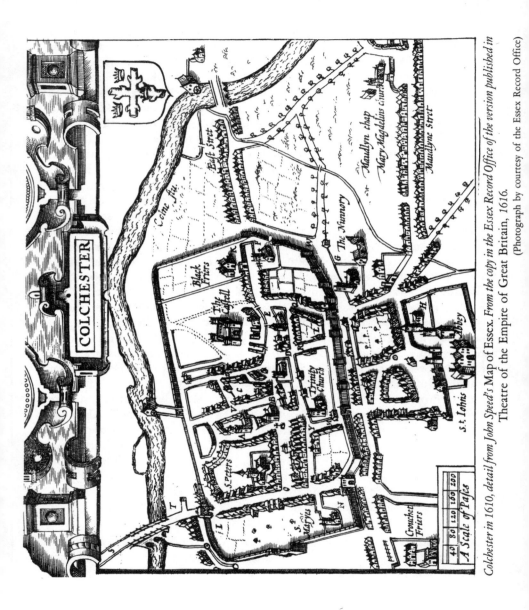

Colchester in 1610, detail from John Speed's Map of Essex. From the copy in the Essex Record Office of the version published in
Theatre of the Empire of Great Britain, 1616.
(Photograph by courtesy of the Essex Record Office)

sums of money in which they were bound.[18] Nevertheless Luskin and Kilden were to remain staunch supporters of Mantell up to the time of his execution.

In 1577, probably in the autumn, Mantell was again arrested, for 'seditious words', spoken in Maldon and other places. He had said not only that Edward VI was alive, but also that he himself was King Edward, adding mysteriously that 'if he could find one that was trusty he could disclose that which should rejoice them all. Howbeit that he could never yet find such an one.'[19] Nevertheless, Mantell did discuss his plans with some people, including Thomas Collins, a Maldon man who later gave evidence against him.[20] His plan for his coup, if it can be called that, was naive in the extreme. He planned to send 500 men, in small groups and wearing 'privy' clothes, to Elizabeth's court. When they were all assembled he would join them there. He then planned to accost the queen while she was out walking, saying to her 'Sister know you not me, I am your brother, do not amaze yourself'. His 500 followers would then draw their weapons and proclaim him king. After the proclamation a knight would be sent (Collins did not say where); he thought his name was Mildmers. The knight intended was presumably Sir Thomas Mildmay of Moulsham, who, far from being involved in any conspiracy, was one of the justices of the peace who later committed Mantell to gaol.[21] There is no evidence that the 500 followers were any more real than Mildmay's involvement.

For this plot, Mantell seems to have been committed to the county gaol in Colchester castle in 1577. Then or later he won over the gaoler, Richard King, who apparently gave him considerable liberty, allowing him the use of an upper chamber in his own house where he was able to receive visitors more or less freely. He was bailed, and had perhaps broken that bail, by January 1578, when Kilden and his wife Jane seem to have been briefly imprisoned for him.[22] By May, however, Mantell was in the Tower of London, 'for abusing Her Majesty's subjects under the name of Edward VI'. He was ordered to be moved to the Marshalsea until he could be brought before the Assizes in Essex.[23] He was duly tried at Brentwood Assizes on 14 July 1578 and found guilty of using seditious words,[24] and was once again committed to Colchester castle.

Five of Mantell's chief supporters worked for him during his imprisonment: Stephen Kilden, the Southwark tailor who had gone bail for him in 1576, with his wife Jane, and their associates William Randall of Ipswich and his wife Catherine, and Elizabeth, wife of Raphael Vessie of London. All of them seem to have been involved in a murky underworld of prophecy, sorcery and witchcraft, which spread beyond Essex and even London.[25] Elizabeth Vessie, in many ways the leader of the group, had heard the rumour of Edward VI's survival *c.*1571, about the time that Mantell first spread it. Her informant, however, was not Mantell but Jane Standlie from Lancashire, who was apparently some sort of 'wise woman'. Jane told Elizabeth 'she should have a marvel of good fortune and should be in great favour and do much for the king of this land, and to be in great trouble for him with the queen and the whole council' nevertheless she 'should

The order to apprehend 'widow Skymell', 12 July, 1579, signed by Thomas Lucas.
(Photograph by courtesy of Essex Record Office. E.R.O. Colch., D/Y 2/8, p.207)

stand to it, as she would answer before God at the day of Judgement, for it was she that was ordained to bring him into his state again'. Jane did not name the king, and nothing more happened until Elizabeth Vessie encountered Mantell and realized, presumably from what he was saying, that he was the man to whom Jane Standlie had spoken. She went up to him and told him everything Jane had told her, and he replied that it was all true.

This was presumably in 1577, as shortly afterwards Mantell was arrested and imprisoned in the Tower, where Elizabeth, with Jane Kilden, visited him. After Mantell's conviction in July 1578 Elizabeth, with the help of her brother William Lewkner and of Stephen and Jane Kilden, tried to obtain his release. Their acquisition of Justice John Southcote's wife's ring may have been part of an attempt to use witchcraft to secure a stay of execution, but their approaches to Henry Macwilliams, the keeper of Colchester castle, and to Sir Thomas Mildmay of Moulsham were more orthodox, as was a later appeal to John Southcote through his wife. Bribery was also used, one Holcroft being paid £20. A petition to the queen was referred to the Master of the Court of Requests, but not enough money could be found to procure Mantell's pardon from him, or so Elizabeth Vessie claimed. Mantell's supporters even tried to appeal to Queen Elizabeth, employing a Mrs Swallowes of Maldon to kneel daily before the queen — until the queen told her to be gone.

At that point, presumably about the spring or early summer of 1579, the mysterious Jane Standlie re-appeared. She was seen in St. Paul's (the main London meeting-place) by Elizabeth Vessie's cousin. By this time Jane would communicate only through 'an old priest' who accompanied her, and then only reluctantly and in riddles. Nevertheless she encouraged Elizabeth in her support of Mantell, and may have suggested helping him to escape. Certainly it was after receiving a 'bill' from her that Elizabeth rode down to Colchester to see Mantell, and to help him to escape.[26]

There is some confusion about the date of Mantell's escape. At the trial of his gaoler in August 1579, and at his own subsequent trial in March 1581, Mantell was said to have been committed to Colchester gaol by the justices at Brentwood on 14 July 1578, and to have escaped that same 14 July.[27] However, according to other assize records he was remanded on 5 April 1579, and he was not listed as 'escaped' in the calendar of prisoners in Colchester gaol until August 1579.[28] The Colchester sources support a date in early July 1579 for the escape. The arrest of his keeper, Widow Simnell, was ordered on 12 July 1579, and on 26 July the town bailiffs protested to Lord Darcy that Stephen Holt, a member of the Colchester town council who had supported Mantell, had been imprisoned in the castle for his part in the escape.[29]

In late 1579 or early 1580, several of Mantell's associates were arrested. Richard King, the gaoler, bore the brunt of the blame. His arrest was ordered on 24 July; he appeared before the justices on 6 August, and was imprisoned in the Marshalsea prison in London, where he remained in January 1580. He was charged with treason, but seems to have been allowed to plead guilty to the lesser crime of escape through negligence.[30] Elizabeth Vessie, too, was imprisoned in London, having been examined on 3 August. She was finally released on bond from the Poultry in London in June 1581.[31] The town bailiffs were ordered to apprehend the Widow Simnell and hand her over to one of the justices of the peace, 'for earnest and weighty causes touching the Queen's majesty's person and safety' on 12 July 1579,[32] but there is no record of her imprisonment, which was presumably brief. Stephen Holt, too was presumably soon released and seems to have kept his place on the common council of the town, to which he was re-elected in September 1580.[33]

Others of Mantell's supporters were charged with 'lewd practices of sorceries and conjurations' not immediately connected with his imposture.[34] Catherine Randall was in Colchester castle gaol on 6 August 1579, and William was in prison as well by 6 October when the Privy Council instructed the bailiffs of Ipswich to allow their children reasonable maintenance from their confiscated goods.[35] Catherine died of a fever in the castle gaol in March 1580, but her husband and his 13-year old servant remained in gaol for most of that year. William was sentenced to death at the end of November, having been found guilty of invoking evil spirits to find hidden treasure.[36] Thomas Luskin or Lufkin and William Warner, a Dedham clothier, both in Colchester gaol on 6 August 1579, had been arrested for 'detestable practices of conjuration' carried out with a Southminster man and a tapster from the New Inn at Chelmsford, but both had also been associated with Mantell.[37] Warner died of an ague in Colchester castle in February 1580; Lufkin was remanded the following March, tried with William Randall at the end of November, and acquitted.[38]

Mantell himself, still maintaining that he was Edward VI, remained free for almost 18 months. He was finally recaptured at or near Lincoln, where he was examined on 3 December 1580. He then claimed to have been ordained priest by Bishop Scambler of Peterborough, and to have served as one at Maxey, Northamptonshire. This may have been an attempt to save his skin by having himself turned over to the church courts, but if so, it failed. He also produced another *alias* Johnson. His examiners, Sir Christopher Wray, chief justice, and Sir Thomas Sainctpoll, concluded, 'he useth many vain and idle speeches as though he were a lunatic person'.[39] Nevertheless the government still considered him dangerous, and by the end of the year he was in Newgate. He was brought to the assizes at Brentwood in March 1581; he confessed and was sentenced to be hanged, drawn, and quartered. The sentence was carried out.[40]

As it was alleged that while he was imprisoned in Colchester castle Mantell was allowed by the gaoler to come and go as he wished, he may have been at least indirectly responsible for some of the rumours and outbreaks of 'conjurations' in Essex in 1579 and 1580. The Maldon labourer, Thomas Playfair, who in March 1580 was imprisoned for saying that the queen had had two children by the earl of Leicester and that he had seen them when they were shipped from Rye in two of the queen's best ships, was almost certainly inspired by Mantell who had been spreading similar stories since *c*.1566. Playfair's interest in the story may have been inspired by fears about the succession to the crown, as at the same time he was sentenced to the pillory for a muddled speech apparently supporting the claims of Mary, Queen of Scots.[41] Gregory Clover of Colchester's allegations, made in March 1579 in Dedham, were less clearly linked to Mantell's, but were made in a place where Mantell had had followers. He said 'that my lord of Warwick and my lord of Leicester are traitors and come of a traitor's blood, and if they had right they had lost their heads so well as others for making away of King Edward'. This was presumably a confused reference to the earls' support of their father the duke of Northumberland in engineering the succession of Lady Jane Grey in 1553, and to suspicions, first voiced in 1553, about the manner of Edward VI's death. Clover was found guilty of trying to deprive the earls of their good names and to stir up trouble between them and the earl of Oxford; he was sentenced to be set in the pillory in Colchester market on market day. Thomas Wixsted, also from Dedham, was accused at the same time of slandering the earl of Oxford, saying that he had been a confederate of the duke of Norfolk (executed for treason in 1572 for his plan to marry Mary, Queen of Scots), 'and as well worthy to lose his head as he'. He too was sentenced to a spell in Colchester pillory.[42] Both the earl and the duke held large estates in Essex, the earl by inheritance, the duke by his marriage to Margaret, daughter and heiress of Thomas, Lord Audley of Walden, and both may have made enemies in the county.[43] In 1580 Humphrey Poles of Maldon was ordered to be arrested for 'conjuration', and the same year Nicholas Johnson of Woodham Mortimer, accused of making the queen's picture in wax (a form of witchcraft), had to be released for lack of evidence against him.[44] Johnson's offence was committed at the Saracen's Head inn at Maldon, and it is possible that he was the Nicholas Johnson who was vicar of All Saints', Maldon 1562–66 and rector of Woodham Mortimer 1567–1611, although he is not described as a clerk in the records.[45]

There is no obvious connection between Mantell and the last occurrence of the Edward legend in Essex, at Hatfield Broad Oak in 1587. A smith, William Francis, reported that there was a man in the Tower who claimed to be King Edward, and explained that the king had been carried by ship to Germany and a piece of lead buried in his place.[46] However, as there is no evidence of another imposter being imprisoned in 1587, Francis's story presumably did refer to Mantell's claims. His allegations do not seem to have been taken particularly seriously by the authorities, presumably because Mantell was already dead.

There are two odd postscripts to this strange affair. First, Mantell acquired, posthumously at least, a following among some of the Catholics in the Colchester area — an odd fate for one who had claimed to be the very Protestant Edward VI. In 1584 Thomas Debell, a servant of the leading recusant Catherine Audley of Berechurch near Colchester, was imprisoned in the borough gaol for several wild speeches. He had suggested to a member of the Dutch community in Colchester that when the queen died there would be trouble in the country, and that the unpopular Dutch 'strangers' would be expelled, although on another occasion he had said it would be the magistrates, ministers and preachers who would suffer, not the common people. He had pointed out that Mary, Queen of Scots was next heir to the throne. He had also maintained that the 'traitors' recently executed had been killed for their consciences, and that 5,000 Catholics were in prison for their consciences. Finally, he had argued that Mantell had been executed on the evidence of only one witness, although the law required two. The bailiffs of Colchester, who considered Debell very dangerous and 'inclined to papistry', reported the matter to the Privy Council, who directed that Debell be further examined. The town clerk also recommended further enquiry, suggesting that Debell's reference to 'Hempe' was 'some blind prophecy', but he finally advised the bailiffs that what Debell had said was not punishable by law, although it was foolish.[47] The previous year, in July 1583, Edward VI may have been invoked by the recusant John Tusser,[48] then of Tolleshunt D'Arcy, who was accused of publishing 'fanatical and false prophecies'. They were obscure in the extreme, but one ran,

> 'And then the poor commonalty shall take the white horse for their captain and rejoice because there shall come into England one that was dead, and with him shall come the royal E, and the dead shall set the crowns of England on his head ... and then shall the royal E which is the best blood in all the world root out all heresies clean out of this realm, restoring the church and the catholic faith. A lion, a horse, and a leopard shall crown E by the help of the great eagle.'[49]

Finally, about 1586 Thomas Collins of Maldon petitioned the Privy Council for a reward, and his expenses, for his part in bringing Mantell to justice. He claimed the affair had cost him £20, and that he had been promised 'a further benefit better worth to me than the £100 which the earl of Sussex said I was worthy of'. He asked for a free victualler's licence for 21 years, enabling him to sell all kinds of grain, beer, mutton, lamb, cheese, bread, bacon, wood and such like, or else a licence to export 400 tuns of beer, or else £40 'at this my necessity'. He alleged that he needed the reward 'to keep me and my poor wife and children, for any of these will not make me amends for my injuries and the wrongs done to me since that said service', adding that witches had lamed him so that he was 'never like to be my own man again, except God preserve me', and concluded by excusing himself from attending the Council in person, 'being not well of my limbs nor yet of my purse'.[50] It is a pathetic ending to an affair which had once alarmed that same Privy Council.

REFERENCES

1 K. Thomas, *Religion and the Decline of Magic*, p.498.
2 M. E. Cornford, 'A Legend Concerning Edward VI', *Eng. Hist. Rev.*, xxxiii, pp.286–7.
3 *Acts of the Privy Council*, 1554–6, p.126.
4 *Ibid.*, pp.221, 228.
5 P.R.O., PROB. 11/61, f.274.
6 J. Strype, *Annals of the Reformation*, 1824 edn., ii (2), p.503.
7 E. Hasted, *Historical and Topographical Survey of Kent*, 1797–1801, viii, pp.60–1. I owe this suggestion to Mr F. D. Price, formerly of Keble College, Oxford, who read and commented on a draft of this paper.
8 J. Strype, *Annals of the Reformation*, ii (2), p.503.
9 *V.C.H. Suffolk*, ii, p.131; L. P. Fairfield, *John Bale: Mythmaker of the English Reformation*, 1976, pp.1, 31–3.
10 B.L., Lansdowne MS. 99, f.92.
11 J. Strype, *Annals of the Reformation*, ii (2), pp.503–5.
12 A. B. Emden, *Oxf. Univ. Reg., 1501–1540*, p.602; J. Foster, *Alumni Oxonienses, 1500–1714*, p.1558.
13 F. G. Emmison, *Elizabethan Life: Disorder*, p.42; E.R.O., T/Z 440/1.
14 F. G. Emmison, *Elizabethan Life:Disorder*, pp.41–2; E.R.O., Colch., D/B 5 Sb2/1, f.22v; and see K. Thomas, *Religion and the Decline of Magic*, p.506.
15 C. Cross, *Church and People, 1450–1660*, pp.78–9; L. P. Fairfield, *John Bale*, p.166.
16 J. Strype, *Annals of the Reformation*, ii (2), pp.503–5.
17 E.R.O., Cal. Essex Q. Sess. Rec., vii, p.58.
18 *Ibid.*, vii, p.208; viii, p.26.
19 *Cal. Assize Rec. Eliz. I*, p.175.
20 P.R.O., SP 12/186, no. 93.
21 *Cal. Assize Rec. Eliz. I*, p.173.
22 P.R.O., SP 12/186, no. 91.
23 *Acts of Privy Council*, 1577–78, pp.146, 223.
24 *Cal. Assize Rec. Eliz. I*, p.175.
25 P.R.O., SP 12/186, no. 91.
26 *Ibid.*
27 *Cal. Assize Rec. Eliz. I*, pp.192, 215.
28 *Ibid.*, pp.180, 189.
29 E.R.O., Colch., D/Y 2/8, p.207; D/Y 2/6, p.13.
30 *Cal. Assize Rec. Eliz. I*, pp.191–2; *Acts of Privy Council*, 1578–80, pp. 194, 371.
31 *Acts of Privy Council*, 1581–82, p.80.
32 E.R.O., Colch., D/Y 2/8, p.207.
33 *Ibid.*, D/B 5 Cr142, rot. 1; the record of the September 1579 election does not survive.
34 *Acts of Privy Council*, 1580–81, p.29.
35 *Cal. Assize Rec. Eliz. I*, p.189; *Acts of Privy Council*, 1578–80, p.277.
36 E.R.O., Cal. Q.B. Indictments, p.84; *Acts of Privy Council*, 1580–81, p.102; C. L'Estrange Ewen, *Witchcraft and Demonism*, p.428.
37 *Acts of Privy Council*, 1580–81, p.23.
38 E.R.O., Cal. Q.B. Indictments, p.84; *Cal. Assize Rec. Eliz. I*, p.194; C. L'E. Ewen, *Witchcraft and Demonism*, p.428.
39 B.L., Lansdowne MS. 99, f.92.
40 *Cal. Assize Rec. Eliz. I*, p.215; *Acts of Privy Council*, 1580–81, p.353.

41 *Cal. Assize Rec. Eliz. I*, p.195; *Acts of Privy Council*, 1578–80, p.405.

42 *Cal. Assize Rec. Eliz. I*, p.191.

43 *Complete Peerage*.

44 *Acts of Privy Council* 1580–81, pp.23, 34, 251.

45 W. J. Petchey, *Prospect of Maldon*, p.197; R. Newcourt, *Repertorium Ecclesiasticum Parochiale Londinense*, 1710, ii, pp.398, 683.

46 *Cal. Assize Rec. Eliz. I*, p.294.

47 E.R.O., Colch., D/B 5 Sb2/4, f.36v; *ibid.*, D/Y 2/7, p.199; D/Y 2/8, pp.319, 323; B. L., Stowe MS. 150, f.33.

48 *Miscellenea*, xii (Cath. Rec. Soc., xxii), p.51.

49 *Cal. Assize Rec. Eliz. I*, p.241; see K. Thomas, *Religion and the Decline of Magic*, p.482.

50 P.R.O., SP 12/187, no. 62.

From Past Historic to Future Perfect: Essex Heritage and the Community

KEN HALL

In 1987 ESSEX COUNTY COUNCIL acquired two thirteenth century timber framed barns at Cressing Temple, together with their associated buildings and some surrounding land. Grants to assist with purchase or repairs were obtained from English Heritage, the National Heritage Memorial Fund and the European Community. It was an enlightened and imaginative initiative to ensure, at least for the foreseeable future, the preservation and conservation of an historic site of international significance. Standing at the hub of a farming complex, the barns had been used, as they were designed to be, for agricultural purposes for more than seven centuries. Now divorced from that larger complex they were, in effect, redundant.

This is a fate which has overtaken many buildings in the past, but as a scheduled Ancient Monument Cressing Temple enjoys statutory protection. A new role had to be defined which would facilitate preservation as well as protect the integrity of the site and its buildings. Altering structures to suit new purposes was not an available option.

It is unlikely that any individual or body, other than the County Council, would have been able to muster the expertise and resources necessary to provide a secure future for Cressing Temple without considerable difficulty. The enterprise involved not only securing the capital needed for purchase and renovation, a considerable undertaking in itself, but also in effect guaranteeing to make available funds in the future for maintaining the site in good repair. To its credit Essex County Council did this and more.

The policy adopted in relation to the site is embodied in:

The Cressing Temple Charter.

Essex County Council having become the custodian of Cressing Temple on behalf of the people of Essex declares that:

The site will be used as a focus for the County's heritage.

The skills and crafts that went into the construction and creation of the buildings, gardens and landscape will be preserved, demonstrated and explained.

149

The walled garden, Cressing Temple.
(Photograph by David Bowyer, courtesy of the Essex Record Office.)

*Opportunities for learning and research offered by a site of such importance will
be used to enable present and future generations to be aware of the County's history
and their personal relationship to it.*
*The buildings and grounds will be made available for public use and
enjoyment.*

The capital expenditure involved in repairing existing structures and providing
the basic facilities, such as car parking and toilets, to enable public access to
Cressing Temple was considerable and there will always be continuing revenue
costs even if the buildings are not used. Such a substantial commitment was possible
because of a conviction on the part of the County Council that it had an obligation,
on behalf of the community, to attempt to preserve and make accessible such a
significant part of the County's inheritance. However, Cressing Temple represents
only a small part of the heritage of Essex. Resources for such purposes will probably
always be limited. Competing demands in the public sector are many. The ethical
and legal constraints associated with many aspects of the heritage often make
unattractive propositions for responsible private or commercial enterprise.
Safeguarding the heritage in such an environment is a challenge which cannot be
met without difficulty and responsibility for the task has to be shared by the
whole community.

To acknowledge the importance of the patrimony and to be seen to be conserving,
extending and enhancing it is not always as easy a political priority to advocate in
Britain as is, for example, the improvement of health or education provision.
This reflects the priorities set by society. Perhaps the apparent lack of an
immediate threat to our heritage by hostile forces during much of our history
has fostered a degree of complacency within the community that often surprises
some of our European neighbours. The physical destruction wrought by bombing
during the two World Wars in the United Kingdom gave only a taste of the
repeated experience of some nations over many centuries.

With regard to the built environment, the reaction of many post-war planners
until the 70s and 80s, was often to sweep away the rubble and to 'modernize'.
Reconstruction or restoration were more commonly adopted as solutions in
continental Europe than has been the experience in Britain. Even where war
damage was not an available excuse the non-selective cultural vandalism which
transformed the centre of many a market town in England is not easily
understood. The growth in civic societies systematically scrutinizing planning
applications during the 1970s can be seen as a symptom of a growing public
appreciation of existing townscapes and a determination to secure greater public
involvement in the decision-making process.

In Essex, as in other counties, the threats to our archaeological inheritance are
most commonly posed by road development or building construction. Recent
planning guidance has at least helped to identify the threats and to create
mechanisms to make resources available sufficient to afford some safeguards.[1]
Slender protection, by comparison, is afforded to archives, other than those of

central government.[2] British legislators have been reluctant to interfere in what are seen as private property rights. Should the owner of the archive of a great estate or of a prominent family wish to destroy or disperse such papers they are free so to do. Fortunately many such owners have chosen to deposit their archives on loan to public archive repositories.[3]

In most cases the threat to records comes from ignorance and neglect, rather than from other causes. The heightened public interest in archaeology, which in part made possible greater statutory protection, has not yet sufficiently extended to the written heritage to effect any real safeguards. An exception is the *Parochial Registers and Records Measure*[4] which has brought into safer custody the parochial records of the established church. That this was achieved may, to some extent, reflect the increasing interest in and use of such archives by local and family historians.

Essex can claim to have had earlier regard for its heritage than can some counties. In 1938 the County Council was one of the first to establish a county record office to afford protection to archives and it has endeavoured to stay at the forefront of development in subsequent years. The creation of a county archaeological service as an integral part of the development control process has set a standard which others seek to emulate and has supplemented and complemented the provision which already existed. Indeed the environmental services branch of the County Planning Department provides a range of services which together help to protect the built and natural landscape and retain the particular characteristics that together constitute Essex.[5]

Apart from its intrinsic value, the heritage constitutes a substantial asset in Essex. It contributes significantly to the quality of life of those who live and work in the county and attracts others to visit and to settle there. In 1992 the County Council published *A Heritage Protection Policy for Essex* which detailed the specific measures by which the authority intended to act in support of the heritage.[6] It outlined statutory responsibilities and adopted policies and was intended to lead the way in encouraging joint action in protecting and developing the heritage and culture of Essex. It was not conceived as a final statement, but rather as an encouragement to the wider community in meeting the challenges presented by the past in the present and for the future.

From May 1996 the Council will provide a sharper focus with the establishment of a Heritage and Cultural Services Board, which will have responsibility for the relevant services and, by means of an associated Forum, bring together in constructive debate the various bodies within the community which have a role to play in safeguarding and making the richness of our past accessible. Potentially this will make it easier to develop a strategic approach in this important field which will co-ordinate and harness the available expertise and resources.

Provision has also been made for a purpose-built headquarters for the Essex Record Office in Chelmsford to open in 1999. This may, itself, be at the hub of a complex of heritage and arts facilities forming an 'Essex Centre'. Together these developments represent important opportunities to ensure a better future for our past, but can they secure a 'perfect' future?

The answer to such a question is, of course, an emphatic 'no'. So many factors have an impact on our heritage that, even if one were able to determine what constituted a perfect future, it would be impossible to guarantee to secure it. One can, however, attempt to encourage a climate of opinion in which the community at large appreciates the value and significance of what is inherited from the past and understands the possibilities which exist to use it to enhance the quality of life for present and future generations. In that sense much has been achieved, but more remains to be done.

A criticism that has been levelled against the various professionals and agencies concerned with the heritage is that they concentrate too much on services tailored to the needs of specialist users. In effect they cater to an elite. Despite the welcoming smiles of staff and the availability of explanatory literature there can be few more daunting experiences for the uninitiated, for example, than an initial visit to a record office. Similarly, few other than the dedicated and determined amateur or specialist are enthused by many of the necessarily technically precise excavation reports available in learned journals. This is not to argue that it is wrong to cater for the specialist. Indeed it is important that we improve provision for such people, but it is also vital that much increased emphasis is placed on making our written, archaeological and cultural heritage accessible and interesting to the majority of people who have neither the time nor the skills of the specialist.

The opportunities which exist to broaden and extend interest in the richness of the landscape of Essex, it archaeological sites, its historic buildings, the oral and written evidence of the county's people and institutions are greater than ever before. The conjunction of the consideration of a centre for the heritage and arts coupled with advances in information technology make it possible to design buildings, services and strategies to interpret the heritage in a manner which captures the interest and imagination of all sections of the community and makes available the raw materials of our past for study and enjoyment in a wide variety of ways and in a diversity of locations throughout Essex and beyond.

The thinking which began in *A Future For Our Past*,[7] which envisaged a new approach to providing access to archives in Essex, is now capable of realization and extension. The new Record Office headquarters will provide ideal storage for archives, to ensure their preservation for the benefit of future generations, and improved facilities for researchers. It will also include a suite of specialist accommodation for the Essex Sound Archive, lecture and teaching facilities and an exhibition gallery. It is also envisaged that public access to the Essex Sites and Monuments Record and the Historic Buildings Record will be available in the same complex.

The ability now exists to make available simultaneously in schools, universities, libraries, museums and, ultimately, homes throughout Essex much of what could be provided until now only in one such central location. The computerization of the Record Office catalogues and indexes is well advanced. The design is such that it is capable of extension to include digital images of original documents and artefacts as well as digital copies of sound and video recordings. Computerization of the Essex Sites and Monuments Record is also in progress and integration of the Historic Buildings Record is planned. It is entirely feasible to make these raw materials of history available via computer networks or by means of CD ROM at remote points. It would also be possible to tailor such material in units relating to particular topics or places and suitable for enjoyment and study by the non-specialist.

If we expect society to make available the considerable resources necessary to protect and enhance the heritage, whether that be with regard to sites such as Cressing Temple, conserving damaged records, or undertaking archaeological excavations, it is of the utmost importance that all sections of the community both appreciate and value it. To achieve this may necessitate a reappraisal of the roles of archivists, archaeologists and museum curators who will need to place increasing emphasis on communicating with a wider constituency of potential users. Essex historians are justly proud of the publishing programme of the Record Office and the County Archaeology section and both of these bodies have achieved much through exhibitions in communicating with the general public. More than ever it will be necessary to engage the interest and support of the layman by interpreting the raw data or the artefacts they hold or the historic buildings they curate using the media which are most accessible to the public.

Cressing Temple is a useful illustration of a part of our heritage adding to the quality of life of the community. Its guardianship by the County Council has preserved its integrity without the necessity for any substantial compromise. However, merely to retain it for its intrinsic interest to those studying timber frame buildings would not have ensured its future. It has also been made available as a venue for the performance of music, drama and dance, the demonstration of crafts and the teaching of history and archaeology. Conferences and charity events as well as historical re-enactments attract a wide cross section of people to visit the site. More recently the garden has attracted a new group of visitors. All of these activities provide a new role for the barns and associated buildings which is very different to their intended and original purposes. It is, however, these new activities which help to make it economically possible to preserve these magnificent examples of the achievements of the past. Without these new, but sympathetic, developments the future would have been uncertain.

The challenge which faces us now is to apply the same principles to the wider Essex heritage in order to ensure that the county's archives, historic buildings, archaeological and historical sites can be made relevant to the whole community and therefore attract the resources to secure their future preservation.

REFERENCES

1 Planning Policy Guidance Note 16: 'Archaeology and Planning', DOE, 1990.
2 Public Records Act 1958.
3 A. A. H. Knightbridge, *Archive legislation in the United Kingdom*, Winchester, 1985, Society of Archivists, contains a useful summary of the relevant statutes.
4 Parochial Registers and Records Measure 1978 (as amended).
5 An account of the development of archaeological services in Essex is contained in D. G. Buckley, 'Essex Archaeology: Retrospect and Prospect'. (Unpublished paper, 1996).
6 *A Heritage Protection Policy for Essex*, Essex County Council, 1992.
7 'A Future for our Past': The Essex Record Office over the Next Decade. A report presented to Essex County Council Library, Museum and Records Committee in 1992.

A Georgian Time Capsule
The Library at Spains Hall, Essex

EDITH FREEMAN

SPAINS HALL

Finchingfield Essex.

IN 1758 ELIZABETH BRISE OF CLARE gave her thirteen year old grandson, Thomas Ruggles, a copy of the recently published *Anson's Voyage round the World*. She chose an exciting book for the orphaned boy who on the death of his father had been placed in the care of his Brise relations. It is the earliest of the acquisitions which were to form the remarkable Library at Spains Hall and Thomas recorded the gift on the fly-leaf just before his death. His appetite for reading was further stimulated by being placed as a pupil at Lavenham Grammar School, where he came under the influence of Arthur Young who was to be his life-long friend. Arthur, a senior pupil, had special privileges which included a room of his own where he had begun to gather a collection of books. Apart from the Bible, the Ruggles family had hitherto not been readers; their energies had been absorbed in a slow struggle to rise in society from yeoman beginnings in Suffolk through various branches of the cloth trade. In the eighteenth century

157

Eliza Brise, School of Hudson, c.1760 *(?)*
(Photograph courtesy of Paul Mellon Centre for Studies in British Art (London) Limited)

the descendants of a John Ruggles who had established himself in the bays trade in Bocking, Essex, became wealthy enough to invest in land and properties.

In 1784, Thomas Ruggles, already enriched through his Brise mother's dowry, was left Spains Hall, Finchingfield, by a cousin on his father's side. It was not until the early 1790s that he decided to reconstruct this old and somewhat neglected house into a fitting residence for a Georgian gentleman. He chose one of the pleasantest rooms to become the Library. It was oak-panelled with a large chimney-piece and windows facing west. Remote from the new domestic offices and nursery quarters it provided privacy for his reading and writing. Nevertheless, it was to become the focus of family life. Shelves were constructed along the entire east wall, curving at the corners (an unusual feature) to fill part of the north and south walls. This arrangement gives a feeling of intimacy to the room.

The volumes to fill these shelves (with a tall-banked overflow by the north door) were collected by Thomas; his son and daughter-in-law, John and Catherine; and catalogued around 1850–60 by their daughter Georgiana; a catalogue still used by the present owner of Spains Hall, Sir John Ruggles-Brise. Only a few books in this index have been lost or sold. Newer books have been accommodated on more recent shelving. The Spains Hall Library cannot compare in the number and rarity of books nor in the splendour of their bindings with that of a huge county seat like Audley End, but it has a special significance. Thomas Ruggles and his family were anxious to establish themselves among the Essex gentry and in the late eighteenth century it was reprehensible for a country-house owner not to furnish it with a library. Unlike some owners, the Ruggles did not buy their collection *en bloc* to make a show. The books were chosen at different times to satisfy their current curiosity or meet a particular need. Thus the Library is a memorial to three generations of the family, as well as a reflection of the tastes of the Georgian gentry of Essex.

It is possible in most cases to determine which member of the family acquired a particular book. As a young man Thomas wrote his name and sometimes the date in a neat, cramped hand on the fly-leaf. When he became the head of the family after the death of his Ruggles cousin, John, Thomas assumed the crest of a castle and stamped this inside his acquisitions. His son John in youth and in a few cases, John's sisters and younger brothers, Samuel and their nieces, wrote their names or initials in books which remained in the Library. After 1827 when John assumed the name of Brise, he used two bookplates; one of these combined the arms of Ruggles and Brise but only bore the Ruggles crest; the other showed only the two crests of castle and griffin. Later descendants copied these book-plates so a counter check has to be made with the catalogue. A few books are to be found in the catalogue but have no indication of who acquired them.

Another puzzle is the stamping of a gold castle on the spine of some of the Georgian books amongst which there appears to be no common factor. Occasionally, although not as often as one might expect, a book contains an interesting inscription.

MEMBERS OF THE RUGGLES-BRISE FAMILY CONNECTED WITH THE LIBRARY AT SPAINS HALL

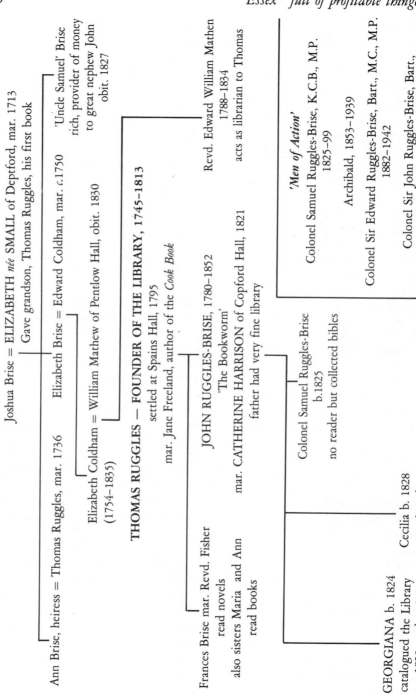

Joshua Brise = ELIZABETH *née* SMALL of Deptford, mar. 1713
Gave grandson, Thomas Ruggles, his first book

'Uncle Samuel' Brise
rich, provider of money
to great nephew John
obit. 1827

Ann Brise, heiress = Thomas Ruggles, mar. 1736

Elizabeth Brise = Edward Coldham, mar. *c*.1750

Elizabeth Coldham = William Mathew of Pentlow Hall, obit. 1830
(1754–1835)

THOMAS RUGGLES — FOUNDER OF THE LIBRARY, 1745–1813
settled at Spains Hall, 1795
mar. Jane Freeland, author of the *Cook Book*

Revd. Edward William Mathen
1788–1834
acts as librarian to Thomas

JOHN RUGGLES-BRISE, 1780–1852
'The Bookworm'
mar. CATHERINE HARRISON of Copford Hall, 1821
father had very fine library

Frances Brise mar. Revd. Fisher
read novels
also sisters Maria and Ann
read books

Colonel Samuel Ruggles-Brise
b.1825
no reader but collected bibles

'Men of Action'

Colonel Samuel Ruggles-Brise, K.C.B., M.P.
1825–99

Archibald, 1853–1939

Colonel Sir Edward Ruggles-Brise, Bart., M.C., M.P.
1882–1942

Colonel Sir John Ruggles-Brise, Bart.,
C.B., O.B.E, T.D., J.P., D.U. (Essex), 1908 –
renewed enthusiasm for the Library

GEORGIANA b. 1824
catalogued the Library
c.1850s and 1860s

Cecilia b. 1828
novel reader

A large number of the books have the initials CRB — Catherine Ruggles-Brise — on inside covers. Catherine's father was John Haynes Harrison of Copford Hall, Colchester. He had a large and highly valued library. Some books he gave to his children during his lifetime; others he willed to them at the time of his death in 1845. While the initials might denote those books Catherine received from her father, other clues suggest that they indicate the works she wished to keep as a widow, reflecting a woman who understood and valued books. In the first paragraph of his will, John Ruggles-Brise states that his wife should be permitted to select up to 500 of any of the books in the Spains Hall Library. It was his intention that she should remove to another residence; if she did so, presumably at her death the volumes were restored to Spains Hall.

Thomas proceeded from grammar school to study the classics at Sidney Sussex College, Cambridge, and then to qualify in law at the Inns of Court. Some texts remain; specially attractive is a beautifully bound volume — *The Institutes of Justinian*, inscribed 'Thomas Ruggles, Inner Temple, 1769'. In a work entitled *The Barrister*, which he published in 1792, Thomas advocates that a young gentleman studying the law should enlarge his reading beyond the legal works needed for his profession. He suggests books which 'may amuse' the young man's 'lighter hours and train his mind gradually to the more polished literary acquirements'. To this end he commends books which will keep up a knowledge of Greek! Both Greek and Latin authors are well represented in Thomas's library. In particular he praised 'the mellifluent periods of Cicero'. His son followed his advice and added a particularly fine set of ten volumes of Cicero's work (1783).

Thomas was trained as a classicist but he was a romantic at heart. He commended to his young gentleman Horace's *Art of Poetry*; he possesed himself of Ovid's *Art of Love* (1757). He seems to have turned to poetry at times of stress and heightened emotion. His sojourn with his dying wife Elizabeth in Lisbon, in 1771, probably explains his purchase of the works of Camoens in Portuguese. While in Bristol with his dying son, he turned to the Rowley poems of Thomas Chatterton, of Bristol birth. Spencer and Thomson appealed to his delight in nature; Byron was evidently a favourite. It is harder to explain his acquisition of Burns and the collection of the anthology of Scottish poems, *The Ever Green* (1761). The purchase of Milton's work was natural for one with the classical training of Thomas. Young's *Night Thoughts* (1813) would appeal to the melancholy streak in Thomas with its atmosphere of 'delightful gloom'. His conservative outlook, and even more that of his son John, would lead us to expect Dryden and Pope among their books and account for the absence of those writers bringing about a revolution in English poetry, Shelley, Coleridge and Wordsworth. (*The Lyrical Ballards* was published in 1798: both Ruggles must have heard the discussions they provoked.)

On the tall stack of shelves beside the north door of the Library are the volumes of Samuel Johnson's *The Lives of the English Poets* (1779–81) but these were probably acquired not so much out of interest for the poets as out of the admiration of Thomas for Dr Johnson. There is an eleven volume edition of his works (1787) and a valuable first edition of Boswell's *Life*. Thomas was fond of quoting from Shakespeare as well as the Classics. There is a ten volume 1790 edition of the works of the poet, very well worn, and an additional copy of a 1729 edition of *King Lear* in which Thomas wrote his name.

Thomas not only believed that a cultured gentleman should be familiar with Greek and Latin but also with modern European languages. For some reason — perhaps later Ruggles extracted texts for study — there are more gaps in the catalogue list of books in this section than in any other. Originally besides the works in Portuguese which the Ruggles family acquired because of their close connection with Portugal, there were copies in Italian of Tasso and Boccaccio and editions of most of the French writers admired in the eighteenth century: Racine; Molière; Diderot, Montesquieu. An amusing little mystery is a slim volume entitled *Les Egarements du Coeur et de L'Esprit* (1765). It is recorded on the fly-leaf that this belonged to Miss Hunter of Gestingthorpe. Who was she and what was Thomas doing purloining her copy?

John was not, like his father, even a dilettante author but he was equally devoted to the Library. Sir John's grandmother records a friend of his great-great grandfather describing the first John as 'a great book-worm'. With more money to spend and ample leisure he added a greater number of volumes to the Library than Thomas had collected.

One would so much like more information about John's dealings with local booksellers, such as Bickmore of Sudbury, identifiable by a tiny label on some inside covers. Some books have fine bindings such as *The History of Henry III* (1783), which John bought in 1820. Others are second-hand copies such as the beautifully bound copy of *Edmondson's Heraldry* (1780).

As new aspirants to the country gentry, Thomas and his son had a strong interest in genealogy, especially insofar as it would provide them with an ancestry of distinction. On the shelves are to be found:

> Dugdale's *Baronage* (1675).
> Nine volumes of Brydges' *Biographical Peerage of England* (1812).
> Debrett's *Peerage of Great Britain and Ireland* (1843).
> Three volumes of *The New Peerage of England, Scotland and Ireland* (1769).
> Five books of *The English Baronetage* (1741).
> Five volumes of Betham's *The Baronetage* (1801).
> Edmondson's *A Complete Body of Heraldry* (1780).
> Dallaway's *Inquiries into Heraldry in England* (1793).

Burke's *Visitation of Seats and Arms* was displayed in the Drawing Room. The enthusiasm of Thomas for working out family trees is shown by his paper on the Cavendishes bound into the *Life of Cardinal Wolsey* written by George Cavendish (1827). Notes made by John on other family trees occur in various books. Thomas set in motion the preparation of the first version of a Ruggles family tree. Georgiana, in the copy of *Debrett*, almost falling apart with use, inserted births and deaths occurring after the printed entries.

In making her analysis of the Library, Georgiana amalgamated in the same section biography (Sir John's favourite reading), history and travel. This was more logical in her time when most biographies were not 'chat shows' for entertainment but an expounding of achievements against a background of the events contemporary with them. Examples on the shelves at Spains Hall are:

> Walter Scott's *Life of Napoleon Buonaparte* (1827).
> William Cox's *Memoirs of Life and Administration of Walpole* (1798).

Boswell's *Life of Johnson* points the way to a new type of biographical literature and Edward Topham, editor of *The World*, gave his friend, Thomas, a copy of his *Life of Elwes*, which approaches Alan Clark's *Diaries* in its racy style and revelations.

In his advice on reading for a young gentleman, Thomas emphasised the importance of studying classical history, so it is not surprising to find among his own special books a 1673 edition of *Tacitus*; inside is his signature and the date 1778. He also owned Plutarch's *Lives* (1727) and Gibbon's *Decline and Fall of the Roman Empire* (1783); whether he was one of those rare owners who actually read the twelve volumes of the latter is not known!

Thomas expected the study of classical history to lead a young man to explore the history of his own country. The collection of books at Spains Hall on English history is extensive as it was of great interest to John as well as to his father. They acquired all the standard works available at the time:

> Fifteen volumes of T. Smollett's *History of England* (1758).
> Eight volumes of David Hume's *History of England* (1798).
> Six volumes of the Earl of Clarendon's *History of the Rebellion* (1732).

Henry Hallam's *History of England* in two volumes was presented to young Samuel when he left Eton in 1842.

Lord Macaulay's *History of England* in four volumes is missing but now replaced by a later edition in five volumes.

'The emphasis of these works is heavily on political history. Thomas' own *History of the Poor* is a rare venture into social and economic issues.

There were originally other books on history in the collection assembled by Thomas. In a codicil to his will of 1811 he left such books as were published by the Society of Antiquaries, of which he was a keen Fellow, to a cousin William Mathews 'the younger' of Pentlow Hall. The Ruggles family of Spains Hall were close friends of the family at Pentlow. In May of 1821, William was a witness of the wedding of Jane, daughter of Thomas, to John Walford in Finchingfield church. Thomas also left his cousin money to pay his subscription to the Society of Antiquaries and to buy further books. He seems to have employed the young man as a sort of librarian and amanuensis. His son had no such employee to care for the library but he kept it up-to-date, especially with historical research by joining the Camden Society and adding 43 volumes of their publications.

Both Thomas and John were interested in Parliament although no Ruggles became an M.P. until John's son Samuel was elected for East Essex in 1868. As there was no coverage by T.V. or radio, printed accounts of the debates were eagerly awaited. On the shelves is a long series of copies of the *Annual Register*, many of which contain summaries of preceedings in Parliament. There are also 21 volumes of collections of *Debates in Parliament* from 1741.

A much greater passion of both father and son was the study of local history, particularly of their own county of Essex. Morant's great history (of which a second copy was added after the catalogue was completed) was supplemented by the more popular *History of Essex by a Gentleman* (1770), with its attractive engravings of country seats. There are fine histories of Norfolk and Surrey and the distinguished account of Hawsted, Suffolk, extracted by Thomas from its author, Sir John Cullum. The prolonged stay of Thomas with a dying son in Bristol accounts for a history of that town. More puzzling is the presence of large works on Manchester and Newcastle.

Closely associated with the pleasure of studying local history was the enthusiasm for exploring such localities as had special scenic and historic attractions. At the turn of the eighteenth century, such tours ranged from day-picnics, like that described by Jane Austen in *Emma*, to the trips Thomas took to the north of Suffolk in his Uncle Samuel's comfortable equipage with the excuse of collecting information on workhouses. William Camden had set a standard for preparing the mind for such outings with the publication of his *Britannia* in 1586, successively re-issued during the two centuries following. The Spains Hall Library contains six volumes of *Magna Britannia* (1720), a revised edition with fine maps by Robert Morden.

Long before Britain was covered by a network of railways, extensive tours had taken place on horseback or with vehicles drawn by horses. Arthur Young rode thousands of miles and described his journeys in print. Unfortunately the Spains Hall Library contains no copy of the accounts of the trips he took with Thomas in Essex which he recounted in *The Annals of Agriculture*. Few copies of this vast publication have survived and it is sad that not one number is to be found at Spains Hall, although Thomas was much involved in the production.

The Romantic Movement in art and literature inspired admiration for the more dramatic scenery on the fringes of the British Isles and for discovery of picturesque ruins. The Library is well provided with works to inspire tours in Scotland, Wales and the remoter parts of Northern England. Among these are the attractive and useful three volumes of *Scotland* (1790) and one of *Wales* (1778) by Thomas Pennant and *England and Scotland* (1791) by Thomas Newt. But there is no evidence that Thomas or John Ruggles were lured into these remoter regions. Both preferred more decorous visits to unruined gentlemen's seats or sitting comfortably contemplating the fine engravings in C. Cordiner's *Remarkable Ruins and Romantic Prospects* (1788).

Yet Thomas urged on his son the benefits of travel in enlarging a young man's mind and John made a trip with a friend as far as Derbyshire, about which he kept a very dull journal. He may have made use of J. Throsby's *Select Views of Leicestershire* (1789) with its fine engravings. Thomas may have used Worsley's fine work on the Isle of Wight with its fold-up map and handsome illustrations to prepare himself for a family visit but there is no account of this visit.

Both men collected maps. To possess accurate road maps must still have been something of a novelty and clear street plans were only just replacing the more decorative picture maps of the early eighteenth century. Mogg's *Map of London* was needed for the occasional visits Thomas made to London before the great landmark of Trafalgar Square. Guide books were changing in character. Instead of volumes too heavy to carry about and packed with factual information, lighter little books were being concocted both to encourage visitors to come and to assist them in exploring. The well-worn copy of the 1829 *Suffolk Traveller*, with a note on the fly-leaf in John's hand is a sample of the former. A year later, *The Stranger's Guide through Cambridge* (1830), a delightful example of the new genre was published and added to the Spains Hall Library. This has a plan of the colleges and charming engravings and is 'laid out in walks' . . . 'to direct the stranger how to perambulate'.

As they grew older both Thomas and John showed an increasing disinclination to leave home and were not to be enticed either to risk the frights or incur the expense of foreign travel. Yet all around them the world was being opened up and writers were exulting in the variety and novelty of far away places. The Ruggles shared in this excitement through the means of their Library. They provided themselves with books on almost every European country. (Thomas as a younger man had taken his dying wife to Lisbon in the hope that the climate might benefit her. He had equipped himself with three solid volumes of *Mappa de Portugal*.) Proud of their own nation's trade and exploration overseas, the Ruggles obtained the best accounts available of a little known world which was being charted as space is in our own time. Good seed had been sown when grandmother Brise gave young Thomas *Anson's Voyage Round the World* (1756). To this was added:

> James Cook's *Voyages*; *A Voyage towards the South Pole and Round the World* (1777).
> Ten volumes of *Modern and Contemporary Voyages and Travels* (1807).
> Five volumes of James Bruce's *Travels to Discover the Sources of the Nile* (1790).
> Four volumes of Irving's *A History of the Life and Voyages of Christopher Columbus* (1728).

The Library was also provided with more detailed studies of scarcely known areas of the world such as the Pelew Islands where Captain Wilson of the 'Antelope' had been wrecked in 1783.

Yet for all this addiction to the wonders of the world, the real concern of the Ruggles was their own microcosm, the development of the house and grounds of Spains Hall. Alas, no book has been identified which inspired Thomas when he reconstructed the house into a Georgian mansion but the practical manual, *The Builder's Price Book* (1789), with which he equipped himself shows the close watch he kept on costs. John, equally careful in spending money, provided himself with the sixteenth edition (1814) of Hoppus's *Tables* for measuring timber, stone, glass and plaster.

It was probably his wife, Catherine, who was most interested in R. Lugar's *Rural Dwellings*, J. C. Loudon's *Cottage Farm and Villa* (1833) and T. D. N. Dearn's *Lodges and Entrances* (1811) when the style of the three lodges in the park was under discussion. There is no Repton's Red Book for Spains Hall but a sketch plan by Humphry Repton survives for the treatment of the water on the south-east side of the house. The copy of Humphry Repton's *Landscape Gardening*, which one presumes Thomas acquired, has alas been sold. John had two water-colours prepared by Ady Repton for the improvement of the south-east frontage but his deviation from the suggested design and his purchase of the three volume work of the younger Repton's rival, Uvedale Price, suggests he was not greatly impressed.

Thomas had gained experience in the lay-out of grounds when as a young man he inherited property in Surrey. It was probably at this period that he bought copies of:

> John Evelyn's *Sylva* (1776).
> John Gerarde's *The Herball or Generall Historie of Plantes* (1634).
> John Ray's *Plant Synopsis* (1724)

These books in which tree-lovers and plant-seekers of his time delighted remain among the special treasures of the Library.

The Ruggles collection of practical gardening books is of particular interest because it reveals how keen country gentlemen were to follow the horticultural fashions of their day. From Uncle Shadrach of Clare was passed on the 'most comprehensive guide to all aspects of gardening', *The Gardener's Dictionary* (1748) by Philip Miller, 'the most distinguished and influential gardener of the eighteenth century'. Thomas up-dated this with Mr Wheatley's *Modern Gardening* (1777). John (or more probably his wife) obtained J. C. Loudon's *Encyclopaedia of Plants* (1829). In the year this was published, John and Catherine were reconstructing their Tudor Walk, preparatory to the laying out of their herbaceous border. John acquired the two volumes privately printed for Revd. William Hanbury, a Leicestershire clergyman, *A Complete Body of Gardening* (1770). He also joined the newly formed Horticultural Society (to become the Royal Horticultural Society) and obtained four volumes (bound in two) of their first transactions; these are most beautifully illustrated with colour plates and drawings (1815–20).

Thomas showed he had an inquiring mind by obtaining two volumes on the use of microscopes. Both he and his son were interested in natural science but the books they acquired, with the exception of Ray's *Synopsis on Plants* and Hudson's *Flora Anglica* (1778), were remarkable for their aesthetic and visual qualities rather than for information. The three volumes of George Graves' *British Birds* (1811) with their hand-tinted illustrations are a delight to the eye. At the period when the Library was collected, an interest in applied science was not common among gentlemen. There are a very few science textbooks, mostly belonging to Samuel, the son of Thomas, who died young. At the age of forty-five, Thomas provided himself with a chemistry manual, and his son John bought himself four volumes *On Air* (1775) by Joseph Priestley.

THE

BELLE WIDOWS:

WITH

CHARACTERISTIC SKETCHES

OF

REAL PERSONAGES

AND

LIVING CHARACTERS.

A NOVEL,

Inscribed to the Beau - Monde.

Detail from the title page of the Belle Widows.

In one important respect there is evidence of a change of outlook in the books collected by Thomas and those his son acquired. It marks the passing of the Georgian into the Victiorian era. Thomas had little or no interest in theology and appears to have moved increasingly towards agnosticism. For John acceptance of the Anglican Church was the badge of a country gentleman. He and his wife Catherine filled several shelves with religious tracts and collections of sermons such as those of the Revd. William Paley and the Revd. Harvey Mariott. Their daughter, Georgiana in compiling the Library catalogue placed Divinity as the first section although Biography begins with B!

Thomas loved women but had small opinion of their intelligence. He would have been astonished to be told that today, an edited version of his wife's cookbook, was selling around the world while his own ponderous *History of the Poor* gathers dust on the shelves at Spains Hall.

Frances Ruggles-Brise

Jane's headquarters were far from the Library, close to the kitchens and nursery stairs. Her daughter-in-law, Catherine, made far more use of the Library and knew the books well. The daughters of Thomas, like the daughters of the Bennets in Jane Austen's *Pride and Prejudice*, might be idle if they chose. Children's books were not attractive as they are today; the print was small, the matter solid and pictures rare. At the age of nine, John was given *The Life of Olaudah Equiano* (1790), written by himself. Dull as it was, his name was crossed out on the fly-leaf and the initials of his two sisters, Marianne and Anne, inserted. Another of the daughters of Thomas became a reader if only of light literature. Frances, later the wife of the Revd. Charles Fisher of Ovington, wrote her name in a two-volume novel entitled *The Belle Widows* (1789), a sketch of real persons, inscribed to the Beau-Monde.

John's son, Samuel, despite his Eton education, never became a scholar. His sisters fared somewhat better than their aunts in that they were provided with governesses and acquired a veneer of culture. On the Library shelves is a handsomely bound set of *The Novelists Magazine* in 21 volumes (1781–85); it had originally been issued as periodicals. It contains complete novels by Richardson and Fielding as well as minor authors and the selection provides a remarkable unfolding of this new genre of English literature. It seems more likely that John, rather than Thomas, acquired the set probably with his daughters in mind. Alas, their reading appears to have approximated closer to that of Jane Austen's heroine Catherine, who raved over the Mills and Boon romances of her time. (Miss Austen's own works are not to be found in the Spains Hall Library.) An example of the preferred reading of Georgiana and Cecilia in the Library is *Anedotes of the Delborough Family* (1772), a novel in five volumes. On the fly-leaf, they have both inscribed their names:

G. R. Brise
C. S. B. Ruggles

(the younger sister retaining the surname of her father until he became his uncle's heir in 1827). A brief quotation reveals the flavour of this treasured novel:

'Despise you, Mariana, I despise you?
Witness awful Creator of the World that I love you to madness!'

Another interesting feature of this book is that it has written on the fly-leaf:
'The Cavendish Society, 1792.'

Was this a circulating library or a literary club? Other books in the Spains Hall Library, not all of them light literature, have a similar inscription. One book has been found with 'Clare Society, 1791', written inside it. So far all enquiries have failed to produce an explanation of these inscriptions. May be this reference will prompt some reader to come up with a clue.

Uare Society 179

THE

INTERESTING NARRATIVE

OF

THE LIFE

OF

OLAUDAH EQUIANO,

OR

GUSTAVUS VASSA,

THE AFRICAN.

WRITTEN BY HIMSELF.

Behold, God is my falvation; I will truft and not be afraid, for the Lord Jehovah is my ftrength and my fong; he alfo is become my falvation.
And in that day fhall ye fay, Praife the Lord, call upon his name, declare his doings among the people. Ifaiah xii. 2, 4.

THIRD EDITION, ENLARGED.

LONDON:
PRINTED FOR, AND SOLD BY, THE AUTHOR.

Sold alfo by Mr. Johnfon, St. Paul's Church-yard; Meffrs. Robinfons, Paternofter-row; Mr. Robfon, and Mr. Clark, Bond-ftreet; Mr. Davis, Holborn; Mr. Matthews, Strand; Mr. Richardfon, Royal Exchange; Mr. Chalmers, No. 81, Old-ftreet; Mr. J. Thompfon, Manchefter; and the Bookfellers in Oxford and Cambridge.
1790.
PRICE FOUR SHILLINGS,
[Entered at Stationers Hall.]

Title page of The Life of Olaudah Equiano, *1790.*

Georgiana, bolting home after forty-eight hours of a disastrous marriage, occupied herself in cataloguing the books her father and grandfather had collected. They are analysed in categories and both the categories designated and the numbers of books assigned to each reveal the preferences of the Ruggles. In making the catalogue, Georgiana, performed a valuable service. John acknowledged his debt to his daughter by providing in his will that she should be permitted to select up to 250 volumes from Spains Hall Library; she seems to have arranged that these should remain on the shelves. Her catalogue has limitations for her mind was not logically trained. Each book was given a letter indicating its shelf-bank and a shelf number but not an individual number and the books in any particular category are not placed together in any one part of the Library. The entries for 'The Georgian Collection' fill pages 1–48 of a foolscap ledger but she only used the right-hand side and Sir John has added notes on the left. The section headings chosen by her are:

Divinity, Theology, etc.	two pages.
Classics, Antiquities, etc.	three pages.
Law	two pages.
Biography, History, Travel	eight pages.
Drama, Poetry, etc.	two pages.
General Literature	six pages.

The last is a real rag-bag containing novels, art and music books, natural history, a few applied science books, practical manuals, works on genealogy.

Sometimes Georgiana enters a book under the name of the author, sometimes under the title, sometimes both or *with variations of them!* A further snare for the book-hunter is that she assigns to Classics almost any book that happens to be in Latin. Thus, together with the works of Horace, we find John Ray's work on plants and *Ignoramus*, a play by George Ruggles of which the family were enormously proud, as King James I came to see performances of it twice at Cambridge. Fortunately for its survival during the time of Sir John's strait-laced grandmother there was no translation in the Library of this lewd comedy.

The Library more than any other room at Spains Hall retains the past. In the deep quiet, one feels the presence of former members of the family, absorbed in reading or maybe nodding off to sleep but the Library was also the meeting point of the family. In this room, at the heart of the house, there took place those domestic dramas which occur in every household. Georgiana knew the Library better than anyone; she handled every book. It was also in this room that she encountered her father's bitter opposition to her marriage. Later in life, she exorcised her ghosts by writing a novel. Modelling it on the style of the romances she had read in the Library as a girl, she used the background of life at Spains Hall and the character of the man who ruined her. The manuscript was never finished. Perhaps it is waiting for another Ruggles to pick up a pen and carry on the story. The Library holds the past for the future.

The University of Essex

MICHAEL SOMMERLAD[1]

At a meeting of the County Council of Essex on Tuesday, 7 July 1959 a motion was proposed by Alderman, later Lord, Leatherland that the Education Committee be asked to inquire into the possibility of securing the establishment of a University of Essex and to report in due course to the Council. A Sub-Committee was set up and its first meeting was held on 23 November, from then on events moved swiftly. On 14 January 1960 very full discussions took place with the University Grants Committee and, after further meetings with the U.G.C., a Conference was held at County Hall, Chelmsford, on 29 March to which a wide range of county figures representing the County Council, the Local Authorities, Industry, Education, the Churches, and other interested parties was invited. Colonel Sir John Ruggles-Brise was present at the meeting and expressed his warm support for the proposal. A University, he said, was one of the marks of an important county.

The Conference established beyond all doubt that there was considerable support for the project within the County. On 5 April 1960 the Education Committee and the Finance Committee were each able to bring before the County Council a recommendation that a University Promotion Committee should be established and that the approach to the University Grants Committee should be formalized. Sir John was asked to head the Promotion Committee and

Wivenhoe Park, the subject of Constable's famous painting now in the National Gallery at Washington, was extensively re-modelled in the first half of the nineteenth century. The house provided administrative and social facilities for the University while the new buildings were under construction. It has now been extended and serves as a Hotel and Conference Centre that is regularly used in both capacities by the University.

he thus began a long and fruitful connection with the University of Essex. His enthusiasm, energy, and application were instrumental in the success of the Essex submission and to the subsequent achievements of the University.

A formal proposal had to be with the U.G.C. by the end of May. This *terminus ad quem* had been known for some time and much of the preparatory work had already been done, including the investigation of possible sites for the new University. Financial matters were also pressing and Sir John wrote to 72 of the County's largest firms seeking their support and asking for an early reply. His elegant letter received a remarkable response and within four weeks 25 firms had given favourable answers; others undertook to do so as soon as possible and when the Proposal was dispatched to the U.G.C. on 26 May Sir John was able to show that the County stood four-square behind him.

An invitation to meet the U.G.C. was received almost by return and Sir John led the Essex deputation to a formal meeting on 16 July 1960. Over the next months the U.G.C. kept in close contact and its members visited possible sites in the County. Matters were still under detailed discussion when on 18 May 1961 the Chancellor of the Exchequer announced in the House of Commons that, in addition to the new universities already being established at Brighton, Norwich, and York, another three should be sited at Canterbury, Coventry, and Colchester.

There were several reasons why the decision was greeted with considerable satisfaction. It had been known from the outset that Norfolk was seeking to establish a university at Norwich and Norfolk's success had been much envied. There had at one time been a suggestion that Essex should associate itself with the Norfolk proposal under an 'East Anglian' umbrella but a strong preference had been expressed for the County to have its own foundation. Although this was largely a matter of understandable local pride there were other considerations. It had always been recognized that there were compelling economic reasons to establish a university in the County for it would bring employment, money, and cultural advantages as well as prestige. The considerable and lengthy discussion about where the university was to be situated engendered by these very practical considerations finally came to an almost deadlocked choice between the rival claims of Chelmsford and Colchester. Sir John, the ever-impartial Lord Lieutenant, pointed out that unless ranks were closed on this difficult decision the chances of getting a University of Essex would be sadly jeopardized. The conflict was only finally resolved when the U.G.C. suggested that a successful submission should contain unanimous agreement as to a proposed site, a suggestion supplemented by a strong hint that the Committee had a distinct preference for the Wivenhoe Park site at Colchester. One reason was that Chelmsford was thought to be so close to London that staff and students might choose to commute and the residential character of the university, thought to be of the highest importance, might be diluted.

There was at that time a national need for a rapid expansion of higher education. Many children were unable to find places and in 1958 alone the secondary schools of Essex produced 70 well-qualified children who were denied a university education. It was clear that in future years the situation would rapidly become worse and that, in particular, there would probably be an increase in the number of girls wanting to go to university. It is greatly to the credit of the Promotion Committee that from the very beginning the University of Essex was conceived · of as a national institution rather than one established to serve specifically local needs, although these were of course not to be neglected. When it was pointed out that this policy could perhaps affect the willingness of local industries to contribute to the appeal fund it was generally felt that the County would rise above this consideration, as in the event it did.

The initiative now passed from the Promotion Committee to an Academic Planning Board consisting of members proposed by the U.G.C. but also including, at Sir John's request, Dr B. E. Lawrence, the Chief Education Officer of the County. The Chairman was Mr Noel Annan (later Lord Annan), Provost of King's College, Cambridge, who was also a member of the planning board for the University of East Anglia, and Essex representation was strengthened by the appointment of Mr D. N. Bungey, the Deputy Chief Education Officer, as Secretary.[2] It was this board that laid the shape of the University of Essex and its work is very evident in the structure of the University as it stands today, one third of a century later.

The Promotion Committee had envisaged a student population of between 2,500 and 3,500 students but the Advisory Board recommended planning for double that number. This was a particularly interesting development because it was at the same time suggesting that the University should not attempt to teach a wide range of subjects:

> 'The general scheme is to establish in the first place a few strong and large departments rather than numerous small departments. We recognize that this will mean omitting in the first decades of the University's existence several important fields of study. But we believe that to do so will be in the best interests of the University for two main reasons, First, good staff are more likely to be attracted because they will not find themselves so isolated in their field of research and opportunities for promotion will be more frequent. Second, the University of Essex will stand in the public eye as a place noted for certain fields of study and will be distinct from other new universities. These large departments should be grouped for the sake of flexibility in larger Schools which will be the main units of academic organisation.'[3]

This paragraph was probably the most important in the whole document.

Later work of the Planning Board was eventually to lead to ensuring that the University had its roots firmly embedded in the County. The governing structure that resulted from its recommendations brought, and still brings, many local people into close and practical contact with the University through membership of its Court and Council and the first lay Officers of the University were the Rt. Hon. Richard Butler (later Lord Butler of Saffron Walden as Chancellor,[4] Colonel Sir John Ruggles-Brise as Pro-Chancellor, and Alderman C. E. Leatherland (later Lord Leatherland of Dunton) as Treasurer. The Armorial Bearings of the University contain the Arms of Essex County Council[5] and the Motto of the University is adapted from the East Saxon poem *The Battle of Maldon*.[6]

The first task of the Academic Planning Board was to appoint a Vice-Chancellor who was in sympathy with its aims and in June 1962 it was able to announce the appointment of Dr Albert Sloman, Gilmour Professor of Spanish and Dean of the Faculty of Arts at the University of Liverpool. Considerable publicity was given to the appointment and this was greatly increased when Dr Sloman was asked by the B.B.C. to deliver the Reith Lectures.[7] The University of Essex therefore had a high profile from the beginning.

When the new universities were established it was hoped that the opportunity would be taken to break away from the traditional pattern of higher education. Certain ideas at Essex, although they are widely accepted today, were ahead of their time and many people were wary of change. In 1963, when the Reith Lectures were delivered, universities were seen as being *in loco parentis* to a student body consisting largely of people under the age of majority. Some parents and teachers thought it unwise to send girls to a University that proposed to house male and female students in the same building without any residential warden in spite of the fact that the sexes were to be segregated by floor. Such arrangements are now commonplace throughout British universities and are no cause for concern. Many students nowadays are mature adults and a few of them have even retired after a lifetime's employment and it can now be seen that Essex's proposal to treat students as responsible adults, which seemed to some to be an alarming development at the time, was nothing more than an accurate anticipation of future trends. This is not to say that members of the university community are left without support in times of difficulty; academic and moral advice is freely available to all through many channels. Another academic rarity was the system of common first year studies designed to make it easier for students to change from a course that they found unsuitable. Today such flexibility is widely found.

runa prð þar seczar ꝼeaht he pæs onʒeþꝥanʒ hyꝥa þꝥeoꝥa bana æꝥ hī ꝥiʒeliner beaꝥn on þā pæle læʒe. þæꝥ pæꝥ ſtið ʒemot ſtoðon ꝼæꝥte. ꝥiʒan on ʒeꝥinne ꝥiʒenð cꝥuncon punðū peꝥiʒe pæl ꝼeol on eoꝥþan. Oꝼpolð ⁊ caðpolð ealle hꝥile beʒen þa ʒebꝥoþꝥu beoꝥnaꝼ tꝥymeðon hyꝥa ꝥinemaʒaꝼ poꝥðon bæðon. ꝥ hi þæꝥ æt ðeaꝥꝼe þolian sceolðon unpaclice pæꝥna neotan. Byꝥhtpolð maþelode boꝥð haꝼenoðe se pæꝼ ealð ʒeneat æſc ac pehte he ꝼul balðlice beoꝥnaꝼ læꝥðe. hi ʒe ꝼceal þe heaꝥðꝥa heoꝥte þe cenꝥe moð sceal þe maꝥe þe uꝥe mæʒen lytlað. heꝥ lið uꝥe ealðoꝥ eall ꝼoꝥ heapen ʒóð on ʒꝥeote amæʒ ʒnoꝥnian se ðe nu ꝼꝥā þiꝼ ꝥiʒ pleʒan penðan þenceð. ic eom ꝼꝥoð ꝼeoꝥeꝼ

The University Motto, 'Thought the Harder, Heart the Keener', is adapted from a line of an Old English poem describing the Battle of Maldon, fought in 991 between marauding Vikings and an army of East Saxons led by Byrhtnoth, Ealdorman of Essex. The earliest printed version, shown here in detail, appeared as an Appendix to Johannis, confratris et monachi Glastoniensis, chronica, sive Historia de rebus Glastoniensibus. Descripsit edititque Tho. Hearnius. (Oxonii, 1726), *vol. 2, p.577.*

The planners of the University certainly looked to the future but it has to be said that their proposals were in no sense revolutionary and in retrospect they look rather cautious. They could hardly be otherwise because the time-scale for the establishment of the University was very short. The first intake of students arrived a mere 36 months after the Academic Planning Board first met and by then staff had been appointed, courses planned, temporary office, teaching, library and laboratory accommodation constructed, a long-term architectural plan drawn up, and the construction of permanent buildings put in hand. It was a heady time and looking back it is hard to believe that so much of substance could have been achieved in so short a period. It says much for the founding fathers that their work remains very evident today and that the academic standing that the University now enjoys is directly due to ideas that were aired at the preliminary planning meetings.

This is not to say that mistakes were not made in the early years. With hindsight it might have been better for the architectural plan not to assume that funds would automatically be made available for several years to come, but that was the general impression given at the time by the Government. Many of the architectural features that now seem less than ideal stem from the unexpected financial cuts in capital provision for higher education in the second decade of the University's life. The residential towers are much criticized but it has to be remembered that high-rise buildings were very fashionable in the Sixties. The proposed social organization on the assumption that the University was a community of adult scholars and that all facilities should be open to staff and students alike and managed in common soon required modification. Staff and students do not necessarily share interests whatever their ages and there will always be a large number of younger students who will benefit from learning to organize and administer their own affairs in a practical and responsible way. There is now a thriving Student's Union employing its own staff, but the original concept is retained in so far as most of the Union's facilities remain available to the whole community. In spite of the changes over the years as the University has faced the ever-varying political and economic climate of the country it has remained largely faithful to the ideas of the founders.

In summary, the original plan was to concentrate initially on teaching a limited range of subjects but to teach them in depth and to recruit the very best academics available. The Departments, where appropriate, were to be linked in Schools of Study and also through a system of Area Studies, in which the Soviet Union, the United States, amd Latin America were selected as the areas in which it would be in the long-term national interest to develop detailed expertise. It was not enough to advertise and hope for good applicants: people of experience and reputation had to be sought out and encouraged to apply, and not surprisingly the early staff appointments included nationals from countries other than Britain. In Dr Sloman the Committee had found the very person to put the plan into practice and during his long service as Vice-Chancellor he never wavered from seeking staff of the highest calibre and he never lost sight of the overall plan.

There is still a wide misconception within the County as to the character of its eponymous University. Some people believe it to be a technological university while others, knowing its strength in the Social Sciences, are surprised to hear of the existence of its large Departments in the traditional sciences, but there has always been a balance. By the time that the first one hundred students had taken their degrees there were eleven Departments teaching and engaging in research in subjects ranging from Art History or Literature at one end of the spectrum of knowledge to Chemistry or Physics at the other. This breadth of interest has always been maintained.

The courses to be offered by the University when teaching began in 1964 showed an awareness of the needs of the County as well as of the country. The decision to concentrate on the Physical Sciences was not only a convenient counter-balance to the University of East Anglia's preference for the Life Sciences, it was also a recognition of the economic situations of the two counties. The establishment of a Department of Physics, soon supplemented by a Department of Electrical Engineering Science, was a direct acknowledgement of the practical importance of these subjects to local industries and the founding professor was recruited from a Government research establishment. It is worthy of note that of the staff recruited within the first three years for this one department three people subsequently became Fellows of the Royal Society and two of these were still teaching in the University 30 years later. On the other hand the establishment of the School of Comparative Studies and, in particular, of the Department of Literature was a deliberate attempt to create a new and wider horizon not catered for in other universities. The founding professor of literature was a Cambridge academic, already established as an eminent poet and literary critic, whose reputation continued to increase for many years after he had left to take up a Chair in the United States. It remained undiminished at his recent death and many of his obituaries mentioned the innovative nature of the courses that he developed at Essex, which aim to expose the students to a wide range of literatures and to place them in a cultural setting to remind them that there is a world outside of, but closely related to, books.

The importance of computers was recognized at an early stage and the founding professor in this case was a man who had been closely involved with the early development of computer programming and whose work at Manchester University had produced the Autocodes for what is thought to have been the world's first commercially available computer.[8] He later headed a small research group that produced the operating system for the Atlas computer and when he came to Essex he was followed by two of his team. The Department of Computer Science was established by people who were known to be at the forefront of their speciality.

The three foundation Social Science departments, Economics, Government, and Sociology were all headed by academics of distinction and they were encouraged to develop expertise within the Area Studies framework, as were those engaged in the teaching of the Humanities. Introductory courses in the

General view of one of the University's five Squares. In the summer the Squares are thronged with
students holding animated discussions in many foreign languages.

appropriate languages were available for students proposing to specialize in any of the areas.

It is possible to establish a university within a matter of a few years but it takes very much longer to establish an academic reputation. Oxford, Cambridge, and London are not to be rivalled overnight and students normally have to have graduated from their universities for some time before they become of any consequence in the world. In most callings careers are not to be hurried but there are of course always exceptions and it has long been possible for a reunion of former Essex undergraduates to gather together a Secretary of State, a Vice-Chancellor, a prominent B.B.C. commentator, and a Booker Prize winner. This is a matter of great satisfaction but of equal satisfaction is the solid range of less public but well-respected figures among our former students. Some hold professorial chairs in the sciences and have been asked to deliver prestigious lectures, others have achieved similar success in the social sciences and the arts. The range is extensive. A whole generation has passed since the first small group of students achieved their degrees and the University is today paid the compliment of receiving applications from their children. After 30 years it is possible to try to make a reasonably sober assessment of how far the aims of the founders have been achieved and even to see if they have been surpassed.

The University is now one of the largest employers in north-east Essex and it has weathered the recession somewhat better than many local businesses, which has been to the benefit of the local community. Public 'Town and Gown' lectures in the Moot Hall are now a regular feature of life in Colchester as are many of the public lectures given on campus, and the University is heavily involved in the production of a Talking Newspaper for the blind of the region. Formal educational opportunities are offered to the County through the University's Continuing Education courses held in various locations throughout Essex and all departments hold Open Days for sixth-form students. Many other contributions are made to educational activity within the County. The Science Centre, for example, has brought countless science teachers and pupils into the University to learn about the latest scientific developments and it has sent university teachers to many schools. It provides a science service on the Internet to schools and the outside world, one element of which is an interactive photographic 'science trail' round Colchester for Primary School children.

The artistic and cultural life of the area has been enhanced. The University has organized many concerts with performances by internationally renowned musicians. There is a modest theatre and an equally modest art gallery, both of which are associated with the academic work of the University and which also offer programmes of professional events. The Gallery's role within the regional context is taken very seriously but it also plays a large part in the M.A. course in Gallery Studies where students are taught by members of the Department of Art, some of whom have been responsible for major exhibitions abroad and in this country at such places as the Tate Gallery, the Hayward Gallery, and the Edinburgh International Festival. The University also has the only public collection in Europe of Latin American art, containing over 200 paintings by many of the most famous artists of that continent. The Department of Literature, which over the years has accommodated a series of distinguished international literary figures and which has on its staff a nationally-known practising playwright, offers a practical element, open to the public, in connection with its academic work on the drama. The University has now established a Centre for Theatre Studies which runs a course on Shakespearean theatre in conjunction with the Royal Shakespeare Company.

Of more specific local interest is the Local History Centre which offers extra-mural courses and lectures in addition to its regular work. In any week between September and April there will be some 75 people in Wivenhoe Park studying local history. For those who find difficulty in getting to the University joint courses with the Essex Record Office are held at Chelmsford. A generous grant from the County has enabled the establishment of an Essex County Fellowship in Local History.

In these and in many other ways the establishment of the University can be seen to have fulfilled the planners' aim of benefiting the County and there have been similar benefits to the country at large. Work in the Department of Physics has developed lasers and their use in measuring light, has investigated the quantum theory of light, and has increased our knowledge of how electrons work in semi-conductors. Recent work on single photons promises to have great significance in telecommunications and this is of great interest to the Department of Electronic Systems Engineering which has made many pioneering studies in this field. The latter Department has helped to develop digital communications networks which provide better quality of speech, facsimile and video connections over national and international networks, and is now helping to introduce 'intelligent' network features stemming from the merging of computers and telecom-munications. The Department of Chemistry has worked in collaboration with industry to produce commercially available products assisting the treatment of heart disease in hospitals. The Department of Biology has discovered one of the most productive plants in the world, capable of producing 100 tonnes of dry matter per hectare per year, a discovery that opens up new perspectives in agriculture. This Department contains one of the country's foremost researchers in the effects of global climate change on crops and native plant species and the effects of pollutants on the ability of wheat to grow, work that is obviously of importance to an over-crowded planet. One of the most interesting developments arising from the original structure has been in the study of languages. Originally founded as a service centre to provide teaching in the foreign languages associated with the Area Studies programme it has gradually developed into a full Department of Language and Linguistics internationally renowned, amongst other things, for its work in the study of First and Second language acquisition in children.

The range of Departments has been extended: Philosophy and Psychology are now taught and Europe and Japan have been added to the Area specialities. It should be mentioned that the Areas are not exclusive; the Department of History, for instance, runs courses on South Africa and China, and the Department of Literature's interests are world wide. There are now two departments, those of Law and of Accounting and Financial Management, that look towards the professions. The individual departments are in general larger than their counter parts in other universities in this country, sometimes markedly so.[9] The student enrolment of 5,423 in 1995 is within the range envisaged in 1962.

It is the custom for each Vice-Chancellor or Principal of any institution of higher education in this country to submit an annual report to the governing body. These reports usually look very similar because they all tend to record remarkable progress and achievement in the face of considerable difficulty whilst maintaining standards of academic excellence. This is hardly surprising because all universities operate under similar constraints and academic excellence is an agreed common aim. It is impossible for all universities to share a common standard by which academic excellence is measured nor is it likely that any university could honestly believe that all of its departments had attained a uniform degree of excellence. Attempts have been made by outside bodies, however, to assess individual departments and the U.G.C. rated six of the then 15 Departments at Essex as being 'outstanding by international standards'. Most of the other Departments had to make do with merely achieving high national rankings but, given the exacting standards set by the U.G.C. this was a very respectable result indeed and a remarkable achievement for a comparatively recent foundation. The policy of establishing a few large departments has proved a success.

It is one of the aims of the University to develop those areas where the interests of the individual Departments overlap. The Brooker Laboratory for Intelligent Embedded Systems provides an innovative approach to teaching computer science by utilizing mobile robots, and it is thought to be unique in allowing such diverse subjects as electronics, computer science and psychology to be supported within a unified experimental environment. This kind of teaching and research is necessary to build the intelligent machines of the future. The Laboratory has been supported by national and international bodies and is now able to provide students with the same hardware and software as is used, for example, by N.A.S.A. for the Mars landing, British Aerospace for 'fly by wire' aircraft, and the French T.G.V. rail system.

It was entirely predictable that the University should acquire a reputation for the quality of its Social Science Departments. The planners had always intended that Essex should be 'a place noted for certain fields of study' and the Reith Lectures pointed to a national need for more research in every aspect of modern societies and to the need to ensure that the demands created by social and economic change are adequately met. From the very beginning Essex offered courses in Economics, Government, and Sociology and each of these Departments can claim to be among the very best in the country. They have developed exceptionally close links and they form a collective powerhouse that has attracted considerable ourside support and in return, as will be seen later, they provide information and

Two Japanese students showing the model of the Aoi Festival Procession presented to the University by Mrs S. Ogawa. The procession is held annually on 15 May at Kyoto, Japan.

direction that is highly important for the governance of the country. Many of the staff regularly appear on television or can be heard on the radio as expert commentators on domestic and international affairs. The Department of Government is particularly well-known in this respect. The School of Social Sciences has an international reputation and has not surprisingly proved to be highly attractive to postgraduate students. The Social Sciences are indeed a field of study for which Essex is particularly noted.

The University is by no means alone in offering certain things that are unique. That is a happy situation for higher education in this country. Essex, however, is unusual in the emphasis that it places on the interdisciplinary character of its activities and there are many ways in which this emphasis has affected the University. The academic staff may each have their own specialities but the undergratuate course structure brings them into close contact with those who profess other disciplines whilst research is greatly enriched by the members of individual departments joining together in Centres of Study of which there are many covering various subject groups.[10] There is even a Centre for Theoretical Studies that has no specific disciplinary orientation but which aims to stimulate contacts between different theoretical approaches and which, for example, discusses models of rationality in such disciplines as economics, political science, and philosophy, or the generalization of linguistic models in the various fields of the social sciences.

It has to be admitted that many achievements similar to those that have been reviewed so far might well be claimed by some, if not several, other British universities. There is, however, one aspect in which Essex is exceptional. It is not one that was specifically intended by the founders but it was certainly in their minds[11] and it stems naturally from the decision to seek a distinctive pattern of research concentrated in a few specialities and linked by an outward-looking system of area studies. This concept attracted an international staff which established an international reputation for the University. Essex is almost certainly the most internationally-minded of all the universities of the United Kingdom; in 1995 31 per cent of its students came from overseas and 104 countries were represented. Of the total of 5,423 registered students 1,671 were from overseas, 671 of whom came from other countries in the European Union.

The value to this country is immeasurable and is not to be considered in crude terms of the money that these students bring to this country or to the County. They will return to important positions in their own countries and it is hoped that their experience here will make them well disposed towards Britain; the real gain, however, is in the exposure of our own nationals to so many different cultures, not only socially but also to the varied and enriching contribution that these students make to seminars on political and social matters. One such student, Dr Oscar Arias Sanchez, who enrolled specifically because of Essex's international reputation in Latin American Studies, and who maintains close links with this country and the University, later became President of Costa Rica and joint winner of the Nobel Peace Prize as well as the individual winner of several other international prizes.

Innovation and co-operation and an international approach are always encouraged. The Department of Law, for instance, has always been active in teaching many of the international aspects of law and is inevitably much involved in teaching the law of the European Union. It soon recognized that this should not be left in the hands of specialists working in this country and that there was a need to bring together a cross-section of the member states. It accordingly took the initiative to found the Pallas Consortium, of which one of its members is Chairman, bringing together six universities in the Union to create and teach an advanced course in European Business Law. This is obviously an important contribution to the expertise available in this country but it is also innovative in the sense that it moves away from the typical programme designed at one institution to which outsiders are invited to contribute, aiming instead at a joint design of a truly common curriculum. As a further benefit, collaborative research projects have already emerged among the network of teachers thus created.

The growth of the University has largely coincided with the evolution of what is now the European Union and it was only to be expected that a university noted for the social sciences would pay close attention to the developments in western Europe. The European Consortium for Political Research was established in 1970 with its headquarters in the Department of Government, largely through the initiative of the founding Professor, bringing together European institutes of higher education primarily engaged in teaching and research in political science. The eight founding members came from five countries but within a year there were 25 members and the E.C.P.R. now encompasses some 215 institutions from 15 countries representing some 4,000 individual political scientists in western Europe. It is an extremely active organization and each year it holds at the University a Summer School in Social Science Data Analysis that has by now been attended by a large proportion of the European political science profession. The E.C.P.R. is now one of the largest and most important scholarly associations in the social sciences in the western world.

The University offers degree schemes specifically based on European themes which are co-ordinated by a Centre that brings together the activities of the various departments. It by no means restricts its interests to western Europe and it seeks to encourage interdisciplinary and comparative studies of the development of all European countries. The University also arranges for many of its students to spend some time abroad through an active 'Year Abroad Programme'. The Albert Sloman Library has been designated as a 'European Documentation Centre' and maintains a comprehensive collection of the Union's official publications.

Other activities on campus look to a wider field than Europe for the University houses a unit of the Scientific Committee on the Problems of the Environment that has since 1983 been recognized as the international centre for information on the environmental consequences of nuclear weapons. Originally

Dr Hans-Dietrich Genscher, Minister for Foreign Affairs and Deputy Chancellor of the Federal Republic of Germany from 1974 to 1992, who received an Honorary Doctorate from the University in 1993.

established by the Royal Society to conduct work on the 'nuclear winter' its remit was later extended to studying the effects of the Chernobyl disaster and of nuclear test explosions.

The emphasis on international aspects does not mean that Britain is in any way neglected. The reputation of the three original Social Science departments together with the University's known ability in computing was instrumental in making Essex a national information centre. The E.S.R.C. Data Archive at the University, which is jointly funded by the Economic and Social Research Council, the Higher Education Funding Council, and the University, houses the largest collection of accessible computer-readable data in the Social Sciences and Humanities in the United Kingdom. It disseminates data throughout the United Kingdom and, by arrangement with other national archives, throughout the world. Founded in 1967 it now houses approximately 4,000 fully catalogued data sets of interest to researchers in all sectors and from many different disciplines. In addition it holds a special collection of about 3,000 commercial opinion polls. Central Government, and in particular the office of Populations Censuses and

The R. A. B. Butler Building that houses the E.S.R.C. Research Centre on Micro-Social Change and the British Household Panel Study.

Surveys, is a major and regular source of data. Of particular importance are the regular repeated surveys such as the General Household Survey, the Labour Force Survey, and the Family Expenditure Survey which collectively represent a major research resource for the study of most aspects of social and economic life in Britain during the second half of the twentieth century. The Archive acts, in conjunction with the University of Durham, as a Resource Centre for access to data on Europe. Its resources are made available at cost to academic researchers but fees are charged to commercial users who are more than happy to pay for such useful public domain information that would otherwise be difficult to recover. To some people this may all seem distressingly contemporary and intrusive. They may be somewhat reassured to know that the Archive contains a rapidly expanding History Data Unit which contains files with information from the nineteenth century censuses, poll books and trade directories and even texts from manor court rolls. The University has always been eager to apply modern technology to historical problems and it was a former member of the Department of Physics who directed the British Museum's inquiry into the dating of the Turin Shroud.

The E.S.R.C. appears to have been well pleased with the work of the Survey Archive because in 1989 it established at Essex one of the first social science Interdisciplinary Research Centres and followed this up in 1993 with a grant to a professor in the Department of Sociology to set up a Qualitative Data Archival Resource Centre. This triple vote of confidence from a national body stands as a testament to the strength of the social sciences at Essex.[12] The Research Centre on Micro-Social Change attempts to identify, explain, model and forecast social change in Britain at the individual and household level. It provides the Government and the country with a large-scale micro-data set derived from an annual national survey of some 10,000 individuals drawn from a representative sample of 5,500 households. The 'Qualidata' Centre has its roots in the Department of Sociology's long-standing work in the development of Oral History where it became apparent that there was a pressing need to identify and archive the wealth of material that was being destroyed or becoming untraceable. The Centre's work in dealing with this problem is now well in hand. All this activity may well seem a long way from the conventional research world of books but the Albert Sloman Library holds strong research collections of national and even European importance in the declared specialist areas of the University, whilst using modern electronic techniques to access and disseminate information from international sources.

A particularly good example of how the University has, from its own resources, brought academics together on a project with world-wide implications is the establishment of the Human Rights Centre which was founded in 1989 by members of the Departments of Law, Government, Philosophy, Sociology and Economics. This interdisciplinary centre aims to give a focus in Britain for teaching and research on the study of human rights and is distinctive in the emphasis that it gives to the integration of human rights theory and practice and in its concern

The Albert Sloman Library, opened in 1967, is probably the most successful of the campus buildings. It now holds more than twice the number of books and caters for twice the number of readers for which it was designed but plans are well advanced for an extension to the wing.

with international humanitarian law. The Centre has good relations with United Nations bodies, the Council of Europe and international and national non-governmental organizations; although it has special interests in Europe, it is world-wide in the scope of its activities and, for example, the Special Rapporteur on Torture appointed by the U.N. Commission on Human Rights is a member of the Centre. Other members have undertaken missions, litigated cases under the European Convention on Human Rights, written specially-commissioned reports, and assisted with training programmes for a variety of international bodies. They have worked for Amnesty International, Article 19, the International League for Human Rights, Helsinki Watch, and other organizations. One of the Centre's members has been involved in a variety of missions to the former Yugoslavia to investigate allegations of ethnic cleansing and of widespread and systematic rape. These wide-ranging activities have established an enviable reputation but they are not allowed to interfere with the Centre's purely academic work and students from all over the world are attracted to the postgraduate courses that it offers. Many of them go on to posts with inter-national organizations or to governmental posts in their native countries. The Centre has been selected by the Joseph Rowntree Charitable Trust to carry out the Democratic Audit of Great Britain, and by the Pew Charitable Trust to write a World Report on Freedom of Conscience, Religion or Belief.

Universities are independent institutions and are not run by the Government or by County Councils; through this independence they aim to preserve and to create the ideas on which this country and democratic societies in general depend. They are, however, far from being remote or divorced from society at large for it is from society that they ultimately draw their support and there has to be common agreement that they are, by and large, a 'good thing'. Over the past 30 years the University of Essex has done its best to be a good thing but like all universities, here and abroad, it has had to adapt to changes in the public perception of the purpose of a university and, inevitably, to the social and economic variations that have affected this country. The University still contains a very few people who have been there since the beginning. They have lived through good times and bad but it seems that, although the current situation is, to say the least, uncomfortable and the management of change has become more and more difficult, the University can be said to be in good shape and has achieved the expectations of its founders. Sir John Ruggles-Brise is perhaps the best person to pass judgement on this, and it is to be hoped that he approves of the institution with which he has been so closely associated.

Acknowledgements

All illustrations in this essay have been reproduced by courtesy of the University of Essex.

REFERENCES

1 The author was, until recently, on the staff of the University but the present essay has been written on a personal and entirely independent basis.

2 The opening paragraphs of this essay owe much to the papers of Mr Bungey that are kept in the Special Collections Room of the Albert Sloman Library at the University of Essex.

3 *First Report of the Academic Planning Board to the Promotion Committee, February, 1962*, University of Essex, p.4, para 8.

4 With the approval of and generous assistance from the Butler family the University has named one of its buildings and a Chair in History after Lord Butler.

5 The armorial bearings are reproduced on p.173. The shield incorporates the ancient arms attributed to the Kingdom of the East Saxons and granted to Essex County Council in 1932. The crest symbolizes the University's situation: the branches of oak, shaped like the Colchester ragged cross, suggest the parkland of Wivenhoe and the ancient forest of Essex. The branches pass through an annulet, or 'O', which with the Wyvern form a heraldic pun on the name Wivenhoe.

6 'Thought the Harder, Heart the Keener'. The Albert Sloman Library possesses a copy of the earliest printed version (1726) of the poem. The relevant text is reproduced on p.177.

7 Published as A. E. Sloman, *A University in the Making*, B.B.C., 1964.

8 The Ferranti Mark I computer, delivered in February 1951. Professor Tony Brooker developed one of the first high-level languages, Mark I Autocode, for the machine in 1954 thus pre-dating the FORTRAN language. A logic door and a Williams tube electrostatic memory unit from the Mark I are on permanent exhibition in the entrance vestibule of the Department of Mathematics.

9 The Department of Government, for example, is one of the largest and most prestigious in Europe, with 25 full-time teaching staff, 26 part-timers and over 160 graduate students, 100 of whom are studying for doctorates.

10 Centres have been established for European Studies; Psychoanalytic Studies; Russian Studies; Theatre Studies; Theoretical Studies; the Study of Theology; Cognitive Science; Contemporary Japan; Human Rights; Latin America; and the United States.

11 *First Report of the Academic Planning Board*, p.9, para 23.

12 The E.S.R.C. has also sponsored an 'East-West Initiative' aimed at developing academic links with Eastern Europe.

People and Pigeons in Symbiosis: Essex Dovecotes

JOHN H. BOYES

STANDING IN THE GROUNDS of Spains Hall adjacent to other farm buildings is a square brick structure of no great architectural merit crowned with a tiled pyramidal roof and crested with a small wooden lover. A building which could readily be passed by without a second glance yet its function reflects a remarkable relationship of man with feral nature. This simple structure, probably of eighteenth century construction, is a dovecote — or in the vernacular Essex a duffus — one of the sadly diminishing number which survive in Essex, indeed in the country as a whole, but which represents the last evidences of an economic tradition of pigeon keeping. Such a tradition is quite distinct from the present day enthusiasm and dedication of pigeon fancying. It is a tradition which has persisted for several thousand years — a tradition which is not only protracted in time but also one that has a widespread geographical distribution, undoubtedly reflecting a continuous transfer of agricultural technology.

But the fundamental question which must be asked is why and how this strange relationship between men and free-flying wild birds first started. Clearly it was a basic step different in concept from that pursued in the domestication of other wild animals and yet it was a successful triumph in progressive agriculture. The Comte de Buffon, the French naturalist writing at the end of the eighteenth century provides a succinct summary of this relationship.

'It was easy to domesticate the heavy and inactive bird, such as the common hen, the turkey and the peacock, but to tame those which are nimble and shoot on rapid wings, required attention and art. A low hut, rudely constructed on a confined spot is sufficient for lodging and raising our poultry: to induce the pigeons to settle we must erect a lofty building, well-covered without and fitted up with numerous cells. They really are not domestics like dogs or horses: or prisoners like fowls; they are rather voluntary captives, transient guests who continue to reside in the dwellings assigned them only because they like it and are pleased with the situation which affords them abundance of food, and all the conveniences and comforts of life.'[1]

193

Dovecote: Spains Hall, Finchingfield.

It is possible that early man noted the addiction of pigeons to nest gregariously in caves and on ledges relatively remote from disturbance, and their natural habit of returning to the same perching position. No doubt he eventually realized that if appropriate accommodation were provided he would derive economic advantage from their presence. Jeremiah, the prophet, alludes to this observation when he writes, 'Oh ye that dwell in Moab leave the cities and dwell in the rock and be like the dove that maketh her nest in the side of the hole's mouth'. Again in those past ages he must have discovered the advantages of forming a relationship. First that the eggs and young birds provided a welcome and readily available addition to his food supply, and second, as he began to understand the techniques of an agrarian economy he would realize that by collecting the droppings he had acquired a valuable fertilizer. This again is referred to in the Bible when we read in the Second Book of Kings, 'And there was a great famine in Samaria; and behold they besieged it until an ass's head was sold for four pieces of silver and the fourth part of a cab of dove's dung for five pieces of silver'. (A cab was a Hebrew dry measure of about two litres.)[2]

Despite its economic value, or perhaps because of it, the pigeon in ancient times was highly regarded as a beneficial sacrifice. The vast quantity of birds available is indicated by the reported sacrifice by Rameses III of 57,000 birds to the god Ammon at the end of 1100 B.C. A thousand years later as a sacrifice it was classed as 'The Offering of the Poor' as recorded by Luke concerning the Virgin Mary following the birth of Jesus Christ, 'And when the days of her purification acording to the Law of Moses were accomplished, they brought her to Jerusalem, to present Him to the Lord; and to offer sacrifice according to that which is said to be the Law of the Lord, a pair of turtle-doves or two young pigeons'.[3]

The pigeon's ability to find its way back to the nest even over long distances was also turned to advantage in early times in using it as a carrier pigeon. There are records of this practice from the Assyrian era and because it was faster than any other contemporary means of transmission the practice survived into the present century and was used in both peace and war. There were many occasions in both World Wars where carrier pigeons released in times of distress were instrumental in saving lives and there are memorials recording those feats.

It is clear that the evidence of the earliest economic use of pigeons is in the Middle East but as civilisation spread the practice followed, first to the Greeks and then to Rome. From there it was taken into Gaul and then in all probability into England. There is, however, as yet no positive archaeological evidence to establish its presence here. Nor is there, so far, any archaeological or documentary evidence of pigeon rearing in this country between the fourth and eleventh centuries. It seems that the Normans, having followed the Gallo-Roman tradition, then established or re-established the practice which has continued to the present day.

Obviously because of the limited scope of early Norman records it is impossible to judge how widespread the construction of specially designed accommodation

Dovecote: The Hall, Wenden Lofts. Exterior showing decorated cornice.

either in separate buildings or integrated in buildings used for other purposes might have been in both Normandy and Britain. Or indeed when the first dovecotes were built. However the rentals of the Abbaye de la Trinité and l'Hôpital de la Maison Dieu at Caen preserved in the Departmental Archives of Calvados suggest that dovecotes were normally to be found on Norman estates by the thirteenth century. A further document legalized the existence of those built before 1256. This being the custom there it may well have been similar to that existing in England.

An indication of their early introduction into England, apart from doveholes incorporated in the towers of e.g. Rochester and Conisbrough Castles is provided by the following extract:

> 'About prime (6 a.m.) on 16 February 1271 Alexander le Gardiner of Potton [Bedfordshire], Lady Christine de Fornival's servant, was digging under the walls of an old dovecote in the garden in Lady Christine's courtyard in Sutton to demolish them and, as he dug, the wall by misadventure fell upon him and broke his head so that he immediately died there. His wife, Alice, came with his breakfast, looked for him, saw his surcoat and cap and the spade with which he dug and so found him dead and his whole body broken. She immediately raised the hue, which was followed, and found pledges. The spade was worth 1½d.'[5]

If this were an old dovecote in 1271 and was being demolished it certainly suggests a probable original twelfth century date. Nevertheless reliable evidence for early dovecotes is difficult to find, though an early date can be presumed for one at Woodstock in Oxfordshire where an order was sent on 28 August 1239, 'To the keeper of the Manor of Woodstock, Contrabreve to cause the king's dovecote at Wodestok to be repaired where necessary'.

The realization that repairs and improvements had to be undertaken at this date suggests that there might be some truth in the theory that a recognition of their economic importance might stem from the return of Crusaders who had seen the value placed upon the keeping of pigeons in the Middle East.

So far as Essex is concerned no early records of dovecotes have come to light. None are mentioned in Domesday Book, where one would expect to find references to such a valuable estate asset, and the earliest recorded structures seem to have been associated, as might be expected, with monastic establishments. Thus the earliest record is that of the Manor of Feering, one of the manors of the Abbey of Westminster. In an extent of the manor dated 25 March 1289, as edited by Dr Clarke, 'The buildings comprised the Manor House, a Hall with a Solar ... within the Courtyard stood also the Chapel and the Manor Dove Cot'.[6]

The unembellished reference to the Manor Dove Cot implies that the acceptance of such structures on manorial land was not unusual at that time. Another early date for Essex is in the accounts of the Convent of Canterbury of 1293 regarding

Dovecote: The Hall, Wenden Lofts. Interior showing nesting holes and the potence. The latter, pivoting on the central column, allowed access to all the holes.

repairs to a pigeon cote at the monastic manor of Milton, Southend-on-Sea, again suggesting a much earlier date as in 1293 repairs were required.[7]

Early fourteenth century references are limited but one is mentioned at Bocking in 1311, also in monastic ownership. In 1319 William of Goldington, a lay owner, held one messuage, one dovehouse, 100 acres of arable land . . . in Aldham; and in 1323 at the Manor of Gibbecrake in Purleigh on a manor held by the de Veres of Hedingham there was a messuage, with a garden and dovehouse as well as a watermill and a windmill.

Documentary references begin to increase in the fifteenth century as more records survive but it remains an open question as to how many dovecotes existed at this time in Essex. Certainly none of those mentioned at this period now survive but later cotes could easily have replaced some of them.

Examples from Feet of Fines are as follows:

1405	Andrew Tele, Thomas Byrchelegh of Wytham *et al* acquired property including a dovecote either in Wytham, Fulkebourne or White Nottle.
1423	17 manors including Langford, Great Totham, Tolleshunt and Little Bentley were transferred, which included 8 windmills, 4 dovecotes, etc. and a comprehensive rent which included *inter alia* 20 roots of ginger, 12 lbs. of pepper and 20 red roses.

It is interesting that the start of increased references coincides with the end of the Wars of the Roses when there was a temporary relaxation of manorial privileges.

1479	The Manor of Leebury, Elmdon, included one dovehouse.
1479	A dovehouse in Chigwell.
1504	John Broke *et al* purchased for Edward Cardemaker the manor of Chingford Earls in Chingford which included a dovecote.

A further economic advantage was developed during this period when it was discovered that pigeon droppings were a valuable source of saltpetre which is an essential ingredient of gunpowder and collection of the droppings was a regular activity until the mid-seventeenth century. It is ironic that the products of the dove of peace became a constituent element in the pursuit of war.

Following the dissolution of the monasteries and the reallocation of estates, documentary references during property transfers became more frequent and a new era of construction begins. That this was also the period of the Great Rebuilding is not without significance and it is the fear of a similar proliferation of dovecotes in Brittany at the same period that led to more restrictions known as 'La Nouvelle Coutume' being issued in 1580.[8]

Dovecote: High House, Purfleet.

From this time there was a clear distinction occurring in Essex between the basic structure necessary for the day to day needs of the less affluent estates and the architectural status symbol of the greater estates. This became very evident in the seventeenth and early eighteenth centuries and can be seen in the surviving cotes today.

Probably the finest surviving dovecote in Essex, and beautifully maintained, is that at Wenden Lofts — though the place-name Lofts has no reference to the existence of the cote; it is a corruption of a personal name. It is a brick-built octagonal structure some 40 feet high with a decorative brick cornice at eaves level with about 1,500 nesting holes in the internal walls. The nests could be reached by a potence — a revolving pole to which are arms carrying a ladder. The flight holes are sealed so that there are no birds occupying the structure today. There is a single dormer window and a fine lover at the summit of the roof. It is possibly of sixteenth or early seventeenth century date. Quendon Hall has a similarly well-designed octagonal cote but on a smaller scale and is again of the seventeenth century. Other octagonal cotes with less architectural pretensions are at Downham Hall, which has recently been re-erected on a new site at High House, Purfleet where there is an outer and inner door for security against theft — the inner door is of iron, and at Castle Hedingham. There is only one surviving round cote in Essex in Writtle Park, though others formerly existed. In the western and northern counties round cotes are not uncommon. Octagonal and round cotes because of their shape allowed the use of the rotating potence to provide easier human access to the nests, though occasionally square cotes are provided with a potence as at Kentwell Hall, Long Melford, just over the border in Suffolk.

In Essex the majority of surviving dovecotes are square and the evidence of many now demolished is that they followed this pattern. Structurally they are either of timber-framed construction on a brick plinth or entirely of brick as at Spains Hall. But why square? Certainly a square structure is a more straightforward building to construct and as a working farm building it is in some ways analogous to similar farm buildings capable of being built by local labour without reference to outside architects. John McCann, however, propounds in a recent paper a very cogent reason.[9] The square structure would have for its roof four hips converging on a centre lover or four gables with their valleys similarly converging. The lover would frequently be similarly formed of four gablets or be a simple wooden cupola. In every case the roof slopes would provide perching positions to allow the birds to enjoy the warmth of the sun or else offer shelter from whichever direction the wind was blowing. This would be essential in counties such as Essex where the wind direction is so variable, unlike other areas where its direction is relatively constant.

Provision for perching is a requisite for pigeons and has been recognized from earliest times as one of the features embodied in the relationship of the birds with man. In the Middle East even today one can see adjacent to the nesting holes the perching poles jutting out horizontally from buildings. These poles are illustrated

Dovecote: High House, Purfleet.
Showing double doors, outer wooden and inner iron for security against theft.

very clearly in Carlo Crivelli's fifteenth century painting of 'The Annunciation' in the National Gallery.

Finally, within the cote itself were the nest holes, generally L-shaped, to allow the pigeons some privacy for laying and hatching their eggs. The nest holes could be formed of various materials including natural stone, brick or wood, and they are designed in tiers up the vertical face of the wall so as to accommodate the maximum number of birds within the structure. A provision which reflects the natural nesting arrangements of the wild birds and which has certainly benefited the birds themselves.

Essex thus demonstrates in its surviving cotes the later stages of man's association over several centuries with a bird which in some ways has become tame in that it is at home in a human environment and yet enjoys the consideration that man has offered but is certainly not domesticated. So in Essex there is a microcosm of economic advantages to man and mutual benefits to man and bird which for thousands of years have developed from this virtually unique remarkable symbiotic relationship.

REFERENCES

1 P. and J. Hansell, *Doves and Dovecotes*, 1988, p.39.
2 Jeremiah, chap. 48, verse 28.
3 Luke 2, verses 22 and 24.
4 'Le Droit de Colombier en Normandie Sous l'Ancien Regime', *Annales de Normandie*, March 1984, p.62.
5 *Bedfordshire Coroners Rolls*, Bedfordshire Historical Record Society, 103, p.47.
6 Cambridge University Library, MS KK 5, 29; *Essex Review*, vol. XXI, p.210.
7 D. Smith, *Pigeon Cotes and Dove Houses of Essex*, 1931, p.61. Quoting from Morant.
8 'Le Colombier: Un Signe Exterieur de Noblesse', *Annales de Bretagne*, tome LXXXVIII, 1 March 1981.
9 J. McCann, 'An Historical Enquiry into the Design and Use of Dovecotes', *Ancient Monuments Society Transactions*, vol. 35, 1991, p.120.

Patrons, Artists and Craftsmen in Essex

IRIS WOODWARD

Introduction — a rich inheritance

'At a certain stage in social development, fluid capital is one of the chief causes of civilisation because it ensures three essential ingredients — leisure, movement and independence. It also allows that slight superfluity of wealth that can be spent on nobler proportions . . . a high degree of civilisation in the purely materialistic sense of the word.' Sir Kenneth Clark was referring chiefly to the seventeenth century in Holland but his remarks are true of any age and are particularly relevant to the study of patrons.

In our appreciation of works of art we tend to neglect those who have collected them, paid for them, preserved them and bequeathed them to this generation — from the churchwardens who put their initials on roof beams as at Writtle, Little Sampford, Gestingthorpe for example, to those who ordered wall painting to be done as at Waltham Abbey, Copford, Terling, Great Canfield, Belchamp Walter and elsewhere, stone and woodcarving on screens and bench ends, ironwork on church doors as at Bocking and Eastwood, pargetting, apart from its practical use, to please the eye as at Saffron Walden, Newport and on countless other buildings.

These are the unknown patrons, but there are unusual and interesting ones such as the Marneys who introduced Italian workmanship in the terracotta window frames of their magnificent gatehouse at Layer Marney along with delightful dolphins, pineapples and winged cherubs. Similarly in the sixteenth century there were murals at Hill Hall, painted in the time of Sir Thomas Smith, the erudite scholarly Secretary of State to Queen Elizabeth, of classical and religious subjects 'without parallel among surviving examples in England'; they reveal the type of interior decoration of great houses in Tudor times and are the only known examples of the art of the 'painter-stainers'. They were uncovered in 1939 and 1951 and were removed to the Victoria and Albert Museum for safety.

Essex has had a long relatively prosperous and undisturbed history with great wealth at various times from the wheatlands and the cloth trade. In addition to the great families who gave their patronage to well-known artists and craftsmen,

Wivenhoe Park, Essex, 1816 by John Constable.
(Photograph courtesy of the Board of Trustees, National Gallery of Art, Washington, U.S.A.)

there were prosperous merchants, some of whom retired from London to form new estates. One of these was Samuel Tufnell who settled at Great Waltham in the seventeenth century and built a house, Langleys, which contained some of the richest Jacobean plasterwork in England, decorated with caryatids, figures of ease and plenty, fruit and foliage. Another was Thomas Paycocke of Coggeshall who built in the sixteenth century a house for his son with handsome carvings, linenfold panelling, naturalistic foliage and oriel windows, or the rich merchants who settled at Dedham and beautified the church.

There are the great families such as for example at Audley End, Ingatestone and St. Osyth where the patrons could offer more permanent and continuous support, not only for painting but in sculpture and furnishings. We have lost some of the most important, as at Wanstead where the art collection was sold in 1712 and 1825 when the house was demolished. We have only Hogarth's painting 'Assembly at Wanstead House' (now in Philadelphia and a sketch in the Tate Gallery) to give us any idea of the magnificence and the grandeur of the ballroom, seen in the late afternoon, with tapestry, furnishings, paintings and sculpture. Copped Hall was destroyed by fire in 1917 but its finest treasures had already gone to Knowle. Moulsham Hall, rebuilt in the eighteenth century for Lord Mildmay, was filled by him with sculptures and paintings, for example, by Honthorst and Wootton, portraits 'at full length' and 'a fowle piece with a peacock in it at large', a Rembrandt among other works, all dispersed and the house demolished in 1864.

Although we connect Gainsborough mostly with Suffolk it is worth remembering his very early painting of Mr and Mrs Andrews at Bulmer in Essex shown in the background of his corn sown and drilled in the latest fashion — a setting obviously demanded of the artist by the proud owner. Constable, too, we connect more with Suffolk but it is a pleasant reminder of the generosity of some patrons that General Rebow encouraged a struggling artist by commissioning portraits to be painted at Wivenhoe and asking for a landscape (now in the U.S.A.) of his house and grounds, albeit with demands which Constable found very exacting, 'the great difficulty has been to put so much in as they wanted and to make them acquainted with the scene'. He had to add strips of canvas to each side of the picture 'so that my view comprehends so many angles'. The grounds had been landscaped by Richard Wood in 1776 and had to be shown to their best advantage. General Rebow was prepared to advance payment to help with Constable's proposed marriage; both are examples of the restrictions and generosity between patron and artist.

There are so many examples of those who encouraged the arts in Essex that I am going to restrict this chapter to some only of the arts and crafts, tempting though it is to describe the architectural background. So we will look at a few examples of the use of 'fluid capital' and 'superfluity of wealth' that were spent by Essex families on the arts and crafts and follow that through to the twentieth century when the whole idea of patronage has changed.

(Photograph courtesy of the Essex Record Office)

Ingatestone Hall, 1829, engraved by R. Acon from a sketch by T. Barber for the Excursions through Essex.

The knightly residence at Ingatestone

Presiding over the family portraits at Ingatestone Hall is Sir William Petre. Over four centuries of family social history are shown in paintings by highly fashionable artists — in addition to collections brought in through bequests and marriage.

His own portrait shows the face of a clever shrewd man, of a man with a cool head and a quiet tongue which enabled him to hold office under Henry VIII, Edward VI, Mary I, and Elizabeth I, and to survive in unique and unbroken service through the cut-throat world of Tudor politics. Almost alone among his contemporaries he escaped the Tower, the block, fines and exile and yet earned the reputation of an honest man, neither rapacious nor a rogue. We do know that he was a distinguished scholar and 'a man of approved wisdom and exquisite learning' according to Camden.

After studying Law at Oxford and five years abroad he returned to Oxford to become a Doctor of Law in 1533 and became assistant to Thomas Cromwell in ecclesiastical matters. He became Master of Chancery, K.C., and eventually Principal Secretary. In 1540 he acquired a small estate with the title of Esquire and Lord of the Manor of Gynge Abbess in Essex for a country retreat and started building Ingatestone Hall in 1540, then within easy reach of London. It is typical that he chose to have a modest house in comparison with Layer Marney and Leighs Priory, too modest for the fashion of the time but sufficient for his own needs. From 'an olde house scant mete for a fermor to dwell on' he created a knightly residence with orchard and gardens and 'a wholly one very fayr and stately gallery or walke mete for any man of honor to come into'. It was a fairly early example of a Long Gallery which was rapidly becoming the fashion set by Hampton Court in 1535. Edward VI at Windsor Castle in 1549 complained bitterly 'methinks I am in prison, here be no galleries nor gardens to walk in'.

In the seventeenth century especially the collecting of portraits became a passion. John Evelyn said that 'only in face painting have the English made their mark'. Portrait painting in England had been dominated by foreigners since the time of Holbein and artists were thought of as mere craftsmen. There was no academy of art here until the early eighteenth century when Kneller formed his School, and not until Georgian times was landscape recorded by competent artists.

Sir William's gallery is well proportioned, furnished and decorated and still has some of its original heraldic stained glass. There we see Sir William in his gown, three-quarter length as was the fashion of the time, and wand of office, gloves, black cap, white ruff, and Chancellor's badge of the Order of the Garter and his coat of arms. A hieratic portrait, too, is that of his second wife modest in black bonnet and dress with white ruffs and cuffs, a watch on a ribbon round her neck, holding gloves and a jewelled pomander — both of 1567 by an unknown artist.

The two portraits of his son and wife of 1590 are much more colourful and relaxed (thought to be by Marcus Gheeraedts) showing fashionable changes in

Mary Waldegrave, wife of Sir John Petre, c.1595, by Marcus Gheeraedts.
(Photograph courtesy of the Essex Record Office)

costume. John Petre, created baron, but a much less forceful character than his father, a diligent landowner and public figure and a competent musician and friend of Byrd, wears a white ruff over a lace collar, embroidered doublet, the popular full breeches, bobbed hair, moustache and slight beard and, in the fashion of the time, the minute patch of hair below the bottom lip. It is unfortunately much restored after the fire at Thorndon Hall. His wife is equally in fashion — the cartwheel-topped skirt, the full upper sleeves and a variation of the ruff open in front to show the neck, a delicate silver tiara and the splendid rope of pearls, 1466 in all. She was fatherless and poor but gave her parents-in-law 'much joy in his choice'.

They employed, too, Cornelius Johnson, a modest painter of specifically English character, quite distinctive, no rhetoric but very sensitive to the sitter. Portraits change with the period and include Robert 'the adventurous baron' and Arabella Fermor who figures so prominently in Pope's 'Rape of the Lock'. He was celebrated for spending six hours a day having his own hair dressed as a wig.

There was a period when less important painters were employed, during the time when the family were barred from public office by their faith, and withdrew from court circles. After the Catholic Relief Acts there were paintings by Romney, one for example of the ninth baron Petre (about whom Lord Petre has written an essay in this book) in his short powdered wig and Parliamentary robes showing a plan of the rebuilding of Thorndon Hall (to which the family had moved soon after Sir William died, using Ingatestone as a dower house or for the use of the married son) and one of his wife by Andrea Casali showing signs of culture with crayons and portfolio of drawings. There is a delightful painting of the ninth Lord Petre with his eldest son and greyhounds and horse by Stubbs. Then comes Raeburn with a characteristic work of the eleventh baron. Other artists brought into the collection by bequests and marriages include J. M. Kneller, Van Loo, Lely and landscapes by Griffier.

It is interesting and a sign of his important rank that Sir William's tomb in Ingatestone Church shows him, as by right, in a Knight's armour, though as David Piper says 'if ever a man was a Secretary by nature and by calling it was he'.

The Fanshawe Patronage

At the southernmost edge of the county is the remarkable collection of the Fanshawe family. It is now safely and elegantly housed in the attractive Valence House Museum, Dagenham, the neighbouring property of the original site of the Parsloes property, owned by the family over nine generations. The house was demolished unfortunately in 1922 and the collection was given to the Borough Council in 1963 by the last survivor of that line.

The family is well recorded, coming from Derbyshire to Ware Park, Hertfordshire and then to Parsloes, Essex. They lived the life of ordinary country

Sir Richard Fanshawe by William Dobson, c.1644.
(Photograph courtesy of Valence House Museum, the London Borough of Barking and Dagenham)

gentlemen, taking part in public affairs, some having a distinguished career as 'king's servants' and in the army and navy, throughout the sixteenth to nineteenth centuries when the family moved to London.

They were patrons of the Arts throughout 300 years, from the time of Elizabeth I, with portraits, manuscripts, maps, letters and other papers. The family used the most well known artists of each generation, beginning with Marcus Gheeraedts and Cornelius Johnson. There is a particularly charming painting by William Dobson an English painter, Van Dyck's successor, of Sir Richard Fanshawe, a classical scholar, poet and translator, with his hound, the god Alpheo and a mask of drama. He took an active Royalist part in the Civil War, was imprisoned after the battle of Worcester, and later as a diplomat helped to arrange the marriage of Charles II to Catherine of Braganza. His wife's portrait by Cornelius Johnson is there too. She was the writer of most vividly interesting memoirs, describing the dangers she shared with her husband in the war and later in Spain and Portugal.

There are paintings also by Lely, in his Van Dyck style and a specially charming double portrait of Sir Thomas Fanshawe and his wife in 1659, some by Hudson, Kneller, Richardson and Romney and some by the school of Reynolds.

There are fewer portraits in the nineteenth and twentieth centuries but fortunately a striking one of Captain Aubrey R. Fanshawe, by Fraser, of 1912, who gave the collection to the Borough. It is housed in suitably charming furnished rooms; one is the original fine panelled room of Valence House itself.

An 'altogether stately palace'

In the eighteenth century Audley End had the good fortune to fall into the hands of a great benefactor, John Griffin Griffin, who had inherited from the Countess of Portsmouth at a time of great dilapidation and who set out to restore and rebuild its fortunes with great diligence and sensitivity.

Described as 'one of the most famous of any stately mansions which have been the glory of the English countryside for the past 400 years', it is situated near Saffron Walden on the site of the former Benedictine abbey of Walden. It was given to Sir Thomas Audley in 1538 at the time of the Suppression and he converted the monastic buildings into his 'chiefe & capital mansion house at Walden'. His black marble tomb lies in Saffron Walden church and is described by Fuller as 'no blacker than the heart of him whose bones lie beneath'. His daughter Margaret married Thomas Howard, Duke of Norfolk, and their son became Baron Howard de Walden, Earl of Suffolk and High Treasurer of England in 1614. He decided in 1603 to create a magnificent mansion in Anglo-Flemish style dramatically larger than the present building, 'too large for a king but might do for a Lord Chancellor' according to James I on a visit there. He overspent and was convicted for embezzlement, heavily fined and deprived of his office.

Sir John Griffin Griffin by Benjamin West, P.R.A., 1772.
(Photograph courtesy of English Heritage, Audley End House)

After the Restoration it was sold in 1669 to Charles II, and at this time described by John Evelyn as 'showing without like a diadem by the decorations of the cupola and other adornments'. Pepys, visiting the house (and playing his flageolet there), commented on the excellent pictures there, though seven years later he said there was not a good picture there. Celia Fiennes in 1697 described it as 'a fine and altogether a stately palace'.

In 1701 it was restored to the family. By 1745 six earls had occupied the house and the cost of maintainance proved crippling in spite of Sir John Vanburgh's scheme of partial demolition. By 1727 Defoe described it as 'the ruin of one of the largest and most magnificent piles in all this part of England'. When the tenth Earl died without issue in 1745 the contents of the house were disposed of and it was left empty.

On the point of demolition in 1747 Lady Portsmouth inherited and rescued the building, bequeathing it in 1760 to her nephew, Sir John Griffin Griffin, who eventually took the title of Lord Howard de Walden and Baron Braybrooke. A former career soldier he was a man of high integrity and, having determined to restore the ancestral state of the house and estate, he did it with good taste.

He was very wealthy with a rich wife and no children — it was a period of greater prosperity for landowners at this time. He had great business acumen and set out to cope with formidable repairs. He employed only the best craftsmen, making use of the material on site as well as having bricks made on the estate, buying stone from Burwell, Ketton and Portland so that the remodelling was done in harmony with the older parts of the house; wood and timber came from the estate and from the Baltic.

Unfortunately the flower of the art collection seems to have been dispersed before Lady Portsmouth rescued the estate. The family had obviously employed the most well-known artists and there were additional paintings added to the collection through marriage to the Cornwallis, Neville and Griffin families.

It was Sir John Griffin Griffin who brought together the collection of sixteenth and seventeenth century owners and purchased other items such as landscapes by van Goyen, Canaletto and Berchem for example and other cabinet pictures. He added valuable furniture, sculpture, ornaments and tapestries suitable for the house and he commissioned William Peck of York to design the windows for the 'Gothick' chapel.

From the earliest portraits thought to be of the first Lord Chancellor Audley and his wife and the Lady Mary Howard, Duchess of Norfolk, beautifully shown in the formal style of Hans Eworth, they ranged through Mytens, Cornelius Johnson, J. M. Wright and Honthorst to Charles Jarvis' touchingly simple rendering of Dorothy Walpole, Viscountess Townsend. Lely's fashionable faces are there in the Grey family along with the more unusual 'self-portrait with Hugh May'. There remain a few polite Augustan masks by Kneller and a likeness of Admiral Matthew Whitewell by Reynolds and include more informal work by Zoffany, Hoppner, Lawrence and Beechey. Then there is a Pine's version of George II, said to have been painted from a closet without the King's knowledge as he

Audley End, the Tea Bridge by Robert Adam, c.1780.
(Photograph courtesy of English Heritage, Audley End House)

detested having his likeness taken. Benjamin West, P.R.A., was chosen by Sir John for his own formal portrait showing him full length as the first Lord Braybrooke and as a General, along with a 'Kit Kat of his Lady and of his late Lady' in the guise of Sibyls.

His real love was the family and he had the saloon redecorated, keeping the magnificent Jacobean ceiling with representations of them with copies from appropriate originals by Biagio Rebecca, along with some earlier portraits to 'commemorate those noble families through whom with gratitude he held these possessions'. While we might have hoped for more distinguished artists working for Sir John, we have to be grateful for his care in preserving so much of the house, property and estate.

With typical enthusiasm he entered into landscape gardening using Robert Adam, not only in the house but also in architectural items to punctuate parkland views. The Lion Gate, the Temple of Victory, complete with menagerie and its beautiful vista over to the house, the Stone Bridge, the charming Tea Bridge and Lady Portmouth's obelisk were all to enhance the estate. The formal garden and parkland in seventeenth century style favoured by Charles Howard, the 9th Earl of Suffolk, was placed in the hands of Capability Brown in 1763. Jacobean formality gave place to gentle grading of the land and to a more natural form of landscape. The course of the Cam was diverted and the planting of deciduous and evergreen trees all added to the delightful scenery.

There were several small pleasure gardens which could be reached from the newly remodelled apartments made by Robert Adam — including Lady Griffin's garden with its ornamental dairy. Placido Columbani was asked to build on Richard Wood's plan to create a more romantic and informal Elysian flower garden.

Several alterations have been made, especially by the 3rd Lord Braybrooke, but basically the grounds are the same as in Sir John's time. It is a magnificent park and a work of art, and the spirit and form of the eighteenth century estate, as arranged by Sir John, remains.

An Essex manor house and its people

Another charming red brick house, which has been described as 'the quintessence of the English manor house', is Spains Hall on the outskirts of Finchingfield. It has been owned by three families since Henry de Ispania held that part of Essex from the Norman Conquest and gave his name to the estate. His coat of arms, along with that of the Kempe and Ruggles-Brise families who succeeded him, appear in the stained glass in the window of the hall.

There are still the remains of the moat and the oldest part of the house and the Elizabethan frontage with Dutch-style gables built by William Kempe about 1585.

A clothier from Bocking, Samuel Ruggles, fell in love with the house (understandably) and bought the estate in 1760 and it was a descendant, John Ruggles, who rebuilt the north-east wing in 1768 and the park was landscaped in 1807 by Adey Repton, son of the famous Humphry.

Sir Thomas Ruggles, pastel by John Russell, R.A., 1789.
(Photograph courtesy of Sir John Ruggles-Brise)

The family have continuously employed artists who are less well-known but of a good standard, such as Benjamin Wilson and Edward Penny, though in the eighteenth century Thomas Ruggles took himself and his wife to have their portrait taken in pastel by John Russell, R.A., the eminent and fashionable artist who did drawings of other members of the family too. Jane Ruggles was the authoress of the delightful *Household Book*.

There is a fine array of family portraits in the house including one by the Hon. John Collier of Evelyn Ruggles-Brise who introduced the Borstal form of treatment of young offenders, at that time a great improvement on the existing system. By that time the name of Brise had been added through marriage. There are landscapes and seascapes and still-lifes collected by the family. Portraits have been commissioned to the present day and the latest one is of Sir John Ruggles-Brise, who has held a wide variety of public offices including that of Lord Lieutenant. This is still a living house with the same family patronage remaining unbroken.

The exuberant elegance of Great Warley

'Perhaps the most complete manifesto of Art Nouveau in England', it is astonishing to find in a corner of south-west Essex the outcome of a patron's individual preference for a style which lasted for only about 15 years in England and is the only church built so uninhibitedly in that style.

The term 'Art Nouveau' originated in 1896 as the name of a shop in Paris owned by Samuel Bing; it blossomed and swept throughout Europe between then and 1910. The style was on the whole more decorative than architectural, characterized by forms with whiplash effect, tendril-like and flame-like shapes, based on the work of the Arts and Crafts movement in England, reacting against the Victorian Gothic Revival.

Mr Evelyn Heseltine, a young stockbroker, cultivated and wealthy, had seen the church at Hascombe and decided to build at Great Warley a replacement for the old crumbling building and nearer the centre of the parish population. It was to be a commemoration of his brother who had died in 1897 and he wished it to direct the congregation's thoughts to the Resurrection and away from the morbid contemplation of death. He daringly chose Harrison Townsend as architect and William Reynolds-Stephens, a worker in metal, stone, marble and jewels, as interior designer.

The exterior is simple, in the Voysey tradition, but the interior is a complete contrast, with symbolic colourful Arthurian paintings in the Pre-Raphaelite style with lavish use of metalwork, woodwork, sculpture and jewelry throughout. A bomb landed in the churchyard in 1940 and vandalism took place in the 1970s; both have meant a great deal of restoration and replacement, but all has been done with great care and sensitivity to convey the symbolic character of the subject.

St. Mary the Virgin, Great Warley,
Art Nouveau decoration by William Reynolds-Stephens, c.1904.
(Photograph courtesy of the Churchwardens)

The coffered chapel ceiling, the low-relief plaster panel, the sculptured font, the vases and the embroidered hangings all have beautiful motifs of curvilinear flowers, comprising vine, poppies, roses, lilies, thorns and pomegranates. There are doves and fifteen winged guardian angels and other symbolic figures all carried through in the most remarkable rich but durable materials. All are embellished with gold and silver-aluminium leaf, with pewter, brass, oxidized copper and mother-of-pearl, ormolu and cornelian with coloured marbles in the font, apse and reredos. The rood screen, exhibited in the Royal Academy in 1903, has a basis of dark green marble with rose trees in brass and mother-of-pearl and the altar rail has a crown of thorns on either side of the opening.

Electricity was in its infancy then but Reynolds-Stephens invented elegant pendant and pierced light-shades and lamp-holders with coloured glass and enamelled panels. In contrast the woodwork, mostly walnut, was very plain with occasional carving in the Bishop's chair and the sedilia, a massive heavy door with iron fittings and with some William Morris-type chairs. The organ case on the other hand is in a variety of metals. Most of the stained glass has had to be replaced except for the side-chapel windows and two small windows on either side of the altar.

It is a remarkably functional building, its interior colours quite impossible to describe in words — the achievement of one forceful patron who generously gave a complete and significant work of art to his parish.

Continuity and change in art and patronage

Patronage, as we have seen it, began to decline in the nineteenth century; lack of wealth on the grand scale and the tradition for men of good taste to collect for future generations largely diminished, and the leisure necessary for that kind of activity became scarcer.

In the twentieth century changes of interest — photography, film, television — have produced a different kind of culture which lacks the permanence of former times but the twentieth century becomes very interesting because the preservation and care of the Arts, with a few conspicuous exceptions, has moved into the hands of institutional groups rather than individuals.

Essex County Council, for example, have beautifully restored the magnificent Cressing barns; Chelmsford Borough Council with Hylands and Hollytrees by Colchester Corporation are other examples. The Harlow Art Trust and Development Corporation has commissioned a number of excellent pieces of sculpture and other works from artists as well-known as Henry Moore, Barbara Hepworth, John Piper and Ralph Brown, all well and interestingly placed around the town.

Two Dogs, a bronze cast by Robert Clatworthy, the Gibberd Garden, Harlow.
(Photograph by Val Cullen, A.R.P.S., courtesy of the Gibberd Garden Trust)

Torso, Horton Stone, carving by John Skelton, the Gibberd Garden, Harlow.
(Photograph by Val Cullen, A.R.P.S., courtesy of the Gibberd Garden Trust)

Two examples of more individual enterprises are to be found in the north of the County. On the outskirts of Harlow in Marsh Lane is a sculpture garden designed and furnished by Sir Frederick Gibberd, the master-planner of Harlow New Town, worked on up to his death in 1984 and continued by Lady Gibberd. It is a highly interesting creation. The garden is planned as a series of 'rooms' with groves, glades and pools; with settings for more than 50 pieces of contemporary sculpture and other artefacts — beautifully and imaginatively situated in the garden. It was left to Harlow Council but because of legal problems a group of Harlow residents have formed the Gibberd Trust to purchase the estate. It ranks as a masterpiece of garden design, with the delight of the juxtaposition of works of art.

The Blue Plough, Saffron Walden, linocut 1962, by Edward Bawden, R.A.
(Photograph courtesy of the Fry Art Gallery, Saffron Walden)

The second example is the collection in the small, beautiful Victorian Gallery in Castle Street, Saffron Walden originally built in 1856 by Francis Gibson to house his largely Dutch collection, and inherited by Lewis George Fry. It was the concept of Iris Weaver and friends who formed the Fry Art Gallery Society and who were allowed the use of the then empty gallery to display a unique collection of works by north-west Essex artists. It opened in 1987 and the introduction to the *North-West Essex Collection* by Olive Cook gives an exciting account of those artists who have lived and worked around Saffron Walden and Great Bardfield — for example Edward Bawden, Eric and Tirzal Ravilious, George Chapman,

John Aldridge, Michael Rothenstein, Duffy Ayres, and the younger generation of artists and friends whose works are the basis of that collection.

Sir Roger de Grey, then President of the Royal Academy, said at the opening 'This area is unique in England for the way internationally famous artists have settled here . . . they are assiduous observers of what is going on in the local scene . . . probably unique in British art'. It is a rich and exhilarating collection of contemporary art and the gallery is a unique outcome of real inspiration on the part of the originators.

So that with a 'slight superfluity of wealth' which Kenneth Clark thought necessary and an even smaller amount of 'fluid capital' — however small compared with the great patrons of the past — the Arts do continue to be supported in Essex in the tradition of patronage. Long may it continue!

BIBLIOGRAPHY

M. Sommerlad, *Wivenhoe Park and J. Constable*, 1984, Essex University Press.

F. G. Emmison, *Tudor Secretary*, 1961, Longmans.

A. C. Edwards, *John Petre*, 1975, Regency Press.

Introduction to Ingatestone Hall, 1972, E.R.O.

H. C. Fanshawe, *The History of the Fanshawe Family*, 1927.

J. Howson, *Fanshawe Family and other Portraits*, 1983, London Borough of Barking and Dagenham.

W. C. Pugsley, *Valence House, a Guide*, 1966, London Borough of Barking and Dagenham.

Dagenham and the Fanshawe Portraits, 1963, Dagenham Public Library.

E. Freeman and Sir John Ruggles-Brise, *The Ruggles of Bradford Street*, 1983.

Edith Freeman, *A Family Story: The Ruggles of Spains Hall*, 1993.

Essex Homes, 1066–1850, 1965, E.R.O.

Audley End – Catalogue of the Pictures, 1954, H.M.S.O.

Audley End – D.O.E. Official Guide Book, 1977, H.M.S.O.

Audley End – Concise Historic Tour, 1952, D.O.E., H.M.S.O.

P. J. Drury and J. R. Gow, *Audley End – English Heritage*, 1994, H.M.S.O.

J. D. Williams, *Audley End – Restoration of 1762–1797*, 1966, E.C.C., E.R.O.

W. Addison, *Audley End*, 1953, Dent.

R. Chamberlain, (ed. R. Gray), *Audley End*, 1986, English Heritage.

M. Sutherill, *The Gardens of Audley End*, 1995, English Heritage.

L. Miller, *Great Warley Church and the Art Nouveau*, 1993, Pisa Piper Bookshop, Brentwood.

H. R. Wilkins and A. W. Wellings, *Great Warley – The Church of St. Mary the Virgin. History and Guide*, 1988.

Olive Cook, *The N.W. Essex Collection*, 1988, Fry Art Gallery Society, Saffron Walden.

Saffron Walden: 'Crocuses and Crokers'

KENNETH NEALE

'About the towne of Walden is great store of a Comodetye w(hi)ch is not generall in England, namelye Saffron, and the aboundance of it about this place gyveth unto this towne the adiunct, Saffron Walden,'[1]

To LOCAL FOLK this attractive small Essex market town — probably the best looking small town anywhere in Essex or East Anglia according to Norman Scarfe's authoritative view[2] —is known as Walden. Its distinctive identity derives, however, to a large extent from the affix Saffron an appellation acquired in the sixteenth century. It is thus the saffron crocus, its cultivation, uses and associations with Essex and this handsome town to which this essay is devoted. I must confess that I hesitated before choosing this subject as part of the tribute to Sir John Ruggles-Brise, despite the town's close association with him and the county's present Lord Lieutenant, Lord Braybrooke. The topic has not been neglected. Various authors have written upon it in the press, periodical magazines, briefly in the extensive literature of the culinary arts and in the journals of local history. Most of these articles are popular in character, but there are also two reliable and useful modern studies.[3] Beyond those there are the standard topographical accounts of antiquarian interest to which I shall make reference in the course of this essay. My initial doubts were put aside in the belief that it would be useful, and hopefully rewarding, to bring the disparate material up-to-date, to extend the available research and to explore some fresh dimensions of the subject in bringing together the accessible knowledge in a coherent and interesting context. It is also a pleasant, fascinating topic about a once locally important aspect of Walden's history and one of the minor rural industries in Essex.

It is evident even from a cursory evaluation of the landscapes of rural Essex for which Saffron Walden serves as a social and economic focus, that farming has dominated the lives of the people who have lived and worked in the area since long before historical records begin. The cultivation of the saffron crocus was but a brief episode, on a comparatively modest scale, in the perspective of the general agrarian background. The chalky sub-soils, alluviums and glacial drifts that characterize the lands of Saffron Walden and the clay-based loams of the surrounding parishes have always defined the nature and pattern of the farming

Saffron Walden, Essex, W. Bartlett, engraved by C. Mottram.

(Photograph courtesy of the Essex Record Office)

activities that were pursued there. Long before Domesday, subsistence farmers worked the fields with their primitive ploughs and husbanded their animals. Sheep, cattle and pigs provided meat, milk and cheese to eat, wool and hide to wear and there were oxen and horses for haulage. Forest and scrub clearances in the twelfth and thirteenth centuries won more land, mostly to create arable farms. It remained thus until that significant medieval phase of extending the agricultural areas, was succeeded by the technical improvements in equipment and practise that enhanced the fertility and management of the farmlands and, in the long run, made them economically viable and eventually profitable. It was not easy. Unremitting labour was necessary, especially before the eighteenth century innovations that enabled the fields to be hollow-drained with beneficial results that made farming a modern commercial enterprise. Saffron was a cash crop and, in the story of Saffron Walden, as already noted, of some consequence. But, even during the period in which the saffron industry thrived, agriculture, husbandry and the associated industrial activities were and remain today, the most conspicuous idioms of life in the area.

The archaeological evidence for pre-historic and Roman settlement in and around Saffron Walden reinforces the generally accepted assessment of the strategic importance of the chalk ridges and river systems to the west of the town. The Roman fort and the walled town at Great Chesterford and the Ring Hill earthworks of Iron Age origin testify to that. Defended and serviced by these then more important settlement complexes the vicinity of Saffron Walden was, as excavation has shewn, continuously occupied and exploited from the Neolithic period. The focal resources eventually established at the present town site, were the consequence of the building and development by the de Mandevilles of the Norman castle and its environs on the mound between the so-called King's Ditch and the Madgate Slade from the mid-eleventh century. Its market town status derives from the same process and the medieval street pattern, most of which still survives, is itself tangible evidence for the market role and the ancilliary trades and crafts. The parallel rows, Mercers, Drapers, Tanners and Fish along with Pig Street, Cheese Hill, Poultry Hill and the Butter Market backed onto the Corn Market. Saffron, although now reflected in the name of the town itself, was not a marketable commodity in the sense that the basic necessities of life were. So it is not likely that any specific topographical features ever carried that name, although it is true that some, like Fuller's Lane, have now gone and others may have disappeared from the records. Philological evidence for the saffron industry rests on the town name and the minor field-names of the area. Few of these remain in vernacular usage, although there are some, of modern designation, but earlier relevance like Saffron Gardens in Wethersfield.

'Coloured with the name thereof'

Thomas Fuller, the genial and scholarly parson of Waltham Abbey, referred in 1662, in his delightful *History of the Worthies of England* to Saffron Walden as a 'fair

market town which saffron may seem to have coloured with the name thereof'.[4]
It was, as we shall see, a commodity to which he acknowledged a personal debt of
gratitude. Before we come to the plant, its cultivation and uses, however, it is
perhaps convenient to consider the derivation of the word and its provenance in
Essex place and field-names with special reference to Walden.

The generally accepted view is that we derive the English word saffron from
the Arabic *Za'faran*. That is, naturally, an over-simplification for the study of the
origin of words is notoriously complicated and frequently unsatisfactory.
Ultimate roots tend to be elusive especially when, as seems to be the case with
saffron, the word may have reached contemporary language from several albeit
related sources. The Middle English form of the word is *saffran* which had its
origin in the Old French *safran* in turn probably derived from Arabic. In
medieval usage the Latinized form was *safranum* which also seems to have had its
source in the Arabic word. In classical Latin, however, saffron, as a noun, is *crocus*
which would seem, at first sight, to be an allusion to the plant rather than the
product. However, the Romans used prepared saffron as a spice, in perfume and
in medicine. My Latin dictionary of 1677[5] translates saffron as *crocus* and
mentions Cilicia 'which abounded in Saffron which is therefore called *Spica
Cilissa'*. It also refers to Ovid's personification of the name Crocus as the
handsome youth who in consequence of his passionate love for Smilax, turned
into a flower (saffron) of his name. Greek dictionaries cast a little further light
on this. The Greek word κροκος is translated as saffron. It is mentioned in
Homer but only as a flower, not as a dye or spice. The words crocus and saffron
seem, as in other languages, to have become inter-changeable in demotic use. It
might be safer simply to acknowledge that the word, whether used in reference
to the plant or the spice is of ancient origin, the Semitic language Arabic having
given it the widest currency.

Place names derived from the names of trees or plants are common in the
nomenclature of English towns and villages. Such are frequent too in field and
minor place-names. Usually they occur in compounds as in Roydon, an adjectival
derivative of rye: or in names with two or more elements such as Hatfield Broad
Oak. In simplex forms they are very rare. The affix in the case of Saffron Walden
is unique which reflects the strength of the town's association with the valued
spice. Interestingly though, Croydon in Surrey — *Crogedena* — in the ninth
century, has been defined as indicating the 'valley where wild saffron grew' or
'saffron valley'.[6] This is difficult to accept on botanical grounds and is more
probably a reference to the autumn crocus (*colchicum autumnale*). So far as Saffron
Walden is concerned it is popularly assumed that it indicates that Walden was the
principal place where the saffron crops grew and flourished. They did, but most
of the saffron was grown in the surrounding parishes. Indeed, there was probably
not a parish in the area where it was not grown at some time. It was because the
town served as the centre for processing and marketing saffron that it attracted
its present name in the sixteenth century. Within the town precincts its cultivation
was on a comparatively small scale.

In its earliest known form the town's name was *Waledana* (Domesday 1086) from the Old English *weala-denu* — 'the valley of the Britons or serfs'. By the early fourteenth century it was *Chepyng* (meaning market) *Walden*. But it is as Saffron Walden that the name has come to be accepted as an attractive and appropriate reflection of a once important aspect of town life.

Although the crop was grown and marketed in Saffron Walden long before, the earliest archival reference we have to the town's name as *Saffornewalden* is in a deed of 1582.[7] The name Saffron Walden was also being used at that time in the works of leading topographers including William Harrison,[8] the Rector of nearby Radwinter (1559–93) and Vicar of Wimbish (1571–81) and John Norden in 1594.[9] Interestingly, in all the relevant Elizabethan wills that I have seen the testators refer only to Walden which suggests that then, as now, local people preferred to use the simplex ancient name even though, on a more formal level the prefix Chipping had been abandoned and Saffron adopted.

As a field-name the occurence of the element Saffron is more common and was used in conjunction with -Field, -Ground, -Piece, -Garden, -Shot, and -Close. These names indicate not only the location of the saffron crops, but also something about the distribution and scale of its cultivation.

'Watchet or pale blewe'

In a footnote[10] to his entry for Saffron Walden, Morant, the prince of Essex historians, but not a botanist, asserts in reference to the saffron crocus 'the flower is of the lilly kind'. The *crocus sativus* (meaning sown or planted, an apt nomenclature) is, in fact, a bulbous rooted perennial of the Iris (*iridaceae*) family. As its Linnaean classification implies, it has been cultivated from time immemorial and does not occur in natural situations as it is now sterile.

The bulb, or corm, multiplies annually, the new corms flowering usually in the autumn of the third year, although a few will do so in the second year. The flower is described in John Norden's words as 'watchet (washed) or pale blewe' but is actually pale to mid-purple. The saffron crocus is thus, in colour, not unlike the spring crocuses (*c.vernus: c.albiflorus*) but rather larger. Each flower has six petals which open towards the tip. Within the corolla is a ring of yellow stamens rising from the perianth with a pale whitish pistil at the centre. From the pistil protrudes the style which is divided into three orange-red filaments, the stigma or chives. It is these which are harvested and dried to become the saffron, or 'hay-saffron' in allusion to the appearance of the spice after processing. As Norden delightfully describes it the marketable product is derived from 'the stringes like unto threades which issue out of the harte of the flowre'.[11] The flower stalks are enveloped in a double sheath the leaves appearing after flowering.

Flowering between September and November and in habit not altogether unlike the autumn crocus (*colchicum autumnale*) the saffron crocus is sometimes confused with it. That is a dangerous mistake for the former, with its local names like 'naked Jacks' (Somerset), 'fog crocus' (Yorkshire) and 'Kite's legs' (Kent), is

Crocus Sativus, sculp. F. Hilliard from The Universal Herbal *by Thomas Green, 1816.*

poisonous if used to excess and precariously called also 'meadow saffron'.[12] The cultivated saffron crocus is widely dispersed across the world and has been used for its various purposes throughout recorded history. It was a familiar condiment in China, where it was introduced by the Mongols, and other countries of the Far East. The Egyptians employed the so-called bastard saffron (*Carthamus tinctorius*), sometimes used to adulterate saffron, and they do not seem to have had the true product. In China it is described in medical science (Pun tsaou 1552–78) but the premier region of its early cultivation, the ancient authorities agree, was, as I have already indicated, Cilicia (Asia Minor) from whence it was introduced into India and later Spain and thence to Europe by the Arabs in the tenth century.[13] It seems to have disappeared from the European inventory, but was re-introduced by the Crusaders and there is a spurious legend, which I will not repeat, about its arrival in England with a returning pilgrim. Readers can pursue this if they wish by reference to an early edition of the *Essex Review*.[14] Nowadays it is mainly cultivated in Spain, France, Sicily and in the Far East especially Kashmir where the great bulk of Indian saffron is cultivated and it is even used as currency. Still the most expensive spice in the world it is known as 'vegetable gold' in Kashmir and 'red gold' in Spain in those localities where it is grown as a cash crop in otherwise poor agricultural country and is therefore very important to the economy. The harvest in November, the fruit of intensive hard labour, is celebrated with a festival of feasting, costume and folk-dance.[15] But let William Harrison have the last word in this brief botanical excursion into the world of saffron:

> 'As the saffron of England . . . is the most excellent of all other: so of
> that which is to be had amongst us, the same that groweth about Saffron
> Walden in the edge of Essex surmounteth all the rest, and therefore
> beareth worthilie the higher price, by six pence or twelve pence most
> commonlie in the pound.'[16]

'The abundance of Saffron there cultivated'

John Evelyn, in recording a visit, in 1654, to Audley End, 'that fine palace', wrote of 'Saffron Walden, famous for the abundance of Saffron there cultivated and esteemed the best'.[17] Little definitive evidence exists for establishing with any precision, the time from which the saffron industry commenced in and around Walden, although it has been accepted that it began to flourish during the reign of Edward I (1327–77). Dorothy Cromarty speculates on the connection between the industry and the development of dyeworks in Walden which were frequently referred to in the court rolls between 1381 and 1440.[18] It is a pity that these entries make no mention of saffron although the dye produced from it could well have been in demand by the local woollen industry. The earliest reference to

The saffron crocus photographed in Saffron Walden by Richard Jemmett

dyeworks in Walden is dated 1359, some 22 years before the court roll series begins. In 1444 a *Composito de Decimus* shews that saffron produced beyond the precincts of the abbey at Walden was then treated as a titheable commodity.[19] By 1500 it was well established in the area and in the sixteenth century was of acknowledged local significance as we have seen. The Charter granted by Henry VIII in 1514 was decorated with various ornamental devices including the saffron flower and the appellative saffron had been acquired for the town name before the end of the century.

The term 'croker' was also being used in reference to the saffron men who cultivated the plant and those who sold it in the market. Walden's place as a centre of the industry was thus widely recognized. There was even a surplus in the mid-sixteenth century as production exceeded demand and some of the saffron grounds were used for growing other crops.[20] It seems however, that Sir Thomas Smith, Queen Elizabeth's Secretary of State and a Walden man by birth, was instrumental in helping to revive the trade to the benefit of his native town and the crokers. William Harrison records the ribald comments on this matter in reporting the 'murmuring' crokers crude reaction to the problem in his *Description.*[21] (Croker: deriv. Crocus-er).

In 1586 William Camden wrote of Walden being situated midst fields smiling with the beautiful crocus.[22] The saffron crocus continued to be grown in the Walden area up to about 1760, although it is said that by 1726 Littlebury was the only remaining site of the industry in the vicinity of the town. By about 1790 it was limited to a small area close to the Gogmagog Hills just south of Cambridge. Curiously, some plants were noticed to have sprouted in newly turned ground in 1843.[23] The crop did, of course, continue to be grown on a very small scale by a few individuals but had ceased to be an industry that supported a local market. It appears that the last of the crokers may have been a farmer called Knott who lived at Duxford and gardened half an acre. He sold his crop, according to the Saffron Walden Almanack of 1880, in London and died about 1820.[24] Lord Braybrooke, in his book of 1836, asserts that the cultivation of the saffron crocus near Walden ceased as a result of the pressure of foreign competition and the disuse of the plant in medicine.[25]

It is interesting to establish, as far as possible, the geographical limits of the area around Walden and other places in the county where the saffron crocus was grown. A century ago William Waller, Treasurer of the Essex Archaeological Society and a notable Essex historian, published a series of tables in the Transactions of the Society to which readers are referred.[26] In these he listed systematically numerous ancient field-names of Essex. Miller Christy, who wrote the account of the saffron industry in the *Victoria County History of Essex*,[27] relied on Waller's lists in defining the pattern of saffron cultivation in the county. His analysis of the field-names with the element saffron in those lists shewed that there were at least 28 parishes in the county (curiously not including Saffron Walden) where the crop had been grown. Twenty-one of these parishes were situated in the

north-western part of the county, most of them within ten miles of Saffron
Walden. Those noted elsewhere in Essex were Alphamstone, Fordham, Great
Waltham, Hatfield Peverel, Horndon-on-the-Hill, Tollesbury and Writtle.

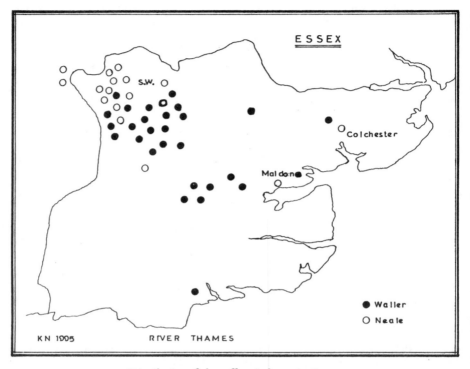

Distribution of the saffron industry in Essex.

I am able, after further research, to extend that analysis to include saffron
field-names which occur in deeds, wills and other archives. For example, a deed
executed in 1616 cites Richard Bullocke, yeoman of Sampford Magna and the
late John Westley, yeoman of Hempstead in respect of several properties in
Great Sampford including 'Kyngs Crofte alias the Safferon grounde'.[28] Among a
considerable number of Elizabethan wills, the abstracts of which are in the late
Dr Emmison's monumental series, we find:[29]

> Jane Runham, a widow of Great Chesterford who, in 1572
> bequeathes to her daughters '1 rood of saffron of 2 years' set, and to
> both another rood of 2 years' set, together with my saffron heads
> commonly called raising ground'.

> William Gooddinge of Walden leaves, in 1579 to his brother '1 rood

of saffron ground lying in a close leading towards Thaxted in the occupation of Alexander Raye, which rood Mark Hille must set of this present season at his own costs'.

Two of these wills are of particular interest as concerning Colchester and illustrating the value of the saffron crop. Thus:

Robert Brown, a grocer and Alderman of Colchester refers, in 1568, to his saffron gardens and leaves 'To the poor people of Colchester £10 where most need shall be considered by the discretion of my exors. to be levied out of the yearly rent of my saffron garden in the parish of St. Leonard in Colchester'.

And Thomas Fairstead of St. Botolph, Colchester, 1582, refers to his gardens '1 called the saffron pane in St. Botolph under the town wall'.

To the field-name forms mentioned earlier which came from Waller's list may, therefore, be added names with the second element of -croft and -pane. Waller's parish list can be extended to include, in the Walden area, Saffron Walden, Newport, Great Sampford, Widdington, Elmdon, Great Chesterford, Little Chesterford, Littlebury, Chrishall, Strethall, Wicken Bonhunt and Hadstock. I can also include Heydon and Great Chishall, in Cambridgeshire since 1895, but formerly in Essex before the County Councils were established in 1888. Beyond these, also in Essex, are Maldon, Colchester and Hatfield Broad Oak, seventeen in all. This is, however, still a limited analysis and is, I am sure, susceptible of augmentation given further research in the county archives. Furthermore it should be noted that some of the testators do not specify the location of their saffron grounds although their own abode is given and that will normally imply, unless otherwise stated, local property. Even with that minor *caveat* the clear inference is that further searches would reinforce the picture that has already emerged. That is, of an intensively worked area of saffron grounds near Walden and into the adjacent areas of Cambridgeshire; and a fairly widespread, but localized, distribution of cultivation elsewhere in the county.

If the evidence for the precise extent of the industry and the chronology of its growth and decline is deficient, information about the processes involved in its cultivation is readily available. Happily, most of the accounts that have survived in topographical, botanical and horticultural studies are broadly consistent, or at least not essentially in conflict, except in minor detail. For these we turn to the doyens, Harrison, Norden and Morant already mentioned. To their learned contributions we may add the knowledge and advice to be culled from the poet of husbandry, Thomas Tusser of Rivenhall who, as Fuller rather unkindly said,'Spread his bread with all sorts of butter yet none would stick thereon'![30] There is too, Thomas Hill who wrote the first popular gardening book in 1577.[31] Most reliable is the account given by Dr James Douglas of the Royal Society in his paper printed in the Society's Transactions of 1727–8.[32] He had studied the industry in the Saffron Walden area between 1723 and 1728. Numerous other

Saffron Crocus (source unknown)
(Photograph courtesy of Essex County Council Libraries, Trustees of the Town Library, Saffron Walden)

authors have described the culture of this plant and it must suffice here to outline the process, but the authorities that I have mentioned are well worth consulting for the detail and insights they offer.

The 'right trusty' Tusser, as Charles Clark of Great Totham describes him in the edition he edited in 1834, says 'Pare saffron between the two S. Marie's daies' — the reference being to St. Mary Magdalene (22 July) and the Assumption of the Blessed Virgin (15 August). Paring was to cleanse the raising grounds of weeds and rubble. The soils of Saffron Walden, light and alkaline, were very suitable — 'it joyeth to be bestowed in a mean and chalkie ground' according to Hill. In the spring, well before the paring which could, in fact, be as late as early September, the ground, normally fallow, would have been ploughed and well manured. The grounds, as is confirmed by the evidence of the bequests in the contemporary wills, were quite small, often less than an acre. Camden's reference to the smiling fields sounds like poetic licence. The raising grounds, or gardens, were fenced with hurdles or hedged to keep out hares, which were a particular problem, and other herbivores. John Roulles of Great Chishall states in his will of 1573 that his saffron garden is 'at the town's end next the hedge'. An acre might contain almost 400,000 'heads', or corms, which were planted about three inches apart in trenched rows by the crokers. Regular weeding was carried out and the flowers emerged in late September. The first year the yield was small but of the highest quality; the second, the yield increased but it was in the third year that the optimum crop was harvested. Thereafter the corms would be lifted and the ground left to lie fallow for some years, a practise which, as Harrison tells us 'our Crokers carefullie observe'.

The flowers were picked at 'sun rising' before the autumn sunshine withered the flower heads, and gathered in baskets after which they were spread on tables and the filaments, or chives, were separated by the 'pluckers', the rest of the flower being useless. The chives were carefully dried over kilns on frames of hair cloth or wire networks, the former being preferred as the saffron was less likely to burn. After this lengthy and tedious process only about twelve pounds of saffron were obtained from an acre of ground. Various calculations have been offered to shew that over 4,000 flowers were needed to prepare an ounce of saffron. Dr Douglas estimated that the costs of culivating an acre of saffron in his period, 1723–28, including the rent, ploughing, manuring, hedging, setting, paring, gathering and preparing the spice was over £23. That is why it has always been expensive. As Norden had it, the culture and harvesting of the saffron crop was 'verye laborious, requiring also noe small charge. But in the ende it pay'th it agayne with advantage.'

Saffron Walden, Camden tells us, was a 'very good mercat town' and it was on that function that the ultimate fortunes of the industry relied. At the height of the saffron industry it was the proceeds of that, along with the prosperity of the maltings, brewhouses, hostelries and the commodity markets that the vigour and growth of the local economy depended. The manor courts record the presentment of the traders and crokers for the fouling of the streets of the town, as they littered the walkways with the discarded petals of the crocus flowers and the debris of the firings during the preparation and drying processes. The borough authorities were responsible for the proper conduct of the markets and the regulation of the quality standards of the goods on sale, including the saffron some of which was confiscated as inferior on occasion. Hay saffron was offered for sale in Saffron Walden from 21 October, St. Ursula's Day which gave its name to the fair which later became the Common Fair. According to Harrison 'Some craftie jackes' adulterated the saffron with scraped brazil nuts and he asserts that there were no bigger rogues than the saffron dealers. The crokers were regarded as hard working and skilled in their craft, even if given to blasphemous language in hard times! There was itinerant labour too. In proceedings at the Essex Quarter Sessions in 1580 concerning one Elizabeth Cole of 'Myllnoll' (Mildenhall) in Suffolk, who was involved with a Mary Watson and Thomas Wheeler in a felony case, it was reported that she was at Walden 'pyckinge of saffron'.[33]

An agreeable aspect of the saffron industry was the practice of giving gifts to distinguished or influential visitors. In such circumstances gifts of food were common; that of saffron peculiar to the Essex market town. Thus, in 1545, a pound of saffron was given to a Lady Paget, probably Anne the wife of Sir William Paget, a senior colleague of Sir Thomas Smith in the Queen's service. William III, at Audley End in 1689, was presented with a silver plate which cost £4 6s. 6d. and fourteen ounces of saffron which cost almost as much, £3 11s. 8d.[34] That is, perhaps, a felicitous note on which to consider the various uses to which this exceptional product was put.

'Highly prized by mankind'

In a pharmacological study in 1879 it was asserted that 'Saffron, either as a medicine, condiment, perfume or dye, has been highly prized by mankind from a remote period, and has played an important part in the history of commerce'.[35] The reputation of the supposed medicinal properties of saffron was once almost universal. Introduced from Iran and Kashmir by the Mongol invaders into China, it was noted by Pun tsaou in the sixteenth century. But long before that it was in widespread use for medical prescription in Europe. In 1535 Bartholomew (Berthelet) opined 'He that drinketh Saffron first shall not be drunken . . . and cureth biting of serpents and of attercops (spiders), and stinging of scorpions . . . and tokeneth passing heat and distemperance of blood in the liver'.[36] Thomas Hill, already cited, states that saffron 'amendeth the hard fetching of breath . . . comforteth the heart . . . procureth the termes' and that it was used for treating 'jaundice, ulcers, gout, swellings, grief of the eyes . . . diseases of the ear'.[37] There was no end to belief in its supposed therapeutic formula. Even the sensible Thomas Fuller described it as a most admirable cordial and 'under God I owe my life when sick of the smallpox, to the efficacy thereof'.[38] Thus he managed to reconcile his touching superstition with his religious mantra.

If its medical efficacy has not stood the test of time its culinary properties have. It is still a highly prized condiment. However, like most unique flavours saffron is an acquired taste. Too much saffron, in the view of Elizabeth David, is 'repellent'.[39] Alexandre Dumas, the French novelist and dramatist, compiled a massive culinary dictionary of more than half a million words. He spared a few to discuss saffron, but he too was tentative — 'Its bitter, aromatic taste is not at all disagreeable'. Nevertheless he praised the spice as a seasoning and as a colouring agent for cakes, butter and vermicelli and even included an intriguing recipe for a chilled *mousse au safran*.[40] Larousse emphasizes the importance of saffron in bouillabaisse, paella, mourtayrol (a chicken soup of the Périgord), risotto, semolina, brioches and desserts. It refers also, engagingly, to the labours of the *safraniers* in the Gâtinais and Angoumois regions where it was grown.[41] Dorothy Hartley, admired for her research into domestic aspects of English social history, says it was used in stews, cordials, possets (e.g. hot milk with beer and spices) and blended with nutmeg or rosemary.[42]

The uses of saffron are or have been, it would seem, virtually endless — but that is not all. Saffron was used in perfumery from ancient days. Strewn on the floors of Greek buildings it was used also as an aromatic agent in the Roman baths. It was said to have been sprinkled in the streets of Rome when Nero entered the city.[43] But a more persistent practise, other than in the sophisticated cuisines, was its use as a dye. As we have seen, its value as such was part of the economic rationale of the industry in Saffron Walden. In Hellenic times the Greeks made good use of the yellow dye obtained from saffron for it was then a royal colour. The fascination and the promotional status of saffron is not, it would seem, confined to the epicureans who enjoy sophisticated cookery. I noticed, on a visit to Estonia where I was working, a company offering financial and currency services and trading under the name 'Safran'. Their rather clever company 'logo' is a stylish representation of the saffron crocus, and an interesting allusion to the symbolic value of this unique spice.

'Have with you to Saffron Walden'

Another, and notorious literary reference of the late sixteenth century that illustrates the formal adoption of the prefix Saffron in the town name, comes from the vivid pen of the satirist Thomas Nashe. His 'confutation of the sinfull doctor', the pedantic scholar Gabriel Harvey, published in 1596, was entitled *Have with you to Saffron Walden*.[44] This ridiculous and infamous literary duel originated in a long-standing grievance and culminated in Nashe's polemic which to modern readers is a farrago of sarcastic, convoluted nonsense. Neither emerged with any credit from this vitriolic exchange of insults. In these concluding paragraphs, however, I shall try to dwell a little further upon the themes of the crocus and the crokers of Saffron Walden on a rather more agreeable if miscellaneous note. For period pieces of that time we inevitably turn to

Armorial bearings, Saffron Walden.

(Photograph   courtesy of Richard Jemmett)

William Shakespeare. We shall not be disappointed. There were few contemporary personalities, topics or items of domestic interest for which the bard's extensive works do not provide at least one felicitous or pertinent reference. Saffron is no exception.

The *Winter's Tale*[45] was a significant success for the playwright after his venture into the genre of Romance had made a hesitant start with *Pericles* and *Cymbeline*. In a rollicking dialogue between the Clown and the rogue Autolycus, the fool utters the requirements for the Sheep-shearing Feast. There must be rice, currants, sugar, mace, nutmegs, ginger and 'Saffron to colour the Warden Pies' — Wardens were baking pears. An allusion to the use of saffron as a dye is to be found in *All's Well that Ends Well*.[46] It is a classic comedy, laced with ambivalence and tangled relationships. In a subtle scene with the sophisticated court jester to the Countess of Rossill, the sagacious Lord Lafew counsels his ageing patroness 'No, no, no, your sonne was misled with a snipt taffeta fellow there, whose villanous saffron wold have made all the unbak'd and dowy youth of a nation in his colour'.

It is no surprise to find the saffron crocus prominently depicted on the town's armorial bearings. These appear to have dated from 1594 when 5s. 4d. was paid for the arms. As is the fate of heraldic insignia these bearings have been susceptible of change and erroneous usage. H. C. Stacey, a former Town Clerk and himself steeped in Saffron Walden's history, has pointed out, in a most interesting and detailed description, the botanical inaccuracies that have persisted and the chronic errors that have confused this subject, as well as a trite punning allusion that I prefer to avoid.[47]

The carvings of saffron flowers in the fine late fifteenth century Perpendicular nave of the parish church of St. Mary the Virgin in Walden are of fine quality. Eight of these flowers, of varying size and arranged to radiate as if from the centre of a circular design are to be seen in the spandrels of one of the arches of the arcade of the south aisle. They may be accepted as contemporary symbols of the industry that flourished in the town in Tudor times and, as such, dispel spurious beliefs about the date of the introduction of the crop to the area. The saffron flower, set in scallops, is depicted also in the lead-work of the lights of the windows in the north and south chapels. Lead-binding in stained and enamelled glass windows was frequently used as an element in the design by the glaziers, similar in purpose to the outlining of scroll-work in medieval illuminated manuscripts.

In a laudable effort to rekindle local interest in that flower, now so special to Walden's identity, a scheme was promoted in 1973 to re-introduce the crocus to the town's gardens. Some 8,000 corms of *crocus sativus* were obtained from Van Tubergen's in Holland and numerous local people — the modern crokers — supported this initiative by planting them.[48]

That would be a happy and positive theme with which to conclude this essay. But, I cannot resist one more perceptive quotation from William Harrison in his *Description* of 1577.[49] 'Would to God', he wrote in this sad little homily, 'that

Armorial bearings, Saffron Walden.

(Photograph courtesy of Richard Jemmett)

my countrymen had beene heretofore (or were now) more carefull of this commoditie! then would it no doubt have prooved more beneficiall to our Iland than our cloth or wooll. But alas! so idle are we.'

REFERENCES

1 J. Norden, *Description of Essex*, 1594, E.R.O., D/DMs P1.

2 N. Scarfe, *A Shell Guide to Essex*, 1968, p.182.

3 M. Christie, *Victoria County History of Essex*, vol. II, 1903, pp.359–66; H. C. Stacey, *Walden's Saffron-Crocus Sativus*, MS, Saffron Walden Town Library, E/SAF 331.7, 1973.

4 T. Fuller, *The History of the Worthies of England*, (1662), Folio Society edition, ed., R. Barber, 1987, p.138.

5 A. Littleton, *Latin Dictionary*, 1677.

6 E. Ekwall, *Dictionary of English Place-Names*, C.U.P., 1970, p.134.

7 P. H. Reaney, *The Place-names of Essex*, C.U.P., 1935, p.537.

8 W. Harrison, *Description of England*, (1577), ed., F. J. Furnivall, 1878, p.50.

9 J. Norden, *op. cit.*

10 P. Morant, *The History and Antiquities of the County of Essex*, vol. II, 1768, pp.544, 545.

11 J. Norden, *op. cit.*

12 G. Grigson, *The Englishman's Flora*, Dent, 1987, p.411.

13 *Encyclopaedia Britannica*, 13th edition, vol. 19, 1961, p.812.

14 A. Clark, 'Saffron and Walden', *Essex Review*, vol. xix, no. 74, 1910, p.58.

15 B.B.C. Overseas Service, 23 November 1994.

16 W. Harrison, *op. cit.*, pp.50, 51.

17 J. Evelyn, *Diary and Correspondence*, vol. I, ed., W. Bray, 1857, p.305.

18 Dorothy Cromarty, 'Chepyng Walden 1381–1420', *Essex Journal*, vol. 2, no. 2, 1967, p.109.

19 M. Christy, *V.C.H. Essex, op. cit.*, pp.359–66.

20 *The Saffron Crocus*, Saffron Walden Museum leaflet no. 13.

21 W. Harrison, *op. cit.*, p.56.

22 W. Camden, *Britannia*, 1586, Trans. Ph., Holland, 1610.

23 S. T. Jermyn, *Flora of Essex*, Essex Naturalists' Trust, 1974, p.220.

24 M. White, *Saffron Walden's History*, 1991, p.49.

25 Richard, Lord Braybrooke, *History of Audley End*, 1836, p.146.

26 W. C. Waller, 'Essex Field Names', *Trans. Essex Arch. Soc.*, (new series), vols. v, vi, vii, viii, and ix, 1895–1901.

27 M. Christy, *V.C.H., op. cit.*, pp.359–66.

28 E.R.O., D/DHt T233/22.

29 F. G. Emmison, ed., *Essex Wills*, series from 1982.

30 T. Tusser, *Hundred Good Poyntes of Husbandrie*, 1577, rep. 1834, ed., C. Clark and *Five Hundred Points of Husbandry*, edition 1794.

31 T. Hill, *The Gardener's Labyrinth*, 1577, ed., R. Mabey, O.U.P., 1987.

32 J. Douglas, 'An Account of the Culture and Management of Saffron in England', *Philosophical Transactions of the Royal Society*, vol. 35, 1727/8, pp.566–74.

33 E.R.O., Q/SR 76/22, vol. IX.

34 E.R.O., T/A 401/2, 'Accounts of the Guild of the Holy Trinity', 1545–61.

35 M. Christy, *V.C.H.*, *op. cit.*, pp.359–66.

36 H. W. Seager, *Natural History in Shakespeare's Time*, (1896), Minet ed., 1972, p.269.

37 T. Hill, *op. cit.*, p.212.

38 T. Fuller, *op. cit.*, p.138.

39 Ellen Szita, 'Demystifying Saffron', *The National Culinary Review*, (U.S.A.), rep. *Saffron Walden History*, no. 31, 1987, p.194.

40 A. Dumas, *Le Grand Dictionnaire de Cuisine*, 1873, p.246.

41 *Larousse Gastronomique*, edition Hamlyn, 1988, p.913.

42 Dorothy Hartley, *Food in England*, 1973, p.452.

43 *Encyclopaedia Britannica*, *op. cit.*, p.812.

44 T. Nashe. *Have with you to Saffron Walden*, 1596.

45 W. Shakespeare, First Folio, 1623, rep. Harrap, eds., C. Porter and H. A. Clarke, 1906, *The Winter's Tale*, iv.3.38.

46 *Ibid*, *All's Well that Ends Well*, iv.5.2.

47 H. C. Stacey, *Saffron Walden History*, no. 24, 1983, pp.225–29.

48 R. Hay, 'Saffron returns to Walden', *The Times*, 15 December 1973.

49 W. Harrison, *op. cit.*, pp.59, 60.

The Plume Library, Maldon:
A New Chapter

FRANK HERRMANN

I BELIEVE THAT OUR VIEW of the Library which Dr Thomas Plume gave to the town of Maldon in 1704 has changed in recent years. The Library has become alive to many more people after slumbering sedately for many years. Undoubtedly this is due in large part to the formation of a body of people interested in its long-term welfare, who called themselves the 'Friends of Thomas Plume's Library'.

They came into being some nine years ago when a local antiquarian bookseller spotted a title for sale in another particularly distinguished antiquarian bookseller's catalogue. In order to prove its notable provenance, it proudly announced that the volume bore the book plate and shelf marks of the Plume Library. We wanted that book back on the Library shelves where it belonged, and a group of Maldon citizens clubbed together to raise the not inconsiderable sum to buy it.

We then discovered that it was by no means the only title which had 'disappeared' from among the 7,000 volumes that Plume had bequeathed to Maldon, and it was thought that we should continue to replace them. Thus, the 'Friends' came into being, initially as a steering committee. As we were uncertain where we were heading, we formulated not a constitution for our long-term governance, but a simple set of only six 'terms of reference', the first of which states that 'The aim of the organization [the 'Friends'] is to support and assist the Trustees, financially and otherwise, in all aspects of the preservation, conservation and accessions to the Plume Library in Maldon, and in any other need that may arise'. Our sixth precept is that 'The executive committee shall be empowered to raise funds in any way that it deems appropriate for the fulfilment of its aims'.

For the first seven years I was chairman of the Friends. I was succeeded by Vic Gray, our former Essex County Archivist who, as Trustee, had been largely instrumental in getting us off the ground, and he, in turn, has now been succeeded by Dr Bill Petchey, author of a particularly thoroughly researched Plume lecture, published in 1985, called *The Intentions of Thomas Plume*.

In 1996 we can point with some pride to the fact that we have funded a great deal of conservation work in relation to the Library's early documentation. Thus we have repaired the bindings of the entire run of the Minutes of the Trustees'

A portrait of Dr Plume which is in the Library in Maldon.

meetings since 1714 and our several early inventories; and have had protective covers made for our collection of 1,600 seventeenth century political pamphlets. We have also purchased replacements for over a hundred missing volumes, in several cases of the *actual* copies with our Library label and shelf marks, the rest being copies of precisely the same edition as we had lost. Furthermore, we have gradually created a much greater awareness in academic and bibliographical circles of the importance of the Library and this, in turn, has led to its increased use.

At our instigation, the Plume Librarian undertook the onerous task of comparing our inventories of 1761 and 1843 in order to establish which of Dr Plume's books had gone missing during the time when the lower floor of the building in which the Library is housed had been in use as a grammar school. In recent years, various scholars have remarked that, despite Dr Plume's wide-ranging interests, there seemed to be lacunae in his purchases, particularly in the areas of literature (essays, plays and belle-lettres) and among books on travel and topography. It now emerged that these topics had proved the most tempting for what we might call 'permanent borrowers'. But it is an amazing fact that, although the books we replace originate almost exclusively in the seventeenth century, they can still be bought today in the London saleroom. Our own interest, which is, of course, known in the book trade, has kindled much wider interest in the period and whereas relatively few booksellers stocked such books a decade ago, the number has doubled, if not trebled, in the last few years. Sadly, from our point of view, there has been a concomitent rise in prices!

What is much more important is that our example has stimulated increased interest in the few remaining, similar, mostly parochial, libraries; also among many more collectors, in that form of seventeenth century literature that is also of interest to us. With the consent and encouragement of the Trustees, we have also added, particularly in the early days of our existence, to the very extensive collection of contemporary sermons which Dr Plume had got together.

It is difficult for us today, with the multitude of methods of communication and leisure interests that envelop us in a materialistic age, to imagine the importance of that weekly message from the pulpit of a church to its adherents. Church-going was virtually obligatory in the seventeenth century, so the man who led the church in each community was all important. He was the guide and mentor in that part of life where thought, imagination and — above all — faith were what mattered. 'A minister of religion', James Thomas Oxley had written in 1609, preaching to his fellow clergy in Durham, 'should be the eyes of the world for his congregation to disperse the clouds of ignorance and give life'. Such a man was Thomas Plume, and he, like his fellow clergymen, worked endlessly at his sermons. To help their efforts, there arose a whole industry of commentators and interpreters who published their ideas for the benefit of ministers of religion, and for the laity too if they cared to read them which, in fact, they did. 8,800 volumes of sermons alone were published between 1660 and 1750, often in editions of a size which present day publishers would find quite acceptable.

An external view of the Library.
The tower is the property of the Church Commissioners; the rest of the building is currently owned by Maldon District Council; the contents of the Library are vested in the Plume Trustees.

We know that Plume, who for much of his life was vicar of Greenwich, was an excellent preacher. Both Samuel Pepys and John Evelyn have told us so. Plume kept a notebook (we have it in the Library) of references to other people's sermons and anecdotes which he might use himself later; items which were not included in his printed books. He also assembled many hand-written notebooks of other people's sermons: again, we have nearly 150 such manuscripts in the Library.

He himself in 1675 published an immense folio volume of *A Century of Sermons, upon Several Remarkable Subjects*, left to him by his friend and mentor, John Hacket, Bishop of Lichfield and Coventry. The average length of Hacket's sermons is 8,000 words; the delivery in each case must have taken a good hour and a half. Hacket was a convinced Royalist, who was banished from London after the execution of Charles I and who, as Plume writes in his dedication to the sermons to Charles II, 'In his ordinary attendance upon your Majesty, your Royal father and grandfather, he had the honour to preach more than eighty times at Court'. So royalty, like the man in the Maldon or Greenwich pew, had its weekly quantum of preaching.

But, of course, the wonder of Plume's Library is the diversity of the subjects it includes besides theology. It was while Plume worked for Hacket, who was at that time residing in Cheam after his banishment from London, that the younger man was sent on regular trips to the metropolis to buy books for Hacket and thus became extremely familiar with the many booksellers in the neighbourhood of St. Paul's Churchyard. We now also know that later in his life, when he had decided that he would leave his Library to Maldon for public use (although of a restricted kind), he attended the first ever book auctions held in the City (and in England: book auctions originated in Holland) in order to widen the range of what had essentially been a working library.

Our detailed knowledge of Plume the man is scanty; but he bought and read books that covered every shade of religious, political and indeed, scientific and philosophical opinions. He must have had an amazingly enquiring mind into most aspects of the growing corpus of knowledge.

He had, for example, Harvey's first work on the circulation of the blood in 1649. Among a host of books on travel and geography, he owned Thomas Mun's *Discourse of Trade from England into the East Indies*, 1621, and Thomas Neale's exceptionally rare *Treatise of Direction on how to Travel Profitably into Foreign Countries* of 1643. He had Sir William Petty's *Essay Concerning the Multiplication of Mankind*, 1686, and Petty's earlier, celebrated *Treatise of Taxes and Contributions* of 1662, two of the earliest works of mathematical statistics. Among the 1,600 tracts and pamphlets I mentioned earlier, Plume owned the infamous and thoroughly venomous *Decree of Starre-Chamber Concerning Printing* of 1637 which ushered in what — because of its extremely repressive nature — has been called the darkest age in the history of the English book trade since Caxton set up his press at Westminster. Plume also possessed Milton's *Doctrine and discipline of Divorce* and the volumes by others that came out in response to Milton's challenging attitude, *and* he had Milton's reply to those.

A page from Christopher Scheiner's Rosa Ursina *of 1630.*
The author was a German astronomer, thought to have been the first to have observed sunspots.
Plume, perhaps because of his long residence in Greenwich, was very interested in matters astronomical
and left money to Cambridge University to found the Plumean professorship of astronomy.

Title page of Thomas Fuller's The Historie of the Holy Warre, *3rd edition of 1647. This very popular history of the Crusades was first published in 1639.*

An interior view of the Library.
Plume's books, as was usual in the seventeenth century,
do not have titles or authors on their spines.

He had William Prynne's notorious and notoriously dull *Histrio-mastix, or the Players Scourge,* of 1633, and no fewer than 35 of Prynne's 200 published pamphlets and books, and he owned at one time the great poetry and drama of the period — works by John Donne, Francis Beaumont, Charles Cotton, Abraham Cowley, William Greenwood, Thomas Heywood, John Milton, Francis Quarles, James Shirley, John Skelton, Edmund Spenser, Sir John Suckling and Edmund Waller.

Not many of these have survived in the Library, but the Friends will continue to search for them. Maldon has much to be grateful for.

A Measure of Essex Cartography

A. STUART MASON

ESTATE MAPS drawn to scale from accurate land measurements first appeared in the last quarter of the sixteenth century. The techniques for their making had been available for some years so it is a puzzle as to why most landowners were tardy and reluctant converts to cartography.

Scale maps of small areas of land were produced from 1550 onwards, pioneered by military engineers who turned from the picture map to the scaled map with ease as they were used to scale drawings of their fortifications. Lawyers needed maps in land disputes heard before courts far from the land disputed: again the picture map gave way to the scaled variety.[1] The first known scale map of a small portion of Essex land was a 'Plan of Northwicke now in variance' drawn and coloured in 1567 and produced at the Court of Requests in a dispute over marshland in Canewdon.[2] The only pictorial element is the painting of the house and barn, hugely out of scale, a work of imagination, not record.

A shining example of English expertise in surveying and mapping was Christopher Saxton's series of engraved county maps (1574 to 1579, with the Essex map published in 1576). This major project was paid for by Thomas Seckford, a lawyer from Woodbridge, Suffolk, and made possible by the Queen's commission.[3] William Harrison of Radwinter pronounced 'Master Seckford's cards' to be 'perfect and exact'.[4] That he should praise the financier not the cartographer reveals an Elizabethan attitude to technicians.

Landowners as educated men were familiar with the use of maps. John Dee, that much travelled mathematical genius, wrote in 1571[5] that men 'liketh, loveth, getteth and useth Maps, Chartes and geographical globes'. Later in this text he turned to estate surveying: 'In these realms of England and Ireland (whether through ignorance or fraud I can not say) how great wrong and injury hath been committed by untrue measuring and surveying of lands and woods . . .' A scaled estate map depended on accurate land measurement for which landowners had scant regard. As late as 1610 the surveyor, William Folkingham, could write that 'it is a world to see the sottish pressures against the admeasurement of land'.[6] He could not understand why people were content to have the 'selling of wares' regulated by weight and measure without bothering with land. He made a good point. Chelmsford, like every shire town, received standard weights and measures from the Crown in 1492 and Clerks of the Peace and manorial courts were kept busy by those accused of selling short measure.[7] There was no legal mechanism to bring the errant land measurer to book.

Essex land has been measured time out of mind. The statute length of the pole at 16½ feet was defined in 1272 although customary measurement with poles of different lengths continued.[8] Monastic lands were enthusiastically measured to fractions of an acre, a nicety beyond the means of measurement. However, the measurements were good enough for Newton,[9] in 1970, to reconstruct the manor of Writtle from those made in 1328 and for Cromarty (1966)[10] to use the measurements of 1400 to map the monastic land in Saffron Walden.

The faceless land measurer was of low social and educational status, unsupported by any trade association. Only one name stands out: John Cracherode was noted in the rolls of Felstedbury manor (1410–13)[11] as being paid 3s. 4d. for measuring the desmesne lands. The task took him four days as he was also paid 8d. for his food at the rate of 2d. a day. The crucial point, most evident after the Dissolution of the Monasteries, was the dichotomy between the roles of the *Supervisus*, a gentleman well versed in all manorial management and the land measurer who was not in a position to gain knowledge of new techniques. The Elizabethan surveyor was indeed a supervisor who did not measure land and appeared unconcerned with the measurer's errors. Edward Worsop said it all in the title of his book (1582):[12] 'A discoverie of the sundrie errours and faults daily committed by Landmeaters ignorant of Arithmatike and Geometrie to the damage and prejudice of many of her Majesty's subjects.'

In fact many of her Majesty's subjects were content with the status quo. The manorial system worked by custom and precedent. If their ancestors had agreed that a meadow contained five acres, landlord and tenant would continue to call it the five acre meadow without questioning its size. For, in Worsop's words, 'the common people are in great fear when survey is made of their lands'. They feared that a survey, being ordered by the landlord, was but a prelude to a rent rise. Worsop was aware that 'most tenants that take lands after the common measuring pay far more than they should' and that 'gentlemen know well enough how to let their lands to the uttermost'. For these reasons he considered that 'it is very requisite for both sides that the land be truly measured. True measurement is not extremitie but good justice.' Of course no tenant would believe that a surveyor employed by the landlord would seek justice at the expense of his employer. Worsop suggested that a college of surveyors be set up to guarantee their skill and probity, measuring and valuing 'according to equity and indifference'. Needless to say his proposals received no support, not even from his colleagues.

Worsop was also an early and keen advocate of the estate map as the best visual display of accurate measurement. But, 25 years later, John Norden[13] recited the conservative countryman's objections to 'modern' surveying by putting them in the mouth of a farmer debating the subject with a surveyor. 'Poor countrymen', says his farmer, 'do not think it good to have our lands plotted out and methinks it is to very small purpose; for is not the field itself a goodly map for the Lord to look upon, better than a painted paper'. For the farmer, with his intimate knowledge of the land he farmed, the new style of surveying was 'an upstart art, found out of late, both measuring and plotting'.

Before the emergence of the new cartographer-surveyors the traditional surveyor compiled a written account of a manor 'taken by survey and the inspection of the copies, leases and other evidence: by the oath of all the tenants and the perambulation and view of all the fields'. This quotation comes from the survey[14] of Chrishall manor made as late as 1592. Although acreages are recorded in such surveys, there is no mention of fresh measurement of the land. By contrast, when the new surveyors, such as Israel Amyce, began to write surveys accompanied by maps[15] the same formula was used with the addition of 'and by measurement of all and singular lands'. The early estate maps were produced as part and parcel of written surveys while other lords of the manor were still ordering the old style of written survey, without new land measurement and maps.

The hesitant start of Essex estate cartography is clear from the date of the first eight surviving maps, each with a written manorial survey: 1576 and 1579 by Amyce, 1584 and 1586 by Walker and one by an anonymous hand, 1587 by Treswell, 1589 by Agas and 1590 by Shene.

The new breed of surveyors who measured and mapped were a diverse bunch. Israel Amyce was born in the manor of Wakes Colne, held by his father. By profession a lawyer, Israel was a property owning gentleman in no financial need to make maps, unlike his older neighbour Ralph Agas of Stoke-by-Nayland who was a professional cartographer. John Walker of West Hanningfield was a yeoman builder, taking after his father, a carpenter and builder.[16] Newton and Edward's monograph *The Walkers of Hanningfield*[17] established the Walkers as the most prolific and best of Essex estate cartographers and linked them to Amcye. Ralph Treswell was a citizen of London, by trade and company a painter-stainer who became a much sought-after estate cartographer. Robert Shene, apart from his plain maps within a written survey of 1590, was really the old style of gentleman surveyor, appearing in 1600, with a written survey, as general surveyor to Lord Rich.

The type of survey, with or without maps, depended on the commissioning landowner. The second Lord Rich was not keen on maps. His steward, John Cooke, produced elegant written accounts of Great Waltham[18] (1563) and Rayleigh[19] (1579) signing himself as 'gent and steward'. But when working for Walter Fysshe, a London merchant tailor, he added 'surveyor' to his splendid written account of Woodham Ferrers[20] (1582). He was presiding over the manor court of Great Burstead in 1593 when Edwin Rich was about to buy the manor from his father. For this transaction the Rich family employed Agas to produce a written survey accompanied by a map of the manor.[21] The wishes of the landowner were paramount. George Golding, Lord Darcy's auditor, employed Worsop to survey his manor of Waltons in Purleigh[22] in 1584. Worsop, the great advocate of estate maps based on fresh measurements, produced the traditional survey, with

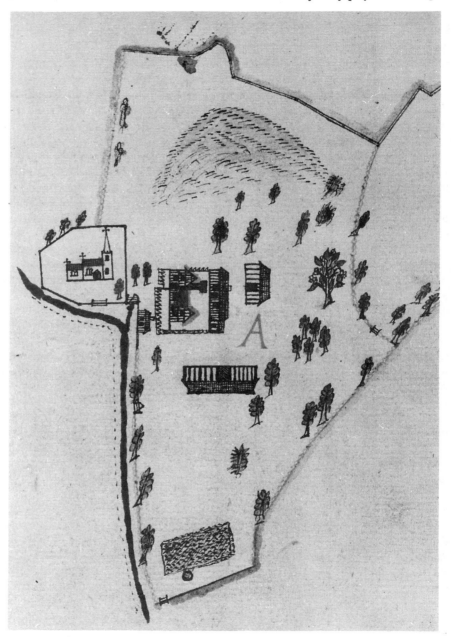

Detail from John Walker's map, 1584 (Manor of West Tilbury, D/DU 23/138).
Typical Walker buildings. The shaded hill was his only attempt to show relief of the land and not copied by his contemporaries.

(Photograph courtesy of the Essex Record Office)

no map. In fact the manor was mapped in 1600 when it had passed to Sir Thomas Mildmay, Walker being the cartographer.[23] When Henry Maynard bought the manor of Tilty from the Crown in 1588 he employed Ferdinando Malyn, a London surveyor commended by Worsop, to survey his purchase and its prospects.[24] So Malyn concentrated on the manor house, reckoning that for 200 marks 'it could be made a convenient and seemly house for an esquire of the best sort'. He recommended new windows for more light 'to avoid melancholy' and noted that the ruins of Tilty Abbey could be a rich source of building materials. Malyn did make a fresh measurement of all the land and called his survey 'A trew platt . . .', a term only applied to maps, apart from this exception. There was no map but Agas made one[25] in 1593. All this makes the first commissioner of estate maps more important.

The first Essex survey[26] to be illustrated by maps was ordered in 1576 by the Dean and Chapter of St. Paul's to show their manor of Belchamp St. Paul's. Amyce, then only 26 years old, made three versions, each with a different number of maps following the written text. The Dean had been quick to realise the importance of maps for an estate so far from its owners. But he was a man of wide scholarship, being Alexander Noel, previously headmaster of Westminster School, whose cousin, Laurence Noel, was an antiquarian and pioneer cartographer.

Amyce's next survey,[27]in 1579, suited his legal training. It was commissioned by the heirs of Edmund Tyrrell, deceased, to aid the partition of his lands in Canewdon, Benfleet and Hockley. Amyce used the same format, and again signed himself as 'gentleman'. On his map of Plomborowe manor he noted for the uninitiated that the fields were set out in 'perfect proportions' with the 'exact buttals and bounds of each'. Correct boundaries were essential to estate management and the prime purpose of a map was to show them. Agas[28] (1596) emphasized the value of a map over a written survey because 'their ancient and faire books can't detect boundary changes and hidden lands', while the survey 'by plat' had 'no such inconvenience'. This was bad news for those who sought after hidden lands in Crown property and for tenants adept at bending boundaries to their profit.

John Walker neatly combined text and map in his surveys of 1584[29] and 1586[30] by putting text and relevant map on facing pages, capital letters on the map being keyed to the text. Both surveys were for minor landowners. The first, of the manor of West Tilbury, was for Andrew Jenour whose home manor was Bigods, Great Dunmow. He must have preferred a map of his distant manor rather than the home property which he knew intimately. Walker's second survey, of Rivers Hall, Boxted, was the owner's home ground. Walker followed Amyce, in telling the user how to use a map. Throughout his career he felt this was necessary, often starting the instructions: 'You shall understand right worshipful and Christian reader . . .'.

The 1587 maps[31] of the scattered Essex lands owned by St. Bartholomew's Hospital were the first to be ordered by the Hospital and Ralph Treswell who

Detail from Robert Skene's map of Little Canfield manor, 1590 (D/DHt M20).
Map drawn in ink-line and the first Essex map to be orientated by a classical wind-rose.
(Photograph courtesy of the Essex Record Office)

made them was the first London surveyor to work in Essex. The changing meaning of the word surveyor is well shown in the Hospital's records. Its original rule book of 1552 laid down that two surveyors be appointed annually to make a general survey of the lands and take care of the leases: the appointees had to be City Aldermen, no other qualification was required. The Governors hired Treswell for the specific task of mapping the lands for the first time. But in 1599 the Hospital appointed as steward Martin Llewellyn who had published a book of sea charts. He took over the maps, making a book of them in 1617, illustrating all the Hospital's holdings, most of them copied from Treswell's work. St. Thomas' Hospital went one better by appointing the great Christopher Saxton as its surveyor in 1587. Prior to this the governors of the Hospital appear to have been responsible for written surveys of their lands. Their manor of Aveley was the subject of a written survey[32] in 1561, with an estimate of acreage and a note that the manor house was 'somewhat in disarray'. A longer survey[33] of 1578 was made in the presence of the bailiff. Without a further written account Saxton mapped[34] the manor in 1593, having previously mapped some of the Hospital's lands in Kent. His Aveley map was a neat working document, so accurate that in 1782 it was copied without revision by Joseph Freeman.[35]

Ralph Agas' first Essex work was a map[36] of the manor of Leaden Roding, belonging to the Waldegrave family, made in 1589: the map is overlaid with too much Latin text, much like his 1593 map of Great Burstead which had a written account as well. An anonymous but skilled hand produced a series of maps[37] to accompany a written survey of Belhus manor, Aveley, at some time betwen 1586 and 1589 as it was made for the widow of Edward Barrett who died in 1586. The last of this list of early estate maps was by Robert Shene whose brief written survey[38] of Little Canfield, posessed by several gentlemen, was followed by two plain maps in ink line without colour. One map is distinguished by orientation with a compass rose, naming eight classical winds of the Mediterranean. This is the first use of a device already familiar on sea charts while other Essex maps had the cardinal points of the compass written in the four margins.

These early years of Essex estate maps show how closely they were wedded to the traditional written manorial survey. The start date of 1576 is not significantly behind the general introduction of estate maps. Probably the earliest example is the 1572 map of land belonging to the City of Norwich made by John Goodwin. He was also surveyor to the Townshend family who, apart from their Norfolk estate, held the manor of Great Bentley. Goodwin advised on this manor but was not asked to map it.[39]

Major Essex landowners, like the Mildmays and the Petres, did not take to estate mapping until after 1590 when the number and variety of Essex estate maps increased markedly. Nor were they flattered by decorative features on the maps which, however well made, were designed primarily for estate management. For some ebullient Elizabethans the sheer size of a map was a symbol of their own importance. Thus, in 1580 Sir William Cordell, Master of the Rolls, had his Long Melford, Suffolk, estate recorded by Amyce on a map[40] measuring 8 by 6½ feet.

A year later this was overtaken by Lord Cheney who had Agas make a map[41] of 11 by 8 feet of his estate at Toddington, in Bedfordshire. Both these maps were of an impractical size, but Agas[42] wrote of making vellum maps using 12 to 16 skins 'for so the owner would have them'. The Lord Chancellor, Sir Christopher Hatton, was more practical in getting Treswell to make a series of maps of his estates in the mid-1580s.

Sir Thomas Mildmay, who inherited his father's estates in 1566, decided on maps to accompany the written surveys of 1591. For the manor of Bishops Hall, which included the town of Chelmsford, the written book of 'survey and admeasurement' was presented to the manor court before Edward Moryson Esquire, Surveyor, John Lathum gent., Steward, and John Walker, measurer. A neat example of the hierarchy that managed a manor. Walker, demoted to land measurer status, signed his splendid map[43] that showed each house in the town as 'Architector'. The other home manor of Moulsham was mapped by Walker[44] at the same time. depicting the 1,700 acres of land. Walker was the only surveyor-measurer to be employed by Sir Thomas for mapping. He mapped[45] the 1,270 acres of Terling manor in 1597 and newly purchased land in Purleigh in 1600.[46]

Mildmay's friend Sir John Petre inherited his estates in 1572 but did not order his first map[47] until 1596. This map of the manor of Ingrave, a late purchase of his father's, was made by John Madison, better known for his elegantly written manorial surveys for Lady Catherine Audley (Great Tey,[48] 1593), Lord Darcy (Kirby,[49] 1597) and for John Paschall (Great Baddow,[50] 1605). These landowners did not want a map and were satisfied with 'the diligent Inspection and Perambulation of John Madison, surveyor'. Madison used Latin for his written surveys and on some of his maps. His map of Ingrave was drawn in black ink framed with a wide border patterned with Cornish choughs and Tudor roses borrowed from the Petre arms. This is the first Essex map to have a decorative border, but the ink drawing of it looks as if it should have been coloured. An anonymous map[51] of the same date of Cranham manor, another late Petre purchase, has a style suggesting that Madison could have made it. The title indicates that it illustrated a written survey, whereas the Ingrave map has an attached vellum giving a full contents list of the map.

Sir John Petre turned to Walker for subsequent maps. The 2,855 acres of the Petre manors in Horndon were shown on one map[52] in 1598, but the next year just one farm of the Writtle manor was depicted.[53] It was not until 1601 that the core Petre estate of Ingatestone was mapped [54] (by John Walker now assisted by his son) and Ingatestone Hall with its demesnes was finally mapped[55] in 1605.

The ancient and huge estates of the de Vere family (Earls of Oxford) were not well represented by maps as the 17th Earl of Oxford spent his time selling land to support his life-style at Court. In fact the estates were in the hands of administrators (including Amyce) from 1580. Soon after his marriage to Lord Burghley's daughter in 1571 the Earl sold his home manor of Castle Hedingham to his

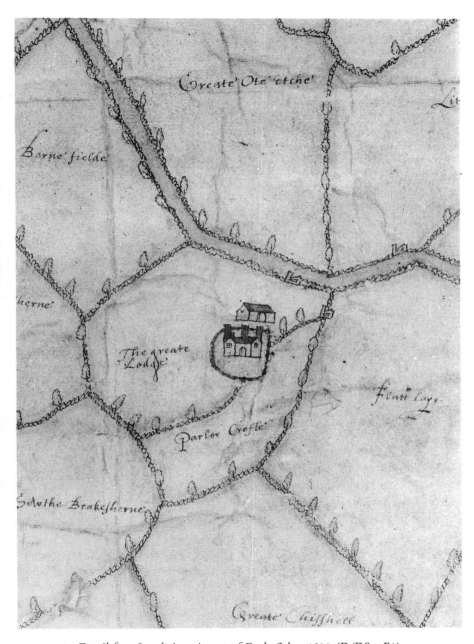

Detail from Israel Amyce's map of Earls Colne, 1598 (D/DSm P1).
Moated house and hedgerow field boundaries typical of his style.

(Photograph courtesy of the Essex Record Office)

father-in-law and in 1584 he sold his manor of Earls Colne and Colne Priory to his steward, Roger Harlackenden. Amyce made written surveys illustrated by maps of both the properties, Castle Hedingham[56] in 1592 and Earls Colne[57] in 1598. To the latter he added a large map showing all the manor but neglected to fill in a title within the box he had drawn for it.

Two institutions which had long held Essex land turned to maps in the 1590s. The Wardens of Rochester Bridge followed the example of St. Thomas' Hospital in appointing a cartographer as their surveyor. Philip Symonson, best known for his unique large scale map of Kent published in 1596, was appointed their Superintendent and Surveyor in 1592 and promptly mapped[58] their Kent properties and their manor of South Hall, Tilbury, in 1594. New College, Oxford, had its Hornchurch lands mapped in 1600. By contrast Christ's Hospital did not get its Essex lands until the death of their benefactor Dame Mary Ramsey in 1596. Ralph Treswell mapped her estate in Rickling in 1597 and the lands in Colne Engaine, Clavering and Berden in 1602.[59]

It was not until the last years of the Queen's reign that first-time buyers of Essex land ordered maps of their new estates. Oliver Style, a London grocer, bought in 1597 a farm in Hornchurch and 'for the better knowledge of the premises' asked the ubiquitous Treswell to map it.[60] Roger Gwynne, a rich apothecary (and hence of the Grocers Company) began buying Essex land in 1596 and by the turn of the century owned some 4,000 acres in Pebmarsh, Great Henny and Bures Hamlet, all of which was well mapped by William Sands, unknown apart from this work.[61]

This ready acceptance of maps was not shared by the previous generation of City men. Thomas Thompson, a haberdasher, bought Shalford manor in 1579: This came to his son, Sir Thomas Thompson in 1590 but he did not have it mapped until 1603 when Edward Eldred of Stebbing, a lawyer with a London practice made a most sophisticated map[62] using a grid for reference to each parcel. The title script is in the finest engrossing hand as befitted a lawyer who was later Clerk of the Peace in Essex[63] (1612). Apart from a written survey[64] of a Stebbing farm there is no other surviving work of this excellent cartographer who died in 1624.[65]

Elizabethan owners who ventured on a map may well have been surprised by the amount of information displayed. Hedgerows and park palings, gates into fields, ponds and streams, highways and driftways were all on the maps of that time, including those by anonymous surveyors. The main advantage of the map, an expression of the newly established accuracy of land measurement, was the setting out of true boundaries for each parcel of land. Moreover the type of land tenure, demesne, copy- or freehold, was indicated by key symbols or letters, or by colour-wash over inked boundary lines. 'Quality' of land (i.e. arable or pasture) was indicated in contents tables as on the map[66] of the lands of Little Dunmow Priory where 'each field noted by the Alphabetical letter which being found in the table do declare the names of the same grounds and their quality and quantity'.

Decorated capital S (of Supervisus) of title of Edward Eldred's map of Shalford, 1603 (D/DSm P6).
As a lawyer Eldred was used to fine scripts
(Photograph courtesy of the Essex Record Office)

The man who made this map was working under orders for he noted some land 'not known to the bailiffe so I have not seen it'. A map[67] of Dancewell Hall has a brown or green wash over field boundaries to denote arable or pasture. John Norden painted the whole field green for pasture or with brown brush strokes to indicate furrowed arable in his map of Berden Hall, his only surviving Essex estate map.[68] The same technique was used on an anonymous map[69] of a farm in Hatfield Broad Oak which used an arrow-like polar indicator with a fleur-de-lis at the north end; both techniques typical of the late eighteenth century.

Decorative features were remarkably rare, the maps were working documents for estate management. A map[70] of New Hall (alias Bremstons), Purleigh, is boldly drawn and coloured, using green over fields belonging to the property, others remaining uncoloured. A simple geometric design forms a cartouche for the title and contents table, yet only part of this is coloured. The area of each field is, as usual, written on the field but given to the nearest acre rather than in acres, roods and perches which are found on all other maps. This map indicates how little uniformity there was in presentation, each cartographer solving the common problems in his own way.

Single maps of small properties, common in the eighteenth century, did not feature in Elizabethan times as mapping was mainly tied to written manorial surveys. Walker provided the one example in 1591 with his excellent map[71] of the 41 acre 'Widdow wealdes land and Tenement' in Broomfield. For Lord Petre he made an unusual map[72] of a section of the road from Stock to Chelmsford, bordered by a wood on one side and the palings of Crondon Park on the other: at least 70 yards of land lies between the two boundaries with a narrow road in the middle, a telling illustration of manorial waste.

When Skelton reviewed[73] the unique collection of Tudor maps in Hatfield House he found no progression or evolution in their cartography. The same can be said of the first 30 years of Essex estate mapping. In particular Amyce and Walker held to their distinctive styles throughout long careers and their early maps were as good and as detailed as their later work. In short, land surveyors were fully conversant with estate cartography and the required accuracy of land measurement for some time before their expertise was sought by landowners. The potential supply was ahead of a reluctant demand.

Landowners, and their bailiffs, who knew their lands at first-hand were probably less enthusiastic about estate maps than we are in viewing them as a unique recreation of the past. Value was what mattered. Maps showed the site of all sorts of buildings but could not indicate the internal layout or state of repair. Nor, on the fields, was anything to denote the quality of husbandry which affected valuation. However more and more landowners were requesting maps in the early years of James I reign, although nothing new was added to the format.

The first textbook to acknowledge the estate map as a routine product of a survey was published in 1616 by Aaron Rathbone.[74] He was a down-to-earth Yorkshireman who did not lament the sins of past land measurers or make a special plea for maps. He described the measurement of land and the making of a map as straightforward jobs of work. He told his readers what to present to a manorial court of survey and then 'repairing home [you] may there perfect your plot . . . and engrosse your survey'.

At that time Rathbone and many others were much involved in the survey of Crown manors that had lain neglected until James I came to the throne. In 1602 Sir Robert Johnson informed Robert Cecil, later the first Marquis of Salisbury, that Crown lands could yield a proper income if well managed and that 'the chiefe foundation of mischief has been the want of authentic surveys'.[75] When Salisbury became Lord High Treasurer in 1608 he found the Treasury 'almost exhausted' and immediately ordered 'the royal manors to be surveyed, what before were but very imperfectly known'.[76] This proved to be an administrative nightmare, not least because of the extraordinary lack of initial information. Salisbury sought information on Essex from William Waldegrave who had been deputy steward of Crown manors in the county since 1580. Waldegrave, then at Little Ilford, 'confined to my chamber by grief', could give no account of the royal forest, could not list the copyholders of Crown manors and did not know the names of the Justices of the Peace. All he knew was that there were 'divers surveys taken heretofore and written in books' in the custody of Sir Edward Elliot of Roxwell but now held by Sir Edward's son.[77] No wonder Salisbury accomplished little before he died in 1612.

The sheer number of Crown surveys commissioned inevitably led to great disparity in the quality of the work done. Both money and time were scarce so most surveys were in written form and relatively few maps were made. Among the experts employed was John Norden who left a very long list of the Crown lands he had surveyed. These included lands in West Ham, Havering and Stapleford Abbots. But not all surveyors took their job as seriously as he did. He complained that John Hercye charged a full fee for surveying manors by 'relation' only, for 'he perambulated none. One day was sufficient for the survey of a great manor.'[78] 'Relation' meant recording the comments of selected manorial tenants, a short cut bordering on fraud.

Two Crown surveys in Essex unearthed the chaos of land titles. H. H. Lockwood in his fascinating study of the 'greedy hunters after concealed lands', described what happened in Barking.[79] In 1616 Robert Treswell, son of Ralph, was commissioned to 'plot' the whole of Barking, its first measured survey. But, three years later, 'this plot ruffe made by the Surveyors' was still in dispute: the map had revealed the problems of land titles but had not solved them. Professor McIntosh described[80] the same problems for the Royal Liberty of Havering. This was mapped[81] in 1617 in meticulous detail by an anonymous hand that may have been that of Robert Treswell. The value of this map to the Crown became obvious in 1619 when the Attorney-General charged 182 tenants with holding illegal land titles. By the following year the Crown had become an open adversary of those within the Liberty, who learnt to their cost that true maps accurately defining boundaries might be true justice but were not to their advantage.

By this time experience had shown people that accurate land measurement was a practical application of mathematics, not to be left to the unskilled, and the map had been accepted as a useful instrument of estate management and sale. The pioneer estate cartographers had ended or were near the end of their careers. Ralph Treswell had been succeeded by his son Robert, and John Walker and his son made their last maps in 1616, leaving a unique legacy of quality. In the years that followed until the Civil War the surveyors remained a disparate bunch of individuals not seeking any corporate identity. Work surviving from these years seems to have been more varied in quality than the earlier maps. Style changed with fashion, particularly with decoration designed to flatter the landowner. No new cartographic concepts were introduced. But all this is another story.

REFERENCES

(Catalogue marks refer to documents in the Essex Record Office, unless otherwise specified.)

1 For a definitive account of manuscript Tudor maps see P. D. A. Harvey, *Maps in Tudor England*, 1993, P.R.O. and B.L.
2 P.R.O., MPI 627
3 See S. Tyacke and J. Huddy, *Christopher Saxton and Tudor Map Making*, 1980, B.L.
4 W. Harrison, *Description of England*, 1577, (from 1968 edition, ed. G. Edelin).
5 J. Dee, 1571, Preface to H. Billingsley's translation of *Euclid's Geometry*.
6 W. Folkingham, *Feudographia*, 1610.
7 See H. Grieve, *The Sleepers and the Shadows*, 1988, E.R.O. A drawing of Barking courthouse made soon after its building in 1567 shows a pillory, large scales with standard weights and a standard bushel in front of it. Drawing in the P.R.O.
8 See A. W. Richeson, *English Land Measuring*, 1966, M.I.T. Press.
9 K. Newton, *The Manor of Writtle*, 1970, Phillimore.
10 D. Cromarty, *The Fields of Saffron Walden in 1400*, 1966, E.R.O.
11 D/DSp M38.
12 E. Worsop, *A discoverie of sundrie errours and faults daily committed by Landmeaters*, 1582.
13 J. Norden, *The Surveyors Dialogue*, 1607.
14 D/DVm 20.
15 D/P408/28 and Guildhall Library, MS25517/1 and 2.
16 See the Petre family accounts for 1550: 'Paid to Walker the carpenter . . . for making three new tenements in Crondon Park', D/DP A10.
17 A. C. Edwards and K. C. Newton, *The Walkers of Hanningfield*, 1984, Buckland Publications.
18 D/DTu 254.
19 B.L., Add. MS 24782.
20 D/DRa M9. See F. G. Emmison's account in Trans. E.A.S., XXIV, 6–16.
21 D/DP M986 (survey) and D/DP P3 (map).
22 D/DHn M7.
23 D/DHn P1.
24 D/DWv M197.

25 T/M 7.
26 D/P408/28 (kept in the parish for years; has least number of maps). Guildhall Library MS 25517/1 and 2 (No. 1 is prime version with most maps; No. 2 is version annotated by the Dean).
27 D/DWt M27 (no maps). B.L. Harley MS6697 (survey with maps).
28 R. Agas, *A Preparative to Plotting Lands*, 1596.
29 D/DU 23/138. Note that the maps with facing text only describe the demesne lands. A written account of the marshlands follows and on the last page is written: 'Beholde this platt following whose scale is alowed 32 rods to every yntch.' The preceeding demesne maps are on twice this scale and no map follows in the document. It would appear that Walker made, or intended to make, a map of the marshland.
30 D/DE1 P1.
31 Maps and documents quoted in this paragraph are in the archives of St. Bartholomew's Hospital. Also see Dr N. M. Moore's history of the hospital.
32 B.L. Add. MS 42114.
33 D/DTh 18.
34 Original map in G.L.C.R.O.
35 D/DTh 18.
36 Bodleian Library (R)MS C17:28.
37 Northants R.O., map 1254. A roll of 10 maps stitched together, written survey missing.
38 D/DHt M20.
39 D/DU 318/1. Letter from Goodwyn, written from Colchester, to Sir Roger Townshend, advising on land disposal in Great Bentley. Goodwyn also wrote a book of customs for this manor. See F. G. Emmison, *Elizabethan Life: home, work and land*, 1976.
40 See A. S. Bendall, *Maps, Land and Society*, 1992, C.U.P.
41 See P. D. A. Harvey, *op. cit.*, (ref. 1).
42 R. Agas, *A Preparative to Plotting Lands*, 1596.
43 D/DM P1 and survey D/DGe M50.
44 D/DM P2. Walker wrote on this map: 'I have right honourable and Christian readers whatsoever you may be set downe a true and perfect platt of a goodly manor . . . surveyed measured and taken by John Lathum, Gent, Steward there, and John Walker Architector.' (Moryson is not mentioned).
45 Map in private custody.
46 D/DHn P1.
47 D/DP P4.
48 D/DCm M1.
49 D/DE M1.
50 D/DWv M69.
51 Acc. 7028, D/DH.
52 D/DP P5.
53 D/DP P6.
54 D/DP P8 and D/DP M1449 (written survey).
55 Map in private custody.
56 D/DMh 1.
57 D/DPr 626; D/DSm P1.
58 T/M 409. Original map with Wardens of Rochester Bridge. William Lambarde, antiquarian and Keeper of Records at the Tower of London, was Warden at this time and commissioned Symonson's map of Kent.

59 Original maps in Guildhall Library.

60 D/DU 296 (documents for sale). Styles' land is shown on the map of Havering marshes made in 1600 by Richard Barnard for New College, Oxford (T/M 126 and New College archives MS5617).

61 D/DU 760/114 (Pebmarsh), Ph 3/10A (Great Henny), D/DU 351/1 (Bures Hamlet). At that time some mathematical instrument makers were freemen of the Grocers Company but William Sands does not appear in the list of freemen (document in Guildhall Library).

62 D/DSm P6.

63 ASS 35/55A/H-112.

64 B.L. MS 40631A, f.161.

65 Will of Edward Eldred D/DA Bw 45/13.

66 D/DYa 1. Map made c.1600 for the Earl of Sussex: the demesnes 'geographically described'.

67 D/DGh P5. Map undated and anonymous: 'a true platt'.

68 D/DU 1458/1. Map dated 1602. The long life of such maps is evident from its endorsement as produced in evidence in April 1860 for tithe dispute.

69 D/DU 737/1. Undated map of 240 acre farm. Brush strokes over fields, green for pasture, brown for arable.

70 D/DGe P1.

71 D/DVk 1.

72 D/DP P7.

73 R. A. Skelton and J. Summerson, *A description of maps . . . with collections made by William Cecil, now at Hatfield House*, 1971, O.U.P.

74 A. Rathbone, *The Surveyor*, 1616.

75 See S. J. Madge, *The Domesday Book of Crown Lands*, 1968, Cass.

76 See entry for Robert Cecil in *Biographia Britannia*, c.1760.

77 B.L. Lansdowne MS 91, f.8. Letter dated 1608.

78 B.L. Maps 198.c.50. (Copy of MS held in Cambridge University Library).

79 H. H. Lockwood, 'Those Greedy Hunters after Concealed Lands', K. Neale, ed., *An Essex Tribute*, 1987, pp.153–70.

80 M. K. McIntosh, *A Community Transformed*, 1991, C.U.P.

81 D/DU 162/1.

Noblewomen and Piety in Late Medieval Essex

JENNIFER C. WARD

THE PARISH CHURCHES OF ESSEX provide visible testimony to the importance of the Church in the Middle Ages. Men and women at all levels of society made use of the Church's sacraments throughout their lives, were guided by its teaching, and hoped ultimately for salvation. Charters and wills show how they endowed churches with land, money and goods. Many of the surviving documents were issued by men, but women were also important benefactors and many were well known for their piety. Late medieval Essex noblewomen have left evidence of their religious practices and patronage, and it is possible to see how their involvement with the Church overlapped with their concerns for their families, estates, retainers and friends. Several of these women had lands in other parts of the British Isles, but most emphasis here will be placed on their activities in Essex.

The leading noble families in late medieval Essex were the Bohun earls of Hereford, Essex and Northampton and their descendants, the de Vere earls of Oxford, the Lords Fitzwalter, and the Bourchier earls of Essex. The last Earl Humphrey de Bohun died in 1373, and his estates were divided between his two daughters, Eleanor who married Thomas of Woodstock, duke of Gloucester, youngest son of Edward III, and Mary who married Henry Bolingbroke, sub-sequently Henry IV. Eleanor's share of the estates passed via her daughter Anne to the earls of Stafford. The Bourchiers were a rising family in the fourteenth and fifteenth centuries, Henry being created earl of Essex in 1461. Other noble families held lands in the county, and two dowagers were especially significant in the fourteenth century, Marie de St. Pol, countess of Pembroke (d.1377), who had a residence at Great Braxted, and her close friend Elizabeth de Burgh (d.1360) who often resided at Clare in Suffolk and at Great Bardfield. In addition, the families of knights and esquires counted as noble in the later Middle Ages, and their culture, interests and attitudes were similar to those of the higher nobility. There are strong parallels between the religious concerns of the wives and widows of the gentry and those women who were above them in the social hierarchy, and this is reflected in mortmain licences and wills.[1] A distinction has however to be drawn between the wife who was legally subject to her husband, and the widow who was entitled to dècide her own actions. Elizabeth de Bohun,

Monumental brass commemorating Lady Elizabeth, (daughter and co-heir of Sir Richard Scroope, widow of William, Vicount Beaumont and Lord Bardolf, second wife of John de Vere, 13th Earl of Oxford, 1537), depicted in coronet and heraldic mantle.

(Rubbing courtesy of H. Martin Stuchfield)

countess of Northampton, referred at the beginning of her will of 1356 to obtaining her husband's consent to her bequests.[2]

The life of the nobility was permeated by religious activity. The daughter of a noble family had the option of either marriage or entrance into the religious life, and at least in the former case the parents had a major say. In drawing up his will in 1383, Sir William Berland made provision for his daughters' dowries, or for their entry into a nunnery if they so wished.[3] Nunneries in the later Middle Ages were known for their noble inmates, and many Essex families had a relative who was a nun. Sir John Gildesburgh, in his will of 1387, referred to his sister Margaret who was a nun at Barking abbey.[4] Isabella, daughter of Thomas of Woodstock and Eleanor de Bohun, became a nun, and subsequently abbess, at the abbey of Minoresses outside Aldgate.[5] There was frequent contact between noblewomen living in the world and in monastic houses, and papal indulgences were granted for visits and entertainment. Matilda de Vere, countess of Oxford, and her son received permission in 1364 for the religious to eat meat at their table. Seven years earlier, Elizabeth de Burgh was allowed to enter the enclosures of Minoresses with five ladies, as opposed to the three previously permitted.[6] Visits were paid to religious houses in the course of the lady's travels, as when Elizabeth de Burgh paid short visits to Tilty abbey and Thremhall priory in the summer of 1347.[7] Monastic houses were occasionally used for confinements; Henry de Ferrers was born in 1356 at Tilty.[8]

There were some similarities between life in the nunnery and in a noble household, and lay households had their own chapels, sometimes with separate chapels for husband and wife. For the widow, it was possible to become a vowess, and live a religious life while continuing to carry out secular responsibilities. Becoming a vowess entailed taking a vow of chastity in the presence of the bishop who blessed the vowess and clothed her with mantle, veil and the ring of chastity;[9] Elizabeth de Burgh took a vow of chastity before 1343.[10] Marie de St. Pol's desire to be buried in the habit of a Minoress may indicate that she adopted certain facets of the nun's way of life; she is known to have had her own chamber in her foundation for Minoresses at Denny in Cambridgeshire.[11]

Religious activity centred on the household chapel which, judging by bequests in wills, was colourfully and richly furnished. Elizabeth Beaumont, countess of Oxford, bequeathed to the parish church of Wivenhoe, where she was buried in 1537, her best vestment and cope of crimson velvet, her best chalice, and her two altar cloths of crimson velvet with a pane of blue velvet in the centre, and a frontal to match; two other altar cloths and frontal were left to the altar of St. John the Baptist.[12] Attendance at Mass in the private chapel is documented in Elizabeth de Burgh's chamber account of 1351–52 which lists the offerings made at the service. The services were attended by household and visitors,[13] and were part of the fabric of daily life. The seasons of the Church determined the food which was served to the household, with fasts and feasts being observed. Elizabeth de Burgh always celebrated the feast of Corpus Christi which was introduced into England in the early fourteenth century, and rapidly achieved popularity. The importance of the feast for Elizabeth is emphasized by her expenditure on food and drink for the feast, £18 16s. 4d. being spent in 1358.[14]

The religious practices of women within the household appear self-contained, and the private and individual nature of late medieval religion has been emphasized by several historians.[15] In addition to the use of the private chapel, this is apparent in indulgences secured from the papacy, possession of religious objects including books, and the practice of pilgrimage. Concern over death, purgatory and salvation was central to late medieval religion, and this was reflected in petitions for papal indulgences. A petition was presented in 1366 on behalf of Henry de Coggeshale and John Gildesburgh and their wives for plenary remission of sins at the hour of their deaths; a similar indulgence for plenary remission by a confessor of their choice was obtained by Earl Aubrey de Vere and his wife Alice in 1398. Other indulgences concerned the celebration of Mass which was the focal point of worship in the later Middle Ages. Several of the nobility had the right to have a portable altar, as had Earl John de Vere and his wife Elizabeth in 1434. A less usual indulgence was granted to Countess Matilda de Vere in 1408, that she might have Mass and the divine offices celebrated in a low voice, behind closed doors, and without bells, in the presence of herself, her servants and five honest persons of her choice in places which were under interdict; if she or any of the others died in such a place, burial might take place in church or cemetery.[16]

Many women had their own images, relics and books which they bequeathed to family and friends, and some showed special devotion to a particular saint. Alice, Lady Neville, in her will of 1393 singled out the amber rosary which she used. In the following year, Joan Heveningham bequeathed to her son John and his heirs a gold cross containing a relic of the true Cross, an ivory tabernacle, a missal and a breviary; her daughter Joan was left a psalter and a silver-gilt tabernacle, and her son Thomas a gold crucifix and a gold and jet rosary.[17] Such possessions were still valued by their owners in the 1530s at the time of the break with Rome. Elizabeth, countess of Oxford, was accustomed to wear a gold cross containing a relic of the true Cross. Her books included an illuminated *Book of Hours*; many of the nobility were able to read and thus had the opportunity to make prayer more personal. Among her images was a gold tablet depicting the Assumption of the Virgin Mary and St. Francis. Her rosary was of jet, ornamented with gold crosses. Her rings also had religious associations, such as the diamond ring with the five joys of the Virgin Mary.[18] Some of the possessions referred to in women's wills were family heirlooms; Marie de St. Pol bequeathed to Westminster abbey the cross which her father-in-law, William de Valence, brought from the Holy Land, and in bequeathing a richly bound, illuminated psalter to her son, Eleanor de Bohun commented that it had been left to her on the condition that it was to pass from heir to heir.[19]

Pilgrimage continued to be popular in the later Middle Ages, and a few women went on pilgrimage overseas. In 1344 Countess Margaret de Bohun was referred to as going to Santiago de Compostella and other places of pilgrimage.[20]

It was however more usual to visit English shrines. Elizabeth de Burgh's vow to visit the Holy Land and Santiago was commuted to other works of piety in 1343, as she felt that having reached the age of forty she could not hope to fulfil it.[21] She went on pilgrimages to Canterbury, Walsingham and Bromholm.[22] The popularity of Walsingham as a centre of pilgrimage until the Reformation is reflected in bequests; Elizabeth, countess of Oxford, left a gift to the priory to be distributed among the poor of the town, to the honour of God and the Virgin Mary.[23]

All these practices and possessions give the impression of religion centred on the individual. Yet simply to emphasize these private elements is to take too narrow a view. When arrangements for funerals and chantries are examined, together with gifts to parish churches, monasteries, and the friars, and involvement with confraternities, it is clear that the noblewoman saw her religious obligations in a wider social context. Participation in the Mass by the lady herself and the celebration of requiem Masses were community occasions, and were not simply for the benefit of a single person or family.[24] Concern with death and salvation was universal, and the Mass was seen as being at the centre of the Church's worship; the decision in favour of transubstantiation in 1215 and the institution of the feast of Corpus Christi in 1264 meant that the Church put increasing emphasis on the Mass down to the Reformation.

It was usual in wills for the testator to bequeath the soul to Almighty God, the Virgin Mary, and all the holy company of heaven. There were some variations in wording, but all the noblewomen under consideration were orthodox in their approach, and there are no traces of Lollardy among them. Men and women made provision for their funerals and requiem masses, these sometimes supplementing existing chantry arrangements. Many women were appointed by their husbands as executors, and so had the responsibility of organising funerals and commemoration. Often they chose to be buried next to their husbands, although this was not invariably the case. Lady Elizabeth Bourchier in 1499 wanted to be buried in the Lady chapel at Beeleigh abbey next to the tomb of her father-in-law, Henry, earl of Essex; her husband had intended to be buried there four years earlier, but his widow had to arrange for the full payment of his bequest to the abbey, and to direct her executors to move her husband's bones from Stebbing parish church to Beeleigh, and to have a tomb built for husband and wife.[25] On the other hand, in 1356, Elizabeth, countess of Northampton, wanted to be buried in the church of the Dominican friars in London, while her husband had previously arranged to be buried with other members of the Bohun family at Walden abbey.[26] There was great variation in the degree of splendour of the funeral, as in the cases of Elizabeth de Burgh and Marie de St. Pol; Elizabeth left £200 for funeral expenses, and 200 pounds of wax for the lights round her body, while Marie, like several other late fourteenth century testators, wanted her burial to be carried out without excessive cost.[27]

Many noblewomen chose to be buried in a religious foundation of monks or friars. Elizabeth and Marie wished to be buried away from their husbands, in the

St. John's Abbey Gatehouse, Colchester, the only surviving monastic building.
Margaret Teye and other Essex families chose to be buried in the abbey. Engraving of 1808.
(Photograph courtesy of the Essex Record Office)

Minoresses' houses outside Aldgate in London and at Denny respectively. Alice FitzRalph in 1471 wanted to be buried in Ixworth priory in Suffolk, or next to her mother in the Greyfriars church by Newgate, depending on whether she died at Pebmarsh or in London. Margaret Teye chose burial in St. John's abbey, Colchester, next to her husband.[28] There are also examples of burials in parish churches, like that of Margaret Chaunceux beside her husband at Canewdon in 1389, and Elizabeth, countess of Oxford, in 1537 next to her first husband at Wivenhoe where their brasses still survive.[29]

The provision made for funerals epitomizes two deeply held convictions in the medieval world, the importance of gifts to the church itself, and of charity towards the poor. The gifts could be of money or goods and inevitably varied in size; Margaret Teye bequeathed to St. John's abbey her old great carpet, her best counterpane and £10 in money. The prayers of the poor were particularly highly valued in helping the soul through purgatory, and alms-giving to the poor at funerals was a continuation of the charity shown in various ways during the noblewoman's life. Alice, Lady Neville, wanted £3 to be distributed to the poor on the day of her burial, and Elizabeth, countess of Oxford, wished the poor to be present at the requiem masses to be held 30 days after her death in the parish churches round Wivenhoe.[30] Additional provision for the poor was made in wills, with hospitals or particular groups of poor people being singled out. Marie de St. Pol wanted all the goods on her manors on the day of her death to be given to her poor tenants, or to the poor in the nearest villages, to maidens, prisoners, widows, orphans (so that they might have a trade), and to poor religious, according to the discretion of her executors.[31]

The belief in purgatory and the importance attached to requiem masses and prayers for the soul explain why the foundation of chantries was so widespread in the later Middle Ages. Chantries were tailored to individual needs. Endowment took the form of land or money and the chantry might be perpetual or for a set number of years. The endowment financed the celebration of daily or weekly masses for the benefit of named persons; alternatively, as became increasingly usual, trustees were appointed to pay the chaplain's stipend.[32] Chantries varied greatly in size, from the colleges of chaplains like those established by Thomas of Woodstock at Pleshey about 1393, and the Bourchier family at Halstead in 1412, to the anniversary masses prescribed by less wealthy testators.[33]

Just as family traditions were important with burials, so chantries often commemorated members of a family rather than an individual, and foundations were made by the husband, or by husband and wife together, or by a widow. William le Baud received a mortmain licence in 1328 to establish a chantry in Corringham church where masses were to be celebrated for his soul and that of his wife Isabella, and the souls of their ancestors and others. The chantries for which John de Sutton of Wivenhoe received licences in 1352 and 1363 were to commemorate the souls of John himself and his wife Margery; the earlier licence for a chantry in Foulton chapel in Ramsey was also to commemorate their fathers and mothers, ancestors and benefactors, while the later one for Wix priory was to commemorate their heirs.[34] Widows acted as founders and trustees, as when a mortmain licence was granted in 1408 for the endowment of masses in Coggeshall abbey for the souls of Margaret de Badewe and her two husbands, Hugh de Badewe and Thomas Coggeshale; the founders included Joan de Bohun, countess of Hereford, Margaret herself, Joan's grandson-in-law Sir William Bourchier, and Sir William Marny.[35]

The lists of those to be commemorated by the chantry underline the fact the social as well as the family element was very important in late medieval religion. Responsibility was felt for friends, and for lords or retainers. The licence for the alienation of Berden to Walden abbey was issued to Earl William de Bohun and his wife Elizabeth, although the establishment of the chantry itself was in William's name.[36] Those to be remembered included Edward III, many members of the Bohun family, the parents of the countess, and all the faithful departed. This chantry was unusual in commemorating brothers and sisters, but it is clear that both men and women made their personal choice of those to be remembered. Margaret Chaunceux in 1389 left ten marks to Richard Lynde, chaplain, for masses for two years after her death for the souls of herself, her husband John, her parents and friends, and all the faithful departed.[37] Alice, Lady Neville, did not want great expense at her funeral, but wanted 300 masses for her soul and all Christian souls within fifteen days of her death. The requiem masses on the thirtieth day after the death of Elizabeth, countess of Oxford, were to include prayers for herself and her husband, her father and mother, and all Christian souls. In addition, her executors were to provide for 200 masses as soon as possible after her death for her, and her husband, father and mother, at a rate of 12d. a mass. As was usual, she specified the type of masses she wanted: 50 of the Trinity, 50 of the Holy Ghost, 50 of the five wounds of Christ, and 50 of requiem.[38] The prayers offered by the chantry priest broadened out from the founder and family to friends and benefactors and all Christians.

How far did individual churches benefit from benefactions by noblewomen? The noblewoman and her family certainly had ties with parish churches, monasteries and houses of friars on their estates and associated with kindred and ancestors, but the degree of involvement varied according to personal preferences, family concerns, and social responsibilities. Relatively little is known of the noblewoman's relationship with the parish church, although it is likely that the household chapel was of greater importance for regular worship; parish church attendance by Elizabeth de Burgh in 1351–52 was occasional.[39] Funerals and chantries, however, with their attendant gifts and endowments, benefited a parish church, as did other bequests in kind and money.[40] The small size of many of the gifts in wills may be an indication that noblewomen were making a token gesture towards the parish church, but they may have made larger gifts in their lifetime of which we know nothing. In her will, Elizabeth de Bohun singled out the parish church of Rochford for the bequest of a pair of vestments, and Margaret Chaunceux left £2 to Canewdon church and £1 to Shopland.[41] Elizabeth de Burgh singled out four parish churches in her will, Clare, Great

Bardfield, Standon and Bottisham; the £3 and a cloth of gold left to the first three, and the £2 and a cloth of gold left to Bottisham were minor items among her religious bequests. However, her accounts show that at least in the case of Standon a larger sum of £20 was given for building work in 1343–44.[42]

Great Bardfield parish church.
The tower dates from the late twelfth century, and much of the rest of the building from the later fourteenth century. Elizabeth de Burgh arranged for a requiem mass to be celebrated in 1352 for her councillor, Thomas de Cheddeworth.

Greater interest was shown in the friars; nearly every noblewoman's will included bequests to the friars although the scale of donations varied widely. Some women, such as Margaret Teye, had a relationship of confraternity with them[43] Her bequests show the importance attached to the prayers of the friars, as she wanted each house to sing a solemn Dirge and Mass for her and her friends immediately after her death. The practice of making small bequests to several houses of friars was common, as with the will of Alice, Lady Neville, who bequeathed 13s. 4d. each to the Carmelite friars of Maldon, the Dominicans of Chelmsford, the Franciscans of Colchester, and the Augustinian friars of Clare.[44]

Elizabeth de Bohun was far more lavish in 1356; she left 100 marks, her own cross containing a relic of the true Cross which she used to wear, and chapel furnishing and books to the Dominican house in London; she wished to be buried in the choir of their church. She also left £20 to the Dominican friars in Chelmsford; the bequests to the Carmelites of Maldon and the Franciscans in Colchester were left blank in the registered copy of the will.[45]

The later Middle Ages was not a great age for monastic benefactions, but many of the nobility maintained connections with the houses established by their ancestors; although heiresses, like Elizabeth de Burgh, kept up links with foundations associated with their inheritance, wives and widows usually patronized the houses connected with their husband's family. Matilda de Vere in 1366 wanted to be buried with her late husband in the de Vere foundation of Colne priory, and she left 100 marks to the monks for work on the church, and £10 for prayers, especially for her soul and that of her husband.[46] On becoming earls of Essex in 1236, the Bohun family became patrons of Walden abbey where Joan de Bohun, widow of the last Earl Humphrey, was given confraternity, often attended Mass on saints' days, and provided for sculpture in the nave of the church, a lead roof and a new tower, and gave vestments, altar vessels, and a gold cross containing several pieces of the true Cross.[47] Gifts and bequests were sometimes associated with providing for a husband's burial and commemoration, as with Elizabeth Bourchier and Beeleigh. Quite apart from family considerations, there was an element of personal choice in some of the bequests; Margaret Teye in 1517 chose to make a gift to Barking abbey, and asked the convent for a solemn Dirge and Mass for her soul, her husband's, and all her friends'.[48] As with the friars, the relationship between noblewoman and religious house was essentially reciprocal; gifts were given in return for prayers and, in some cases, confraternity. This relationship was regarded as important; Marie de St. Pol wanted all the religious houses where she had received confraternity to be informed of the day of her death, and to receive one of her relics, vestments or images for the greater remembrance of her soul.[49]

When new houses were founded in the later Middle Ages, it was the stricter orders which were favoured. Marie de St. Pol planned a Carthusian foundation at Horne in Surrey, but this proved abortive; she made small bequests to Charterhouses in her will.[50] Other references to Charterhouses are rare in the wills of noblewomen connected with Essex, although Elizabeth, countess of Oxford, in 1537 left small sums to the Charterhouses of Sheen and London, and to the Bridgettine house of Syon.[51] Where noblewomen associated with Essex stand out is in connection with the Minoresses and with the university of Cambridge, and these foundations show the same reciprocal relationship of gifts in return for prayers. Four houses of Minoresses were established in England. The London convent outside Aldgate was patronized by Elizabeth de Burgh, and her grandson-in-law, Lionel, duke of Clarence, established the house at Bruisyard in Suffolk in 1364–67. Waterbeach in Cambridgeshire was founded in 1294 by Denise de Montchensy, and it was this house which was moved to Denny in the

1340s by Marie de St. Pol. Marie and Elizabeth de Burgh are also well-known for their foundations of Pembroke and Clare colleges at Cambridge.[52] The Minoresses are occasionally mentioned in Essex women's wills, the most significant bequest being that of Matilda, countess of Oxford, in 1412; she wished to be buried at Bruisyard, and granted the nuns her manor of Wrabness.[53]

The later Middle Ages saw the growth of religious gilds which, especially in the large towns, attracted the membership of gentry and nobility as well as townsmen. St. Helen's gild at Colchester was refounded in 1407 in St. Cross chapel, and supported five chantry priests and thirteen poor people in the hospital; a feast was held on St. Helen's day, and prayers were said for Henry IV and the brothers and sisters of the gild. Of the women members of the gild, the most notable in 1418 was Joan de Bohun. Joan was described as countess of Hertford, but, as this title did not exist in 1418, it is most likely that the countess of Hereford was meant.[54] The existence of the gild provided yet another opportunity for prayers and requiem masses. Joan's membership signalled her importance within the county, as well as her piety.

In examining piety, it is clear that the overriding concern was for the fate of the soul after death. At the same time, religion permeated daily life, and religious and social concerns were intertwined, while family, wealth, property and piety were inextricably enmeshed. These considerations were as true of men as of women in the later Middle Ages. At the same time, an element of individuality comes out in religious activities. In addition to family and social considerations, women were exercising a measure of choice as to their place of burial, the destination of their gifts, and the degree of their generosity.

From our viewpoint in the late twentieth century, noblewomen's piety took a tangible form. Gaps in the evidence, especially concerning gifts during the woman's lifetime, and a lack of letters, which might have thrown light on religious attitudes and motivation, make it dangerous to assume that some women were more pious than others. Probably there was much variation in the depth of religious feeling, and an interest in religious matters may have developed with age. In the existing state of the evidence, it is clear that, while all women conformed to the general religious practices, some, and not necessarily the wealthiest, devoted much time, energy and money to the Church. Of the women connected with Essex, Marie de St. Pol stands out. Married as a teenager to Aymer de Valence, earl of Pembroke, in 1321, and widowed without children three years later, she spent over 50 years of her life as a widow. She was unusual in the number of her religious foundations and benefactions, and in making these over a long period of her life, from 1336 until her death in 1377. She probably had an early interest in the Franciscan order, and this explains her determination to establish and eventually to be buried in the abbey of Denny. Her interests extended to France where she held lands and where she tried but failed to found a college in the university of Paris. In the obituary written by Thomas Walsingham of St. Albans abbey, she was described as an outstanding woman who during her lifetime spent her goods to the honour of God and the glory of her house, and for the benefit of the poor. Her good works made her an example to the nobility. On her death she left all her substance to her servants, churches, or the poor.[55]

Religion was not a matter in which the woman thought only of herself. Elizabeth de Burgh was concerned in her foundations as in her will to commemorate her three husbands, other members of her family, and her household and retainers. Joan de Bohun, described by Walden abbey as a woman devoted to God, watching in the temple of the Lord,[56] combined her religious observance with family and social obligations, acting as the leading magnate in Essex after Henry IV's accession; as Henry's mother-in-law, she was trusted by king and gentry alike, and in supporting chantry foundations of retainers and gentry Joan's religious and political roles overlapped.

Noblewomen's piety has to be seen as an integral part of their lives. It was influenced by personal considerations and circumstances, as well as by husbands and families, by ancestral tradition as well as by contemporary ideas. When Elizabeth, countess of Oxford, died in 1537, having drawn up a traditional late medieval will; the Reformation was already under way, some monasteries had already been dissolved, and in a few years prayers for the dead would become a thing of the past. Within a short space of time, the practices of the later Middle Ages were shattered.

REFERENCES

1   After Edward I issued the Statute of Mortmain in 1279, a mortmain licence had to be obtained from the Crown when property was given to the Church.

2   Lambeth Palace Library, Register of Simon Islip, fo.122a–b.

3   The will is printed in translation in Jennifer Ward, ed. and trans., *Women of the English Nobility and Gentry, 1066–1500*, Manchester, 1995, pp.34–5.

4   Guildhall Library, London, Register of Robert Braybrooke, fos.433b–434b.

5   *Calendar of Fine Rolls, 1399–1405*, pp.201–2; *Calendar of Patent Rolls, 1416–22*, p.364; *Calendar of Entries in the Papal Registers relating to Great Britain and Ireland. Papal Letters, 1396–1404*, p.385. The Minoresses were Franciscan nuns, following the rule laid down by Isabella, sister of Louis IX of France.

6   *Calendar of Entries in the Papal Registers relating to Great Britain and Ireland. Papal Petitions, 1342–1419*, pp.300, 490.

7   P.R.O., E101/92/30, m. 5d, 8d.

8   *Calendar of Inquisitions post mortem*, XIV, no. 347.

9   R. N. Swanson, trans.,*Catholic England. Faith, Religion and Observance before the Reformation*, Manchester, 1993, pp.166, 173.

10 *Calendar of Entries in the Papal Registers relating to Great Britain and Ireland. Papal Letters, 1342–62*, p.113.

11 H. Jenkinson, 'Mary de Sancto Paulo, foundress of Pembroke College, Cambridge', *Archaeologia*, LXVI, 1915, p.432; R. Gilchrist, *Gender and Material Culture. The Archaeology of Religious Women*, London, 1994, p.120.

12 P.R.O., Prob. 11, 11 Dyngeley.

13 P.R.O., E101/93/2; Jennifer Ward, ed. and trans., *Women of the English Nobility and Gentry, 1066–1500*, Manchester, 1995, pp.220–1.

14 M. Rubin, *Corpus Christi. The Eucharist in Late Medieval Culture*, Cambridge, 1991, pp.199–201; J. C. Ward, *English Noblewomen in the Later Middle Ages*, London, 1992, pp.75–6; Jennifer Ward, ed. and trans., *Women of the English Nobility and Gentry, 1066–1500*, Manchester, 1995, pp.221–2.

15 E.g., J. Catto, 'Religion and the English nobility in the later fourteenth century', in H. Lloyd-Jones, V. Pearl and B. Worden, eds., *History and Imagination. Essays in honour of H. R. Trevor-Roper*, London, 1981, pp.45–50.

16 *Calendar of Entries in the Papal Registers relating to Great Britain and Ireland. Petitions, 1342–1419*, p.531; *Papal Letters, 1396–1404*, p.126; *Papal Letters, 1427–47*, p.515; *Papal Letters, 1404–15*, p.140. Church services were not normally permitted to be held in a place under interdict.

17 Guildhall Library, London, Register of Robert Braybrooke, fos.443b, 445a–b.

18 P.R.O., Prob. 11, 11 Dyngeley.

19 H. Jenkinson, 'Mary de Sancto Paulo, foundress of Pembroke College, Cambridge', *Archaeologia*, LXVI, 1915, p.433; J. Nichols, *A Collection of all the Wills of the Kings and Queens of England*, London, 1780, pp.181–2.

20 *Calendar of Patent Rolls, 1343–5*, p.350. Margaret was the widow of Earl John de Bohun who died in 1336.

21 *Calendar of Entries in the Papal Registers relating to Great Britain and Ireland. Petitions, 1342–1419*, pp.22–3; *Papal Letters, 1342–62*, p.112. In 1343, Elizabeth was about 48 years old.

22 P.R.O, E101/92/12, m.10d–11d; E101/92/30, m.10d; E101/92/2, m.12d.

23 P.R.O., Prob. 11, 11 Dyngeley.

24 E. Duffy, *The Stripping of the Altars. Traditional Religion in England c.1400–c.1580*, New Haven, pp.109–16, 121–2.

25 P.R.O., Prob. 11, 27 Vox; 32 Horne.

26 Lambeth Palace Library, Register of Simon Islip, fo.122a–b; B.L., Harley MS. 3697, fo.258a–b.

27 J. Nichols, *A Collection of all the Wills of the Kings and Queens of England*, London, 1780, p.23; H. Jenkinson, 'Mary de Sancto Paulo, foundress of Pembroke College, Cambridge', *Archaeologia*, LXVI, 1915, p.432.

28 P.R.O., Prob. 11, 2 Wattys; E.R.O., 98 CR2.

29 Guildhall Library, London, Register of Robert Braybrooke, fo.433a–b; P.R.O., Prob.11, 11 Dyngeley.

30 Guildhall Library, London, Register of Robert Braybrooke, fos.443b–444r; P.R.O., Prob. 11, 11 Dyngeley.

31 H. Jenkinson, 'Mary de Sancto Paulo, foundress of Pembroke College, Cambridge', *Archaeologia*, LXVI, 1915, pp.433–4.

32 K. L. Wood-Legh, 'Some aspects of the history of chantries in the later Middle Ages', *Transactions of the Royal Historical Society*, fourth series, XXVIII, 1946, pp.47–60; C. Burgess, ' "By quick and by dead": wills and pious provision in late medieval Bristol', *English Historical Review*, CII, 1987, pp.837–58.

33 R. Gough, *The History and Antiquities of Pleshy in the County of Essex*, London, 1803, pp.169–70, 175–81; *V.C.H. Essex*, II, London, 1907, pp192–5.

34 *Calendar of Patent Rolls, 1327–30*, p.264; *ibid. 1350–54*, p.350; *ibid. 1361–64*, p.382.

35 *Ibid. 1405–08*, p.389.

36 *Ibid. 1343–45*, p.62; B.L., Harley MS. 3697, fos.258a–259a.

37 Guildhall Library, London, Register of Robert Braybrooke, fo.433a–b; she laid down in a codicil that an extra seven marks were to be allocated if possible.

38 *Ibid.* fo.443b; P.R.O., Prob.11, 11 Dyngeley. Elizabeth was married twice, to William, Viscount Beaumont, who died in 1507, and subsequently to John, earl of Oxford, who died in 1513. She did not specify which husband was to be commemorated, but she chose to be buried with her first husband at Wivenhoe.

39 J. C. Ward, 'Elizabeth de Burgh and Great Bardfield',in K. Neale, ed., *Essex Heritage*, Oxford, 1992, pp.56–7; Jennifer Ward, ed. and trans., *Women of the English Nobility and Gentry, 1066–1500*, Manchester, 1995, pp.220–1.

40 C. Burgess, ' "For the increase of divine service": chantries in the parish of late medieval Bristol', *Journal of Ecclesiastical History*, XXXVI, 1985, pp.46–65.

41 Lambeth Palace Library, Register of Simon Islip, fo.122a–b; Guildhall Library, London, Register of Robert Braybrooke, fo.433a–b.

42 J. Nichols, *A Collection of all the Wills of the Kings and Queens of England*, London, 1780, p.33; P.R.O., SC6/1110/12, m.1, 1d. N. Pevsner and B. Cherry, *Hertfordshire*, second edition, Harmondsworth, 1977, p.340, refers to mid-fourteenth century work at the west end of Standon Church.

43 E.R.O., 98, CR2.

44 Guildhall Library, London, Register of Robert Braybrooke, fo.443b.

45 Lambeth Palace Library, Register of Simon Islip, fo.122a–b. The mark was a unit of account and was worth 13s. 4d.

46 G. M. Benton, 'Essex wills at Canterbury', *Transactions of the Essex Archaeological Society*, new series, XXI, 1933–37, p.263.

47 W.Dugdale, (J. Caley, H. Ellis and B. Bandinel, eds.), *Monasticon Anglicanum*, London, 1817–30, IV, p.140.

48 E.R.O., 98, CR2.

49 H. Jenkinson, 'Mary de Sancto Paulo, foundress of Pembroke College, Cambridge', *Archaeologia*, LXVI, 1915, p.434.

50 *Ibid.*, p.433; *Calendar of Patent Rolls, 1345–48*, p.141.

51 P.R.O., Prob. 11, 11 Dyngeley.

52 A. F. C. Bourdillon, *The Order of Minoresses in England*, Manchester, 1926, pp.1–25; J. C. Ward, *English Noblewomen in the Later Middle Ages*, London, 1992, pp.158–60; D. R. Leader, *A History of the University of Cambridge*, I, *The University to 1546*, Cambridge, 1988, pp.82–4.

53 Lambeth Palace Library, Register of Thomas Arundel, II, fo.161a–b.

54 *V.C.H. Essex*, IX, ed. J. Cooper, Oxford, 1994, pp.64, 307; P. Morant, *The History and Antiquities of Colchester*, second edition, Chelmsford, 1815, p.150n, App.13–14.

55 E. M. Thompson, ed., *Chronicon Angliae*, Rolls Series, London, 1874, pp.137–8.

56 W. Dugdale, (J. Caley, H. Ellis and B. Bandinel, eds.), *Monasticon Anglicanum*, London, 1817–30, IV, p.140.

Essex Springs and Shaws

JOHN HUNTER

A WRITTEN SURVEY of Cressing Temple Manor, dated to 1656, is preserved in the Essex Record Office.[1] Under 'woods' it lists 16 *springs*, the largest just over two acres in size, but most just under one. They are all coppice and the survey gives the growth in years of underwood. The springs are named from the adjacent fields, and it is clear that they are the narrow linear woodlands following field boundaries that can be seen on many estate maps of the sixteenth and seventeenth centuries. Their numbers declined in the nineteenth century and they are rare in today's Essex. Before looking more widely at the nature and origin of these distinctive landscape features, we will consider the later history and demise of the Cressing springs, as their fortunes may be typical of the hundreds that once graced the Essex scene.

In 1656 ownership of the Templars' estate and home farm had fragmented and the former open fields had been sub-divided into smaller units favoured by the farming practice of that time. The extensive manorial woods in the north of the parish had been sold and the springs may have been established to compensate for the loss of woodland produce. Moreover they would have given shelter to stock and provided game cover — a point I shall return to. It is certainly difficult to view them as natural survivals of the period of clearance (1150–1300) when the Templars established their efficient arable demesne while owning a plentiful woodland resource near at hand.[2] It would seem then that the springs were created at a later date, perhaps by natural seeding from the hedgerows that bounded the open fields or, more likely, by planting.

An estate map of 1727 of New House Farm, Cressing, lying on land formerly part of the Templar demesne, depicts springs bounding the former Ash Field, now divided into three,[3] but they had vanished by 1800 when the Ordnance surveyors produced their draft survey of Essex. A map of Cressing Temple Manor of 1794,[4] the reduced core of the demesne, shows no spring surviving. This is hardly surprising as rising corn prices in the late eighteenth century, culminating in the French Wars when prices went through the roof, brought pressure on surviving woods, greens and heaths to convert to ploughland. On well managed, stable estates, woodland survived the pressures, but on fragmented areas of land ownership such as Cressing parish little remained. In 1840 some

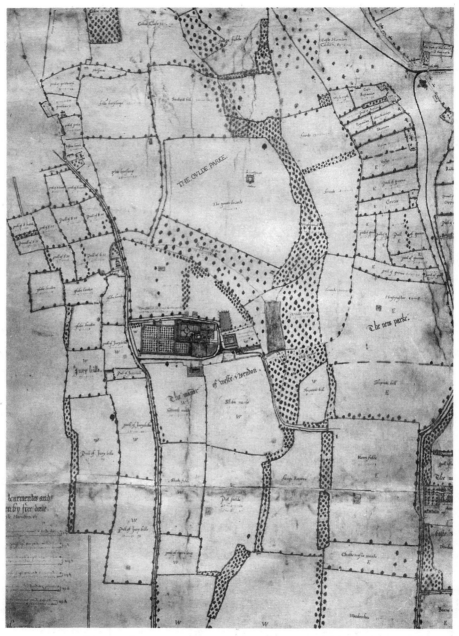

Survey of West and East Horndon by John Walker (senior), 1598 (D/DP P5).
(Photograph courtesy of the Essex Record Office)

small spinneys retained for game birds were the sparse remnants of the former woodlands and springs.

Perhaps the best cartographical record of springs is John Walker's fine map of the Thorndon estate in 1598 (page 284). Here we see Thorndon Hall situated on the ridge line (not the site of the present hall). To the north the landscape is a patchwork consisting of greens and tofts, commons and deer parks, but to the south lies the rectilinear landscape of the south Essex plain, with squared fields relating to north/south boundaries which may stretch for several miles. This is a planned landscape, but when and by whom is unknown, although there have been several guesses. Springs, here termed *shaws*, mostly follow major boundaries on the north/south axis, some fenced, others left open for cattle to browse. It would seem unlikely that they were strips of woodland left when the land was cleared as there were considerable woodland reserves on the high land north of the Hall. But as the woodland gave way to wood-pasture on the commons, or to exclusive wood-pasture in the parks, springs may have developed as a substitute resource. Some fragments remain today and could be under-planted and renewed — illustrated below.

Relict shaw near site of the old Thorndon Hall.

A third example is from another Walker map (below) of the small estate of Little Leighs Hall in 1609. The former park, itself small at some 140 acres, has a linear belt along its northern boundary, shown unfenced and open to grazing, and probably not managed as coppice at that time.

A transcription of the area of the former park, showing spring and clumps.
From 'A trewe platt of the Manor of Little Leighs Haule within the Countie of Essex',
John Walker, 1609 (T/M 320).
(Photograph courtesy of the Essex Record Office)

Many other examples can be found on early maps and written surveys in Essex, but few survived the 'terramania' of the later eighteenth century and the French wars, to be seen on the tithe maps of the 1840s. To discover the nature of springs in their heyday we must look to the counties south of the Thames where many still survive and research has shown their structure and management. But first, we must consider the terminology. *Spring* is a term for coppice and is generally found in north and central Essex. *Shaw* is more usually found in south Essex and is general south of the Thames.

The *Shorter Oxford English Dictionary* defines a shaw as 'a thicket, a small wood, copse or grove, a strip of wood or underwood forming the border of a field'. The *Dictionary of the Sussex dialect*[5] defines it as 'a small hanging wood, a wood that encompasses a close'. The same dictionary also refers to *rews* and *rues*. Peter Brandon noted *rewes* on the Low Weald of West Sussex,[6] and writing in 1974, deplored the destruction of shaws as uneconomic despite their rich plant and animal life.

In Kent, as in Essex, shaws were early targets of agricultural 'improvers'. Furley, writing in 1871, claimed that the clearance of shaws and woodlands, together with improvements in drainage, had caused an increase in agricultural output of 50 per cent over the previous 40 years. 'If the civilisation of a district is to be tested by the state of its agriculture, the condition of its roads, and the means of transport which it possesses, what rapid strides the Weald of Kent has made since the commencement of the present century — I may say, since the beginning of the reign of George IV! Very small fields and enclosures were then invariably to be met with (too many still remain), separated by wide shaws and hedgerows, filled with wide-spreading and thriving oaks, luxuriating in stiff clay. The activity also displayed in grubbing-up these shaws and hedgerows of underwood and timber is completely altering the face of the country and bringing large areas of fresh soil into cultivation.'[8] How Furley would have welcomed the consequences of the Agriculture Act 1950.

On a happier note, I would strongly recommend a visit to the Weald and Downland open air Museum at Singleton in West Sussex, a remarkable achievement in any case, but suggested here because springs have been planted as elements in the landscape setting to the Bayleaf Farmhouse. They were designed after careful research into the content and structure of Wealden shaws by R. and A. Tittensor.[9] They found that shaws were traditionally often two rods wide (33 feet) and were intensively managed as coppice with standards. Trees were deliberately sown, mainly oak and elm and produced good timber. In a 30 yard stretch there were likely to be 4–5 standards, and overall there were at least 15 species of tree and shrub in a shaw, sometimes as many as 22. Interestingly, fruit trees are common in shaws and include species such as bullace, crab apple, wild pear, cherry and damson. Beech, birch, sweet chestnut and sycamore are uncommon, but hawthorn and hazel are widespread. Hornbeam is often found in Kent. The shaws designed by the Tittensors have a central line of timber trees (oak and

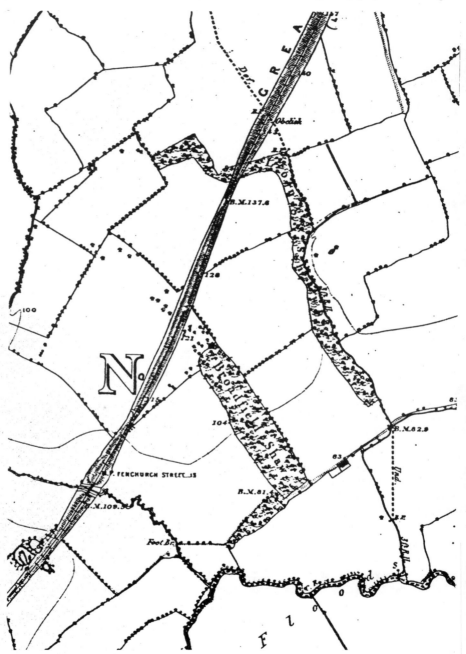

The Loughton demesne shaws as shown on the O.S. 6 inch map surveyed in 1870.

ash), a matrix including hazel and maple on each side and a thorn hedge along the edges; other species are scattered in the matrix.

Despite the research, the origin of the Wealden shaws is unclear, although many date from the Middle Ages. It was mooted in the past that some may be strips of woodland left in the process of forest clearance and so represent primary woodland cover. However, former assumptions of the Weald as an area of primary forest cleared by the Anglo-Saxons are open to question, rather as the Essex claylands which we now know to have been farmed in the prehistoric and Roman periods. So turning to Essex, what conclusions can we draw on the origins and age of the springs and shaws, now mostly vanished, that are depicted on the older maps?

We have noted that the Cressing springs were most probably established much later than the field system of the demesne farm, which was completed in the latter half of the thirteenth century. The hedged boundaries of the large fields would have sheltered the early growth of the new springs, which were intended for coppice management. The Thorndon shaws were established at a far greater distance in time from the original land clearance, perhaps well over a millennium. The small surviving fragments suggest planting with oak in contrast to the field hedges which were predominantly elm.

A few examples of complete shaws survive. One is Bovingdon Rows at Bovingdon Hall, Bocking; the survivor of a cluster of springs shown on a parish map of 1809. The springs lay within the home farm and occur nowhere else on the Tabor estate of some 2,050 acres. The term *rows* appears similar to the Sussex *rews*. The wood is ancient but not primary as the outline of two ditched enclosures can be discerned in the woodland floor, and these occupied a substantial part of the present wood. Moreover, small-leafed lime is absent although it is abundant in nearby woods.

Two other examples can be seen from the M11, on the left travelling north just past the Bank of England works at Debden (pages 288–92). These are Broadfield Shaw and Long Shaw, both described as lying within the demesne of Loughton Hall and depicted with today's boundaries on the Loughton Tithe Award of 1850.[10] Long Shaw is of particular interest with a rich ground flora containing bluebells, yellow archangel and ransoms as well as the inevitable brambles. A natural watercourse forms most of the eastern boundary and a modest ditch and bank the western. The northernmost section was severed by the construction of the Loughton and Ongar branch of the Great Eastern Railway. The species include coppice hornbeam, maple, woodland thorn and wild service, and also crab and apple trees. Of particular interest are a scatter of ancient oak and hornbeam pollards which indicate that the present wood was once wood-pasture, either a common or parkland. The adjacent field is named Seventeen Acre Field and the hedges have the look of late enclosure. The Tithe Award names the wood Seventeen Acre Shaw and a reasonable conclusion is that the woodland was established in the seventeenth or early eighteenth century. The

Hornbeam pollard within Long Shaw, Loughton.

rich flora could have colonized outwards from the sheltered habitat along the brook.

Broadfield Shaw is a coppice with standards woodland. It contains no pollards and gives a sense of age greater than that of Long Shaw. A rough copy made in 1900 survives of a map of 1820 which uses where possible field names taken from a demesne survey of 1739. Broadfield Shaw is named Hods Row and Long Shaw, while present, is un-named.

So it would seem that springs and shaws in Essex were a feature of the sixteenth and seventeenth century landscapes, appearing in localities with strong landlord control — there is no evidence for springs in the small scale 'peasant' landscape that covered much of the northern half of Cressing parish and is depicted on the Tithe Map. Their function was to provide timber and underwood, perhaps to compensate for the loss or clearance of woodlands previously owned. This would be true for Cressing Temple Manor, but hardly for Bovingdon Hall. Further functions would be the provision of welcome shade and shelter for animal husbandry and also game coverts. Field sports developed in the seventeenth century into a form we would recognize. The development of the shot-gun replaced hawking and resulted in the rapid destruction of game birds and the recognition that the supply was no longer inexhaustible. 'Perching', shooting pheasants on the bough, began to give way to 'shoot flying', a more difficult art as often practised on horseback. Conservation of game stocks gave rise to a law passed by the Cavalier Parliament of 1671 by which freeholders of under a hundred pounds a year (the yeoman farmers) were prevented from killing game, even on their own land — a deeply divisive measure. I am advised that well-managed springs would be ideal for game, so the sporting concerns of the squirearchy of this period could well be a factor in the creation and location of springs.

A fourth factor could be fashion. As we have seen, springs and shaws tended to locate on demesne land, and landowners from the sixteenth century onwards were often as swayed by changes of fashion in their landscape and estate management as they were by architectural styles. Take, for example, the extensive gardens and designed parks that are such a notable feature of English cultural history. In the study of a hyperthetical historic park that has survived into the late twentieth century, we may find that in Stuart times, a vogue for radial and axial avenues saw such features superimposed on the wood-pasture landscape of a medieval deer park, and the fish ponds converted into a formal canal. Later on, a reaction towards 'natural' design and the desire for an Arcadian ambience could see the avenues thinned into irregular clumps, the canal converted into a serpentine lake, and artful temples and monuments erected by, or in the style of, the architect currently in vogue. Later still, exotic trees would be introduced and exotic gardens planted. Over the same centuries we might find that knot gardens near the house gave way to parterres and broderies, then to lawns, and then again to formal parterres in the Italian style. The functional landscape of farming was

Long Shaw, Loughton.

Broadfield Shaw, Loughton.

also subject to innovations and change, and in the eighteenth century Essex was in the forefront of progressive agriculture. In this context, it would hardly be surprising if features such as springs and shaws, imported from south of the Thames, enjoyed a vogue.

After speculating on the origin and uses of springs and shaws, there are other linear wooded features which do not come into this category and should not be confused. These would include the peripheral belts planted around parklands in the eighteenth and early nineteenth centuries to shut out views of the functional countryside beyond the pale, and also silvan approaches to country houses planted in the late nineteenth century, such as can be seen at High Trees, Little Sampford, and the northern approach to Debden village. The magnificent belts around Newmarket are certainly not springs; they were planted to give shelter for the racehorse training and breeding industry at the end of the last century and early in this.[12]

Springs and shaws are now rare in Essex; many, such as the Cressing springs were lost long ago when corn prices peaked, rather than during the destructive decades following the Second World War when so much was lost in haste in the drive for modernization. By 1970 the devastating effects of a new strain of Dutch elm disease had become apparent and Essex County Council held a conference in 1972, *Landscape in Decline*, at which I well remember Sir John giving the concluding address. Tree planting with advice and grants were offered and the initiative found a welcome amongst many farmers. I prepared a booklet suggesting ways in which areas of tree and shrub planting could be accommodated in the new farming scene of large fields and a predominance of arable cropping. It is interesting to look back: field corner planting was acceptable but new hedgerows were definitely not, and the considerable lengths being planted today would not have found favour. After all, in the early '70s farmers were still being paid to grub out hedgerows. I also suggested belt planting, rather on the Newmarket model, being unaware then of the earlier tradition of springs and shaws. But this found little favour, too much land was involved, and no one then suspected a time would come of surpluses and Set-aside. Two belts, however, were planted, appropriately enough on the Essex Show Ground and they are now an established part of the scene.

The Essex initiative was unique in eastern England in 1972 and planted the seeds for a most successful county Farming and Wildlife Advisory Group and for the widespread planting we see carried out today. Now at last, trees are legally accepted on Set-aside land and this could include 15 metre headlands, which coincides with the 15 metre minimum width required by the Woodland Grant Scheme. Perhaps three rod wide springs might again be planted to enrich the landscape scene in the first century of the next millennium.

REFERENCES

1 E.R.O., D/DAc 96 and 101.

2 J. M. Hunter, 'The Historic Landscape of Cressing Temple and its environs', in *Cressing Temple — A Templar and Hospitaller Manor in Essex*, E.C.C., 1993, pp.33–5.

3 E.R.O., T/M 504/1.

4 E.R.O., T/M 529.

5 W. D. Parish, *Dictionary of the Sussex dialect*, 1875, reprinted 1957 by Gardner's of Bexhill.

6 P. Brandon, *The Sussex Landscape*, Hodder and Stoughton, 1974.

7 I am indebted to Dr Nicola Bannister for information on Kentish shaws.

8 R. Furley, *A History of the Weald of Kent*, John Smith, London, 1871.

9 I am most grateful to the Tittensors who lent me a copy of their report, *Wealden Shaws: A Landscape Setting for Bayleaf Farmhouse*, 1986.

10 E.R.O., D/DCT 225(A). I am grateful to Emma Hay who drew these interesting woods to my attention while researching woodlands belonging to the County Council.

11 E.R.O., T/M 89.

12 C. Taylor, *The Cambridgeshire Landscape*, Hodder and Stoughton, 1973.

Eliza Vaughan of Finchingfield

ALAN JONES

Eliza Vaughan of Finchingfield, drawn by Martin Angel.

'EYES DARK, hair turning grey. Height, 5' 5". Place and date of birth, Brixton 19 June 1863.' Fortunately, these passport details are supplemented by her photograph shewing an intelligent if rather severe face with hair parted centrally and combed tightly back. Thus we are introduced to Miss Eliza Vaughan, aged at the time 58, author, antiquarian, naturalist and amateur artist; the seventh child of the Reverend Matthew Vaughan, Vicar of St. John the Baptist Church, Finchingfield, in the County of Essex.

There would have been much rejoicing in the Brixton vicarage when Mrs Vaughan, also an Eliza and at the age of 34, gave birth to her only daughter after having had six sons. One year later in 1864, Matthew Vaughan took possession of the living of Finchingfield where he was to remain until his death 25 years later in 1889. A splendid coloured marble memorial tablet recording his ministry is to be found on the south wall of the church. The large Victorian vicarage (now turned into flats) is opposite the school with a rear garden leading down to the river. Of this garden Eliza was later to write, 'My earliest recollections are connected with a large and picturesque garden wherein certain portions were separated from others by high hedges, with attendant ditches whose banks were covered with primroses and periwinkles. A little plot was given me in which my hoe and rake might be freely used, and there, accompanied by two wooden horses and several cats, some of the happiest hours of childhood were spent.'[1]

This imaginative gesture by her parents formed in her an abiding love of gardening seen clearly in her later notebooks where it becomes almost obsessional. She further comments on this early period, 'Another source of happiness came to me when, in my teens I was given a copy of John's *Flowers of the Field* and began, by myself, the study of field botany, thus making the walks in lanes and woods of even greater interest than before'.[2]

June . 1921.

Page from Notebook, June 1921, recording visit to St. Peter's on the Wall, Bradwell-on-Sea.

Her brothers were boarded at Felsted School after receiving a grounding in the classics from their father. Her own education appears to have been at home by governess, although she informs us that she and her two youngest brothers received lessons from the local headmistress if 'the orthodox governess was absent'.

Friendships were made with contemporaries from Spains Hall which lasted into adulthood. 'Sometimes my two younger brothers and myself were asked to spend the day at the Hall, a beautiful Elizabethan house about a mile from the village. After lunch we used to assist in harnessing a large piebald donkey to a small tumbril with straw at the bottom, and in this attractive conveyance we would ride off with our young friends to the woods, along narrow field-tracts by the side of deep ditches.'[3] There was considerable empathy between the Ruggles-Brises of Spains and the vicarage, for when Matthew Vaughan became vicar he had as Churchwarden Colonel S. B. Ruggles-Brise who had been appointed to the office in 1858. It is worth recording that since then, the office of Vicar's Warden has always been held by a member of the family and the present occupant, Colonel Sir John Ruggles-Brise, Bt., has established something of a record in occupying the position for over 50 years, an achievement recognized by the Parochial Church Council in 1993, when he was presented with a framed certificate of appreciation.

Authoress

After the death of her father, Eliza, together with her mother, removed to Kelvedon, living there until the death of Mrs Vaughan in 1895. Later (in 1902), the family had another, smaller marble tablet erected to the memory of their parents which was placed on the north side of the Norman arch leading into the tower from the church. The inscription reads, 'The Chimes in this tower are dedicated by their sons and daughter'. Bereft of her mother, Eliza moved to her final home at Rayne. Turners is a delightful house fronting the main road, dating back to probably the sixteenth century. From there she researched and published her first book *Stephen Marshall — A Forgotten Essex Puritan*.[4] It carries the inscription, 'To The Dear Memories of Matthew Vaughan (Sometime Vicar of Finchingfield) and Eliza, his wife. Their daughter dedicates this little book.' The year was 1907. Stephen Marshall had become Vicar of Finchingfield at the invitation of William Kempe of Spains Hall, and was instrumental in ending the self-imposed seven-year silence of that unhappy man. Marshall was called to London at the inception of the Long Parliament in 1640, being appointed special preacher to the House of Commons. The book, full of local as well as of general historical interest was well received.

Nineteen years were to pass before the appearance of her second book, *The Stream of Time*, subtitled, *Sketches of village life in days gone by*.[5] This work is wholly concerned with the Finchingfield she once knew together with recorded memories of older village worthies. It was a labour of love, an evocation of her

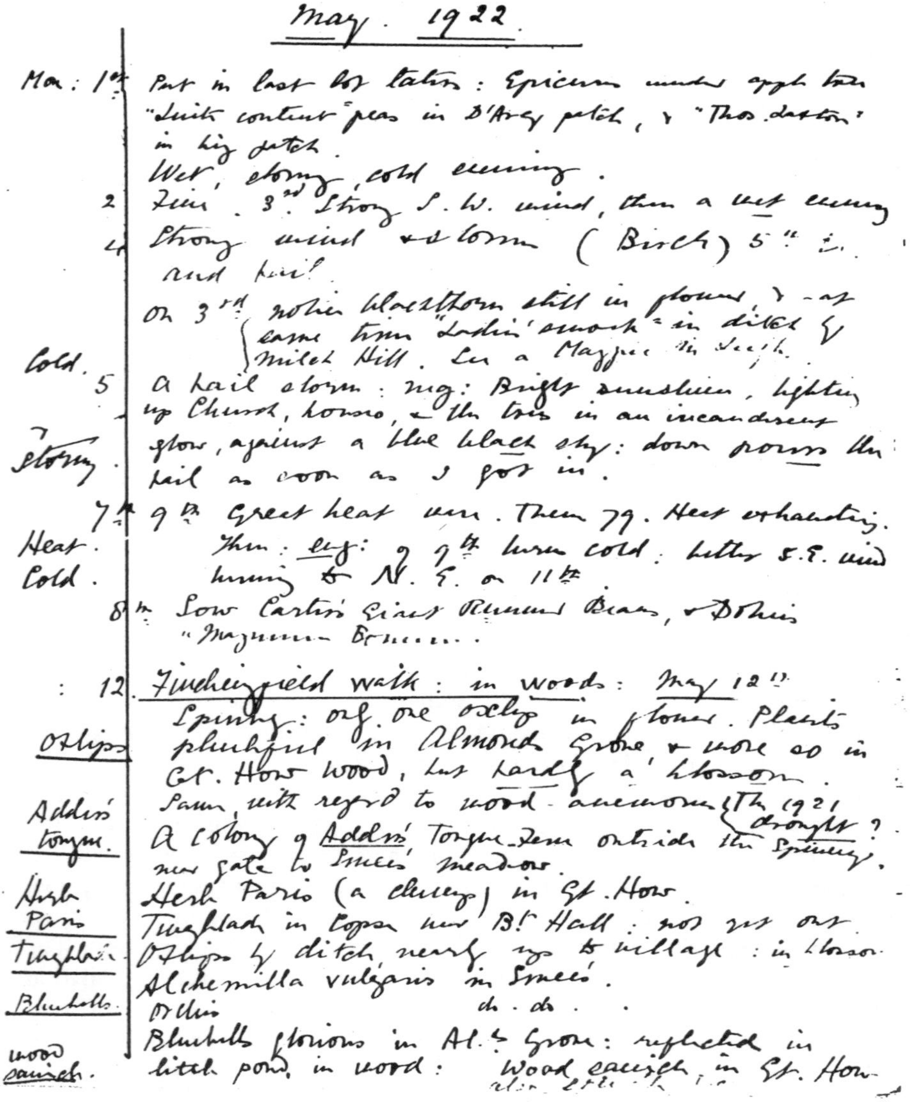
May. 1922.

Mon: 1st Put in last lot taters: Epicure under apple tree "Quite content" peas in D'Arcy patch, & "Thos. Laxton" in big patch.
Wet, stormy, cold evening.
2 Fine. 3rd Strong S.W. wind, then a wet evening
4 Strong wind & storm (Birch) 5" ... and hail!
On 3rd noticed blackthorn still in flower, & - as came from "Ladies' smock" in ditch of Mill Hill. Saw a Magpie ...
Cold. 5 A hail storm: mg: Bright sunshine, lighting up Church, houses, & the trees in an incandescent glow, against a blue black sky: down pours the hail as soon as I got in.
Stormy.
7th 9th Great heat ... Therm 79. Heat exhausting.
Heat. Therm: eveg: of 9th turns cold: bitter S.E. wind turning to N.E. on 11th
Cold.
8th Sow Carters Giant Runner Beans, & Dobbies "Magnum Bonum".
12. Finchingfield walk: in woods: May 12th
Oxlips Spinney: only one oxlip in flower. Plants plentiful in Almonds Grove, & more so in Gt. How wood, but hardly a blossom.
Adders' tongue. Same with regard to wood-anemone (The 1921 drought?) A colony of Adders' Tongue-fern outside the Spinney: near gate to Smees' meadow.
Herb Paris Herb Paris (a clump) in Gt. How.
Twayblade Twayblade in Copse near Bt Hall: not yet out.
Oxlips by ditch nearly up to village: in blossom.
Alchemilla vulgaris in Smee's.
Bluebells Orchis do. do.
Bluebells glorious in Al.s Grove: reflected in little pond in wood: Wood sanicle in Gt. How
wood sanicle.

Page from Notebook, May 1922 recording a walk in woods near Finchingfield.

own past. She speaks of her friends as 'belonging to another age which has vanished never to return', adding, 'there is a danger of the old age and its memories being forgotten as it recedes further into the distance. It has therefore seemed to me that we err greatly in allowing any records, however ordinary, that speak of old times, to be consigned to oblivion and the following pages represent a humble attempt to preserve some fragments of rural life as it was in my youth, when it still retained, as it were, the touch of a venerable antiquity.'[6] She is as good as her word for the book is an antiquarian's delight enabling us to share in her sentiment that, 'Not the least interesting part of the intercourse with my village friends was their intimate connection with the past, and no doubt a more abundant harvest of recollections might have been preserved if one had realized in youthful days the priceless store ready to hand. As it is, the gleanings that remain are doubly cherished.'[7]

Her literary and historical talents were now in full flood with a new volume appearing two years later in 1928. Dedicated to the memories of her two brothers, Matthew Vaughan formerly Assistant Master at Haileybury College and John Vaughan, late Residentiary Canon of Winchester Cathedral, *The Essex Village in Days Gone By*[8] is more discursive in content. There are the inevitable chapters on her beloved Finchingfield, but for her opening foray she delves into 'An Old Clerk's Register' from Rayne. She strays into neighbouring Suffolk for the reminiscences of an elderly dame, only to return to Essex for an essay on Sir Eliab Harvey of Hempstead, Captain of the *Fighting Temeraire*, inspired, so her preface informs, by her late brother Matthew. In this same preface is a tantalizing acknowledgement 'of encouragement and help' to Miss F. M. Mayor, by now famous as the author of *The Rector's Daughter*. Further tribute is paid to Flora Mayor in her final book, *These for Remembrance*[9] in wishing, 'Never to forget that but for her inspiring aid none of my records of the past would ever have been written'.[10] One would love to know more of the friendship between these two clergy daughter-writers. In this her fourth and final book she admits to going further afield for her literary wanderings. However in her penultimate chapter she returns to Essex and its countryside, taking us down an Essex lane. First appearing in *The East Anglian Daily Times, The Wayfarer's Garden*, is a botanic *tour de force*, and becomes a personal *Te Deum*. One assumes it gave her immense pleasure to pen these quite glorious lines.

Notebooks

I have in my keeping four notebooks kept by Miss Vaughan. The first covers the years 1921–26; the second, 1927–30; the third, 1931–33, and the fourth, 1937–38. One obviously appears to be missing. It has to be said that all four are a veritable hotch-potch, a miscellany of bits and pieces. Her main concern is in recording the vagaries of the weather. There are pressed flowers and newspaper cuttings and proposed planting-out schemes for Turners. But there are also ink sketches, plus a few cameo watercolours and photographs of places visited. Unfortunately,

Duck End Mill. from the fields.

Page from Notebook, September 1924 showing a sketch of Duck End Mill at Finchingfield.

personal references are few and far between though small nuggets of information can be gleaned. For example, she was in great demand as a speaker at Women's Institutes and these engagements took her to places as far apart as Heybridge, Bocking, Dedham, Theydon Bois, Felsted, Chelmsford, etc. Indeed, for many years she travelled the county far and wide. Her subject matter expressing her own deep and varied interests. At Wethersfield, she spoke on 'Days Gone By'; at Bocking, 'Old Village Local Government'; at Great Bardfield, 'Old Essex Roads'; at Felsted, 'Folk Medicine'. Her interest in the Ruggles-Brise family was unceasing, recording that at the General Election of 1924, Archibald Ruggles-Brise was returned with a majority of 3,886. Between 4 and 7 March 1925, she stays at Keswick Hall, just outside Norwich and the family home of Agatha Gurney, mother of Sir John. She visits nearby Earlham Hall, forever associated with the remarkable Gurney family and the early years of Elizabeth Fry (née Gurney). Perhaps her visit was in company with her childhood friend, Florence Ruggles-Brise, aunt of Sir John who at the time was living at Dairy Lea, the farm opposite Spains Hall.

In common with many of her class and background, Eliza Vaughan enjoyed painting and became an accomplished water-colourist. Her first two books rely entirely upon photographic illustrations, but the third, *The Essex Village*, reproduces her painting of an old mill at Finchingfield, one of several no longer in existence. Of the five illustrations in her last book, *These for Remembrance*, she is confident enough to include three of her own watercolours of scenes on the Suffolk coast, Dunwich, Blythburgh and Beccles. She attended art classes, probably locally, and was given the nickname 'Poplar'. On the back of one in my possession her tutor writes, 'As it was in the beginning, is now and — please Poplar, give us a variation!'. It seems she painted too much in the same district (Finchingfield), and much the same subjects. Never-the-less her watercolours and sketches are both competent and charming.

When writing this essay my attention was drawn to the diary of the Reverend Andrew Clark, 1914–19 under the title, *Echoes of the Great War*, edited by James Munson.[11] Mr Clark was Rector of Great Leighs and friend of Miss Vaughan who made frequent visits to his rectory. His entry for 22 November 1915 gives the information that she was under-housekeeper for the V.A.D. Hospital, Braintree. A footnote adds: 'Miss Eliza Vaughan, a local government rate collector, lived in the nearby village of Rayne', then a separate village west of Braintree. Through her interest in Essex history, her many contacts with local people and her work in the hospital, she would become one of the Rector's most important sources. He affectionately referred to her as 'Miss Eliza Vaughan, the suffragette of Rayne'. From further references in the book there emerges a portrait of a woman with a dry sense of humour, a keen observer of the human scene and one with considerable determination. This latter quality comes to the fore in an incident recounted by Mr Clark in his entry for Tuesday, 3 October 1916, 'Miss Eliza Vaughan's (the suffragette of Rayne) great ambition has been to see a Zeppelin. Hearing that Zeppelins were expected on Su. night (1 Oct.) she went out, with a bag of

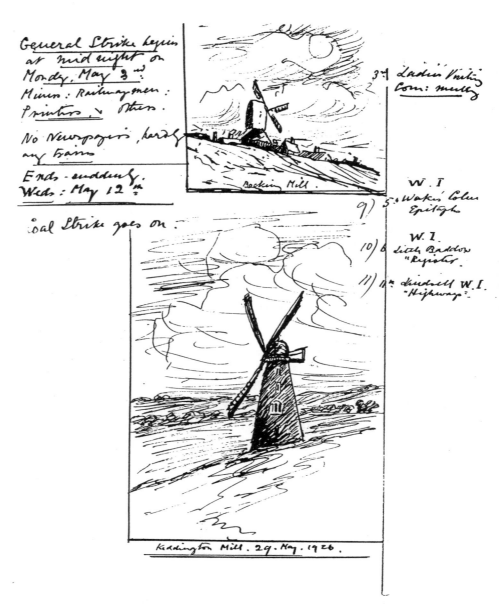

General Strike begins
at midnight on
Monday, May 3rd.
Miners : Railwaymen :
Printers & others.

No Newspapers, hardly
any trains

Ends - suddenly.
Weds : May 12th.

Coal Strike goes on :

Bocking Mill.

Kiddington Mill . 29. May. 1926 .

3.| Ladies Visiting
Com: meeting

W. I

9) 5. Wakes Colne
Epitaphs

W. I
10) 6 Little Baddow
"Register"

11) 11th Sandwell W. I
"Highways".

Page from Notebook, May 1926 with a record of the General Strike.

peppermint bulls-eyes, at 9.30 p.m. and sat on the bridge at Rayne in the midst of all the roughs of the place. Just before midnight, when her mouth was sore with sucking peppermints, and she was bored with the conversation of the yokels, she managed to see the Zeppelin.'[12]

I am indebted to Mr Leonard Whitehead of Colchester for memories of Miss Vaughan. His family received visits from her when living at Great Saling. He mentions that she had an intimate knowledge of the old Essex dialect and was able to speak it to perfection. Not only of course to speak it, but more difficult perhaps, to write it down. There are excellent examples of this particular gift given in *The Stream of Time*.[13]

The sobriquet 'Suffragette of Rayne', indicates her sympathies and convictions, perhaps the result of being the only daughter in a large family. In the Epilogue to *Echoes of the Great War*, it is recorded that she not only got the vote, but in time, local fame as an authority on Essex life and history. Several of her articles were published in *The Essex Review*, but they are, in the main germinal to, or derived from, her books. In 1940, the editor of *The Essex Review*, invited a contribution from her on *The Village in Wartime, Past and Present*. This duly appeared in vol. 49. She writes, 'To begin with, it seems that with all its dreadful and wholesale slaughter in the field, we country folk took the Great War more light heartedly than the present one. We were so interested in it. For one thing, we were able to help in ways now denied us.' It is not a perceptive article and I think had she been asked to contribute perhaps a year or so later when the conflict was well under way, her analysis might have been much different. As far as I am aware this was her last excursion into the literary field. She died at home on 2 February 1949, aged 85. Her own lifetime had bridged two very contrasting centuries. The old order had well and truly passed. Faces she had known and loved had been carried away by that inexorable stream of time. Entry no. 769 in the Burial Register at Finchingfield church records that she was buried on 7 February in the same plot as her parents and but a yard or so to the south of that occupied by members of the Ruggles-Brise family.

REFERENCES

1 *The Stream of Time*, Benham, Colchester, 1926, p.4.
2 *Ibid.*, p.7.
3 *Ibid.*, p.6.
4 *Stephen Marshall — A Forgotten Essex Puritan*, Fairbairns, London, 1907.
5 *The Stream of Time*, Benham, Colchester, 1926.
6 *Ibid.*, p.2.
7 *Ibid.*, p.48.
8 *The Essex Village in Days Gone By*, Benham, Colchester, 1928.
9 *These for Remembrance*, Benham, Colchester, 1934, p.6.

10 Flora Macdonald Mayor, *b.*1872, *d.*1932. Her father was a Cambridge scholar clergyman. Her novel *The Rector's Daughter*, published in 1924, received wide acclaim. It has been reprinted in Penquin Modern Classics.

11 *Echoes of the Great War*, OUP, 1985, p.95.

12 *Ibid.*, p.161.

13 *The Stream of Time*, Benham, Colchester, (many pages but see *The Essex Dialect*, p.2).

Acknowledgement: Oxford University Press for permissiom to quote from *Echoes of the Great War*, edited by James Munson, 1985.

Finchingfield Town Meetings, 1626–1634

F. G. EMMISON

O N THE OCCASION of my first lecture tour in New England in 1953, I was able to study two of the oldest surviving Town Meeting books there. I noticed the similarity between some of their phraseology and that used in the Finchingfield and Braintree books, a similarity I had already seen in the Town Meeting minutes of Chelmsford, Massachusetts.[1] In 1968 Harvard invited me to give a public lecture based on the Braintree and Finchingfield vestry books. The material appeared on the 350th anniversary of the sailing of the Pilgrim Fathers, who included a number of Essex emigrants.[2] These north Essex records are by far the most detailed early vestry minutes in the whole county.[3] In England every village was called a 'town' at the period: much later of course 'town' became a short word for market-town. The two books are complementary in contents in various ways. The parishes are, however, different in type. Finchingfield, a rural village whose inhabitants were mainly engaged in agriculture; Braintree, largely in cloth manufacture. Both volumes are signed at the end of each meeting by all members present at the Vestry. It is somewhat surprising that nearly all could write their names. But the likenesses are perhaps only superficial. Whereas Dr Samuel Collins, the Vicar of Braintree, is struggling with inhabitants whose heads are 'full of whirligigs', Stephen Marshall, the Vicar of Finchingfield, is a powerful Puritan preacher (his fame is already spreading abroad) and keeps his parishioners more united. Before 1640 he is outwardly conformable to the Established Church.

By the Act of 1601 each parish is responsible for its own poor, and every means is used to minimize the number of paupers or potential paupers, in order to keep down the rates. Each individual parish enforces its own immigration regulations and deports all who try to gain illegal entry or intrude without right and are discovered. Hence, Finchingfield resolves that two vestrymen, James Chaplein and Edward Choate, 'shall talke with (a pet formula) Peter Stubbin about sending away the strangers which are at his house'. Two townsmen 'shall goe upon Thursdaye next to the quarters sessions & shall indyte Thomas Cragg for takeing in to house the wife of Gyles Elman contrary to the mynde of the towne' (another common phrase). Is it possible to see a parallel, half a century later, in the minutes of the Town Meeting of Dedham, Massachusetts, where

At the meeting at mr Kempe at spaines Hall octob: 23 1626

ffirst, It is agreed that none of us shall releeve any roague or vagabond but shall bring them to the constable to have their punishment

Item It is agreed that John Crook & Henry Taylour shall talke with goodman How about serving to the towne to drive the towne of spanish Booth, or if he will not then he to deale with nahanisth naile about removinge thither

Item for the preventing of more inmates of poore no man shall let a cottage to any of an other towne, nor to new maried people who were not borne in the towne and if any man shall refuse to agree to this order, his cottage shall be indited if it be within compass of the statute which they will consent to let it to the overseers, or put none into it, without their appoint

And for the veiwing what cottages are in the parish: Goodman John Crook... Alexander Bay: shall get the names of all cottages about... towne end, James Crapkins & Edward ..., & John fitts ... for spaines end & ... zath end, Robert Harrington & John Hamond for How street, John Crook & Henry Taylour for Barton Hall end, Thomas Livermore, Mathy Hart & Arthur Crapkin for Asfild Hall end, and to get a perfit note of all against the next meeting

Item that James Crapkin & Edward Crook shall talke with peter Stublin about sending away the strangers now at his gate, and to tell us on Saturday next, that if they be not gone, we may take order to send for a warrant

Item that yf said Stublin ... Henry Tailor with 23 lads ... servants they have ... to ... towne for the towne ...

Jeremi: KEMPE

Stephen Marshall

James Crapkine

John ...

John Taylor

Edmond ...

ffrancis Burton

Thomas walford

Edward Crook

John ×

Henry Tailor

Alexander ...

John Diamand

John ffletcher

Extract from Town Meeting Book, 1626 (D/P 14/8/7).

'contrary to the mind of the selectmen' occurs in a similar inmate case? The Finchingfieldians' watchfulness is not confined to strangers. It is an equal offence to take in brother-in-law or son-in-law, 'without the consent of the parish', if likely to become a charge. The immediate penalty is dispatch to the nearest justice of the peace, who after examination orders removal if settlement at Finchingfield cannot be proved. Control of cottages is also thorough. Like Braintree, the Vestry resorts to pulling down dwellings as a safeguard against potential paupers getting a settlement: 'Goodwife Lounte shalbe removed & placed with the widow Cater and the cottage to be pulled downe where she now is'. She shows obstinacy, so two vestrymen are to see it done. In another billeting case the telling clause, 'to try how they can' appears.

Sick pay is sometimes given out of the 'Communion money', either to the patient or to a relative 'who hath taken great pains' or 'something allowed him for a while until it please God his wife recover her health'. The Vestry's kindest act is seen in their agreeing to bear the cost of a blind boy's journey with a guide to Northamptonshire 'expert in kuringe of those that are blynde', together with the fee. But in vain, and two years afterwards the blind lad is taken to Thaxted, perhaps to see another expert, or a quack.

The social disciplines exercised by the Town Meetings are illustrated well in the following extracts.

'At the meeting at Mr Kemps   October 23 1626
at Spains Hall

It is agreed that none of us shall receive any roague or vagabond but shall bring them to the constable to have them punished.

It is agreed that John Choate and Henry Taylour shall talke with goodman How about security to the towne to discharge the towne of Francisse Benson, or if he will not then they to deale with Nathaniell Waite about removing him.

For the preventing of more charge of poore no man shall let a cottage to any of an other townes, or to new maried couples who were not borne in the towne, and if any man shall refuse to agree to this order, his cottage shall be indited if it be within compasse of the statute unlesse they will consent to let it to the overseers, or put none into it, without there approbation. And for the inquiring what cottages are in the parish: Goodman Loker, Thomas Walford, Alexander Bayly shall get the names of all cottages about the towne end, James Chaplein, Edward Choate and John Fitch for Spaines end and Cornish Hall end, Robert Harrington and John Hamond for How Street, John Choate and Henry Taylour for Boeton Hall end, Thomas Livermore, Matthy Hart & Arthur Chaplin for Ashfeild Hall end, and to get a perfect note of all against the next meeting.

James Chaplein and Edward Choate shall talke with Peter Stubbin about sending away the strangers which are at his house, and to tell us

The Gild Hall, Finchingfield, c.1920
(Photograph courtesy of the Essex Record Office)

one Saturday next, that if they be not gone, we may take order to send for a warrant for the said Stubbin.

John Hamond to talke with John Cracknell, Henry Tailor with Bland about servants they have intertained, to come to the townes men.'

The scope of the business transacted by these village worthies is evident from the minutes of the second meeting at Spains Hall:

'At the meeting at Mr Kempes   December 2 1628

A warrant to be feched for John Richardsone for beinge found drunk on the Sabboth daye.

A warrant to be fetched for John Stubbinge for takeinge in of an inmate in to his house. Alexsander Bayly & Giles Walford are appoynted to speake with Stubbinge the next Sabboth daye.

John Chote, Edward Dix & John Goodah are appoynted to goe to Claksones & take notice what moveables Anne Mott hath.

The overseers and churchwardens shall remove Anne Cragg from the town house & another putt in hir roome to helpe ould Taylor & the rest.

The overseers shall paye 6s. 8d. to Clacksons wife for Anne Mottes dwellinge.

Robert Steevens 2 eldest boyes should be placed in fitt services as soone as maye be.

John Chote should carry the faggottes that are in Finchingfild Parke to Mr Marshall & is to have 8s. for the cariage of it.

The overseers shall paye to ould Hissone to helpe to releeve him 6s. 8d.'

Typical of other acts of charity are those in the minutes of the meeting at 'Gyles Wolfes' on 24 February 1631:

Goodman Chaplyn, goodman Wolfe and goodman Chote shal goe to Waldone to bye some corne for the poore.

Edward Johnsone shall have somethinge allowed him for a while untill it please God his wife recover her health . . .

John Brewster should be allowed somethinge out of the common monye now in the tyme of his sicknes.'

Thus is the life of this small community managed for the benefit of public order, the sick and the needy.

To Stephen Marshall and his flock, drunkenness is a grave vice, 'none of us', they determine in 1627, 'shall give our consentes' to further alehouses except with the authority of 'the whole companye' (the only occasion on which the term is used): it is an extra-legal decision, as licensing is the justices' prerogative. At least one alehousekeeper is a painful thorn pricking their moral senses. He and 'divers others' have been admonished for disorder and drunkenness; should they not reform, 'we will take some course with them to punish theme for the same'. Finchingfield must not become a sink of iniquity. The fight waxes fiercely. 'Some of us in our severall endes [hamlets] of our towne shall go out in the night tyme in the maner of privie watche' and search in suspected places and houses.

Distress is first evident in this country parish in 1630, when the large sum of £100 is borrowed and laid out 'for the use of the poore', the loan to be secured by the vicar, three chief vestrymen and the four overseers of the poor. With soaring prices of food, the money is invested in corn. The problem occupies the Town Meetings during the winter of 1630–31. Interesting decisions of 1628 relate to the summer storage for the supply of winter fuel to the poor in need. A minute of July reads: 'Of the 400 lb. of faggottes which are bought for the poore, 300 shalbe laid in to Mr Marshall yard, and soe to be sould out by his man to the poore.'

The monthly meetings are held, not in the vestry, but in the homes of all its members and in rotation, which starts with Robert Kemp of Spains Hall, John Berners of Petches, Stephen Marshall of the Vicarage, and James Chaplin of Cornish Hall. The list continues with John Mead, Francis Burton, Robert Cracknell, Thomas Livermore, Robert Harrington, , Matthias Hart, Thomas Walford, Edward Chote, John Guye, Henry Taylor, John Chote, Alexander Bayley, Gilbert Harrington, John Hammond, John Fitch, and Giles Walford. After the second round, again beginning with Robert Kemp, there is a hiatus, March 1630/1–December 1633 inclusive, the record ending with the months January and February 1633/4, a few alternative names occurring after the first round.[4]

Thus, these immensely valuable archives, so well preserved by Finchingfield folk for over three hundred years, enable us to watch this little oligarchy, neither partial nor corrupt, trying according to their lights to provide good standards of local government. Their chronicle is more intimate and less formal than the county quarter sesions records. A little later, but only once in our book (16 January 1626/7), the Finchingfield Vestry was often referred to as 'The Company of the Four and Twenty'.

REFERENCES

1 W. Waters, *History of Chelmsford, Massachusetts*, 1917.
2 F. G. Emmison, *Early Essex Town Meetings, 1619–36; Finchingfield, 1626–34.*
3 F. G. Emmison, ed., *Catalogue of Essex Parish Records*, (revd. edn., 1966, E.R.O. Pubn. no. 7); ref. D/P 14/8/1.
4 F. G. Emmison, *op. cit.*, p.117, n.157; For transcript of leaf (of Vestry minutes, 24 February 1630/1), now missing, see *Essex Review*, viii, p.128.

The Bow Street Mounted Patrol on Essex Highways

HERBERT HOPE LOCKWOOD

W HEN I WAS A SCHOOLBOY I learnt — as many doubtless still learn — that the Metropolitan Police Force established by Sir Robert Peel in 1829 was the first in Britain, and the model for all others. This young, vigorous and well-trained force, quickly nicknamed 'Bobbies' or 'Peelers', took the place of the poor old 'Charleys' or night-watchmen, and of part-time unpaid parish constables — so I was told.

I learnt later that the truth — as ever — was more complex. Peel had not pulled the idea of his 'New Police' out of thin air; the concept of a 'preventive police' maintained from the public purse had been evolving over the preceding eighty years.

The first initiatives may fairly be credited to playwright and novelist Henry Fielding and his half-brother, Sir John Fielding, 'the Blind Beak', presiding at the Bow-street Magistrates Court in the mid-eighteenth century. Henry recruited the small band of officers which came to be called Bow-street Runners.[1] Sir John published his *Plan for Preventing Robberies within Twenty Miles of London* and experimented with nightly horse patrols.[2] Although Home Office funding was withdrawn for these latter, the Gordon Riots in 1780 were followed by the formation of a Bow-street Foot Patrol of 68 men in 13 Parties, each under a Captain, who patrolled the streets of London at night but were also available to assist the Runners at other times if required. They wore no uniform but were armed.[3]

In 1792 an Act was passed which created seven new Police Offices in London on a similar pattern to Bow-street, each with three stipendiary magistrates and eight to twelve paid constables (Runners) attached to each. The City, jealously maintaining its independence, organised its own night and even day patrols to police the 'square mile'.[4]

Meanwhile in 1798 Patrick Colquhoun and Captain John Harriot organized the Thames River Police controlled from an additional Police Office at Wapping. The 68–74 members of this force, who patrolled the Docks and river, again wore no uniform.[5]

311

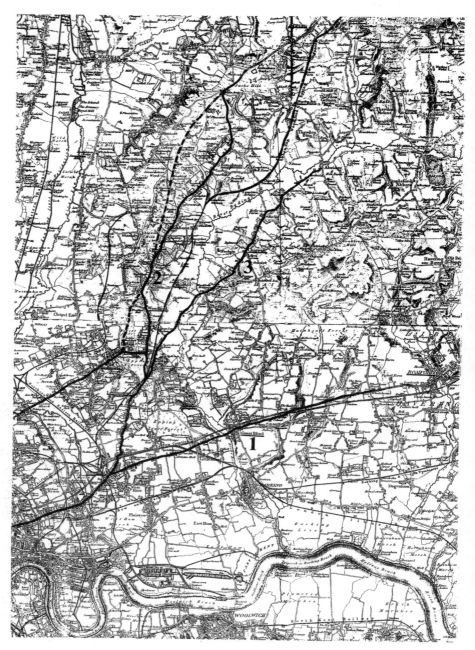

Essex roads patrolled by Bow Street Mounted Patrol.

These new bodies also co-existed — by no means harmoniously — with the ancient institutions of parish constables and night watchmen.[6] So by 1800 the word 'police' was acquiring something of its modern sense, though this piecemeal structure fell far short of providing a modern police force even for the Metropolis. John Gifford, Chief Magistrate of Worship Street (Shoreditch), complained in 1816 to one of the series of Select Committees set up by Parliament to examine the problem, 'the different Police Offices keep their information to themselves, and do not wish to communicate it to others, that they may have the credit and advantage of detecting offenders'.[7] Such 'advantage' included the public and private rewards upon conviction of criminals — nicknamed 'Blood Money' — which could supplement the quite inadequate salaries of their police officers. To many therefore police remained just 'thieftakers' or, even more odiously, 'paid informers'.[8]

Bow-street, with the support of the Home Secretary, retained the unique position it had acquired in the time of the Fieldings. Their eight Runners not only provided Royal Protection but acted as a sort of central C.I.D. — 'they are properly speaking, police officers for the whole country at large, than for any actual service to us', their Chief Magistrate observed.[9]

In January 1805, under the presidency of Sir Richard Ford, Bow-street again took the initiative and, with a further subsidy from the Home Office, formed the first uniformed police force in Britain:[10] the Bow Street Mounted Patrol. A body of 52 ex-cavalry troopers, under two Inspectors began a nightly patrol of the main roads leading into the capital up to a 20 mile radius. An official account says that the 'Horse Patrol . . . was first suggested in consequence of the many Highway Robberies committed on the roads round London'. The lack of crime statistics makes it impossible to say whether an actual increase in these offences prompted so robust a revival of Sir John Fielding's earlier experiments.[11] The evidence from metropolitan Essex is interesting though not conclusive.

On this side of London three roads (see map page 312) — all of which had been turnpiked during the preceding century — were considered necessary to patrol. First and foremost there was the 'Great Essex Road' through Romford, which ran on to Colchester and maintained communications not only with much of Essex and Suffolk but with the continent of Europe via Harwich. Next, increasing in importance, was the road through Woodford, Loughton and Epping which ran on to Cambridge, and via Newmarket to Norwich. Finally there was the old road through Woodford Bridge and Chigwell to Ongar, which had carried more distant traffic before the Loughton–Epping link had been completed during the early seventeenth century.[12]

The first two highways received most attention from robbers because they carried the more lucrative traffic and passed through the most open country; Stratford Common, Wanstead Flats and Chadwell Heath on the first, and wide tracts of Epping Forest on the second.[13] During 1790 two masked and 'well mounted' highwaymen held up several post chaise and carriages on the Woodford–Epping road before one of them was eventually hunted down at

'The Bow Street Mounted Patrol on Duty'
An artist's interpretation specially drawn by John Bryning, 1996.

Battlesbridge. In 1793 Sir William Plomer driving through the forest with two companions was relieved of his watch and 14 guineas by a highwayman in broad daylight.[14]

Yet such attacks seem to have been even more frequent in the late seventeenth century and earlier in the eighteenth — including those popularly attributed to Dick Turpin.[15] Plausibly the transmission of money in the form of banknotes and bills, more easily identifiable than coins or bullion, and the increasing numbers of turnpike gates and enclosures of waste may have put some mounted highwaymen out of business before 1805. But it has also been suggested that improvements in the policing of the inner London streets were driving more footpads into the environs.[16]

Nobleman in post-chaise attacked by Highwaymen, 1750 (from Newgate Calendar).

A particularly daring and vicious attack by five of the latter took place on the Romford Road in 1795.[17] On the evening of Friday, 10 December, two King's Messengers carrying despatches and money to Switzerland and Italy were travelling to Harwich in a chaise-and-four in company with a Leghorn merchant. All precautions had been taken: the three were well armed, and the two postillions had been instructed to increase speed if challenged, and to shout a warning to their passengers if forced to stop. Yet around 7.30 p.m., between Ilford and Romford, near the cross-roads at Goodmayes where Barley Lane and Stoup Lane (now Goodmayes Road) meet the High Road, the chaise halted without warning.

Armed men wrenched open the doors, and one of them, realizing the occupants were also armed, instantly discharged his pistol, fatally wounding one Messenger.

The other two passengers continued to defend themselves and even though three of their pistols missed fire (the unreliability of firearms at this time was a fact of life — and death!), managed to fire three shots in answer to seven or eight. The robbers dragged the dying man out onto the footpath and brutally pistol-whipped him but the other Messenger and the merchant, though wounded in the arm, succeeded in escaping in the darkness to a neighbouring farmhouse.

The footpads fled with a rich haul, including 60 Louis d'Or, gold coins intended for Florence. Officers despatched at once from Bow-street were unable to catch them. The postillions were suspected of complicity, but nothing was proved. James Martin, the Messenger who died of his wounds, was buried at Romford. Plainly the menace on the highway from gangs of footpads could equal that from the classical highwaymen.

The new Mounted Patrol was prepared for either. Recruits had to have served with credit in a cavalry regiment, to be under 40, literate and married. They were well armed — with truncheon, sabre and two pistols — and well mounted. When going on duty the pistols were to be loaded and the sword worn on the outside of the coat. Strict regulations were laid down for the care of the horse.

The uniform comprised blue riding coat with yellow buttons, worn over blue trousers, and a scarlet waistcoat which earned them their nickname, 'Robin Redbreasts'. This dress was completed by black Wellington boots with spurs, white gloves, leather stock and a reinforced leather top hat. The headgear was apparently intended to give a civilian rather than a military touch to the uniform and was copied by the Metropolitan Police in their early days. The patrole[18] had to pay for this uniform, but a riding cloak was issued together with his weapons and harness. He was also instructed to identify himself to carriages and horsemen met on the road by calling out 'Bow Street Patrol'.[19]

He went on duty in the evening — the exact time varied with the season —and patrolled his highway until after midnight. There was always some traffic on the roads; coaches outward bound from London in the evening — the last cleared Epping, for example, at midnight — then the inward flow of slow, unlit market carts began. He was expected to ride at a steady pace reaching the limit of his beat at a set time and halt for ten minutes before returning. Patroles on the same road were to meet up at a halfway point on their journey to exchange information and to provide mutual assistance if required. They were to keep to the main road except when in pursuit of offenders; here William Day, the Inspector who became Conductor and effective head of the Patrol in 1813, insisted that they must use their judgement and discretion.[20]

This system was obviously open to the criticism that it assisted criminals to work out times when the coast was clear. But in fact it was the Patrol's chief means of communication between themselves and with the public. Any failure to rendezvous would alert a colleague to possible trouble and had to be reported next morning to an inspector. It has to be realized that the telegraph, telephone and radio lay far in the future and that the Patrol's manpower was strictly limited.

We do not know much about the personnel or working of the Bow Street Mounted Patrol in the opening years. There is reason to suspect that their establishment of 54 was not always maintained and only limited use was made of their services.[21] Nor was it easy for them to overcome popular prejudices against police. In 1811 John Fowler, Horse Patrole from Romford, asked the Becontree magistrates to bind over Thomas Ingram of Chadwell who had 'at various times assaulted' him 'threatened to do him some bodily harm, and to take away his life'. As late as 1823 Joss, patrole from Loughton, similarly charged Edwards, a troublesome 'pot-valiant' plumber of Leytonstone, of attempting to unhorse him 'by laying hold of his leg as he was riding along the road'.[22]

Yet by 1816, Day could boast 'we have had scarcely any highway or footpad robbery since the establishment [of the Horse Patrol]; and in those which have happened, the parties have been apprehended, with very few exceptions'. Since he was also Keeper of Criminal Registers it was unfortunate that he could give no actual figures to the Select Committee. But others supported him, like William Fielding, magistrate at Queens Square (son of Henry Fielding), who declared 'I think the horse patrole of the Office at Bow street has been of a very considerable degree of service in putting down that class of depredators.'[23]

In Essex, patroles had been stationed at Stratford, Romford, Woodford, Loughton and Woodford Bridge and more accounts of their work begin to appear in the Press.[24] During the winters of 1815 and 1816 John and Thomas Clement and James Gibbs, members of the Patrol then stationed at Romford, were busy apprehending groups of unarmed footpads operating on the road through Chadwell Heath. Their victims had included a sailor who had been celebrating in the Greyhound after being paid-off at Deptford, and a number of carters on their way to market.[25]

This was cold but routine work, in contrast to that which the Woodford patrole, Richard Boucher, found himself doing the following winter. The drama really began just after 10 o'clock on a bright January morning in 1817 when James Graves of Ilford was driving through Epping Forest with his 14 year old son in a one-horse chaise. South of Epping, he was stopped by three men and one of them with his hat pulled down over his eyes demanded 'your money or your life'. Astonished at this sudden attack in broad daylight, the gentleman asked if he was serious. The response was a volley of oaths and a double-barrelled pistol which was plainly loaded, and Graves realized that one of the others was also armed. He surrendered what money he had — about £5 — and they also took his gold watch, chain and seals — worth £40. They seized a gun from the chaise but tossed it back when they found it was not loaded. The robbers who had Irish accents then fled into the forest.[26]

Ten days later John Windus, son of a local solicitor, was driving from Epping to London and had given a lift to a young gentleman at the Epping Turnpike. Between 8 and 9 a.m., they too were held up by three men with Irish accents who presented pistols to their heads saying 'Your money or your life; be quick about it'. This time the robbers had only a poor haul of three one-pound banknotes before they ran off westward into the forest. The whole incident lasted only a few minutes after which Windus drove on to Woodford and alerted Boucher about 9 o'clock (Orders laid down that a Patrole should be in his stable for at least an hour after 8 a.m. to feed and groom his horse). Boucher remounted and set off in pursuit. Obviously well acquainted with the terrain and probably well informed about the previous attack, he followed tracks towards Sewardstone and eventually spotted three men and a boy hurrying ahead.

Alone in the forest with armed suspects, his problem was to identify and arrest them. So he deliberately rode past them, dismounted and, walking his horse slowly to let them catch up, engaged them in conversation. Confident now that he had the right men, he accompanied them for a little way to a point where the forest opened out on a group of houses where men were working. Shouting for assistance he seized and secured two of the gang called Hunt and Hindley. The third, called Claffy, and the boy, succeeded in running away, but a farmer's son rode after Claffy and eventually cornered him in some marshes. Hunt had a double-barrelled pistol which he had tried to conceal in his hat, and another pistol was found in the marsh near Claffy. The bank-notes were found on the prisoners; Claffy tried to use one to bribe the farmer's son to let him go.

Boucher escorted the three men to Bow-street where they were examined and one of them was recognised by a Foot Patrole as having escaped after a robbery in Islington Fields some months before. They were committed for trial at Essex Lent Assizes; Hindley escaped on the way, but Hunt and Claffy were convicted. Subsequent events showed just how daring and resourceful John Claffy was. Awaiting transportation, he successfully organized a mass break-out from Chelmsford Gaol. Ten convicts were eventually recaptured — two of them by the Horse Patrol at Chadwell Heath — but Claffy eluded all pursuit.[27]

This case illustrates both the possibilities and limitations of the Mounted Patrol. Obviously they were unable to offer 24 hour policing even of the high roads. Frequently they had to act alone (or appeal for public aid) in dangerous situations and take difficult decisions. Plainly Boucher had to use his own judgement whether to seek assistance from a Loughton colleague or to leave the main road on his own to follow three armed men. According to one account he even entrusted his own horse to the farmer's son to catch Claffy — a direct breach of standing Orders. Some ex-soldiers accustomed to the rigid army discipline of the period must have found it difficult to adjust to a regime of personal responsibility under William Day. Was this one reason why the Home Office took over direct control of appointments in 1813 when giving Day full operational control? Certainly Day's policy of retaining men at the same station was vindicated by Boucher's familiarity with the area and local people.[28]

The enquiry of 1816–17 gave only very qualified approval, 'The Horse Patrol would be a most useful body, if it could be properly superintended and directed, but on the present system that is impractical. The stations are so wide apart and the men are left so much to themselves, that but little comparative good can be derived from their services.'[29]

Between then and the early 1820s a number of adjustments were made. A new training section was introduced for filling vacancies in the Mounted Patrol. Though similarly uniformed and equipped it operated on foot and was confusingly named the 'Police Horse Patrole Dismounted'.[30]

Further developments were initiated in 1821 whilst Viscount Sidmouth was Home Secretary and continued under Robert Peel (1822–27). The old Bow Street Night Foot Patrol which had interfaced with the Horse Patrol on a four to five mile radius was withdrawn into inner London and its strength increased. The Dismounted Patrol, greatly augmented to 100 strong took its place in the environs. At the same time the Mounted Patrol establishment was increased to 72 in four Divisions, each under an Inspector. With two exceptions on the Enfield road, all the 'stations' of the 4th Division lay in Essex.[31]

Another Select Committee in 1822 were 'strongly impressed' with these developments and earnestly recommended 'the further extension of the principle' by the creation of a day patrol. Peel, who had chaired the committee, immediately sanctioned a Bow Street Day Patrol for the central area, albeit on the very modest scale of 24 men and three Inspectors. Unlike the Night Patrol, they were given a uniform modelled on that of the Mounted and Dismounted Patrols. Mostly ex-soldiers themselves, Peel felt 'they would be proud of their establishment if they were dressed as their mounted colleagues'.[32]

Actually Peel appears to have brought about a new emphasis on the wearing of uniform in the Mounted Patrol itself. The Orders of 1813 only mentioned the compulsory wearing of uniform at monthly inspections. William Day was casual about it even when giving evidence to the 1822 Committee 'it was in order that they should look a little respectable when they assembled as a body, they only wear it at that time'. But the Orders for 1827 are specific that uniform is to be worn 'on Nightly Duty' and even at other times when 'from home'.[33]

It is plain from the Essex evidence that these developments resulted in a recruiting drive between 1821 and 1823 producing a new generation of the Horse Patrol. With ages between 24 and 34 many would have seen active service in the Napoleonic Wars as young cavalrymen. Whilst not knowing details of their war service, we know their names and vital statistics because they were still serving in the Horse Patrol in 1836 when first preparations were being made for a takeover by the Metropolitan Police.

From the same source we know the places where they were stationed in 1836. To the five listed in Essex in 1816 (see above) we can add six, probably seven, by 1836, *viz.* Lea Bridge Road, Snakes Lane (Woodford), Epping, Leytonstone, Chigwell, Ilford, and probably Leyton. Some of these additions were needed to cover new stretches of road — Woodford New Road (opened 1829–30) and Epping New Road (by-passing Loughton, 1833—34).[34]

A change had also taken place in the nature of their accommodation. In 1816 they were in lodgings — sometimes unsuitable with stabling at a distance. By 1836 each patrole was accommodated in a purpose-built four-roomed house with adjoining stable and loft. This was a development foreshadowed by Day

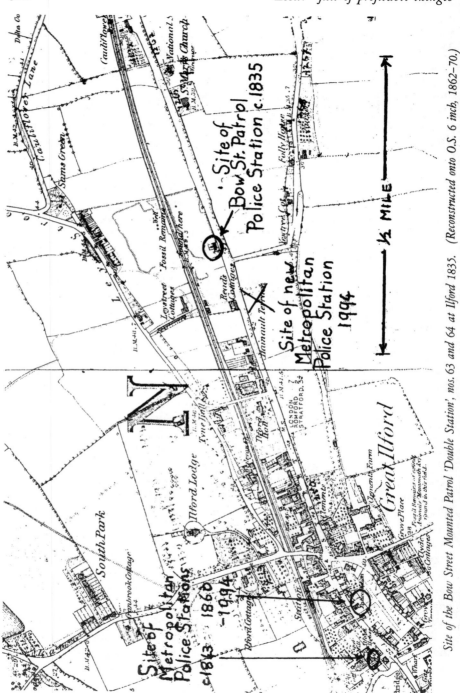

Site of the Bow Street Mounted Patrol 'Double Station', nos. 63 and 64 at Ilford 1835. *(Reconstructed onto O.S. 6 inch, 1862–70.)*

before the 1822 Committee and largely achieved by 1833. Each residence was termed a 'station'; Stratford, Woodford and Ilford had what Day termed 'double stations'.[35] In the case of Great Ilford I have been fortunate in locating the exact site of the pair of cottages on the north side of the High Road (Romford Road), on the outskirts of the village just east of the present junction with the Green Lane (see map page 320).[36]

In one (Station No. 63) lived Patrole John Aris with his wife Sarah and family: in the other (No. 64), Patrole James Othen, wife Margaret and family. Hampshire born, Othen had joined the Mounted Patrol in 1821 and had been stationed in Ilford since at least 1829. But at that date he seems to have had lodgings in Back Street in the village itself and Aris may have been stationed at Woodford. The earliest certain date for the Ilford station houses is 1835.[37]

During 1836, Aris would ride eastward to the 10th milestone on the Romford Road, near the Whalebone Turnpike at Chadwell Heath, where he overlapped with George Weston, the patrole from Station No. 65 at Romford. These two, having stretches of three miles or less to patrol were expected to make four journeys, meeting each other at the set times, before completing their tour of duty. Meanwhile Othen would have ridden westward for three and a half miles to meet with Samuel Gutteridge from No. 62 Stratford, this pair making three return journeys.[38]

Weston, also Hampshire born and enlisted in 1821, was 6' 2", one of the tallest men in the force and a very active policeman. In 1824 he arrested in the forest, an ex-naval seamen calling himself John Mitchell who had stolen a stock of shirts stamped 'Chelmsford Workhouse'; a character so resolute that he had to be placed in irons as well as handcuffs to get him back safely to Chelmsford. On the way the prisoner declared that 'had he known Weston's pistol had not been loaded with ball, he would not have been taken.[39]

In November 1832 a gang of three poachers who had been shooting deer in Hainault Forest were surprised by keepers and in the ensuing fight the keepers got the worst of it and one of them, William Hill, was so savagely beaten about the head that he lost eight teeth and part of his nose. The Mounted Patrol were informed and tried unsuccessfully to catch the gang. But the following September, Weston recognized one of them, James Cooper, near the Whalebone Turnpike — a powerful man known around the forest as 'Gypsy' Cooper — and promptly arrested him.[40]

More remarkably still, in February 1836, Weston, who had been present at the subsequent trial of Cooper and Boon, the second member of the gang to be caught, succeeded in arresting John Boreham, the third man. Boreham, it was said, had shouted to the two beating Hill, 'Kill him! Kill him! Kill the ------ before you leave him'.[41]

Weston worked with Samuel Gutteridge and James Othen on a more sophisticated crime in September 1830. On the evening of the 7th, three valuable bales of raw silk had been despatched by carrier wagon from London to Colchester. One of the bales containing four bags of silk had been strapped in the rear of the wagon not quite covered by the tilt. Arriving at Brentwood about 11.30 p.m. the wagoner found it was missing, although he had seen it there when he reached the Greyhound, Chadwell, at 8.30. The alarm was raised and by 9 next morning Othen, who had gone to investigate, found loose skeins of silk and a wrapper had been picked up near the roadside beyond Hare Street (Gidea Park) by several travellers during the night. Nevertheless over 150 lbs. of raw silk was still missing, worth at least £100. We may guess the wagoner, having imbibed too freely at the Greyhound, was dozing when robbers boarded his vehicle lumbering over Romford Common and cut the bale free — using 'considerable ingenuity' as the Grand Jury were told.

By next night the Patroles were on full alert — experience suggested the thieves would have come from London and could soon try to get back with their loot. Near Chadwell about 11.30 p.m. a gig passed Gutteridge travelling in the direction of London, he called out 'Bow Street Patrol' and they replied 'Good night'. In the moonlight he saw their faces plainly: he had reason to be suspicious because they answered to the description of two men who had been seen by Weston travelling in a similar vehicle towards Romford earlier on the previous evening. He followed them — they increased speed — but by breaking into a gallop he kept them in sight to Ilford. He then went on to meet Weston. Together they left the High Road to follow the gig across Wanstead Flats (making probably for the Lea Bridge Road). Eventually they saw it stop and rode up to question the men.

When the officers offered to search the chaise, their suspects made violent efforts to escape. Weston knocked one down and drew his sword; Gutteridge threatened to draw his pistol on the other. The prisoners were taken to the Eagle at Snaresbrook and searched; three damaged bags of raw silk were in the gig, the men had knives and an iron tool to which traces of gummy filament adhered. They were subsequently found guilty though they secured a clever lawyer. The system of 'parliamentary rewards' (Blood Money), which had so fuelled public prejudice against the police, had been abolished: but it is probably fair to surmise the officers received some private reward for their efforts in this case.[42]

In 1834 Weston and Gutteridge were highly commended by the local magistrates for their skill in tracking a load of hay stolen from a shed in Romford to a loft in Walthamstow and in identifying the culprits, Abraham Punt, a jobber, and James Guerton. They noted that Punt's horse was peculiarly shod and the wheels of his cart had an unusual width between the strakes, and these corresponded to wheel tracks and footprints observed outside the shed and on the road. And they noted that Guerton's own shoes tallied with footmarks there. Weston had even taken the precaution to cover some of the prints with a board to preserve the evidence.[43]

Gutteridge sometimes operated with his neighbour, Yorkshire born, David Johnson, who lived at Stratford station No. 61 and patrolled the Epping road up to the Woodford Turnpike Gate — a six and a half mile stint which he did twice in a night. In 1834 they apprehended a couple of labourers who had stolen a gallon of rum and two quarts of gin from the Thatched House at Wanstead and were caught the next day in the Eagle and Child at Forest Gate completely intoxicated and smelling of rum.[44]

The following year they conducted a more serious investigation in connection with the Thatched House. They established that over a couple of years Featherstone the ostler there had been receiving quantities of stolen goods from visiting carters (mainly taken from local employers). A cart-load of assorted property was found in a stable there after Johnson had obtained a search warrant, and Featherstone was even discovered to have lodged part of his proceeds in the Bank of England. The under-ostler had also been concerned in this (not so uncommon) scam. They and a couple of wagoners were charged at Lambeth Street Police Office; Featherstone ultimately received two years imprisonment. The local Bench suspended the licence of the widowed landlady, Mrs Sophia Renwick, because of many complaints of disorder against the house. Gutteridge and Johnson were much praised.[45]

By 1827 orders specifically permitted the Mounted Patrol to take prisoners 'before a Justice of the Peace more immediately situated' so saving man and horse from the frequent journeys to Bow Street on the morning after.[46] Additionally this improved relations with local magistrates. Co-operation with the parish constables also appears to have increased. James Othen developed a close relationship with Samuel Davis, the Ilford Parish Constable.

In 1832 Othen was called upon to assist Davis in trying to quell one of the few riots ever recorded in Ilford. It began one evening in March when six men besieged the house of the Assistant Overseer demanding more poor relief and threatening to throw him into the village lock-up. When they refused to disperse a sympathetic crowd started to gather and Othen had to seek reinforcements before he and Davis could arrest the men and drag them across the High Road to lock them into rooms in the Angel Inn. One attacked Othen with a shovel and only his pistol holster saved him from serious injury. Eventually Richard Brassey, Esq., the nearest magistrate (he lived in Cranbrook Road), had to read the Riot Act to a crowd, now estimated at several hundred, which had gathered outside the inn.

Even then it was an hour and a half before they ventured to open the gates and run the gauntlet of the remaining rioters to take their prisoners to the new gaol at Little Ilford. One of the stones thrown at them, so Constable Davis stated, 'struck Othen the Bow St Patrole on the hat and stove it in; if it had hit him a little lower it must have knocked him off his horse'. Subsequently at Essex Quarter Sessions seven rioters received prison sentences from two to six months; and two bystanders were fined for failing to aid and assist the officers when charged in the King's name.[47]

On New Year's Day 1836, Othen helped Samuel Davis (a butcher when he found time to practice his trade) to find and arrest Charles Deller and John Burton for stealing a lamb from a farmer in Ilford and slaughtering it. Convicted at the Old Bailey, Deller aged 21 and Burton 18 were transported for life. (Neither had ever had regular work, and had no previous convictions!)[48]

On Tuesday, the 18 October 1836, James Othen, informed at 5.15 pm. that an Ilford widow had been burgled that afternoon and two suspicious characters had taken the road to London, rode after them 'with the activity that has characterised him on former occasions' (according to the *Essex Standard*) accompanied by Samuel Davis. They overtook the culprits near Stratford and retrieved all the stolen property — including some already pawned — within an hour. One of their prisoners, Alfred Ruff, the widow's grandson, previously jailed for threatening his father, was eventually transported for seven years; the other, a boy of 13, was jailed for a year![49]

It could be argued — indeed it was argued by Day himself — that such cases as the foregoing were outside the remit of the Horse Patrol. 'I have had great difficulty to keep the men strictly to the line of duty for which they were specially appointed . . . many of them would be rather engaged in looking after burglars or other offenders than patrolling the roads'. On the other hand Day had admitted earlier to the same Select Committee of 1833 that 'independent of patrolling the roads they are a great local protection to the inhabitants' who invariably protested if a station was changed. Like it or not, his men were only responding to the logic of their situation as part of the community; public expectation was over-riding job specification.[50]

As most examples given above show, the Mounted Patrol generally got a good press — when it got any press at all. But the further they became involved in matters of general policing and public order, the more likely were they to encounter problems and adverse criticism.

On the night of 29 October 1834, patrolling the High Road near Goodmayes at about 10.40 p.m., George Weston noticed a large fire away to the south and went to investigate. Two miles away he found the rickyard of Lodge Farm ablaze, with a number of people already fighting the flames. He was joined by Gutteridge, Aris and a parish constable. Farmer Gray was adamant that the fire could not have started accidentally and suspicion fell upon James Hunt who had raised the alarm and his friend Stephen Sawkins. The Patrol detained them and whilst Aris guarded them in the kitchen of the farmhouse, Gutteridge and Weston interviewed each in a separate room. Next day they brought them before a neighbouring magistrate, Revd. John Fanshawe of Parsloes (brother of the Vicar of Dagenham) who released them. He evidently considered the evidence too circumstantial and wanted no 'Tolpuddle Martyrs' on his patch.

A committee of local farmers and landowners, fearful of an outbreak of incendiarism such as accompanied the agricultural unrest in the Eastern Counties four years earlier, now appealed for help to the Home Office who offered a £100 reward in addition to the £100 promised by Gray for any information leading to a conviction. The Lambeth Street Police Office at Whitechapel sent Samuel Miller, their experienced Head Constable to assist. Weston and Othen also took part in a further investigation, apparently designed to discredit Hunt whom they re-arrested together with Sawkins. The entire local Bench now re-examined the case — with Fanshawe prominent in questioning — and remanded the prisoners in custody for a fortnight. They finally discharged them for want of further evidence. It looks as if the Patrol had got themselves involved in a competition to find a scapegoat for a crime which may never have been committed. Strangely, there was an even more disastrous fire at Lodge Farm, Barking, in 1836.[51]

Peel's Police Act of 1829 followed close upon the heels of another Parliamentary Select Committee in 1828 and brought the 3,000 strong Metropolitan Police force into being at the end of September 1829. The Bow Street Night and Day Patrols, together with the Dismounted Horse Patrol were absorbed into the 'New Police'. Day's modest proposal to expand the Dismounted Patrol by 300 men and extend its operational radius to 12 miles was a non-starter. But, as we have seen, his Mounted Patrol continued to exist, and even to show some increased activity. Essex saw little of the New Police yet; the local magistrates did not seek their help over the Lodge Farm fire in 1834, although they did hire 14 constables from the Metropolitan force to keep order at Fairlop Fair in 1836.[52]

The smouldering rivalry between the Bow Street Magistrates and their opposite numbers at New Scotland Yard (not yet dignified as Commissioners) was obvious to a further Select Committee in 1833. The pride which both sides seemed to be showing in the small cooperation between their police forces could not be in the public interest. The solution was probably inevitable — an Act of 1836 placed the Horse Patrol under the control of the Metropolitan Police with effect from 1 October 1837.[53]

Even then the last Patrole in Essex did not ride finally into the sunset. The Metropolitan Police was not fully operational across the River Lea until 1840. In the meantime the Horse Patrol continued to work under the command of 'K' Division Inspector William Richardson who had himself been a Deputy Inspector of the Bow Street Mounted Patrol which he had joined in 1826. Not surprisingly the Patrol still operated along much the same lines, as the following incident indicates.[54]

Two journeyman sawyers from South Ockendon were tramping home from London one Sunday night in August 1838. At a point on Romford Road near the later site of Seven Kings Railway Station they were set upon by a man, one of a group of four or five sitting in the road, who claimed to have some grievance against them. He knocked them both down several times with his fist, kicked one of them, swearing 'he would knock my bloody guts out' and, having snatched the poor man's handkerchief and hat, vanished across the fields with two other men. Seeking help, the battered sawyers walked on to a public-house at Chadwell (the Greyhound, or the old White Horse opposite) where they waited for the Patrol.

George Weston rode up about 9 o'clock accompanied by Inspector Richardson. They took one of the sawyers to Kemp's beerhouse in the Green Lane — the Old Thatched House, now the Lord Napier — where he identified their assailant, who was promptly arrested. He dropped the stolen handkerchief as he got up, and a woman customer retrieved the stolen hat from under the bench where he had been sitting. The culprit, a twenty-year-old Ilford man with a previous conviction, was sentenced at the Old Bailey to 15 years transportation — a harsh sentence, but prior to Peel's law reforms he would probably have been hung.[55]

Inspector Richardson, incidentally, had a more difficult time the following July when he was in charge of police at the Fairlop Fair. A squad of six Metropolitan Constables and three or four Parish Constables escorting a handcuffed prisoner to gaol were overwhelmed by a hostile crowd, Richardson was knocked flat, and the prisoner escaped.[56]

Of those listed as members of the Bow Street Mounted Patrol 4th Division in 1836, John Aris, David Johnson, and George Weston, together with Richard Watkin (No. 52, Enfield) and Charles Whitman (No. 59, Leytonstone) were still serving under the Metropolitan Police when the take-over was completed. All these resigned with effect from 24 August 1840, doubtless under superannuation arrangements, having served since the early 1820s. The former 4th Division Inspector, Ben Pritchard, continued to serve, like Richardson, as an Inspector in the Metropolitan Police until the beginning of 1846 although he too had joined in 1821. Thomas Jaques (No. 57, Loughton), who had joined in 1826, served with the Met. until August 1842. William Hogg who only joined the Mounted Patrol in 1837 — possibly as a replacement for Gutteridge — became a Sergeant in the Metropolitan force.[57]

The remaining 10 or so members of the old 4th Division resigned before 1840. In the instance of James Othen we can carry the story further. The last record of him as a Bow Street Horse Patrol is in December 1836 when he gave expert evidence on wheel marks in a case where one Ilford jobber accused another of stealing a cart-load of turnips. We may presume he resigned between then and the Metropolitan takeover in October 1837. In July 1837 Margaret his wife died and in the last quarter of the year he remarried. His new bride was Frances, widow of James Wood former landlord of the Three Rabbits in Little Ilford. So James Othen thus achieved a convenient transition from policeman to publican. It may be noted that Frances was a Hampshire woman and that the Three Rabbits — facing onto the High Road and backing onto Wanstead Flats — was a familiar landmark on Othen's accustomed beat.[58]

In 1839 the Eastern Counties Railway had reached Romford, by 1843 it reached Colchester; the stage-coaches were galloping into a romantic past and the Turnpike Trusts gloomily contemplating bankruptcy. Between 1801 and 1841 the population of West Ham (Stratford and Plaistow) nearly doubled and that of Great Ilford more than doubled though it was still only a village. Between 1840 and 1843 Metropolitan 'K' Division opened their own police station at Roden House on Ilford Hill, nearer the centre of the village. Up to 1860 they continued to rent quarters on the north side of the High Road before constructing a purpose built station opposite, on the site which they were to occupy for well over a century.[59]

Already in the 1840s they had an establishment for 13 policemen — a far cry from that tiny force of the Horse Patrol who had first made safe the road into London. Even so it was decided in 1840 that the Metropolitan Police should not after all operate as far out as the Horse Patrol had done and Romford was placed under control of the newly formed Essex Constabulary (until 1965). Now by a curious coincidence the large new Metropolitan Police Station opened in 1995 along the High Road Ilford has been erected within yards of the site of the two cottages which served as a 'double station' for the Bow Street Mounted Patrol nearly two centuries ago (see map page 320).[60]

So far as the Essex experience is concerned, the defence of Sir Frederick Roe, Chief Magistrate of Bow Street, before the 1833 Committee, might make a fitting epitaph for the old Mounted Patrol, 'Highway robberies have been put down, and no complaints made of the inefficiency of the corps, but great approbation expressed of it ... Considering there are 20 roads protected by only 70 men.'[61]

Acknowledgements

I am most grateful to Peter Lawrence and Bryn Elliott for starting me off with essential extracts from the MEPO files, to Les Waters for his kindness in giving me a copy of his valuable Bow Street 'Handlist', and to Christopher Forester for his generosity in sending me the opening chapters of his draft History of the Mounted Branch. My thanks are due to Elizabeth Sellers for sharing part of her research into Essex police families, and also to Andrew Phillips. Essential support has been given by Nicola Thomas and Bryan Weaver.

REFERENCES

The following abbreviations are employed in these references:

GA   Gilbert Armitage, *The History of the Bow Street Runners 1729–1829*, 1932.

PP   Patrick Pringle, *Hue and Cry*, 1955.

WH   B. Weinreb and C. Hibbert, eds., *The London Encyclopedia*, 1983.

CF   C. C. Forester, *The History and Development of the Metropolitan Mounted Branch*, forthcoming.

MEPO   Metropolitan Police Files, Public Record Office (Kew).

OBSP   *Old Bailey Session Papers*.

SC   *Select Committee of the House of Commons on Police of the Metropolis*.

Newspapers:

CC   *Chelmsford Chronicle*.

EH   *Essex Herald*.

EM   *Kent and Essex Mercury*.

ES   *Essex Standard*.

1 GA 56–9. GA is the chief authority used for basic facts relating to Bow Street in succeeding paragraphs.

2 GA 61, 64–6; PP 166–7. There seems to be some doubt about the precise size and duration of this early horse patrol.

3 GA 61, 123–7; PP 198. Pringle is probably correct in maintaining that the Night Patrol was actually introduced after Sir John's death in 1780. The anti-papist 'Gordon Riots' in June of that year, fomented by the unbalanced Lord George Gordon, alerted even radicals to the dangers from an ignorant and loot-hungry London mob. Rioting was suppressed by the military, the parish constables being totally unable or unwilling to contain the disorder.

4 GA 122–3; SC 1822 has a detailed account of the establishments of the various London Police Offices including the City of London; *The London Ambulator*, 12th ed.,1820,'Account of the Metropolis', pp.39–40 gives the general location of the Offices.

5 WH, s.v. 'Thames Police' neatly explains the foundation but exaggerates the size of the force, for which see SC 1822.

6 Mr J. Stafford, Bow Street Chief Clerk and Inspector of the Foot Patrol, said in evidence to SC 1822, 'the watchmen have a general idea that the Bow-street patrol are a sort of spy upon them, and accordingly they hate them most cordially'.

7 Evidence of Sir John Gifford, SC 1816.

8 'Blood Money' — particularly rewards of £40 for information leading to a conviction for Burglary or Highway Robbery and some other offences — all of which, before Peel's reforms, carried the death penalty. Leading Runner, John Townsend, whilst arguing that police seldom obtained more than a small share, admitted 'officers will always be tempted to obtain a conviction even against their consciences', SC 1816. For a near contemporary treatment showing the degree of public concern, see C. Knight, ed.,'Sketches of the History of Crime and Police in London', *London*, 1841, pp.225–40. For another cause of prejudice against police, see note 19 below.

9 Evidence of Sir Richard Birnie, SC 1822.

10 It could perhaps be said that the issue of blue greatcoats to the City Day Patrol in 1782 foreshadowed police uniform, WH s.v. Police (607).

11 GA 129ff; (History) MEPO 2/25.

12 On the 2nd and 3rd roads see *V.C.H. Essex*, V, p.116 and VI, pp.342–3.

13 Chapman and André, *Map of Essex*, 1777, Sheets XVI and XXI; OS 1" 1st ed., 1805, Sheet no. 1.

14 W. B. Ramsey and R. L. Fowkes, *Epping Forest Then and Now*, 1986, p.80.

15 *Ibid.* pp.76–9; C. B. Sworder,'Epping Highways', *Essex Review*, 32, 1923, pp.84–7.

16 Sir F. Roe's answer to Q.1377, SC 1833; CF 6. Forester also cites the arming of guards on stage-coaches with the blunderbuss as contributing to the decline of highwaymen.

17 CC 19.12.1794; Romford Burial Reg. 14.12.1794.

18 'Patrole' was the official spelling and I have retained it in quotations or when referring to an individual police officer. The convenient term 'patrolman' appears to have been a later introduction from the U.S.A.

19 'The Regulated Uniform', 'List of Appointments', MEPO 2/25; 'Orders . . . November 1813', delivered by Wm. Day to SC 1816. The civilian touch to the uniform may have been intended to distinguish them from European gendarmerie popularly regarded as agents of foreign despotism.

20 *Ibid. SC* 1816; Day in evidence to SC 1816, SC 1822, SC 1833, held to the line that an officer must use his own judgement and discretion. See especially his answers to Qs. 1356, 1357 also to 1344–7, SC 1833.

21 Virtually no documentation from this period has survived, it has been plausibly suggested that much of the Bow Street archive handed over to the Metropolitan Police in 1837 was discarded

and destroyed in the 1880s (info. Print Room, Guildhall Library); Day's answer to the 4th question by *SC* 1822 regarding 'the history of this establishment' is confused and evasive. Admittedly he was not himself in full charge until 1813.

22 ERO PBR/I 25.1; *KEM* 18.3.1823.

23 Evidence of Wm. Day, of Wm. Fielding, *SC* 1816.

24 'Statement delivered in a Card' by Wm. Day, *SC* 1816.

25 *EH* 18.7.1815, 19.3.1816; *CC* 27.12.1816.

26 *CC* 17.1.1817, 21.3.1817; *EH* 21.1.1817, 18.3.1817.

27 *EH* 21.1.1817; *CC* 24.1.1817; *EH* 25.1.1817, 15.4.1817, 22.4.1817, 5.8.1817.

28 Day's answers to Qs. 1264, 1265, *SC* 1833.

29 Recommendations, *SC* 1816/17.

30 GA, pp.130–1 and CF p.11 state that the 'Dismounted Horse Patrol' was created in 1821, but Orders for that force dated 1816 were exhibited by Day to *SC* 1816.

31 See previous note. Re. increased establishment, see Day's evidence, *SC* 1822 and CF p.14. For stations see '4th Division The Horse Patrol 1st October 1836', MEPO 2/25.

32 Recommendations, *SC* 1822; GA, 128; A. A. Clarke, *Police Uniform and Equipment*, 1991, p.4.

33 'Orders . . . November 1813', delivered by Wm. Day, *SC* 1816; Evidence of Wm. Day to *SC* 1822; 'Orders 1827' MEPO 2/25.

34 'Stations, 1836' MEPO 2/25.

35 Evidence of Wm. Day, *SC* 1822; Wm. Day's answers to Qs. 1156–71, *SC* 1833; List — Stations and Landlords 1836, MEPO 2/25.

36 Map is based on OS 6″, 1st ed. 1862–71 and E.C. Rlwy. Plan 1835, ERO Q/RUm 1/56. Schedule 1835 shows the two properties indicated as 'Police Station', landlord Thos. Curtis, a Stratford builder who also owned brickfield to rear. List of Horse Patrols, Stations and Landlords 1836, MEPO 2/25, shows pair at Stratford (Nos. 61 and 62) and at Ilford (63 and 64), landlord 'Mr Curtis, Stratford Green'.

37 Lists etc. 1836 MEPO 2/25; Barking (St. Margaret's) Baptismal Reg. 13.8.1828, George Othen; Barking Rate Valuation, Ilford Ward no. 678, 1829; Woodford (St. Mary's) Bapt. Reg. 30.9.1827, Sarah Elizabeth Aris.

38 List — Stations and Roads Patrolled, etc., MEPO 2/25.

39 *Ibid.*,; *KEM* 1.6.1824.

40 *ES* 24.11.1832, 5.10.1833.

41 *ES* 19.2.1836, 11.3.1836.

42 *EH* 26.10.1830.

43 *ES* 22.5.1834.

44 Lists etc., MEPO 2/25; News cutting 1834, Hiram Stead Coll., 133 (Stratford P.L.).

45 *Ibid.*, 1835 (2).

46 Order no. 3 1827, MEPO 2/25. Compare Order no. 3 of 1813, *SC* 1816.

47 ERO Q/SBd 7/2; *ES* 7.4.1832, 14.4.1832. Despite the year this riot had no political significance. For further details see, H. H. Lockwood,'When the Riot Act was Read in Ilford', Ilford and Dist. Hist. Soc., *Newsletter*, 37, Nov. 1993.

48 *OBSP* 1835–6, pp.590–3.

49 *ES* 28.10.1836; *OBSP* 1836, 1092–3.

50 Wm. Day's answers to Qs. 1273, 1264, 1261, *SC* 1833.

51 *CC* 7.11.1834, 14.11.1834; *ES* 7.11.1834, 14.11.1834, 28.11.1834, 12.8.1836. Site of former Lodge Farm is in Lodge Avenue near junction of Porters Avenue.

52 GA, pp.258–9; 'Proposed plan . . . from Mr. Day, addressed to Mr. Stafford, 26 Aug. 1829', MEPO 2/25; *ES* 17.6.1836, 1.7.1836.

53 Commissioners' and John Wray's answers to Qs. 177, 239, 1075–82, *SC* 1833; Day's to Qs. 1278, 1334–40, *SC* 1833; CF 17; 16/17 Wm. IV cap. 50 (13 Aug. 1836); Directions from Whitehall re. Transfer on 1 Oct.1837 (dated 20.9.1837), MEPO 2.

54 *Ibid.*, — promotion of Wm. Richardson to Inspector of Met. Police is endorsed, MEPO 2; Bryn Elliott, *Ilford Police*, (Pamphlet, Waltham Abbey 1993),2; Bernard Brown, 'Romford Police', *Romford Record*, 22, 1990, 25.

55 *OBSP* 1938, pp.737–40.

56 *OBSP* 1839, pp.554–5.

57 Lists of 4th Div. Horse Patrol and stations 1 Oct 1836, and those 'who were transferred to the Metropolitan Police, and were serving therein 7 Dec. 1837' (date of 'removal', added), MEPO 2/25.

58 *Ibid.*, MEPO 2/25; *ES* 9.12.1836; Barking (St. Margaret's) Burial Reg. 21.7.1837, Margaret Othen, Great Ilford; Central Reg. Off., Marriage Index, Dec. Qtr.1837, Othen James/Wood Frances, Bishopsgate Sub. Reg., 2.19; Census 1841, Little Ilford, Three Rabbits Inn.

59 *V.C.H. Essex*, V, 3; ERO DDSa Sales 8.12, Lot 2; B. Elliott, *Ilford Police*, p.2.

60 B. Brown, 'Romford Police', p.26.

61 Sir F. A. Roe's answers to Qs. 1359, 1370, *SC* 1833.

Drewry and Cornwell: Two Essex Naval V.Cs.

IAN G. ROBERTSON

WITH A COASTLINE some 300 miles long and a well-attested maritime tradition,[1] which included providing men for the Royal and Merchant Navies, a ship-building industry, a thriving coastal trade and fishing fleet, it comes as no surprise that two of the inhabitants of the historic County of Essex should be awarded the Victoria Cross, and are amongst the 582 recipients of the V.C. in the Great War.[2] Although of different social standing and naval rank, the two lads, Midshipman George Leslie Drewry and Boy First Class John Travers Cornwell, had much in common; they were both under the age of majority, then set at 21, both lived near to each other in Forest Gate and Manor Park respectively, areas to become part of the London Borough of Newham, and between them represented the carrying out of two of the traditional roles of the Royal Navy in time of war, namely, ensuring that soldiers are landed, which Drewry was endeavouring to do at Gallipoli in 1915, and engaging the enemy on the high seas which was Cornwell's task in what became known as the Battle of Jutland in 1916.[3]

The question, for at least the local historian, is why was it that, of the two young men from adjacent parishes both awarded the supreme recognition of gallantry in action, one, George Drewry, V.C., should drop from public recollection, while the other, Jack Cornwell, V.C., remains even after nearly 80 years probably the most famous Victoria Cross winner of all.[4] The answer is suggested by a perusal in the National Army Museum of the files kept by Canon William Lummis, and now maintained by the Military Historical Society, in which he collected press cuttings and other printed or typescript material relating to the recipients of the award.[5] It will be argued that these press cuttings show that there was a well-coordinated attempt to promote the war effort by the exploitation of Cornwell's heroism with the active intervention of the national press; this was possible because Cornwell's Victoria Cross, unlike Drewry's, was a posthumous award.

The son of Thomas Drewry, Works Manager of the Peninsular and Oriental Steam Navigation Company, and the former Mary Kendall of Weelsby, Lincolnshire, George Leslie Drewry was born at 58 Claremont Road, Forest Gate, in the County Borough of West Ham on 3 November 1894 and subsequently educated at Merchant Taylors' School at Blackheath.[6] On leaving school he joined the

George Leslie Drewry.

Mercantile Marine becoming an apprentice on *The Indian Empire*, a sailing ship out of London, subsequently moving to P. & O. as an officer in 1912. As a member of the Royal Naval Reserve from 1 July 1913, Drewry was at Port Said when he was called up for active service on 3 August 1914 and was posted first to H.M.S. *Egmont*, a guardship at Malta, then to *H.M.S. Hussar*, a torpedo gunboat, from which the midshipman was tranferred to *H.M.T. River Clyde*. The next year found him involved in the ill-fated Gallipoli expedition and it was off 'V' Beach that, under Commander Unwin, Midshipman Drewry won his Victoria Cross. The plan was that *H.M.T. River Clyde*, a collier converted to take large numbers of troops and disgorge them rapidly through specially cut openings in the sides, was to be run aground and the troops would land by crossing a bridge to the beach composed of lighters.

In the event this landing had to be effected under intense fire from the Turkish Forces and in the course of attempting to complete the Navy's task of seeing the troops ashore Commander Unwin, two midshipmen including Drewry, and two seamen were all awarded the Victoria Cross for their gallantry. The *London Gazette* citation (16 August 1915) is as follows:

> 'George Leslie Drewry, Midshipman, Royal Naval Reserve, H.M.S. *Hussar*. Dates of Acts of Bravery: 25 and 26 April, 1915. Assisted Commander Unwin at the work of securing the lighters under heavy rifle and Maxim fire. He was wounded in the head, but continued his work, and twice subsequently attempted to swim from lighter to lighter with a line.'

This account was amplified by his friend Surgeon P. Burrowes-Kelly, R.N., D.S.O., who noted in his diary that:

> 'Midshipman Drewry (now Lieut.) R.N.R., V.C., was executive officer of the *River Clyde*. When the time arrived to run ship ashore was placed in command of the "Greek Hopper" which accompanied us, and ran ashore on our portside. On his way through the water to the shore picked up a dangerously wounded Munster Fusilier in the shallow foreshore water, and endeavoured to carry him to safety. The man was shot dead in his arms. After lighters, etc., broke adrift, Drewry, though laid out from wounds of the head on a drifting lighter, succeeded in effecting to make lighter fast again, and then jumping overboard, he was seen to swim with rope or hauling line round his neck to the other part of his task. Shortly afterwards he was brought into the *River Clyde* in an exhausted and delirious condition.'

In a more lengthy account in the *Daily Chronicle*, endorsed by Burrowes-Kelly as accurate, it is reported that having jumped overboard with a rope and swimming towards the lighters Drewry

> 'when halfway across found that the rope was not long enough, and

The Bystander, August 25, 1915

271

Heroes of "V" Beach
WHERE THE "RIVER CLYDE" WAS RUN ASHORE

Photograph   C.N.
MIDSHIPMAN GEORGE LESLIE DREWRY, R.N.R., V.C.

SEAMAN GEORGE SAMSON, V.C.

Photograph   *Russell, South ea*
COMMANDER E. G. ROBINSON, V.C.

Midshipman G. L. Drewry, V.C.

The photograph, taken by Midshipman George Drewry, V.C., shows the beaching of the Collier "River Clyde"—a perilous operation undertaken, as Admiral de Robeck's recently published despatch tells us, in order to "form a convenient breakwater during future landing of stores, etc." The photographer gained his Cross during the operation

had to remain in the water until Lieut. Morse and Midshipman Malleson arrived with a picket boat and completed the operation.'

After the award of the Victoria Cross had been published Surgeon Burrowes-Kelly who was then the medical officer on *H.M.S. Hythe* wrote on 3 September 1915 to Mr and Mrs Drewry, the parents of the V.C. winner as follows:

'I am taking the liberty now — I meant to take it before, but could not get the address, of writing to you just a few lines about your most gallant of sons, our beloved Midshipman who has made himself and incidently all those with him famous. I maintain that I am the only person living who can ever know what Commander Unwin and your son did on April 25th both before and after they were knocked out. Why both were not killed I cannot tell you and one must look to someone higher for the reason, God alone can only know — I saw them flushed with victory, faced with defeat and death and so on turnabout. When the Commander lay in a dangerous condition your son took over sole charge. When your son was finished Commander Unwin was ready although unfit to relieve him. George has a tremendous future in front of him, because his fame will not affect him, but only tend to elevate him still higher. His absolute contempt of death, love of duty and modesty were proverbial amongst us all, both Military and Naval. You must indeed be proud of this splendid fellow, and that he will be spared for many years to gladden your hearts is my one wish.

To have been with such a body of Naval men has been a great honour indeed, and I shall never forget that I was their Doctor who did what little I could for them all. All were great but River Clyde Drewry as he is now known was the greatest. He and Seaman Samson, the leading Seaman, have borne out Nelson's old dictum "My guns may change, my ships may change, but the spirit of my men remains".

Trusting you will pardon this intrusion on my part and again asking you to accept my warmest congratulations on being the parents of such a son.'

The award of the Victoria Cross clearly aroused much interest in the press, the *Daily Express* of 17 August 1915, for example, ran a story entitled 'Midshipman's VC's Adventures' which was based on an interview with Midshipman Drewry's father at the family home in Claremont Road which included personal details not readily obtainable elsewhere, not least the information that George Drewry's 'elder brother is a certificated merchant service engineer, and his younger brother is preparing to join the Royal Navy'. Further recognition was accorded Drewry in that 'The Imperial Merchant Service Guild presented him with a sword of honour, as the first officer in the RNR and in the Merchant Service to win the Victoria Cross'. However, an undated newspaper report in the Lummis

The War Budget,
September 2nd, 1915.

V.C. for a Brave Boy Middy

Warriors nowadays are not made by age and experience. There is the glorious story of two midshipmen who, although mere youths, have received the coveted honour of the V.C. for courage which may be emulated, but never beaten, even by seamen who saw active service almost before these two youngsters were born. The heroism of one of them, Midshipman George L. Drewry, R.N.R., is depicted in the above drawing. On the occasion of the landing on Gallipoli from the River Clyde, Drewry helped to secure the lighters under heavy fire. He was wounded in the head, but continued his work, and twice subsequently attempted to swim from lighter to lighter with a line.

77

File suggests that he was in fact the second after Flight Sub-Lieutenant R. A. J. Warneford, R.N., who had also served in the Merchant Navy before the outbreak of war.

Having been promoted to Acting Lieutenant R.N.R. in 1916 he was serving on the Northern Patrol in command of *H.M.T. William Jackson* when it was reported that 'Lieutenant Drewry was fatally injured on Friday evening, the 2nd Aug. 1918, at sea . . . A block fell from the end of a derrick and struck him heavily on the head, fracturing his skull and breaking his left arm. He died shortly afterwards.'[7] Drewry certainly seems to have been fearless and may be regarded as fortunate in having reached the age of 23 given that he was as a boy knocked unconscious by a motor vehicle, fell from the mast of a ship into the sea and was nearly killed during his early sea training, (his rescuer received the Medal of the Royal Humane Society), survived the shipwreck of *The Indian Empire* and reached a desert island, being rescued by a Chilean gunboat; there were then the extremely dangerous circumstances in which he was awarded the Victoria Cross and ultimately he lost his life in an accident in command of the *H.M.T. William Jackson*. After George Drewry's death his brother officers of the Northern Patrol erected a memorial window to him in All Saints' Church in Forest Gate. His original medal group including the Victoria Cross was presented to his old school, Merchant Taylors' in 1981.[8]

The award of the Victoria Cross to George Drewry was thought to be relevant not simply in naval terms but also to wider issues of a social nature, especially the problem perceived by many of the degeneracy of British youth. The connection may be demonstrated by quoting the editorial in the *Daily Express* of 17 August 1915 which was entitled 'Hats Off to the Boy'; in this the two Midshipmen, Drewry and Malleson, who were both awarded the Victoria Cross, are eulogized in the following terms:

'There is no more wonderful and lovable thing on earth than the average natural British boy. He stands in a class by himself. His morality is his own, based on common sense, and scornful of mere convention. He loathes sentimentality. He is not remarkable for imagination. His literature is his own. He feeds his soul with Marryat, Henty, and Ballantyne, with Stevenson, and sometimes with the elder Dumas, and nowadays with the Kipling of "The Jungle Book", though rarely with the Kipling of "Stalky and Co.". He submits to authority, but invariably apologizes to himself for his obedience by jeering at all masters behind their backs. He loves soldiers and cricketers and all animals. He is shy and self-conscious with women and foreigners. He hates bullies and "swank" and everything that is conspicuous and unusual. There is very little difference between the British boy at Eton or Marlborough or Tonbridge and the British boy in a well-managed elementary school. The British boy is Peter Pan. There are thousands of him, bearded and grimed, in the Flanders trenches.

THE DAILY MIRROR, Tuesday, August 17, 1915.

YOUNG MIDSHIPMAN WINS THE V.C.: THE IMMORTAL STORY OF THE LANDING AT GALLIPOLI FROM THE RIVER - CLYDE.

Midshipman Drewry (centre figure) photographed on shore after his heroic deed, and Surgeon Kelly (clasping his knee). It will be seen that his ankle is bandaged.

The boy has come to his own in Vice-Admiral de Robeck's belated account of the Navy's part in the landing in Gallipoli. Of five V.Cs., two were given to midshipmen for splendid courage in attempting to secure lighters that had broken loose. These youngsters swam, under a heavy rifle and machine-gun fire, from lighter to lighter, carrying lines with them. One was wounded, but he did not stop. They failed and they tried again. Marryat never conceived a finer deed. D'Artagnan was never braver. George Drewry and Wilfred Malleson are magnificent young heroes of whom the nation is proud indeed, but they would tell you — and they would be telling nothing but the truth — that they have had the luck and that hundreds of other fellows would have done just the same if they had the chance. That is a splendid thing to know, and the knowledge makes all the talk of national decadence more than ridiculous. We may thank God for the British boy.'

The purpose in quoting the editorial in full is to show how George Drewry, the modest midshipman from a professional family in Forest Gate could, by courtesy of the *Daily Express*, join an idealized company of heroes representing all that the best in British boys. The allusions in the piece and the underlying concern, not least the issue of national decadence, would have been clear to contemporary readers. The fear of moral degeneracy had troubled many since the 1890s and especially exercised Robert Baden-Powell contributing substantially to the establishment of the Boy Scouts.[9]

John Travers Cornwell was some six years younger than George Drewry being born on 8 January 1900 at either Ilford or Leyton, the son of Eli and Alice Cornwell. Eli Cornwell, who came from Bottisham Lode, near Cambridge, was a former soldier, having campaign medals from both Egypt and South Africa; he rejoined the Army and died a few months after his son. John Travers Cornwell attended Walton Road School in Manor Park, East Ham, which had originated as the Bessborough Road Board School built in 1900 by the Little Ilford School Board; it was renamed the Jack Cornwell school in 1929.[10] The Walton Road area of Manor Park was poorly built and 'soon became slums'.[11] He also belonged to the St. Mary's Mission, Manor Park Troop of Boy Scouts; with his Tenderfoot Badge, 2nd Class and Missioners Badge he was regarded as a keen Boy Scout and Scoutmaster J. F. Avery of the 21st East Ham Troop reminisced as follows: 'I knew Cornwell well as a working boy. He was always a good boy at work and carried out his duty with cheerfulness.' His mother recalled his wish to go to sea, 'He always wanted to get on in the Navy', she continued in an interview with the *Daily Mirror* of 16 September 1916, 'It was his one ambition. It was strange for the son of a soldier, wasn't it? but somehow or other the Army never appealed to Jack. Over and over again he would get a line down in the back garden and rig up a ship on the fence. From the time he was a tiny boy he talked about the Navy — always the Navy.' Despite that ambition it is reported that he became, on leaving school, a boy on a Brooke Bond's Tea van. When war broke out, his father rejoined the Army and he enlisted in the Navy.

JACK CORNWELL.

" Just an ordinary boy."

Completing his training at Keyham in April 1916, Jack Cornwell was posted as a Boy First Class to *H.M.S. Chester*, a new fast light cruiser forming part of the Third Battle Cruiser Squadron under the command of Rear-Admiral Hood. Action was not long in coming as *H.M.S. Chester* was ordered forward in what were to be the early stages of the Battle of Jutland. On 31 May 1916, 16 year old Boy Cornwell was on duty at the left-hand side of the shield of the forward six-inch gun. He was the sight setter for this forward gun; through the telepad which he wore across his head and over his ears he received direct messages for the gun crew from *H.M.S. Chester's* gunnery officer. As soon as battle was joined this forward gun turret was hit by enemy fire leaving alive only three of the nine men who formed the gun crew. Another enemy shell resulted in just Jack Cornwell standing, although badly wounded. With communications interrupted he looked towards the bridge for visual signals which he could pass on to any relief gun crew who might be sent forward. After the engagement *H.M.S. Chester* returned to the Squadron; as soon as practicable the wounded were taken ashore and it was in the hospital at Grimsby that, with his mother on her way to see him, Jack Cornwell died on 2 June 1916.

The bravery under fire of this lad from Manor Park clearly affected those who witnessed his behaviour. As the captain of *H.M.S. Chester* wrote to his mother:

> 'I know you would wish to hear of the splendid fortitude and courage shown by your son during the action of 31 May. His devotion to duty was an example to all of us. The wounds which resulted in his death within a short time were received in the first few minutes of the action. He remained steady at his most exposed post at the gun, waiting for orders. His gun would not bear on the enemy; all but two of the ten crew were killed or wounded, and he was the only one who was in such an exposed position. But he felt he might be needed, and, indeed, he might have been; so he stayed there, standing and waiting, under heavy fire, with just his own brave heart and God's help to support him. I cannot express to you my admiration of the son you have lost from this world. No other comfort would I attempt to give to the mother of so brave a lad, but to assure her of what he was, and what he did, and what an example he gave. I hope to place in the boys' mess a plate with his name on and the date, and the words, "Faithful unto Death". I hope some day you may be able to come and see it here. I have not failed to bring his name prominently before my Admiral.'

Indeed he had not, and Admiral Sir David Beatty in his official despatch noted:

> 'Boy (First Class) John Travers Cornwell, of the Chester, was mortally wounded early in the action. He, nevertheless, remained standing alone at a most exposed post, quietly awaiting orders till the end of

By special permission of "The Sphere."

JACK CORNWELL

The Story of
John Travers Cornwell, V.C
"Boy-1st Class"

BY THE AUTHOR OF "WHERE'S MASTER?"

JACK CORNWELL

1/3 net

HODDER & STOUGHTON

the action, with the gun's crew dead and wounded all round him. His age was under 16½ years. I regret that he has since died, but I recommend his case for special recognition in justice to his memory, and as an acknowledgement of the high example set by him.'

That despatch was reported in the press in July 1916.

At the end of the month on 26 July Lord Beresford asked in the House of Lords whether it was proposed to award the Victoria Cross posthumously to Jack Cornwell; the answer given on behalf of the Government by the Duke of Devonshire was 'that at present no recommendation had been received'. It was not until 15 September 1916 that the details of the award of the Victoria Cross appeared in the *London Gazette* as follows:

'John Travers Cornwell, Boy (First Class), O.N.J. 42563. Mortally wounded early in the action, Boy, First Class, John Travers Cornwell remained standing alone at a most exposed post, quietly awaiting orders, until the end of the action, with the gun's crew dead and wounded about him. His age was under sixteen and a half years.'

The Times on 16 September commented: 'Nothing connected with the battle has stirred the imagination of the people more than the story of John Travers Cornwell, and the award of the V.C. in his case will be most popular.' In an interview in the *Daily Mirror* published on the same day Jack Cornwell's mother gave her reaction, saying simply: 'It's a great honour, but I wish my boy had lived to enjoy it.' Mrs Cornwell received the Victoria Cross posthumously awarded to her son from the King at Buckingham Palace on 16 November 1916.[12]

It is appropriate to pause at this point and emphasize that the crucial difference between the ways in which George Drewry and Jack Cornwell have been remembered is entirely dependent on the fact that the latter's award was posthumous. Although George Drewry was ultimately killed on active service, he received his Victoria Cross and returned to duty. It is inconceivable that a serving member of the Armed Forces could be treated in the way in which Jack Cornwell was; had he lived it is very unlikely indeed that he would have become so famous. How this very high public profile was established may be traced, not in closed or confidential documents, but by an assiduous reading of the press cuttings and other ephemera collected with such care by Canon Lummis. These disclose a number of strands: first, there were the efforts of the national newspapers, especially the *Daily Sketch*; then there was the positive attitude of the Admiralty; third was the philanthropic response of the public and lastly the harnessing of Jack Cornwell's reputation to promote the cause of patriotism through education, linked with scouting.

It was the *Daily Sketch* which sensed a human interest story by concerning itself with where and how Jack Cornwell was buried in the months *before* the award of the Victoria Cross was gazetted. This newspaper ran a campaign, which it thought presumably would find favour with its readers, based on the fact that Cornwell's body had been brought back from Grimsby and buried in a common grave in Manor Park Cemetery because of the poverty of his immediate family. The way the *Daily Sketch* saw the story was reviewed in its issue of 16 September 1916 when Boy Cornwell's Victoria Cross was announced in the press. Having reported the award and quoted the *London Gazette* announcement, the *Daily Sketch* continued as follows:

'. . . There was a time when it looked as though the nation's debt to Boy Cornwell was not to be paid. He had died a hero, but he had gone to his grave, not indeed, unwept, yet unhonoured and unsung. The *Daily Sketch* discovered that his body was lying in a nameless grave. Admiral Beatty had written of him: "I recommend his case for special recognition in justice to his memory and as an acknowledgement of the high example set by him." And yet there he lay, in a common grave in Manor Park Cemetery. No stone marked his resting-place; not even his name was there to allow the passing stranger to note "A hero is buried here". All there was at the foot of the mound was a white-painted strip of wood, with the figures 323 upon it. They meant simply that this number corresponded with one in the records of the cemetery. When the *Daily Sketch* made this painful discovery there was only one possible decision to be arrived at: Cornwell's remains [the *Daily Sketch* said] must not forever rest in a common and half-forgotten grave. We told the public so; and the public agreed. We informed the Admiralty of what had occurred — that, instead of a naval funeral, there had been a simple, cheap, private interment, the cost of which the boy's mother had borne. The Admiralty expressed itself, through one of its officials, grateful that the facts had been brought to its notice. "But", said the Admiralty, "we cannot do anything unless the boy's mother writes to make an application". Mrs Cornwell did wish to make the application. A woman in humble circumstances, with her sorrow heavy upon her, it had not occurred to her that the nation would honour her son . . . and she asked the *Daily Sketch* what course she had better adopt. The *Daily Sketch* assisted her to send the Secretary of the Admiralty Board the necessary letter with the result that she received the glad tidings one day that her prayer would be answered and her boy would be buried afresh as a hero would be buried. Meanwhile England had been waking up. It had read of the unworthy injustice to one of the bravest of its sons and it was startled into protest. Letters began to pour into the *Daily Sketch* office. Offers were received to provide a grave plot, a tombstone, wreaths and other tributes. On Saturday, July 29th, the agitation of *Daily Sketch* was brought to fruition. The body had been exhumed, and in the afternoon it was reburied, in a grave which the Manor Park Cemetery Committee had given near the gates of the cemetery . . . with all the honours the nation could give. London thronged the streets of Manor Park in its thousands, nine to twelve deep. The procession started from the Town Hall, the steps of which were literally smothered with flowers. Admiral Beatty himself sent a wreath of lilies and immortelles. Dr. Macnamara, Parliamentary Secretary to the Admiralty, was among the followers. The Bishop of Barking read the service, three volleys were fired by a detachment of Blue Jackets from the *Crystal Palace*, and the Last Post was sounded by naval buglers. But Britain, once aroused, was not even then satisfied. The Lord Mayor of London called a Mansion House meeting to establish a Boy Cornwell Memorial to take the form of cottage homes for disabled sailors and marines and their families and the endowment of naval scholarships. The Grimsby and District Hospital where Cornwell died, decided to have a special cot in his memory with the tablet recording his deed of glory. The Boy Scouts, of whom he had been one, began to arrange for more scholarships, and are now to have a badge and medal in his name. And now the King has awarded him the Victoria Cross. Surely never in the history of the British Navy have so many and so full honours fallen upon one whose memory seemed in danger of being allowed to fade. When the *Daily Sketch* called yesterday to congratulate Mrs. Cornwell, it was found her son had been awarded also the Scouts' V.C. by the 1st St. Mary's, Ilford, Troop, of which he was a member. It was a new Mrs. Cornwell who spoke to the *Daily Sketch* about her boy. In the bad old days of early summer, when his remains lay unhonoured, she was a heart-broken mother. Now she talked with pride and gladness of the recognition that had come of the noble way in which her son had died.'

Nor was this account sufficient for the *Daily Sketch* because in its editorial of the same day it is remarked:

'Yet there are only three V.Cs. — one for the Boy Cornwell, who, but for the urgency of the Press, would have slept in a common grave . . . Surely these men were worthy, but was no other man of the Jutland fight worthy of the supreme reward for valour? Either the Army gives too many such rewards or the Navy gives too few.'

There is no doubt that this campaign struck a chord with the public and no one has denied the role of the *Daily Sketch* in taking a lead.[13] The extent of the embarrassment caused may be guessed by a quotation from *The Times History of the War* repeated in the classic history of the Victoria Cross where it is noted that when Boy Cornwell had been wounded

'Some time elapsed before the steadfast courage of the boy was made known. Meanwhile he had been brought ashore, he had died at Grimsby of his wounds, and through one of the stupid blunders which are inseparable from officialdom he had been buried in what was no better than a pauper's grave. No sooner was the truth known of the lad's last hours of life and the manner of his death than public

**BOY 1ST CLASS, JOHN TRAVERS CORNWELL, V.C.,
OF H.M.S. "CHESTER."**

The Battle of Jutland, May 31—June 1, 1916.

*By F. O. Salisbury, painted for the Admiralty on board H.M.S.
"Chester." From the print published by the Fine Arts Publishing
Co. Ltd. on behalf of the Jack Cornwell Memorial Fund.*

"Mortally wounded early in the action, he nevertheless remained standing alone at a most exposed post, quietly awaiting
orders, till the end of the action, with the gun's crew dead and
wounded all round him. His age was under 16½ years."—*Admiral
Sir David Beatty's Despatch.*

opinion demanded a befitting reinterment. Accordingly the body was exhumed, and there was an impressive funeral in Manor Park Cemetery.'[14]

If the press had sensed the mood of the public, the Government was not slow to exploit developments in the interests of the war effort. It will be recalled that Dr T. J. Macnamara, Parliamentary and Financial Secretary to the Admiralty, had attended Jack Cornwell's reinterment at Manor Park Cemetery and indeed had made a speech in tribute after the committal service; this, it should be remembered, was a full six weeks *before* the award of the Victoria Cross was announced in the press. *The Times* for 14 September 1916 recorded Dr Macnamara's words at the launch of the public appeal for funds for the national memorial to Jack Cornwell when he said that:

> 'The teachers of the Walton Road Council School, East Ham, builded better than they knew when they taught young Cornwell to learn the British lesson and to be filled with the British spirit. The Jutland fight gave young Cornwell his chance. How he played his part when it came all the world knows. And, of course, there is not a man or boy under the white Ensign, there is not a soldier of the King who is not inspired at the back of everything by just the same steady ideal and purpose as the good lad whose memory we seek to perpetuate. He died kindling a great inspiration, the harvest of which neither you nor I can measure if we take occasion by the hand and teach the story faithfully . . .'

These sentiments were echoed in a substantially blunter fashion by Sir Edward Carson, First Lord of the Admiralty, when he accepted on 23 March 1917 at the Mansion House, on behalf of the Board of Admiralty, Frank O. Salisbury's picture entitled 'John Cornwell, V.C. on *H.M.S.Chester*'. Without mincing his words Sir Edward Carson said:

> 'The act of John Cornwell is worthy of the best traditions of the Navy. The high example set by the boy is what we want to perpetuate. The man who is not prepared to make every sacrifice to bring about the result which that boy was aiming at is not worthy to be called a British citizen. I am disappointed that from time to time some of the men in some of our shipyards delay the repairs to our ships by striking and by other methods. I ask them to think of Jack Cornwell. It is not a question now between capital and labour. I feel that Jack Cornwell, the boy who met his death at the post of duty, sends this message through me, as First Lord of the Admiralty, to the empire: "Obey your orders, cling to your posts, don't grumble, stick it out".'

One effect of the promotion of Jack Cornwell's memory by the popular press with the support of the government of the day was the development of a popular philanthropic movement exemplified by the meeting at the Mansion House on

13 September 1916 when Mrs Cornwell, Jack's mother, sat on the platform beside the Lord Mayor of London when a public appeal for funds was inaugurated for the national memorial to John Travers Cornwell. As *The Times* reported the form of the national memorial to Jack Cornwell would be the establishment and endowment of cottage homes for infirm and disabled sailors, as well as the foundation of naval scholarships; for the whole project a sum of approximately £50,000 was required. The scale of the appeal was substantial as was demonstrated by reports in the press at the time.

On 9 February 1917 the Queen accepted a cheque for £18,000 in aid of the Star and Garter Home, which sum had been collected in schools throughout the United Kingdom for a permanent memorial to Jack Cornwell. Consent to make the collection was obtained from 278 of the 321 English and Welsh Education Authorities and from most of the Scottish School Boards.

> 'During the month of August envelopes were addressed to the head teachers of all departments of the elementary schools in England, Scotland, and Wales, and the schools were circulated early in September, each school receiving a packet of literature, according to the number of scholars. Some 52,528 schools were circularized in all. Correspondence was very heavy from Sept. 20 until the end of November. On one day there were over 2,300 letters, mostly containing remittances, and for more than three weeks the committee received an average of more than 1,000 letters daily. The staff dealt with upwards of 50,000 incoming letters, of which 26,710 contained remittances, between Sept. 18 and Dec. 1. Appeals have been made to Sunday Schools in certain towns, to schools in Ireland, and to 5,000 secondary schools, the results from the latter being excellent. Up to date the committee have received remittances from 28,400 schools and 485 individual subscribers amounting to £21,849 13s. 11½d; this, with the sale of booklets and pictures and the interest on money on deposit, totals £22,209 8s. 2½d. The total expediture to date, which includes the printing of 11,000,000 portrait stamps of Jack Cornwell, 250,000 booklets, 175,000 posters, 500,000 collecting cards, and the postage of more than 100,000 parcels and letters, amount to £4,821 8s. 6½d. The picture of the young hero standing by his gun, with Admiral Beatty's report of the incident, occupies a position of honour in more than 12,000 schools. This picture will serve to remind future generations of British children of the heroism of a British boy. Jack Cornwell's exploit will go down to history, and his noble deed will be an inspiration to British boys and girls for generations to come.'

It is in this report, showing what had been done since the establishment of a small Jack Cornwell Memorial Fund Committee in August 1916 with Lord Beresford as President and Honorary Treasurer, that demonstrates the grip that was taken on the public imagination by Jack Cornwell's brave action and the way in which it was incorporated into the life of schools with the significant support of the representative on the Memorial Fund Committee of the National Union of Teachers, Sir James Yoxall. J. H. Yoxall had been elected President of the N.U.T. in 1891 and in the following year became General Secretary. He and T. J. Macnamara, both teachers, were highly committed N.U.T. activists and 'seem to have begun working together in January 1887'. Yoxall was Liberal Member of Parliament for West Nottingham from 1895 until 1918. It is worth stressing the fact of N.U.T. participation in the campaign because Dr Macnamara himself was not only born in a barracks in Montreal, the son of a soldier, but he had trained as a teacher in England, been head of a board school in Bristol for eight years, edited the *Schoolmaster*, the publication of the National Union of Teachers, and been elected President of the N.U.T. in 1896. He was returned to Parliament in 1900 as Member for North Camberwell, which he represented as a Liberal for 24 years, 12 of them, 1908–20, being Parliamentary and Financial Secretary to the Admiralty.[15] If one reflects on Dr Macnamara's words after the burial of Jack Cornwell and the formal presence of the N.U.T. on the Memorial Fund Committee in the person of Macnamara's old N.U.T. colleague, J. H. Yoxall, it is suggested that their views as distinguished educationalists accorded on this matter with that of the public at large and the popular press in particular, as well as, presumably having a substantial effect on the views of the teaching profession in disseminating details of the Jack Cornwell Memorial Fund throughout the schools of the United Kingdom.

Sir Robert Baden-Powell did not let the opportunity slip by of raising money for a Scouts' Memorial to Jack Cornwell and he made a typically forthright pitch at a meeting in Bournemouth as reported in the *Yorkshire Post* of 13 September 1919 when he said:

'that he was himself more than ordinarily moved in telling the story of a boy who used to clean bottles in the East End, who was always late at his work and untidy in appearance. One day he came to work early and clean, and his explanation was that he had joined the Boy Scouts. He won all sorts of badges. As a missioner he went to poor homes to be of service in small jobs. He learnt signalling, and when the War broke out he joined the Navy. "He became a V.C.", added Sir Robert, "and he died. His name was Jack Cornwell".'

There is in the Lummis file a letter dated 15 March 1917 from Sir Robert to Lieutenant W. M. Lummis in his capacity as a scoutmaster acknowledging his donation of £1 10s. towards the Cornwell fund, 'on behalf of the 1st Shorncliffe, 1st Cheriton, 1st Aldershot, 2nd Aldershot and 1st Coddenham Troops'. There is no independent evidence, incidentally, that Jack Cornwell was as scruffy as Baden-Powell suggested, but certainly he was an enthusiastic member of the Scouts, clearly with his mother's approval. In the interview with her published in the *Daily Mirror* on 16 September 1916 it is remarked that

'Upon the mantel shelf of the little parlour in Mrs Cornwell's house

Boy Cornwell's Legacy To His Mother.

Mrs. Cornwell showing a neighbour the V.C., the Special Naval Medal, and other decorations, the legacy of the heroism of her son, Boy Cornwell, of Jutland fame.

was a casket. Opening it, she displayed two treasured mementoes —
one the 'Fidelity' Star, presented by Miss Agnes Weston; the, other
Sir Robert Baden-Powell's Bronze Cross. "I believe" she said, "this is
the first time the Bronze Cross has ever been awarded to a dead
scout".'

As the years passed by various events contributed to keeping alive the name of
Jack Cornwell. In January 1921 the Liberal M.P. for Romford, Sir John Bethell, is
reported as offering a site for East Ham Cottage Homes for Disabled Sailors and
Marines in memory of Jack Cornwell, the gun beside which Boy Cornwell stood
had been removed from *H.M.S. Chester* and was placed on exhibition at the
Imperial War Museum at its first site at Crystal Palace, the Union Jack from
H.M.S. Chester was hung in Chester Cathedral and as late as 1929 the *Sunday Despatch*
raised the state of Jack Cornwell's grave; in the issue for 29 September 1929 is
the report:

'Near the entrance of the little cemetery at Manor Park, in East London,
is to be seen a silent spectacle which has moved many visitors this
Christmas. All the graves lining the side of the drive have been
reverently covered with a brilliant array of holly, chrysanthemums,
lilies, and laurel leaves except one. Alone in the cemetery the simple
memorial of Jack Cornwell, the boy V.C. of Jutland, has throughout
the year stood absolutely desolate and forgotten. "Yes, everyone in
East Ham seems to have dropped poor Jack completely out of their
thoughts", said an official of the cemetery. "At first he was a national
figure, and crowds thronged his flower-strewn burial-place but now
—. It must be at least a year since anyone laid a tribute on his grave.
But I believe it is the first Christmas that he has gone unremembered.
I have seen women mourning someone else so upset when they chanced
to catch sight of his neglected grave that they tore sprigs from their
own wreaths and planted them in the soil." . . . Mr. Wade, of Colvin
Road, who is Vice-President of the East Ham Branch of the British
Legion, admitted that at the Legion "they had pretty well
forgotten Jack".'

Reminiscent of the campaign run in 1916 by the *Daily Sketch*, in the 5 January
1930 issue of the *Sunday Despatch* there was a follow-up to the report of desolation:

' "Never again will the grave in the cemetery at Manor Park, E., of
Jack Cornwell, the boy who won the V.C. at Jutland, go unremembered
and undecorated. Immediate steps to prevent the recurrence of such
a thing have been taken locally as a result of the disclosures made in
the *Sunday Despatch* last Sunday, when it was pointed out that at least
a year had elapsed since so much as a wreath was laid on the grave." A
Commander Frederick Medway, R.N. of Southsea offered to look
after the grave as did Mr. R. F. Hamlett of Barking Road, head of the
local Boy Scouts organization and President of the East Ham Branch

of the British Legion. "I was astounded when I read of the way Jack had been forgotten", he said yesterday, "It shall never occur again during my lifetime. The Legion is considering taking up the duty of placing wreaths at intervals on the grave. If they do not do it I promise to have it done by the Scouts. Jack Cornwell was once in our troop. You can take my guarantee that the boy V.C's. memory will be adequately honoured henceforth." Since last Sunday admirers of Jack Cornwell have left wreaths. There is also a proposal under consideration for the children of the "Jack Cornwell" School in East Ham to take care of the grave.'

On 27 November 1968 the family handed over Jack Cornwell's Victoria Cross medal group to the Imperial War Museum; his elder sister, Mrs Alice Payne then aged 78 of Woodford Green, Essex, is quoted in the *Daily Telegraph* of 28 November as saying, 'Jack was a quiet boy, very patriotic. The Scouts were his main interest before he joined the Navy. We are grateful that so many remember him today.'

Although there is no doubt that members of his family respected his self sacrifice, nevertheless the glare of publicity which was focussed on their home brought difficulties which could not readily have been foreseen before the War. The *Daily Sketch* campaign in September 1916 had made it blatantly obvious to everyone that the family was poor and the situation of Mrs Alice Cornwell, Jack's mother, did not improve after the death of his father not long after the Battle of Jutland in which she lost her son. The press reported that of the money collected in the Jack Cornwell V.C. Memorial Fund some £500 was set aside 'to provide a substantial increase in the income of the boy's mother during her lifetime. That sum will revert to the "Star and Garter" Home on the death of Mrs Cornwell.' In the event Alice Cornwell did not live long, being found dead on 31 October 1919, aged 54, in bed at her then home in Commercial Road, Limehouse. Her only surviving son, a brewer's labourer, said that she had been ill since the previous Sunday and a verdict of death from natural causes was returned. Within less than a month of Mrs Alice Cornwell's death and as the remaining members of the family coped with poverty and unemployment, Admiral of the Fleet Earl Beatty, who had sent the wreath of immortelles bearing the inscription 'With Deep Respect' to Jack Cornwell's funeral, was guest of honour of the Cheshire Society in London and in a report of his speech published in the *Daily Telegraph* on 26 November 1919 he said that:

> '. . . The story was in the minds of the whole Empire how a boy showed what a boy could do in the way of making history, and giving an example of how English boys should live and English boys should die. The story of the Boy Cornwell, of *His Majesty's Ship Chester*, was a record which added to the glorious pages of England . . .'

The member of the family who received most attention in the press was Jack Cornwell's sister, Lily, whether it was because she received a present of a piano bought out of the proceeds of a booklet written on her brother's exploit by Mr T. C. MacCormack of Northampton or the fact that she sailed to Canada having failed to secure work at home or, perhaps, on account of her unguarded comments. One sees in an unattributed press report in the Lummis File how precisely the circumstances of this family were exposed in the press:

> 'This week Lily Cornwell, the orphaned sister of Jack Cornwell, V.C., the boy hero of the Battle of Jutland, must say good-bye to the country for which her brother and father died. Unable to secure work, she has, like other members of the gallant sailor boy's family, been reduced to distressing straits. With her sister, Mrs. Payne, Mr. Payne — who was disabled in the war — and their family of three, with whom she has occupied a house in a poor quarter of Leyton, Lily has pluckily decided to start life afresh in Canada. She will join there her younger brother George. They will leave behind Ernest Edward Cornwell, their eldest brother, who also served in the Navy. Their old home in Commercial Road, Stepney, has been built over by a war memorial hostel, and Ernest occupies rooms nearby. He will be the only member of the family remaining in England, for Mrs. Cornwell collapsed and died under the strain of the precarious conditions in which she was left to live. While Lily, who is only 18, and other members of the family have been living in penury, a huge sum of money has been collected for memorials to Jack Cornwell. About £6,000 has been subscribed for the erection of cottage homes for disabled ex-servicemen, and £35,000 has been collected by the Red Cross Fund. The Star and Garter Home at Richmond has benefited largely, but a huge sum of money raised to do honour to the name of Jack Cornwell still lies idle.'

In a press report of 1923 it is stated that:

> 'Miss Cornwell is in very poor circumstances ... referring to the £40,000 which was raised by public subscription in memory of Jack Cornwell, Mrs. Payne said it did seem a shame that a large amount of this money should be lying idle when such a small portion of it would have done wonders for those of the family who survived. She spoke in highly appreciative terms of the Navy League, declaring that but for that organization she did not know what they would have done.'

Further press coverage continued the unhappy theme:

> 'With a sprig of white heather in her black frock, Lily Cornwell, sister of Jack Cornwell, the naval Boy V.C., took a tearful farewell of London yesterday afternoon, and sailed from Southampton last night in the Cunarder *Antonia*. She is on her way to Canada where she hopes to get a better start in life than she has done in this country. "Since Jack was

killed I seem to have had nothing but trouble", she told the *Daily Sketch*. "Perhaps I am leaving trouble behind now. I hope so." Miss Cornwell is going with her half-sister, Mrs. Payne, her brother-in-law, Mr. Payne, and their three children, to Windsor, Ontario. George Cornwell, Lily's brother, who is at present a steward in a liner, hopes to join them there in the near future.'

Other press cuttings show that the Star and Garter Home responded to criticisms pointing out that George and Lily Cornwell had been helped to the extent of about £60 a year, that the expenses for the journey to Canada had been met largely by a grant from the Navy League and in addition the British Red Cross Society had requested its representatives in Quebec to meet Lily Cornwell to help her and her relatives to find work, which, it is reported, did indeed happen.

In conclusion, it will be clear that the difference between George Drewry and Jack Cornwell was that because the latter died in action, the promotion of his reputation and the use of his name for philanthropic purposes were possible in a way that was inconceivable in the case of George Drewry. It is important to stress the unique conjunction of different interests, whether the Admiralty, the National Union of Teachers, or the *Daily Sketch* and the popular press, all of which successfully combined to demonstrate the merits of the behaviour and bravery of Jack Cornwell to the country at large and the younger generation in particular. It is also necessary to emphasize that this involved no falsification of what had occurred — Jack Cornwell was as brave as the citation stated — and therefore no 'de-bunking' by later generations. Rather it is an early twentieth century example of that quintessentially twentieth century activity, the promotion to as wide an audience as possible of a person or issue. For the local historian there is much merit in pondering the role of the national press in this classic human interest story and the effects that posthumous fame of one of its members had on an ordinary family from Manor Park.

Acknowledgements

This paper could not have been attempted without the use of the Lummis V.C. Files in the National Army Museum. Thanks are due to the National Army Museum's curatorial staff, especially Dr Linda Washington and Mrs Lesley Smurthwaite, who produced material and answered questions, and Ian Jones, who prepared the illustrations from difficult originals. The final word of gratitude must be to Mrs Elizabeth Carpenter who has rendered the text of this paper into a publishable format.

All illustrations in this essay have been reproduced by courtesy of the National Army Museum.

REFERENCES

1 *V.C.H. Essex*, II, 1907, pp.259–312.

2 For the number of V.Cs. awarded, see M. J. Crook, *The Evolution of the Victoria Cross*, 1975, p.170.

3 For an account of the naval operations in context, see P. G. Halpern, *A Naval History of World War I*, 1994–95, esp. pp.109–24, 310–29.

4 Demonstrated, for example, by the fact that there is apparently no reference to George Drewry in *V.C.H. Essex*, VI, 1973, while Jack Cornwell is mentioned in connection with the renaming of a school after him, p.40.

5 All references and quotations in this paper, unless otherwise attributed, are taken from the relevant Lummis V.C. Files in the National Army Museum.

6 For the development of Forest Gate and Claremont Road in particular, see *V.C.H. Essex*, VI, 1973, pp.55–6.

7 This and other quotations in the Lummis File, apart from Burrowes-Kelly's letter to Drewry's parents, appear to derive from the late Sir O'Moore Creagh, V.C., and E. M. Humphris, *The V.C. and D.S.O.*, London, n.d., *c.*1920s, — a most important source.

8 D. Pillinger and A. Staunton, *The Victoria Cross Locator*, 1991, p.5, shown as 'not publicly held'.

9 T. Jeal, *Baden-Powell*, 1989–91, pp. 357–415.

10 *V.C.H. Essex*, VI, 1973, p.40.

11 *V.C.H. Essex*, VI, 1973, p.5.

12 It is worth remarking that the Warrant of 1856 instituting the Victoria Cross did not specifically authorize posthumous awards; indeed, it was Rule Four of the 'Warrant Effecting a Further General Revision and Recodification of the Conditions of Award of the Victoria Cross' (PRO.WO32/3443) of 1919 that did so for the first time. See M. J. Crook, *op. cit.*, p.89: 'The only authority therefore upon which the many posthumous V.Cs. of the First World War were awarded was that there was nothing in the rules that precluded it.'.

13 The *Daily Sketch* had been founded as recently as 1909 by Edward Hulton (1869–1925) as an illustrated morning paper. In view of the content of the extract given above, the comment from the *D.N.B.*, 1922–30 may be noted: 'Hulton's interests as a newspaper proprietor were purely commercial . . . His newspapers, if they were without literary merit, were at least free of the charge of political interference. He recognized that the public wanted news, and set himself to supply it in its simplest form . . . He was always ready to lend the aid of his newspapers in raising money for public causes.' p.442.

14 Sir O'Moore Creagh, V.C. and E. M. Humphris, *op. cit.*, p.217.

15 See *D.N.B.*, 1922–30, pp.930–1: Sir James Henry Yoxall (1857–1925). See *D.N.B.*, 1931–40, p.89: *Thomas James Macnamara (1861–1931)*. Also Asher Tropp, *The School Teachers*, 1957, p.152. The significance of Dr Macnamara on the statutory municipalization of the education service nationally has been reassessed in R. Betts, 'Dr Macnamara and the Education Act of 1902', in the *Journal of Educational Administration and History*, vol. 25, no. 2, 1993, pp.111–19.

Early Stuart Essex:
Seedbed of American Democracy and Independence

J. R. SMITH

THE IMMEDIATE CAUSES of the American Revolution, which in 1783 culminated in victory for the American revolutionary army led by George Washington and the recognition of American independence under the Treaty of Paris, have been identified, analysed and discussed in numerous studies by scholars far more qualified in the subject than the author of this essay. For some time, however, the author had been mulling over the idea that in the actions, beliefs and personalities of the early adventurers and lay and clerical colonial leaders were to be found the origins of the American belief in democracy and freedom which manifested itself in the revolutionary fervour of the 1760s and 1770s. With this in mind when invited to contribute to Sir John's *festschrift* an essay dealing with American-Essex connections and history, the author suggested that a suitable topic might be an exploration of that idea. The essay would concentrate on highlighting the roles of some of the leading adventurers and colonists who had close connections with Essex. To this suggestion editor Kenneth Neale readily acceded.

The essay comprises two parts. The first is a brief examination of the religious, political and economic situation and of the Puritan community and network in Essex in the first four decades of the seventeenth century. This is relevant for these were the factors which shaped the lives of the people of Essex and the community from which came the hundreds of men and women who sailed to the American colonies in the 'Great Migration' of 1629–40. The second part looks at the careers of a few of the many Essex people who played leading roles in the early development of the colonies and whose contributions may be seen as having had a crucial and long-term influence in forming the distinctive characteristics of the colonial Americans, recently described by Roger Thompson as 'an individualistic, restless, questing people', a people prepared to break free from the constraints of hierarchies and institutions and in love with freedom and the new.

357

The Essex Puritan community and network, c.1601–c.1640

During Elizabeth's reign more than half the Puritan ministers in England had come from the counties of Essex, Suffolk and Norfolk. After 1600 'the brains and energy of the puritan party' were to be found in Essex and Lincolnshire while the greatest concentrations of Puritan gentlemen were to be found in Essex and Suffolk. Henry Jessey, Baptist divine and friend of John Winthrop senior, praised Essex and Suffolk in 1624 as the home 'of famous preachers and many precious Christians'. In Essex the Puritans were already the dominant party in political and religious life and formed a clearly defined and cohesive group bound by ties of marriage and kinship, patronage and preferment, education and the shared experience of persecution. Such ties were also to unite the early colonial communities and families. Soon after Jessey made his observation Essex Puritans were engaged in widespread opposition to the policies of Charles I and William Laud (which in turn led to the migration to New England of hundreds of men and women seeking political and religious freedom) and in support for the Parliamentarian cause and Cromwell's New Model Army.

The marriage and kinship links between Puritan families were numerous and complex. At the top of the hierarchy the friendship between Oliver Cromwell and Robert Rich, 2nd Earl of Warwick (M.P. for Maldon, 1610–19, and Lord Lieutenant of Essex from 1625) undoubtedly facilitated the marriage of Rich's grandson Robert to Cromwell's daughter Frances. Also related to Cromwell was the family of Sir Francis Barrington of Hatfield Broad Oak, premier baronet of Essex, whose mother Lady Joan Barrington was Cromwell's aunt. In fact Lady Joan was linked, by blood or marriage, to almost all the families who provided Parliamentary leadership in the early 1640s including that of Sir William Masham of Otes in High Laver (M.P. for Maldon, 1624–26, and Essex, 1640–54), Sir William having married Elizabeth Altham, the widowed daughter of Sir Francis Barrington. At a somewhat less exalted level the Harlackenden family of Earls Colne Priory was related to the Haynes family of Copford Hall through the marriage, c.1636, of John Haynes, then governor of Massachusetts, to Mabel Harlackenden.

The Harlackendens were also related to the colonial Winthrops (formerly of Great Stambridge Hall and Groton, Suffolk) through the marriage of Richard Harlackenden to Alice Mildmay, daughter of Sir Henry Mildmay of Graces in Little Baddow and niece of John Winthrop, senior, governor of Massachusetts. The Winthrops, in turn, were related to the Tyndals of Great Maplestead through the marriage in 1618 of John Winthrop, senior, to Margaret, daughter of Sir John Tyndal, and associated with the Puritan divine and martyr Hugh Peters (executed in October 1660 as an abettor of the execution of Charles I) through the marriage of John Winthrop, junior, to Peters' step-daughter Elizabeth Read. The hotheaded Peters, then curate and schoolmaster at Laindon, had wooed and c.1624 married a woman about 30 years his senior. She was Elizabeth, daughter of Thomas Cooke of Pebmarsh, a member of a large and influential family of gentlemen and clothiers, and widow of Edmund Read of Wickford, a leading Puritan layman in the area. This marriage both strengthened Peters' ties with the Essex Puritan community and gave rise to the sexual innuendo which was to entangle him for much of his eventful life.

The most important forms of patronage and preferment were the appointment of Puritan clergymen and lecturers and the employment of Puritan chaplains. The Rich family alone had the advowson of at least 17 Essex parishes. Appointments by Sir Robert, 2nd Earl of Warwick, included William Fenner to the rectory and Edmund Calamy to the lectureship of Rochford in 1629 and 1636 respectively, John Bedle to Barnston vicarage in 1632, Thomas Pecke to Prittlewell vicarage in 1634 and Nathaniel Ward, junior, to Hadleigh rectory in 1639 and to Hawkwell rectory in 1640, while Sir Robert's kinsman Sir Nathaniel Rich appointed Nathaniel Ward, senior, to Stondon Massey rectory in 1628. Preaching Rich's funeral sermon in 1658 Calamy described the Earl as 'a great patron and Maecenas to the pious and religious ministry'. Chaplains appointed by the Barringtons included Ezekiel Rogers (son of Richard Rogers lecturer at Wethersfield) who subsequently became pastor of Rowley, Massachusetts, while appointments by the Mashams included Roger Williams, later to gain fame as the founder of Rhode Island colony, and John Norton who migrated in 1635 and whose subsequent career in Massachusetts was marked by doctrinal controversy.

A number of Cambridge colleges, notorious for their nonconformity and Puritan graduates, served to form important and long-lasting educational friendships and ties. For the purpose of this essay far and away the most important was Emmanuel College, founded in 1584 as a Puritan seminary and a source of 'painful' (i.e. painstaking) preachers. Its founder, Sir Walter Mildmay (?1520–89) of Danbury Place, had entered a clause in the statutes favouring Essex. The list of Emmanuel graduates who went on to become lay and clerical leaders in Essex and in the American colonies is extensive and includes Sir Robert Rich, Thomas Hooker, Stephen Marshall, John and Nathaniel Rogers, Samuel Stone, Thomas Shepard and Nathaniel Ward. Indeed, as Tom Webster has recently pointed out, 'the list of Emmanuel *alumni* in Essex pulpits includes most of the great names of clerical puritanism in the county'. Operating as part counselling centre and part labour exchange, and with an extensive old-boy network, Emmanuel provided an introduction to the godly network of East Anglia second to none. Additional contacts and friendships were made in the Puritan household seminaries of which those founded by the Revd. Richard Blackerby at Ashen in 1604, by Alexander Richardson at Barking and by Warwick's pious daughter-in-law Mary at Leighs Priory in the 1640s, are the best known. Blackerby's seminary is of particular interest and those who passed through its doors included Daniel Rogers, Samuel Stone, Thomas Weld, Jonas Proost (minister to the Dutch congregations in Colchester and London) and, in all probability, Stephen Marshall. Blackerby provided four days' study each week for young clerics who had graduated from Cambridge, usually in preparation for the Master's degree, and introduced them into the patronage networks of East Anglia and Essex.

During John Roger's lectureship at Dedham parish church, 1605–36, the town became a major centre of Puritanism. His son, Nathaniel, became co-pastor of Ipswich, Massachusetts, in 1638.

(Photograph courtesy of the Essex Record Office)

Although Essex Puritan ministers were bound by no formal ties of organisation or establishment, many attended meetings of the irregular *classis* which had been formed in the 1580s. This informal group met at various places in the county and discussed doctrinal matters. Two of the *classis* leaders were Richard Parker and Edmund Chapman, respectively vicar and lecturer of Dedham. Chapman's successor in 1605 was John Rogers, 'roaring Rogers of Dedham' (a near relative of Richard Rogers, lecturer of Wethersfield), who made Dedham one of the major centres of Essex Puritanism.

The Essex Puritan ministry and opposition to Laud

When Elizabeth I came to the throne in 1558 she saw it as her mission to end the religious disputes and persecutions which had divided the country since the Reformation. The enforcement of general religious conformity was seen by the Queen and her advisers as a necessary step towards the achievement of national unity and the issuing in 1559 of a new version of the 1552 *Book of Common Prayer*, revised to make it slightly less Protestant, and the passing in the same year of the Acts of Supremacy and Uniformity, were together intended to satisfy the spiritual needs of the vast majority of her subjects. But it quickly became apparent that these measures, known collectively as the Elizabethan Settlement, were going to satisfy neither the Roman Catholics nor the extreme Protestants, or Puritans as they were soon called. The Puritans wanted to remain within the Church of England but also wanted a purer and simpler form of worship with longer sermons and objected to everything that reminded them of the Church of Rome. They criticized many of the forms of worship, such as making the sign of the cross, kneeling to receive Communion, bowing at the name of Jesus, wearing the surplice and using the ring in marriage. Their words and deeds frequently led them into trouble with Church authorities and to appearances at ecclesiastical courts.

The conflict between the Puritans and the Church of England establishment increased under James I whose belief in the principle of the Divine Right of Kings led him to align himself with the bishops, upholders of that principle within the Church and opponents of the Puritans. Although James had misgivings about the political wisdom of the bishops and refused to promote the able and ambitious William Laud (whose first Church appointment was the Essex rectory of West Tilbury, 1609 to 1616) he was in an impossible position for, when in financial difficulties, he relied on money from the Church and the bishops controlled the Church government of which he was head. The alliance proved fateful, with political as well as religious consequences, for politics and religion were inseparable. The king was head of both Church and State while the bishops were often officers of State as well as of the Church. Through his bishops and loyal priests James had the support of the pulpit, the greatest propaganda organ of the seventeenth century, and the clergy could, and did, preach on the duty of subjects to pay taxes as well as on their religious obligations. It was not surprising then, that just as James' political opponents were branded as religious dissidents and Puritans they in turn labelled as Papists the High Church extremists. James' leniency towards his Roman Catholic subjects, his pro-Spanish foreign policy and his support of the Church establishment all combined to provide his opponents with a powerful propaganda weapon of their own. The growing polarization of political and religious attitudes was to prove a disastrous legacy for his son and successor, Charles I.

The accession of Charles led to his favourite High Church cleric, William Laud, arch-enemy of the Puritans, becoming predominant within the Church establishment and to a consequent heightening of religious tensions. Protestant teaching in the Church was now combined with elements of Roman Catholic ritual and the bishops who ruled the Church were appointed by a king married to a French princess and who upon his betrothal had pledged himself to toleration for all English Roman Catholics. The Puritans now feared the advance of the Counter-Reformation and Charles' pro-Catholic sympathies alarmed and alienated a growing number of his subjects. What was needed was compromise and toleration but Charles pursued the opposite course, appointing Laud Bishop of London in 1628 and Archbishop of Canterbury in 1633.

In no English county were these religious tensions felt more keenly than in Essex. Preaching ministers were demanded by Puritans agitating for moral reformation and reform within the Church but a survey of 344 Essex ministers in 1604 had found only 94 'diligent and sufficient preachers'. In their absence Puritan towns and villages began appointing 'lecturers' to preach on Sunday afternoons and well-to-do Puritan families employed chaplains in their households. These lecturers and chaplains, for the most part ordained ministers who objected to subscription or conformity and who as a result were unable to obtain a benefice, were under no obligation to conform to the ceremonies of the Church. Radical congregations formed around a number of prominent lecturers and Puritan ministers who exerted influence far beyond the bounds of their own parishes to a regional or national level and who as a result became a particular target for Laud and his agents. An eye-witness account of a sermon by John Rogers, lecturer at Dedham, a major emigrant centre, from 1605 until his death in 1636, describes a crowded church with no room for latecomers and 'the people . . . deluged with their own tears' when taken to task for neglecting to read the *Bible*. In the opinion of a Laudian official Rogers 'hath troubled the country these thirty years, and did poison all these parts for ten miles round about that place'. Stephen Marshall, lecturer at Wethersfield from 1618 and vicar of Finchingfield from 1625 to 1651, was said to 'govern the consciences of all rich Puritans in those parts and in many places far remote', while Thomas Hooker, appointed lecturer at Chelmsford in about 1626, attracted a large following 'and the light of his ministry shone throughout the whole county of Essex'. Samuel Collins, vicar of Braintree, remarked in 1629 that 'Our people's palates grow so out of taste that no food contents them but of Mr. Hooker's dressing', while Sir Thomas Barrington sent his sons to board with Collins 'whose name God hath made precious among the saints'.

To the opponents of Puritanism the activities and influence of the lecturers and nonconforming ministers meant factionalism and disorder. The conflict between the High Church establishment and the Essex Puritans heightened following the appointment of Laud as Bishop of London in 1628. Laud was determined to restore 'order and decency' in the Church and Essex lay within the bishopric of London. In January 1629 Laud appointed Robert Aylett, son of Leonard Aylett of Rivenhall, to be his commissary in Essex and Hertfordshire. For the next 11 years Aylett vigorously enforced Laud's policies and reported on the Essex clergy, giving particular attention to instances of nonconformity and the activities of Puritan ministers and preachers. In 1633 Laud became Archbishop of Canterbury and adopted the policy of compulsory uniformity of action on the part of churchmen. In the following year he appointed his nephew Edward Layfield to the office of Archdeacon of Essex and thereafter Layfield joined with Aylett in enforcing Laud's policies.

The impact of Aylett's enquiries and reports to Laud were quickly felt. Hooker resigned his lectureship in 1629 and fled to the Netherlands in 1631 and his protégé Thomas Shepard, lecturer of Earls Colne, was silenced by 1631. Other early victims were Daniel Rogers, suspended from the lectureship of Wethersfield in 1629, Samuel Stone, ejected from the curacy of Stisted in 1630, and Thomas Weld, ejected from Terling vicarage in 1631. Hooker, Shepard, Stone and Weld were all later prominent in New England.

Lay opposition to Laudian church policy was headed by Robert Rich, described in a letter from Lord Conway to Laud as 'the temporal head of the puritans'. Sir Edward Hyde, Earl of Clarendon, recorded that Rich by 'opening his doors and making his house the rendezvous of all the silenced ministers . . . and spending a good part of his estate . . . upon them, and by being present with them at their devotions . . . became head of that party and got the style of a godly man'.

Laud's ascendancy to the primacy in 1633 was quickly followed by the reissue of the antisabbatarian *Book of Sports*. Originally issued in 1618, the avowed aim of the book was to protect 'dancing, playing, church-ales', delights laid down as permissible on Sunday once church service was concluded. It declared that the prohibition of sports on Sunday bred discontent and deprived the 'commoner and meaner sort of people' of their only opportunity for recreation and physical exercise 'seeing they must apply their labour and win their living in all working days'. In reality James I had issued the book in order to curb the influence and practices of the Puritans, especially the sermons by parish lecturers. Essex Puritans were outraged by the reissue, which they regarded as gratuitous provocation, for if obeyed the book's injunctions would remove the only chance many had for discussion as well as hearing sermons. In the opinion of Hugh Peters the reissue was the final straw that led many to make the decision to leave for New England.

Opposition to the policies of Charles I

The early years of Charles' reign were marked by conflict between monarch and the Commons which refused to finance his inept foreign policy and adventures. Charles was driven to ever more extreme measures including the pawning of the Crown jewels to help pay for the disastrous Cadiz expedition, 1626. The raising of a second fleet by levying ships from the coastal counties caused bitter resentment in Essex. A majority of leading Essex families were prepared to assert their independence against extensions of royal power and in 1626 several of the principal gentry suffered imprisonment for refusing to lend money to the King under compulsion. They included the aged Sir Francis Barrington, who spent more than a year in the Marshalsea prison, and Sir William and Lady Elizabeth Masham. Early in 1629 the Commons opposed the King's desire to levy the taxes of Tonnage and Poundage by prerogative rather than with Parliamentary authority. Charles dissolved Parliament on 10 March and governed the country by personal rule until the summoning of the Short Parliament in April 1640.

Another source of grievance was the unpaid expenses for billeting troops newly levied for Charles' foreign expeditions and the violence of ill-disciplined soldiers. Essex suffered more than most counties in this matter and in 1629 the Grand Jury recorded the vigorous protest of the people of Essex who remained unpaid for billeting, stating that 'the country is much grieved that they have not as yet the monies paid unto them which they dispensed . . . upon promise from the . . . Lords of his Majesty's Council'.

The revival of the forest laws alienated many landowners and Essex opposition was led by Robert Rich who confronted the Attorney-General, Sir John Finch, at the forest court held for Waltham Forest in October 1634. But the opposition was unable to prevent Charles from wringing £300,000 from Essex owners of encroachments made since 1301. Rich also led the county opposition to the King's demands for Ship-money for which challenge to royal authority he was dismissed from the office of Lord Lieutenant in 1635. Dislike of taxation was combined with growing unease over its military uses. In particular there was widespread fear that if the King could raise money without Parliamentary authority and consent he would replace the local militias with a professional army and stamp out dissent and opposition.

Sir John Bramston of Skreens in Roxwell summarized in his autobiography the situation in 1635. 'The people in all his kingdoms seditious, apt for rebellion, the disaffected partie pushinge and striveinge to inforce the Kinge to call a Parliament, the King useing his prerogative to rayse monie without Parliament . . . by knighthoods, loanes, benevolences, and by ship-writs . . .'.

Economic depression, 1620–40

At the beginning of the seventeenth century the counties of Essex, Suffolk and Norfolk were the most economically advanced and densely populated in

England and the region was internationally renowned as a cloth-producing area. In Essex the industry was chiefly concentrated in towns and villages in the north of the county, all of them strongholds of Puritanism. Colchester, the largest town in Essex, was also the main centre of manufacture. Other centres included Bocking, Braintree, Coggeshall, Earls Colne, Dedham, Halstead, Stisted and Witham. Fifty thousand inhabitants of the Stour valley were said to be employed in the textile industry. The outbreak of the Thirty Years' War, 1618, played havoc with exports and compounded problems already caused by government interference, changing fashion and foreign competition. The industry was plunged into recession causing immense hardship among the families of the landless wage-earning labour-force of combers, spinners and weavers. In 1629 the weavers of Bocking and Braintree complained that 'trade hath been decayinge for this seaven yeares or thereabouts to theire utter undoinge. Now they have noe work at all . . .'. In Witham in 1630 and 1631 spinners and weavers died from malnutrition.

There were problems, too, with agriculture. Early writers had all commented on the rich and fertile character of Essex and John Norden, writing at the end of the sixteenth century described the county as 'the englishe Goschen . . . most fatt, frutefull, and full of profitable thinges . . .'. Subsequent reports were soon to paint a somewhat different picture. Much farming was commercially oriented and inland Essex, well suited to tillage, was an important supplier of grain to the ever-expanding London market while the coastal marshlands were valued as pasture for cattle and sheep which in turn provided meat, leather, wool and milk for butter and cheese. By the beginning of the seventeenth century population pressures and the growth of the lucrative London market had led to an active trade in land and to escalating prices. In some areas rents quadrupled in the first two decades of the century. Writing in the 1620s John Winthrop declared that 'our land is over-burdened with people', a theme shared by other observers. There were still many middling and small farmers and holdings of five acres or less at the end of Elizabeth's reign but land ownership was becoming more concentrated in the hands of wealthy gentlemen farmers and owners of large estates whose prosperity depended on the cheap labour of thousands of landless agricultural workers.

Bad weather in 1621–23 caused reduced harvests, increased food prices and much hunger and hardship. The first year of Charles' reign was marked by a fearsome plague epidemic. Worse was soon to follow. A series of disastrous harvests in 1628–30 doubled the price of corn and turned the nightmare of starvation into reality for thousands of poor landless workers. There were food riots in Colchester and Maldon. A woman and three men were hanged in 1629 for the theft of corn at Maldon.

The Great Migration begins

When early in 1629 the New England Company was reorganized as the Massachusetts Bay Company, a trading company with the function of establishing a colony that should be both a religious refuge and a profit-making plantation, the 26 Company members named in the charter of incorporation included five Essex men. The first plantation fleet sailed from the Thames in April and May and passengers included the Revd. Francis Bright, curate of Rayleigh from 1625, and his family, John and Samuel Browne from Roxwell, lawyer and merchant respectively and both Company members, and William Jennison from Colchester. The so-called Great Migration had begun. Shortly afterwards, in July 1629, 12 puritan gentlemen, six of them Company members, met at Cambridge and signed an agreement — the Cambridge Agreement — binding themselves to embark for New England 'by the first of March next . . .'. Their number included William Vassall of London and Eastwood, William Pynchon of Springfield and John Winthrop of Groton and Great Stambridge.

Charles' period of personal rule eventually ended in April 1640 as a result of his increasing difficulties with the Scots, Laud's tenure as Archbishop of Canterbury ended in December with his impeachment by the Long Parliament, and the economic depression and Great Migration are generally considered to have ended in the same year. Shortly after the calling of the Short Parliament the Essex freeholders petitioned against 'innovations in matters of Religion . . . tending to the hazarding of mens soules, the increasing of errours and heresies, the decreasing of mens estates, the cherishing and augmenting of schisms among ourselves, and Dissaffection one to another and the greate endangering of the peace of the Commonwealth'. But it was all too late. England was now on the verge of civil war and John Pym, leader of parliamentary opposition to the King and prime mover in Laud's impeachment, lamented that the oppression of recent years 'hath lost the King many of his subjects and soe the Kingdome much weakened, they being fledd into the desarte of another world, because they could not injoye the libertye of their consciences here . . .'.

The Essex influence on early colonial development

Having looked at the religious, political and economic background to migration and at the Puritan community and network in Essex it is now time for us to look at the careers of a few of those men with strong Essex connections whose activities helped shape early American society and who may be said to have embued it with the distinctive qualities described at the beginning of this essay. These men came from three main categories: nobility, gentry and clergy. It was the gentlemen who were chiefly responsible for launching and organizing migration and colonization. The clerics, often reluctant refugees, led the second and third waves in the 1630s as Laudian persecution increased and although, as Roger Thompson has recently pointed out, 'they claimed to be only cleansers and purifiers of corrupted English ways, they helped create in both church and state a reoriented society'. In all 11 clerical companies or groups migrated between 1630 and 1638, of which five were led by Essex clerics.

A nobleman leader

Robert Rich, 2nd Earl of Warwick, was one of a small number of men who never set foot in America yet who wielded enormous power and influence in early colonial settlement and expansion. Some of his Essex connections and activities as leader of the Puritan party in Essex have already been been mentioned and we shall now concentrate on his colonial role.

His interest in colonial development had begun by 1614 when he was one of the original members of the company for the plantation of the Somers Islands or Bermudas. By 1620 he and his kinsman Sir Nathaniel Rich headed one of the two factions fighting for control of the Virginia Company and his interest in New England had already begun by the same year when he was granted a seat on the Council of the New England Company. It was in his capacity as a member of the Council that he was one of the signatories in June 1621 to the patent which gave land title jointly to the investors and settlers of the tiny Plymouth colony. When the second Plymouth patent was granted to Governor William Bradford in January 1630 Rich was president of the Council. It was through his influence and support that in March 1628 the newly formed New England Company in Massachusetts was granted a charter to colonize the land between the Merrimac and Charles rivers and that a year later the royal charter to the Massachusetts Bay Company was granted. Rich was equally closely connected with the founding of Connecticut, granting in March 1632 'the old patent of Connecticut' under which the town of Saybrook was established and John Winthrop, junior, became first governor of the colony in 1635.

In June 1632 Rich was defeated by Sir Ferdinando Gorges in the election for presidency of the New England Council and for the next decade he was chiefly occupied in leading the Essex opposition to Laud and the King. With the election of the Long Parliament his influence increased and in April 1641 he became a member of the Privy Council. In July 1643 he secured control of the fleet for Parliament and in November his connection with the colonies was renewed with his appointment by Parliament to head a commission entrusted with the government of the colonies. He bore the title of Lord High Admiral and Governor in Chief. In December he and his fellow commissioners granted to the colony of Massachusetts the territory around Narragansett Bay and three months later, in March 1644, granted to Roger Williams a charter incorporating Providence and three other infant settlements under the title of Providence Plantation, shortly afterwards changed to Rhode Island and Providence Plantations.

In his individual capacity Rich consistently used his influence to defend religious freedom in the colonies. By supporting Williams and the liberties of the Providence settlers against the threat from the Massachusetts authorities and the New England Confederation he gave tacit approval to a policy of religious freedom and toleration which made Rhode Island colony a haven for sects such as Antinomians, Baptists, Quakers and Seekers, and to the separation of Church and State. He also gave support to Samuel Gorton, founder of a sect known as

the Gortonites, who had migrated to Massachusetts in 1636 and who, having
fallen foul of the Massachusetts authorities, fled to Rhode Island in 1643 where
he purchased land at Shawomet from the Narragansett Indians. Gorton was
imprisoned for heresy at Charlestown later in 1643 and returned to England the
following year. Warwick then intervened on his behalf with the Massachusetts
authorities. When Gorton returned to Shawomet in 1648 he renamed his little
settlement Warwick in honour of his protector. Rich's zeal for religion and
toleration was further demonstrated by the support which he gave to John
Eliot's missionary work with the New England Indians.

Three gentlemen leaders

Great influence in early colonial development was wielded by four gentlemen
migrants with close Essex connections. They were the two Winthrops, John
Haynes and William Pynchon, all of whom were regularly elected to colonial
governorships or assistant governorships and were important shapers of policy
and attitudes. Of this quartet, one, John Winthrop, senior, became profoundly
conservative after migrating to Massachusetts in 1630 and we shall concentrate
on the remaining three because cases can be made for them having been entrepre-
neurial, innovative, liberal, progressive and receptive to change. We shall begin
by looking at the career of William Pynchon if for no better reason than that he
was the first of the trio to migrate.

William Pynchon

William Pynchon was born in Springfield in 1590. His father was John Pynchon
(d.1610), a gentleman with property in Broomfield, Springfield, Widford, Writtle
and other neighbouring parishes. His mother, baptized Frances Brett, came from
Terling. John's brother, Sir Edward Pynchon, married Dorothy Weston whose
family owned the extensive Skreens estate in Roxwell and neighbouring
parishes. Sir Edward and his wife are commemorated in a magnificent monument
in Writtle parish church and the Pynchon family was included in the *Heralds'
Visitations of Essex* in 1612 and 1634. William was therefore born into a family of
wealthy landowning gentlemen. He was probably educated at Cambridge. He
developed business contacts and interests in London, was in partnership with a
City mercer by 1621 and served as churchwarden (then an important parish
office) at Springfield in the 1620s.

His colonial activities began in 1629 when he was one of the patentees named
in the Massachusetts Bay Company charter and a signatory to the Cambridge
Agreement. Later that year he was busily engaged in acquiring ordnance for the
Company fleet (subsequently known as the Winthrop or *Arbella* fleet) being
assembled at Southampton and sailed the following spring with his wife, Anna,
and three daughters in company with his friend John Winthrop. His son John
migrated on a later ship. It is not known how the Pynchon-Winthrop association

began; it may have been through Sir Henry Mildmay who was lord of the manor of Springfield and husband of Winthrop's sister Alice.

Pynchon brought considerable capital to the infant colony and quickly established himself as a prosperous fur trader at Roxbury, which settlement a few miles from Boston he helped to found and where he was the first signatory to the church covenant. He was one of the original assistants elected to the Massachusetts General Court and in 1632 was elected treasurer of the colony. By 1633 he was working with John Winthrop, junior, in a consortium exporting beaver skins to London and importing English goods. In 1635 he served as a member of a commission for military affairs set up by the General Court. Throughout these early years of Massachusetts' development Pynchon played the role of a wise and moderate counsellor helping the colony to establish itself on a firm basis of law and sound government.

In 1635 the Connecticut valley was in the very earliest stages of colonization and the Massachusetts authorities appointed Pynchon one of the commissioners to govern development there. His active interest in the new colony began in the summer of 1635 with the selection of a site for a settlement at the junction of the Agawam and Connecticut rivers and with the initial work at that settlement, named Springfield in 1641 after his home in England. He was there again in May 1636 when he signed an agreement relating to land allotments and appointing a minister. He was joined by his family in the same year.

The Massachusetts General Court had already taken steps to govern the new settlements being established along the Connecticut River but in March 1637 the settlers in effect set up an independent government by electing magistrates and sending 'committees' of deputies from each settlement to a Connecticut General Court. Pynchon was one of those to be elected a magistrate. In the following year he fell out with Thomas Hooker, who had been instrumental in the founding of Hartford some 25 miles south of Springfield, and the new Connecticut authorities over a matter of supplying corn during the Pequot War. He was fined by the Connecticut General Court, unjustly in his view, and thereafter supported the claim of Massachusetts to Springfield and took no further part in the government of Connecticut. Situated at the head of deep water navigation, Springfield was admirably placed to dominate the pelt trade of the Connecticut River and its tributaries. Pynchon invested heavily in the central Connecticut valley and Springfield developed rapidly and vast quantities of furs were shipped to London from Pynchon's warehouse. In 1639 the Connecticut authorities accused Pynchon of trying to monopolize the Indian trade. The charge was refuted, Pychon claiming to be the colony's defender against Indian racketeering.

Separated from Boston by 100 miles of wilderness, Springfield developed as a company town under Pynchon's patronage and as a virtually independent community. Pynchon was the largest investor and landowner and virtually ruled the community with a cabinet consisting of his two sons-in-law and the pastor, George Moxon. He was chosen magistrate by the inhabitants in February 1639 and the town was established on a firm basis of English legal procedure and sound government.

Pynchon's interest in Massachusetts government was renewed in 1642 when he was re-elected to his former position as one of the assistants of the General Court (then headed by his friend Governor John Winthrop) a position of authority he was to retain until 1651. In 1650 he visited England and had printed in London a theological tract, *The Meritorious Price of Our Redemption*, which attacked the calvinistic view of the atonement. It was a valid and constructive criticism which anticipated later conclusions of more liberal theologians but when it reached Boston the General Court referred it to a committee of clergy headed by John Norton. Both book and author were denounced as heretical and when Pynchon returned to Boston he was greeted with a storm of indignation. The General Court ordered the author to appear before it in May 1651 and the book to be burned. Pynchon's old friend John Winthrop had died in 1649, he was not re-elected to the General Court and, having amassed a fortune, decided to retire to England, then seen by many as more tolerant than Massachusetts. He passed his New England property to his son John and his sons-in-law, and the family continued to develop and run Springfield and the surrounding territory for the rest of the century. Pynchon, accompanied by his wife and George Moxon, who shared his views, sailed for England in September 1652.

John Haynes

John Haynes was born about 1594. His parents were John and Mary Haynes of Old Holt in Birch. Little is known of his early life except that some time before 1624 he purchased the Copford Hall estate, including the lordship of the manor, and Copford Hall became his home. By his first wife, Mary Thornton, who died prior to 1633, Haynes had two sons and a daughter. The younger son, Hezekiah, fought with the Parliamentary army in the Civil War, attained the rank of major-general and inherited the Copford Hall estate. Haynes appears to have fallen under the influence of Thomas Hooker and when he migrated in 1633 it was with Hooker's band of devotees aboard *Griffin*. They subsequently enjoyed a close association in New England. At the time of his migration Haynes was described as 'a gentleman of great estate'.

Taking up residence in New Town (renamed Cambridge in 1636) he became an assistant of the Massachusetts General Court in May 1634. He was placed on a commission charged 'with all military affairs whatsoever' and supervised the construction of an ammunition house at New Town. At the next annual election, in May 1635, he became governor, which office he accepted with some reluctance, declining the salary 'partly in respect of their love showed towards him, and partly for that he observed how much the people had been pressed lately with public charges'. Together with other Massachusetts leaders he was interested in the possibilities of settlement in the Connecticut valley. He was responsible for halting the activities of the Dutch along the Connecticut River and was one of the organizers of a group of 60 settlers which went there in October 1635 but which was forced to return because of the severity of the winter. During his year of office he also accused John Winthrop of having 'dealt too remissly in point of justice' and pronounced sentence of banishment on Roger Williams. Although he later expressed regret for his treatment of Williams, these incidents have been cited as evidence for Haynes having been profoundly conservative, a criticism not supported by the evidence of his later career.

In May 1636 he was superceded as governor by Henry Vane but remained an assistant and in December was appointed colonel of a Massachusetts regiment. It was about this time that he married at New Town his second wife Mabel Harlackenden, a member of the Harlackenden family of Earls Colne, who had migrated in 1635. By her he was to have three sons and two daughters.

A more vigorous and successful effort had been made to colonize the Connecticut valley when a party of 100 New Town people led by Hooker marched there in the spring of 1636 and settled at a place named Hartford and in May 1637 Haynes, accompanied by his family, removed thither 'to become the father of the new colony of Connecticut'. He immediately assumed a leading role and was actively engaged in the Pequot War which broke out later in 1637. The Pequots were the most warlike of the New England Indians and although there was much bloody fighting before they were vanquished in 1638 Haynes refused to sanction the killing of Indian women and children. In the same year that the Pequots were defeated a treaty was made between Connecticut and the Mohican and Narragansett Indians, to which Haynes was a signatory.

In January 1639 representatives from the Connecticut settlements of Hartford, Wethersfield and Windsor met and enacted the 'Fundamental Orders', a confederate plan of government based on the popular consent of the freemen, and in April Haynes was elected first governor under the Orders. The Orders prohibited any governor from being re-elected for a consecutive term but Haynes was elected governor every alternate year until his death, usually serving as deputy-governor in the intervening years. From 1637 to 1643 he worked with Hooker to establish a union of the four New England colonies of Connecticut, New Hampshire, Massachusetts and Plymouth. The chief purpose of the New England Confederation, formed at Boston in 1643, was military, in response to Dutch territorial incursions and the threat of Indian uprisings. He represented Connecticut at meetings of the Confederation commissioners in 1646 and 1650.

Haynes died at Hartford in 1654. He became more liberal in his views as he grew older and was held in high regard by his contemporaries. Roger Williams described him as 'that heavenly man, Mr Hains ... though he pronounced the sentence of my long banishment ... was very friendly at Hartford'. In the opinion of the Connecticut clergyman and historian Benjamin Trumbell 'He was not considered in any respect inferior to Governor Winthrop', while the historian George Bancroft described him as 'of a very large estate and larger affections; of a heavenly mind and spotless life; of a rare sagacity and accurate but unassuming judgment; by nature tolerant, ever a friend to freedom'.

John Winthrop

John Winthrop, junior, was born in 1606. His paternal grandmother's family owned property in Edwardstone (Suffolk) and Prittlewell and his father had inherited an estate at Groton (Suffolk) and subsequently acquired estates in Essex by two marriages. His mother was Mary Forth of Great Stambridge. His childhood was divided between Groton and Great Stambridge where the preaching of the rector, Ezekial Culverwell, one of the outstanding Puritan apologists of his generation, had a profound effect on his father. When his mother died in 1615 he inherited a moderate fortune. He studied law in London and was admitted to the Inner Temple in 1625 but gave up the law shortly thereafter and through the influence of his uncle Joshua Downing, a Navy Commissioner (husband of his father's sister Lucy), became secretary to a Captain Best and in 1627 served with Buckingham's ill-fated La Rochelle expedition. In the following year he thought of joining John Enderby's expedition to New England but instead embarked on a 14 or 15-month tour of Europe, visiting Contantinople, Venice, Padua, Leghorn and Amsterdam amongst other places. Winthrop had already shown himself to be possessed of an adventurous and restless nature.

When his father migrated in March 1630 Winthrop stayed in England to settle business affairs and to sell the family estates. In February 1631 he married his cousin Martha Fones (daughter of London apothecary and businessman Thomas Fones) and in August embarked for Massachusetts with his wife, stepmother Margaret (daughter of Sir John Tyndal of Chelmshoe House in Great Maplestead), brothers, sisters and servants. They arrived at Boston on 4 November. Winthrop was elected an assistant of the Massachusetts General Court in March 1632 and in 1633 was the leader of a small group which founded the settlement of Agawam (shortly afterwards to be renamed Ipswich), 30 miles north of Boston. At the same time he formed a consortium with William Pynchon and Emmanuel Downing in London to export beaver skins and import dry goods into the colony. His wife and infant daughter died in the autumn of 1634 and he immediately returned to England, surviving shipwreck in a storm on the west coast of Ireland on the way.

In 1635 Winthrop's father's friends Lord Say and Sele and Lord Brooke, and several others, including John Hampden and Sir Richard Saltonstall, undertook to start a plantation on a large tract of land in the Connecticut valley which had been granted to them in 1632 by Robert Rich, then President of the New England Council. Winthrop was chosen to be governor and his commission, issued in July, appointed him to that post for one year after his arrival at Connecticut. About the same time he married Elizabeth Read, daughter of the late Edmund Read of Wickford, through which marriage he became associated with Hugh Peters. In late July or early August Winthrop set sail for New England on *Abigail*. Among his party were his wife, Peters and the young Henry Vane.

Abigail reached Boston on 6 October and an advance party was immediately sent to build a fort at Saybrook, at the mouth of the Connecticut River. Winthrop followed in March 1636 and remained until the birth of his daughter

Elizabeth in the autumn when he returned to his family in Massachusetts and settled once more at Ipswich where he was appointed lieutenant-colonel of the Essex County Militia and elected one of the prudential men of the town. Ipswich developed into a major cattle market and trading centre, second in wealth only to Boston. It had a committee for furthering trade and an endowed grammar school. Its industries included malting and an ironworks set up with Winthrop's encouragement. He remained there for three years before moving to Salem, to the great regret of the inhabitants of Ipswich, of whom a considerable number claimed in a petition that they had been induced to settle there only on condition that Winthrop would remain with them for life.

Shortly after moving to Salem, Winthrop began the manufacture of salt and tried to interest English investors in setting up ironworks. In order to promote his industrial schemes he sailed for England in August 1641. He returned two years later with a group of skilled workmen and in 1644 set up ironworks at Lynn and Braintree, Massachusetts, and founded a settlement and ironworks at the mouth of the Thames River in eastern Connecticut, at a place called Pequot, where he built a house for himself and his family. He was elected a magistrate for Pequot (renamed New London by 1658) and when his father died in March 1659 decided to remain permanently in Connecticut. About the same time he declined re-election to the Massachusetts General Court, having served that body continuously for 18 years. Winthrop was now on the threshold of his period of greatest influence.

In 1650 he was admitted a freeman of Connecticut and in May 1651 was elected to the General Court. In the middle years of that decade he set up ironworks in New Haven and in 1657 was elected governor. His consequent removal to the colonial capital, Hartford, marks the permanent attachment of his energies and interest to Connecticut. Connecticut law not permitting one man to serve consecutive years as governor, Winthrop was elected deputy-governor in 1658 but such was his reputation and influence that the law was then altered and he was governor from 1659 until his death. The most important of his many services to the colony during his 18 years as governor was his mission to England in 1661–63 with a petition for a royal charter. His charismatic personality made him popular at court and his interest in natural science brought him into contact with influential men. To this was largely due his success in obtaining in May 1662 the most liberal charter for any colony, making Connecticut almost an independent state and including within its boundaries the former small colonies of Guildford, Milford and New Haven.

While in England Winthrop was able to indulge his passion for science and shortly before his return to Connecticut in 1663 was elected a member of the Royal Society. In New England his knowledge of medicine was much in demand. He was ahead of his time in that his interests were scientific rather than theological and he believed that New England's future prosperity lay in commerce and manufacturing rather than in agriculture. The two papers which he contributed to the *Philosophical Transactions* and his letters to scientific friends in England testify to his enquiring mind and deal with a wide range of subjects including agriculture, astronomy, banking, manufacture and trade.

Winthrop died in April 1672 and was placed in his father's tomb in Boston. Sometimes depicted as a forerunner of Benjamin Franklin and one of the most able, engaging, energetic and versatile New Englanders of his generation, Winthrop was a restless mover and great organizer of projects. Wherever he settled it was with the greatest reluctance that his associates would let him move on. Of a tolerant and conciliatory disposition he played a leading and crucial role in the founding of Connecticut and for 18 years successfully guided the infant colony through its formative period. By his second wife, Elizabeth, Winthrop had five daughters and two sons, Fitz John, born in 1638, who became governor of Connecticut, and Waitstill, born in 1642, who became chief justice of Massachusetts.

Four clergymen leaders

In the third and last category of migrant that we are discussing, the clergy, we shall be looking at the careers of four men: Thomas Hooker, George Phillips, Nathaniel Ward and Roger Williams.

Thomas Hooker

The most influential and important member of that group, Thomas Hooker was born in Leicestershire, probably in 1586, and educated at Emmanuel College, Cambridge, where he was awarded the degrees of B.A. in 1608 and M.A. in 1611. He remained at Emmanuel on a fellowship until 1618. In 1620 he became rector of Esher, Surrey. Whilst there his Puritan leanings became more pronounced and he fell under the influence of John Rogers of Dedham.

Hooker's close connection with Essex began in 1626 with his appointment as lecturer at Chelmsford. His immense influence while there has been touched upon earlier in this essay. He attracted the attention of Laud and his agents and in 1629 was forced to resign the lectureship. In that year his first written work was published, an epistle 'To the Reader' prefixed to John Rogers' *The Doctrine of Faith*. Following his resignation he moved to Little Baddow where he opened a school with the celebrated John Eliot as his assistant and where his advice and guidance continued to be sought by Puritan ministers for whom he commenced a monthly meeting 'for fasting and prayer and profitable conference'. But Laud was determined to continue his persecution and having been ordered to appear before the Court of High Commission Hooker delivered a farewell sermon at Chelmsford in April 1631 and fled to the Netherlands.

In 1632 a group of Puritans from central Essex, known as Mr Hooker's Company because they had been his followers there, migrated to Massachusetts under the leadership of William Goodwin of Bocking. Hooker was invited to join them in

New England and in 1633 he returned to England to arrange his affairs and, having narrowly escaped arrest in London, set sail in company with John Haynes and his close friend and protégé Samuel Stone, formerly curate at Stisted. Reaching Massachusetts in September, Hooker, Haynes and Stone joined the migrants led by Goodwin who had already settled at New Town. In October Hooker was elected pastor with Stone as teacher. In 1635 the leading lay member of the New Town community and congregation, John Haynes, was elected governor of Massachusetts. The New Town people had for some time been looking at sites for a new colony, the complicated reasons for which need not concern us here, and the decision in 1635 to move to the Connecticut valley was opposed by the Massachusetts General Court. In May 1636 Hooker led about 100 people across the wilderness to a riverside site which had been purchased from the Indians by Stone. The name Hartford was adopted in 1637.

In August 1637 Hooker returned to Massachusetts to serve as one of the moderators at the synod held in connection with Anne Hutchinson and the Antinomian controversy. He took advantage of the occasion to continue his discussions with John Winthrop on the possibility of creating a confederation of the New England colonies but progress was made difficult by a dispute on the subject of democracy. Hooker was a born democrat whereas Winthrop and most of the other Massachusetts leaders were autocrats. A few months later, in May 1638, Hooker preached a sermon at Hartford in which he expressed the view that political power should rest on the consent of the governed. This was followed in January 1639 by an assembly at Hartford of the freemen of the Connecticut settlements of Hartford, Wethersfield and Windsor which adopted the 'Fundamental Orders', a confederate governmental plan embodying Hooker's democratic ideas. It was to remain in force, with amendments, until 1818. Often cited as the forerunner of the United States' Constitution, it accounts for Connecticut's nickname, 'the Constitution State'.

Hooker's long cherished plan of a confederation of New England colonies finally came to fruition in May 1643. Later that year he was one of the two moderators at a synod at Cambridge, Massachusetts, assembled for the purpose of combating Presbyterian tendencies and re-emphasizing the 'Congregational way'. He was asked to reply to books recently published in England and to defend the Congregational system. His book, *A Survey of the Summe of Church-discipline*, published in 1648 (a year after his death), contains a statement of Congregational principles which was approved by all the ministers of Connecticut and many in other colonies and is the supreme exposition of Congregational church polity, expressing not merely New England ecclesiastical theory but political doctrine and concepts of law, nature and reason.

One of the founding fathers of Connecticut, the inspiration behind the democratic Connecticut constitution and the most eloquent of puritan preachers, Hooker fell victim to an epidemic sickness and his death, in July 1647, was mourned as a public calamity.

Chelmsford parish church, now the Cathedral, Thomas Hooker, lecturer here from 1626 to 1629, had an immense influence throughout Essex and was systematically persecuted by Laud and his agents.

(Photograph courtesy of the Essex Record Office)

George Phillips

George Phillips was born in 1593 and educated at Gonville and Caius College, Cambridge, where he was awarded the degree of B.A. in 1614. In the following year he became curate at Boxted where he was to remain for the next 16 years. He was recommended, probably in 1629, to John Winthrop by his parishioner John Maidstone, nephew of Winthrop's wife Thomasine. Taking with him his wife and three children Philips migrated on *Arbella* in 1630 in company with Winthrop and the other leaders of the Massachusetts Bay Company settlers. He was one of the seven signatories to and very likely the author of *The Humble Request*, a letter of farewell to their fellow countrymen and a statement of the settlers' reasons for migrating.

Phillips' wife died shortly after they reached Massachusetts and in the autumn he accompanied Sir Richard Saltonstall (one of the original Massachusetts Bay Company patentees) to found a settlement on the Charles River six miles west of Boston, to which the name Watertown was given. He became the first pastor there and was the first Massachusetts minister to put into practice the Congregational form of church government.

In 1632 Governor John Winthrop and the assistants of the General Court arbitrarily levied a tax of £60 on the settlements, including Watertown, to finance the building of a palisade around New Town. Phillips led the Watertown settlers' protest and was summoned to Boston where the matter was debated. Although the tax was not remitted it was agreed at the next meeting of the Court that the governor, deputy-governor and assistants should be chosen by and from the freemen, though a limitation was placed upon the freemen's choice of governor by the requirement that he be taken from among the assistants. It was also agreed that in future no taxes should be levied without the Court's consent. The origins of the principle of no taxation without representation (in 1773 to become a rallying cry of the New England revolutionaries) and of representative government in Massachusetts can be traced to the Watertown protest led by Phillips.

A sturdy puritan and man of learning, Phillips died in 1644 having served as pastor of Watertown for nearly 13 years. He was succeeded by John Sherman, born at Dedham, who had migrated in 1634. Phillips' eldest son, Samuel, who had migrated with him, became an eminent pastor of Rowley, Massachusetts. By his second wife, whom he married at Watertown, Phillips had seven children.

Nathaniel Ward

Nathaniel Ward was born at Haverhill, which parish then lay in both Essex and Suffolk, in 1578. His father was vicar there and his mother Susan had previously been married to Richard Rogers, the famous Wethersfield lecturer. He was educated at Emmanuel College, Cambridge, and was awarded the degrees of B.A. in 1600 and M.A. in 1603. For at least a decade he practised law before taking holy orders in 1618. Following a number of clerical appointments he became rector of Stondon Massey, the advowson of which belonged to Sir Nathaniel Rich. It was doubtless through his connection with Rich that in 1629 Ward was recommended to the Massachusetts Bay Company as pastor, which offer he declined. Four years later, in 1633, Ward was removed from his living, having several times been reprimanded by Laud for his nonconformity.

In 1634 Ward migrated to Massachusetts with his wife and some of his children and settled at Ipswich, founded the previous year by John Winthrop, junior, where he became the first pastor. He resigned the cure in 1636 through ill health. In 1639 the deputies of the Massachusetts General Court (two or three from each township, elected by the freemen), anxious to curb the elder John Winthrop's arbitrary government and the power of the magistrates, called upon Ward and John Cotton to submit draft codes of laws. In December 1639 Ward's code was chosen and a year later was adopted as law under the title of *Body of Liberties*. His reward was a grant of 600 acres of land near Pentucket, shortly afterwards renamed Haverhill in honour of his birthplace. This land he subsequently gave to Harvard College, the first institution of higher education in colonial America. *The Body of Liberties* was a remarkable piece of work setting out a system of civil safeguards and procedures and which championed the cause of democracy against theocracy. It was to remain in force for three years and, if found satisfactory, be made permanent. But the deputies thought it left too much authority in the hands of the magistrates and renewed their agitation. In 1645 Ward was appointed to a committee set up to revise the laws and in 1648 the *Body of Liberties* was replaced by the *Book of the General Lawes and Libertyes* which Ward had been active in formulating and for which he was largely responsible. The book, which built on the *Body of Liberties*, was the first modern legal code in the western world and pointed the way to democratic, social and political institutions which were to be gradually incorporated into the legal structures of other colonies, including Connecticut, and other nations.

Meanwhile, in 1646, Ward had returned to England, partly due to ill health, partly because Laudian persecution had ended but chiefly perhaps to see through the press a remarkable piece of work which he had written in 1645 under the title *The Simple Cobler of Aggawam in America. Willing to help 'mend his Native Country, lamentably tattered, both in the upper-Leather and sole* . . . in which he championed political tolerance to the extent of defending the King. His subsequent career in England, though interesting, important and influential, is not germane to this essay. We may note, however, that he received the living of Shenfield in 1648 and died there in 1652. He had at least three children. His son John was rector of Hadleigh from 1633 to 1639 and pastor of Haverhill, Massachusetts, from 1633 to 1693. His daughter married Giles Firmin, John Cotton's deacon at Boston and later vicar of Shalford (Essex). Champion of political tolerance, noted for his plain speaking and famous for his incisive wit, Ward was also a man of judgment and gravity, and is chiefly remembered for his important work in framing the Massachusetts legal code.

Roger Williams

Our fourth and final clerical example is Roger Williams. The son of a London merchant, Williams was born about 1603 and educated at Pembroke College, Cambridge, where he was awarded the degree of B.A. in 1627. He then took holy orders and became chaplain to Sir William Masham and his family at Otes, High Laver, an appointment which enabled him to enter the Essex network of puritan divines and to receive offers of preferment, all of which he declined, mainly, it would appear, owing to his dislike of the Anglican liturgy. While at Otes he met Jane Whalley, niece of Lady Masham's mother Lady Joan Barrington, who lived with the Barringtons at Hatfield Broad Oak. Early in 1629 Williams asked for Lady Barrington's consent to a marriage. His request was denied and in December Williams married instead Mary Barnard, a member of the Masham household. Meanwhile Williams had already had a call from New England and in December 1630 migrated on *Lyon*. He subsequently claimed that he had been 'pursued . . . out of the land' by Laud.

Williams was welcomed in Massachusetts as 'a godly minister' but his rejection of a call from the Boston Church on the grounds that it had not formally withdrawn from communion with the Church of England and his criticism of the Puritan system incurred much hostility. In April 1631 he accepted the post of assistant 'teacher' or minister at Salem, but the Boston magistrates put pressure on the Salem authorities and within a few months Williams had moved to Plymouth where he became assistant pastor. Here he developed a friendship with the local Indians and studied their language. Although the Plymouth settlers were more tolerant than the Boston congregation even they found Williams' opinions and thinking too advanced and extreme and in the autumn of 1633 he returned to Salem. He was soon in difficulties with the Massachusetts authorities for his criticism of the Puritan system and imposed religion, for his advocation of the separation of Church and State and for attacking the colony's charter as a violation of Indian rights. Although Williams was now *persona non grata* with the Massachusetts authorities Salem made him minister and teacher in 1634 in defiance of the General Court. Williams' guidance of Salem to a more democratic church system roused the fears of the governing class for its own supremacy and in October 1635 the General Court found him guilty of disseminating 'newe and dangerous opinions, against the authoritie of magistrates' and ordered him to be banished. In January 1637 a ship was despatched to Salem with orders to arrest him and take him to England but acting on Governor John Winthrop's advice to 'flee into the Narrohiganset's country, free from English Pattents', Williams bade his wife and baby daughters goodbye and fled with a handful of companions. Their long journey through the snowy wilderness eventually ended in May at Slate Rock on the Seekonk River where Williams purchased land from friendly Indians. There he was soon joined by his family and followers from Salem. Thus began the settlement to which Williams gave the name Providence.

The government of the new settlement was based on the separation of Church and State, on complete religious freedom and the humane treatment of the

Otes, High Laver, home of the Masham family. John Norton and Roger Williams were chaplains here before migrating.

(Photograph courtesy of the Essex Record Office)

Indians and it subsequently became a haven for Baptists, Quakers, Seekers, Jews and others seeking refuge from persecution. In 1639 Williams founded at Providence the first Baptist church in America but a few months later left the Baptists to become a Seeker. In other parts of Narragansett Bay more settlers were now appearing, including, in 1639, a group of Antinomians inspired by the counsels of Williams' friend Sir Henry Vane (grandson of Thomas D'Arcy of Tolleshunt D'Arcy and governor of Massachusetts 1636–37) which settled at Newport. The little settlements were united by fear of Massachusetts and their unease was increased by the consciousness that they had no other title to their land than that granted by the Indians. In the spring of 1643 the colonies of Connecticut, Massachusetts, New Hampshire and Plymouth were organizing the New England Confederation and were determined to snuff out independent settlements. In June Williams set sail for England to defend the Narragansett Bay settlements. On the long voyage he wrote his first book, *A Key into the Language of America*, the first attempt to put into print the Narragansett language.

Williams was welcomed in England by Vane, now virtual leader of the House of Commons, who introduced him to the Commissioners of Plantations headed by Warwick. In March 1644 the Commissioners granted him the charter that he sought and which permitted the four Narragansett Bay settlements of Providence, Portsmouth, Newport and Warwick to unite as the independent colony of Providence Plantation and to establish a general assembly. While in England Williams became involved in a controversy with John Cotton. This led to him writing his second book, *The Bloudy Tenent of Persecution*, in which he expounded his views on religious toleration and the doctrine of the liberty of conscience. Williams sailed about the time of publication, probably in July 1644, and it was perhaps as well that he did, for the book caused a great sensation and in August was denounced by the Commons and ordered to be burned. Following Williams' triumphant return the newly established General Court ordered that Aquidneck Island be henceforth called Rhode Island and the colony became known as Rhode Island and Providence Plantations.

A new threat to the colony arose in 1651 when William Coddington obtained in England a commission which split the colony and made him governor of Aquidneck Island for life. In November Williams embarked for England hoping to procure the abrogation of Coddington's authority and to secure protection for the colony's boundaries against encroachments by Connecticut and Massachusetts. Once again Williams was supported by Vane, now at the height of his influence, and wrote to Providence that 'the great anchor of our ship is Sir Henry'. During his two and a half years' stay in England he carried on anew his pamphleteering for democratic principles and religious liberty and enjoyed the friendship of Hugh Peters (who had returned to England in 1641 and was a regular preacher at Whitehall) and Milton. Coddington's commission was rescinded in 1652 and following Williams' return to New England in the summer of 1654 he re-united the colony and was elected governor or president of Rhode Island,

Engraving by J. C. Armytage of the painting by A. H. Wray depicting Roger Williams meeting the Narragansett Indians in the wilderness in the winter of 1635–36, published by George Virtue, c.1835. Williams purchased a tract of land from Chief Ousamequin and founded the first Rhode Island settlement, Providence, in 1636.

(Reproduced by permission of Chicago Historical Society)

which office he held for three consecutive years until 1657. During his presidency the first Jews settled in the colony and in 1659 they were followed by the Quakers, then hated and persecuted in the other New England colonies. Although Williams abhorred the Quakers' views he refused either to expel or persecute them, despite threats and remonstrances from Massachusetts and elsewhere. When in July 1663 the colony was granted a new charter by Charles II guaranteeing religious freedom Williams became one of the assistants under the new governor, Benedict Arnold, and was re-elected in 1667 and 1670.

The last years of Williams' life were darkened by religious controversy, especially with George Fox and the Quakers, and the bloody King Philip's War (1675–76). Despite Williams' friendship and efforts on their behalf he was unable to prevent the Narragansett Indians casting their lot with the Mohawks and other brethren. The Rhode Island settlements in turn cast theirs with their fellow countrymen in Connecticut and Massachusetts and Williams, now a septuagenarian, took part as one of the two captains in command of the Providence militia and saw Providence and Warwick reduced to ashes and the once great Narragansett tribe cut to ribbons. After the war Williams remained active in Providence public life for another half-dozen years, his most unpleasant duty being to serve on a committee which allotted the captive Narragansett survivors as slaves among Providence families. He died at Providence early in 1638.

Although regarded as rash and hasty in his judgement by New England contemporaries, none doubted his sincerity, zealousness and godliness. One of the leading New England figures of his generation, he left an indelible mark on the colony which he founded. Religious liberal and one of the fathers of American democracy and freedom of conscience, Williams' enduring fame justly rests upon his humanity and breadth of view, his unceasing devotion to the cause of democracy and freedom of opportunity, and upon his long record of opposition to authoritarianism and persecution.

Conclusion

The projection backwards to the early colonial settlers for the roots of American democracy and spirit of independence and of the distinctive American qualities described at the beginning of this essay is neither a new nor universally accepted idea but one that remains subject to debate by scholars on both sides of the Atlantic. It has not been the purpose of this essay to enter that debate (and so limited a work could scarcely make a useful contribution) but rather to present evidence and examples to support the simple proposition that early colonial pioneers and settlers who had in common strong connections with one English county, Essex, did indeed play crucial roles in the shaping of American history, roles so crucial and decisive as to merit early Stuart Essex being seen as a seedbed of American democracy and independence.

Further reading

Readers' attention is drawn to three recent publications:

1 J. R. Smith, *Pilgrims and Adventurers: Essex (England) and the Making of the United States of America*, E.R.O., 1992.

2 R. Thompson, *Mobility and Migration: East Anglian Founders of New England, 1629–1640*, University of Massachusetts Press, 1994.

3 T. Webster, *Stephen Marshall and Finchingfield*, E.R.O., 1992 (excellent for information on the Puritan community and network in Essex, *c.*1620–50).

Boarded In-fill: Alternative to Wattle and Daub?

D. F. STENNING

THE VAST MAJORITY of medieval, timber-framed buildings have in-fill panels of wattle and daub. Whilst there are regional variations in the construction details, the principle of reinforced clay, applied to an armature of relatively slight timbers can be seen in all carpentry areas.

Excavation in recent years, on the Thames river front, have revealed remnants of early buildings involving a variety of construction techniques. Of particular interest are those incorporating timber plank construction which clearly represent a mode of construction with especially archaic origins.

It is becoming increasingly apparent that plank walling once enjoyed a certain popularity as more and more examples are coming to light. Being an early construction method, the evidence is fragmentary and the picture is still confused and in need of interpretation.

My interest was first aroused by a recently renovated building, 30 Kings Street, Kings Lynn. This thirteenth century building originally stood on the quayside and has a curious first floor gallery. The framing of the upper floor, front elevation, has grooves to accommodate vertical wall planking (Parker, 1971). Similar grooves can be detected in the external walling of Hurst Farmhouse, Chilham, Kent, a remarkable, wide, unaisled, hall house of the late thirteenth century (VAG, 1992). Nearer to home, the late thirteenth century, aisled hall at Purton Green, Stansfield, Suffolk, had vertical planking in its 'service-end' wall (Walker, 1994 and Hewett, 1969). In the same county and seemingly of similar date, 47 Abbeygate Street, Bury St. Edmunds, had walls clad with vertical clapboarding (P. Aitkens per. com.).

The first mentioned Essex example remains open to more than one interpretation. The service cross-wing at Tiptofts, Wimbish, is probably late thirteenth century, is intriguing in all its details and is clearly earlier than the famous, hammer-beam roofed, hall. Each member of its frame has a pair of grooves, one either side entrapping the long wall braces. At the junctions, the coincidence of the grooves is far from perfect, to an extent difficult to explain by differential movement. The possibility of thin board cladding is favoured by some, but some kind of wattle interweave may be another possibility (Hewett 1980).

Tableau, Cressing Temple.
Wheat Barn — new oak boarded wall as in original construction with figures of thirteenth century
carpenters at work.

No such doubts need to be entertained at Fyfield Hall, near Ongar, despite the baffling nature of this extraordinary building. This is one case where a dendro-chronological survey (tree ring dating) has seemingly confused rather than assisted the unravelling of its history. Nevertheless the two surviving corner posts were probably earthfast, are likely to date from the late eleventh to the mid-twelfth century and remain in a remarkably good state of preservation. Each post has vertical striations involving alternating half rounds and triangles strongly reminiscent of late Saxon stone structures. The faces of the posts contain deep grooves on both the internal and external edges and it is clear that they represent the fixing for elaborate boarded walls.

Similarly at the thirteenth century Wheat Barn at Cressing Temple, where the details of the wall construction can be readily ascertained. Here stout vertical boards were fitted into slots in the aisle plate, studs and wall posts. Whilst no boards survive, having been replaced by brick nogging, the barn now contains a modern reconstructed replica (Stenning and Andrews, 1993).

Another more or less contemporary monastic barn at St. Paul's Hall, Belchamp St. Paul, Essex, seems to have had walling of identical type. Re-used in this barn is a 0.5 metre wide elm plank, which may have originated in the aisle wall construction. That this was not just a local technique is proved by the remnants of a barn at Copton Manor, Sheldwich, Kent.

Such a method of walling provided, at considerable expense, a secure and vermin-proof enclosure. The disadvantage of the system lies in the difficulties with repair as the boards could not be replaced, without dismantling the complete building.

This problem seems to have been solved at Manor Farm Barn, Frindsbury, Kent (early fourteenth century) where the vertical boards are fixed to grooves and horizontal rails on secondary, non-structural posts. As a result of this clever innovation, Frindsbury Barn still retains boarding, much of it the result of later replacement (Rigold, 1966).

A less sophisticated example, but again involving horizontal rails, can be seen at The Monks Barn, Netteswellbury, Harlow (late fourteenth or early fifteenth century). Again, all the original boards have gone, but have been partially replicated in recent times (Hewett, 1969).

That such a technique was the sole property of monastic carpenters is indicated by a small 'vernacular' farm building at Borley Green, in Essex, where rail-fixed boards were again employed. There is some evidence to suggest that the mid-fourteenth century Kentish barns employed horizontal boards, set into rebates and thus easier to replace.

It would appear that solid, vertical plank walling, such as in the Cressing Wheat Barn, would also be used in high status, non-agricultural buildings. The mid-thirteenth century parish church of St. Lawrence, Rushdon Spencer, Staffordshire, exhibits grooved plates and wall posts of an identical type (Meeson 1983). In this useful article, Mr Bob Meeson describes the findings of his investigations and compares the result with archaeological evidence from elsewhere.

A variation of the technique is illustrated by structures which have walls of alternate studs and planks. Certain medieval houses in the Welsh borders and at least one in Shropshire are completely of this mode and this, together with the sheer size of the scantlings, indicates an abundance of first class timber.

In Essex, the most spectacular example is the so-called granary at Grange Farm, Little Dunmow (Hewett, 1969). This peculiar building has a crown-post roof with moulded capitals suggestive of *c.*1300. It consists of two bays, forming two equal 'rooms' with a door arrangement reminiscent of a pair of service rooms. The roof is hipped at both ends, and an extra groove, suggesting a sliding door, between the two spaces, is a particularly unusual feature. Obviously a monastic building and part of the Little Dunmow Grange, the carpentry is generally first class.

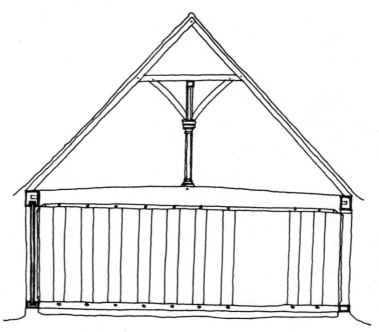

Section drawing, Grange Farm, Little Dunmow by D. F. Stenning.

Smaller medieval buildings that are constructed in this manner and are obviously granaries, exist at Colville Hall, White Roding (VAG, 1984) and at Navestock Hall (EHBG, 1992). A further example at Church Hall, Kelvedon, has extra thick studs, in order to accommodate an inner timber plank and an external in-fill of brick nogging.

Numerous Kentish houses utilize an internal dais end partition of stud and plank construction (sometimes called 'plank and muntin'). It has been reasonably suggested that such partitions are a late reminiscence of complete stud and plank construction, with this expensive technique being limited to this most important of walls. In Essex, only four walls of this type are now known to exist: two in Newport, one in Saffron Walden and a recently discovered example in Great Dunmow. It is probably no coincidence that all these are in the west of the county, where most of the houses of Kentish 'Wealden' type happen to be located.

Easthorpe parish church porch.

A number of timber-framed church porches in Essex and elsewhere also employ stud and plank construction. That at Stambourne in this county is a particularly useful example, in that unlike many, it has escaped major restoration. The porch at Easthorpe is especially interesting in that, although no boards survive, the post spacing is extremely wide and one retains its fixing groove.

Easthorpe parish church porch with boarding groove.

The parish church of St. Leonard's at Hythe, in Colchester, has a two-storied stone porch. Recent renovation work revealed that within the stone structure, remnants of an older building survived. This appears to be a fifteenth century upper porch room constructed of butt-jointed planks and a minimal number of studs. Whether this represents the survival of an old idea or whether it was intended to achieve a high level of security is open to debate. The fact that the floor joists were closely spaced could add credibility to the latter.

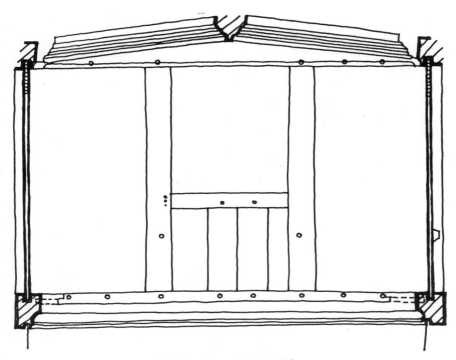

St. Leonard's at Hythe, Colchester.
Reconstruction of fifteenth century upper porch chamber by D. F. Stenning.

As can be seen, evidence for boarded walls provides a complex picture that is just beginning to take shape. Whilst this phenomenon can be encountered in many timber-framing areas, the Essex examples have their particular significance. It would appear that boarded walls, of various forms, were an important feature of early buildings, but one that gradually fell from favour. Nevertheless, they retained their popularity in ecclesiastical circles, where expense was no obstacle and for granaries, where their impenetrability remained useful.

Bibliography

Vanessa Parker, *The Making of Kings Lynn*, 1971, Phillimore.

Vernacular Architecture Group, Spring Conference Itinerary, 1992.

J. L. Walker, 'Purton Green, Stansfield: Some later observations on the early aisled hall', *Proceedings of the Suffolk Institute of Archaeology and History*, vol. XXXVIII, Part 2, 1994.

C. A. Hewett, *The Development of Carpentry, An Essex Study*, David and Charles, 1969.

C. A. Hewett, *English Historic Carpentry*, 1980, Phillimore.

D. D. Andrews, ed., *Cressing Temple, A Templar and Hospitaller Manor in Essex*, Essex County Council, 1993.

S. E. Rigold, 'Some Major Kentish Timber Barns', *Archaeologica Cantiana*, vol. LXXXI, 1966.

Journal of the Vernacular Architecture Group, vol. 14, 1983.

Vernacular Architecture Group, Spring Conference Itinerary, 1984.

'Historic Buildings in Essex', *Journal of the Essex Historic Buildings Group*, 6, 1992.

Essex Gentry and the General Election of 1865

ANDREW PHILLIPS

THIS IS AN ANATOMY of the General Election campaign of 1865 in the vast and rambling constituency of North Essex, an exercise made worthwhile by the survival of an important archive, hitherto unexplored.

In March 1866, with the details of the 1865 contest barely concluded, the Revd. Sir Charles Page Wood, head of a colourful and important Essex family and the Chairman of the Liberal Election Committee for North Essex, died. At his request the bulk of his election correspondence was sent to John Gurdon Rebow of Wivenhoe Park, the driving force behind the Liberal campaign. The papers were still there four years later when Rebow himself died. We cannot know whether they were intended for posterity, but Rebow did keep this collection of 265 letters and receipts intact, though most were of a confidential and, at that date, sensitive nature. Ignorance of their existence (they did not reach the Essex Record Office until 1985) has meant they have not previously been consulted for the insight they shed on the workings of the mid-Victorian political process.[1]

1 — The 1865 General Election in North Essex

In order to analyse processes, some brief outline of context is needed. Nationally the 1865 election was called because the existing parliament had all but run its course, and the elderly Prime Minister, Lord Palmerston, showed every intention of retaining his vigour and his premiership. He was also popular. His impeccable Tory background, plus his leadership of the newly-emerged Liberal Party, enabled him to appeal to a wide range of the electorate. The Liberals called the 1865 election to give themselves a majority while Palmerston was still an asset.

Since their establishment by the Reform Act of 1832 both the North Essex seats had been successfully held by the Conservatives. A serious challenge was only mounted in 1847 by a single Whig/Liberal candidate, John Gurdon Rebow, who, despite being early in the field and well-prepared, failed by 750 votes to secure a seat. Thereafter the Liberals regarded North Essex as a lost cause, and no real challenge was offered at general elections in 1852, 1857 and 1859. By 1864

Sir Thomas Burch Western, Bart., 1795–1873, a drawing of 1851, with (left) a contemporary view of his seat, Felix Hall.

both sitting members, Major Beresford and Charles du Cane, had been spared a contest for 17 years and the lists of registered Conservative electors had become seriously neglected.

Against this background the North Essex Liberals took their opponents by surprise in vigorously contesting the Registration Court of 1864. Technically the task of drawing up a list of eligible electors from parish rate books lay with the Overseers of the Poor, but these unpaid and elected officials had become such a by-word for inefficiency that in practice local political parties employed solicitors of their own political persuasion, or even a professional agent, to check the initial lists and attend the annual Registration Court, there to persuade the Revising Barrister to remove (often on technical quibbles) known supporters of the opposing party and to include known supporters of their own who had in error been omitted or not correctly listed — thereby risking their possible removal by the other side. As a result the increasingly complex and confrontational Registration Courts became a major factor in winning or losing a constituency in any forthcoming General Election. Such appears to have been the case in 1864 when, according to their own figures, the Liberals of North Essex made a gain of at least 500 and arguably as many as 1,000 names in a total electoral register of just under 5,000 voters.[2]

By December 1864 the press was announcing that Sir Thomas Burch Western, Bart., of Felix Hall, Kelvedon, was expected to contest North Essex in the Liberal interest. Having hit the ground running, the Liberals intended to stay ahead until election day, whenever that might be. The Conservatives now faced a dilemma: the combination of the Liberal's registration coup and a popular candidate like 'squire' Western brought home the likely cost of a contest. Having two sitting members the Conservatives were bound to defend both seats; the Liberals however would tell their own side to 'plump' for Western, while seeking to persuade Conservative or undecided voters to split their two votes between Western and one of the Conservatives. Of the two du Cane was both a rich man and a significant and resident landholder; Beresford was neither.

In February a damaging row exploded in the press over allegations that du Cane had upset his tenant farmers by the over-protection of his game at Braxted Park and by rearing semi-tame foxes. In March the news broke that a closed meeting of Conservative gentry at Faulkbourne Hall, seat of the Revd. Walter Bullock, had presented Beresford with an ultimatum — to pay for his own re-election campaign. His response was to resign as a candidate. Within days Ruggles-Brise of Spains Hall had offered himself and been accepted as a second candidate. This however was overtaken by an outcry against the treatment of Beresford by 'the 45 at Faulkbourne'. Spokesmen claiming to act for Conservative tenant farmers demanded a public meeting and offered to raise their own fund to pay for Beresford's re-election expenses. Quick to disassociate himself from the Faulkbourne decision, which had clearly backfired, du Cane in turn resigned. The Conservative *Essex Standard* ran the strident headline 'North Essex at Sixes and Sevens'.[3]

Sir Charles du Cane, 1825–89, with (right) *the view of Braxted Park in 1832.*

(Photograph courtesy of the Essex Record Office)

In fact, as we shall see, these events may have had little effect on subsequent voting behaviour. A Conservative rally in March 1865 not only 'persuaded' Beresford and du Cane to reconsider their resignations, but agreed to raise a fund to finance the return of both the sitting members. Not till late June was the date of the election — July 21st — known. There was in consequence a five month election campaign, fought in the traditional fashion. Behind the hyperbole it is clear that neither side was quite certain of the likely outcome. In the event it was extraordinarily close, votes being cast as follows:

du Cane	2,081
Western	1,931
Beresford	1,882

Western had beaten Beresford by just 49 in nearly 6,000 votes cast by 4,904 electors. This was mainly due to those persuaded to 'split' between du Cane and Western. Although the Liberals expected it, the Conservatives did not lodge a petition against the result on grounds of corrupt practices.[4]

2 — Constituency and Candidates

The great Reform Act of 1832 had first divided Essex North and South for parliamentary purposes, thereby creating something that was more than an artificial boundary relevant for only a few weeks every election. After 30 years North Essex had taken on an identity of its own, with its own leading families and sense of geography. It was certainly large enough: 235 parishes across seven Polling Districts centred on Castle Hedingham, Braintree, Colchester, Thorpe, Witham, Dunmow and Saffron Walden. The advent of the Great Eastern Railway had done little to break down this parochialism, if only because the railway did not run west-east.

In his classic study of Victorian elections, Professor Hanham has rightly stressed the special nature of the English county constituency and the prestige which a county seat carried.[5] One should not however exaggerate the traditional divide between the large, rural county constituencies, dominated by agriculture and landlords, and the tight, urban, borough seats, dominated by family, craft allegiance, religious affiliation and incipient democracy. What North Essex demonstrated was a complex merger of both: wholly rural, landlord-dominated parishes and substantial urban communities, like Braintree, Halstead and Saffron Walden, whose electoral behaviour was much like any other town of comparable size which happened to enjoy the status of a parliamentary borough. Maldon is the obvious example.

More than this, there were several senses in which the political fortunes of borough and county seats were inter-related. Firstly, there was the press, which in politics was wholly partisan. Readers throughout North Essex, unless they were very close to the inner caucus of one of the two parties, were largely dependant on newspapers for an overall narrative of events. Liberals in particular regarded their own *Essex Telegraph*, founded in 1858, as a key reason why, after 33 years' failure, they might wrest one seat from the Conservatives. The ultra-Tory *Essex and West Suffolk Gazette* was largely controlled by the Conservative leader, William Warwick Hawkins, while its great rival, the *Essex Standard*, despite reflecting the Protestant and occasionally populist views of its owner-editor, John Taylor, was equally Conservative, as was the Chelmsford-based *Essex Chronicle*. All four papers fully reported all five Essex contests, the Conservative press looking to celebrate the ultimate electoral triumph of returning a 'Conservative Ten'.

Secondly, there was a significant overlap among the electorate: 365 Colchester residents, 31 from the Maldon constituency and 45 from Harwich were eligible to vote in North Essex as well as, in many cases, their own borough contests. They represented almost 10 per cent of the North Essex electorate, and, but for the partisan nature of the register, it is likely that a good many more potential multiple voters existed.[6]

Finally, both contests were conducted by much the same people. The dominant figure of Liberalism in North Essex was Gurdon Rebow, the former candidate, who was now the Liberal candidate at Colchester. The established godfather of Colchester Liberalism, John Stuck Barnes, Rebow's personal solicitor, was both offered the post of party agent for Colchester, while being chief adviser to Liberalism's inner circle for the North Essex contest. A key figure in that campaign was Sutton Western, son and heir of the Liberal candidate, Sir Thomas Western, and simultaneously the defending candidate for Maldon. Here he initially faced J. T. Selwin, (later contesting the South Essex constituency instead), the brother-in-law of Charles du Cane, the North Essex Conservative member, who had himself been a candidate at Maldon in 1852. Chief orchestrator of the Conservative cause in North Essex was William Warwick Hawkins, a former M.P. for Colchester, who with his brother Charles Henry Hawkins was the dominant political figure in that town and its election. Both sides thus saw the contests as a whole; both knew that success in one could rub off on another; that to engage the enemy's efforts (and gold) in North Essex reduced its freedom to muster forces elsewhere. As Sutton Western put it in a letter to Gurdon Rebow shortly before his father's candidature was announced:

> '. . . if this golden opportunity is allowed to slip by, the boroughs as well as South Essex will not be relieved of the pressure which is so important for the success of the Liberals, particularly at Colchester and Maldon.'[7]

This explains very clearly why Gurdon Rebow and Sutton Western were so interested in the North Essex contest.

In one sense however a county contest did function on a different plane to a borough one. To be a county member was a signal honour, not far short of the greater honour of the Lord Lieutenancy. Among the county community of resident gentry, meeting at Quarter Session, only the most respected owners of wide acres were deemed suitable for the post. A great disgrace would rest on any party who put forward a mere carpetbagger, however willing he were to spend money. Such men should seek a borough contest: Maldon or Sudbury, for example. For this reason there were a strictly limited number of men ideally suited to be a candidate. Both parties had examples of those like Selwin who had been progressed from a borough contest to the greater honour of North or South Essex, notwithstanding the greater expense. For here was an added problem: a county contest would probably cost a candidate £4,000. This further narrowed the field.

In point of fact mid-Victorian Essex was surprisingly short of rich, resident landlords. Of 74 Essex landlords holding 3,000 or more acres (not necessarily all in Essex) 40 lived outside the county. In North Essex perhaps 15 resident landlords boasted 3,000 acres, several of whom by age, sex or inclination might not be parliamentary candidates.[8] For this reason the Conservatives had found themselves in some difficulty in 1847 when Gurdon Rebow contested the seat. The sitting Conservative members, Sir John Tyssen Tyrell, Bart. and Charles Grey Round, ideally fitted the formula. They had 3,000 and 4,000 Essex acres respectively and impeccable county pedigrees. At this point Round, a devout Evangelical, felt led to sacrifice his Essex seat to stand against the youthful, High Church Gladstone for Oxford University. At short notice the North Essex Conservatives had no replacement. In their hour of need, and amidst some outcry, they turned to Major Beresford, younger son of an Irish landed family, and currently M.P. for Harwich, who had neither a fortune nor one square inch of Essex soil to his name.

Beresford proved a spirited candidate, won the seat and won the affection of many of the tenant farmers — the yeomen, as they were still quaintly called for political purposes. He happily embraced (and also cultivated) the title, 'The Farmers' Friend'. He also proved a competent politician, becoming Secretary at War during the brief Conservative government of 1852. This and 24 years services as an Essex M.P. did not prevent a continued irritation among a section of the Conservative leadership about Beresford's appropriateness and the obstacle he presented to any aspiring county candidate. Hence the infamous meeting at Faulkbourne Hall on 20 February 1865 at which 'only five farmers' were present. In the outcry that greeted this 'clique of county gentry' William Hawkins found it necessary to give some explanation at a public meeting. The issue at stake, he claimed, was the problem of financing the contest: Beresford had honourably resigned because he was unable to fund himself and also because

'. . . I had been assured that there was a strong feeling on the part of many influential farmers that the time had come when you yourselves wished for a county man. [loud cries of "No, no" and counter cries of "it is so"] . . . I can state further that several gentlemen who met me after the Hon. Mr Strutt had become Senior Wrangler . . . suggested his name, young as he is, as Major Beresford's successor.'[9]

Rivenhall Place, home of the Revd. Sir John Page Wood, 1796–1866.

The Page Wood archive makes clear this was not the full story. On 8 February Sutton Western had written to Wood:

> 'I have just seen Mr Noyes who has come up from Terling and he tells me a message has been sent to Major Beresford requesting him to retire in favour of young Strutt for the Northern Division and that Beresford has applied to the Carlton for money for the contest but that they have refused to help him and the Tories expect this circumstance will force him to retire. *Is it not very much in our interest to offer to split votes with Beresford in order to keep him in the field as Strutt will be a more formidable opponent?*' (my italics)[10]

Wood therefore wrote to Beresford, his political opponent, who replied:

> 'Your letter came with many others today tending to show me that there is treachery. Oh King Ahaziah! I cannot help it if they chose so to demean themselves.'[11]

Beresford remained in direct, clandestine correspondence with Wood for some time, seeking on two occasions to arrange private meetings, the outcome of which are unknown, but they did permit Wood to declare at the Hustings the following July:

> 'For 18 years the Tories have been trying to drop Beresford — and I can prove it.'[12]

No one challenged this claim.

In the event Beresford's candidature was saved by the outcry within his own party. This merits some analysis. The first public move against the '45 at Faulkbourne' came when the *Essex Standard* newspaper, whose populist editor had clashed with the Conservative Party leadership before, carried a paid advertisement and supportive leader outlining what had happened at Faulkbourne. This was followed by letters to all four county papers by Joseph Beaumont of Coggeshall and Simon Viall of Baythorpe Hall protesting at the dropping of Beresford. Most revealing was an anonymous letter from 'A Conservative Elector':

> 'As you truly remarked in your leader of last Saturday, the Gentlemen have made a great mistake. If they wish to retain any influence with the yeomen they must rectify that mistake at once. The farmers are willing and anxious to co-operate with the gentlemen, but they will not allow their old and valued representative, who has well-earned for himself the title of 'The Farmers' Friend', to be unfairly treated. Nor will they permit their wishes and opinions to be so utterly ignored as has lately been the case. The farmers of Herts. and other counties have been obliged to take election matters into their own hands; the Farmers of North Essex will do the same. Beresford is the Farmers' Candidate; Beresford they mean to have; let the County

Gentlemen make their arrangements accordingly. In my neighbourhood
I will undertake to say, that parish after parish shall take its Conservative
voters to the poll, and it shall not cost the Major a farthing!'[13]

At an open Conservative meeting held at Braintree on 15 March, Beaumont,
Viall and Frederick Finch (also of Baythorpe End) led a similar attack on the
leadership of the party, moving a motion that Beresford and du Cane should
remain the party's candidates. It was at this point that William Hawkins launched
his damage-limitation account of the events at Faulkbourne, inviting the yeomen
to raise £1,000 towards Beresford's expenses, undertaking that the gentlemen
would find the rest. Beaumont tried twice to replace this offer with the more
participative idea of parish committees raising the money to finance both
candidates. This however was by-passed by the leadership and, at a reconvened
meeting at Colchester, poorly attended because of its postponed start and a
blinding snowfall, they set up the traditional central committee, dominated by
the leadership.[14]

Nor was a determination to keep election finance in the hands of a few confined
to North Essex Conservatives. When, in the aftermath of the election, the
Liberals were experiencing great difficulty in raising sufficient to finance Western's
expensive campaign, his son, Sutton Western, wrote:

> 'There are a large number of the well-to-do farmers who doubtless
> would give their £5 or £10, but of course we must not descend too
> low or we shall bring ourselves into discredit with our own party, and
> the ridicule of our opponents . . .'[15]

Making every allowance for Conservative voters' sense of fair play, it is clear
that the sub-text of the Beresford affair was that tenant farmers and small town
solicitors like Beaumont were pushing to be equal participants in the party
political process and that county gentry were less than willing to concede more
than a token presence. Over on the Liberal side the Page Wood archive
demonstrates the extent to which their campaign was conducted by a small, self-
selected Finance Committee, largely controlled by Page Wood, Gurdon Rebow
and Sutton Western, while dealings with their allies, the Dissenters, were
brokered by the ubiquitous John Stuck Barnes, Rebow's personal solicitor.

It is also significant that it is the *tenant* farmers' wish to keep Beresford as a
candidate which runs like a *leitmotive* through this uneasy period of the Conservative
campaign, even though their spokesmen were a solicitor and four *independent* farmers
(or sons of independent farmers) who were sufficiently politically active to send
letters to the papers.[16] For what political service had Beresford done the tenant
farmers, other than the usual round of gladhanding and holding the correct view
on the need for the abolition of the malt tax? His appeal lay less in what he had
done for the farmers, as in what the Essex gentry had done to him — pulled rank
on him. What we are witnessing is a qualified testing of the role of deference in
English society. There is a parallel in the rise of trade unionism after this date, a

phenomenon so disturbing to E. H. Bentall, the Maldon agricultural engineer and employer of 300, that he forsook his hereditary allegiance to the Conservative Party to stand — successfully — as a moderate Liberal and paternalistic employer at Maldon in the General Election of 1868.[17]

Conventional historical wisdom has for long seen the 20 years after the repeal of the corn laws as a 'Golden Age' of agriculture; of rising profits in which landlord and tenant farmer benefited alike, and in which good relations flourished between the two. Certainly farmers' rents rose. New estimates however suggest that agricultural performance after 1846, particularly in predominantly arable areas like Essex, was less impressive and that:

> 'British farmers were unable to compete . . . because an excessively large share of net farm income was allocated to rent to support the social and administrative institutions of the elite landowning class.'[18]

It is perhaps necessary to see Beresford's de-selection and re-selection in this light, particularly given that other conventional wisdom that after 1846 the Conservatives became the only party of the land, a claim which, as we will see, needs qualifying. The Beresford affair and others like it in southern county constituencies anticipates the Farmers Alliance of 1879. Much of what this body stood for formed part of the North Essex farmers' unspoken agenda in 1865.

If North Essex Conservatives thus did themselves no good by undermining one of their own candidates, Beresford, it seems equally odd that they should 'talk up' their only opponent. The announcement of Sir Thomas Western's candidature put them, wrote Sutton Western, in 'a mortal funk'. In November 1864 he was privately approached by Onley Savil Onley, a senior North Essex Conservative and chairman of many of their meetings, with the offer of uncontested seats at Maldon (Sutton Western's own seat) and South Essex, if his father did not stand.[19] And while it is understandable that the Conservative press, particularly the more open *Essex Standard*, should declare that Western was 'the best candidate the Liberals might have', it is rather surprising that Conservative speakers should say the same thing at their own political rallies. It was one thing to 'avoid personalities', refraining from criticising an opponent personally, for gentlemen of both parties not only sat together at Quarter Session, but hunted and shot on one another's estates; however it was rather different to paint them in glowing colours at political rallies. In speech after speech throughout the election campaign Beresford and du Cane declared that they had nothing but personal respect for Western, only disagreement with some of his opinions and horror at the darker forces (i.e. Radicalism) within the Liberal Party.

The explanation for such Conservative behaviour-lies not only in Western's eminent suitability for the post of a county M.P., but also in the less than hidden agenda which ran parallel to the strict party political contest. A General Election was a potentially disruptive time, not just because election day was boisterous and still something of a public carnival, but more because it enabled men whose political objectives were equally unacceptable to Whig or Tory landowners to sound those views abroad. Radicalism had a growing strength in most North Essex towns and their objectives included a widening of the franchise as well as an emerging class hostility to the privileges of the landed gentry. Such views played no part in the political agenda of Sir Thomas Western. Although he had inherited from a distant cousin, his status in North Essex was beyond dispute. Possessing over 10,000 acres, most of them in Essex, he had one of the largest rent rolls in the county, a significant proportion of which had gone towards those considerations small and great which gave a squire a reputation for upholding the standards to which his tenants had become accustomed. Without ever pushing matters into open debate the 'good' landlord would forgo a degree of profit by pegging, even reducing, his rent income; while by looking benignly on a host of customs and practices, not least in paying claims for damage done to crops by the hunt, he could retain his tenants' respect. Owners of wide acres were in a better position to do this. Failure to do it could become a political embarrassment, as we have seen with du Cane.

The allegations against du Cane carried less weight by coming from his recently-dismissed estate agent. But this one-man press campaign against his former master did involve detailed and doubtless accurate quotations from letters written or comments passed by du Cane's tenants, complaining about their lot and about poor farming practices. The Liberal *Essex Telegraph* made the most of this embarrassing public squabble between a landlord and his dismissed agent — because, of course, du Cane was a Conservative sitting member. However, there was no move by the paper from the particular to the general: no move to denounce all landlords. Whatever may be happening in Manchester, the politics of class was no part of this election campaign.[20]

Rather the forces of deference were all too clearly upheld. This may not have been a golden age of farming; it was still a golden age for feudal fantasies. County elections still retained quaint symbolic ceremonies: riding to the poll at the head of your tenantry, girding swords round the two elected knights of the shire, removing the horses to haul your victorious candidate round the town. The Page Wood archive contains only a few of the squids and posters that normally accompanied an election, but the following poem, printed on orange paper and doubtless widely distributed, shows a shrewd exploitation of Western's image as a benign and grand seigneur:

> Arouse old town of Braintree and don thy best array
> From roof and windows to the breeze let orange streamers play;
> Today the good Sir Thomas is coming with his train,
> And Braintree good Sir Thomas greets with all her might and main.

A landlord kind and courteous, as witness we shall see
This score of stout and trusty men, his faithful tenantry —
O'er many a fertile hill and dale his acres broad extend
And of all within his wide domain Sir Thomas is the friend.

Ride on, ride on Sir Thomas our champion leal and true,
Before our orange banner's blaze shall pale the sickly blue;
Before the Liberal sun's bright beam dull Tory shades shall flee.
Ride on, our good Sir Thomas, ride on to victory.[21]

Such doggerel played its part in the wider context of the 1865 election in which neither Whig nor Tory leadership sought to disturb the existing social order. It did not however reflect the interests of Braintree Radicals.

3 — Issues and Allies

The one significant item of disagreement between the two parties in the North Essex election of 1865 and between the two sets of election addresses was Western's open support for the Abolition of Church Rates, a cause long dear to the Dissenters' hearts, and for most of them a staging post towards the wider goal of Disestablishment. Samuel Courtauld, silk manufacturer, the largest employer and perhaps richest Dissenter in North Essex, was prominent both in the national campaign and in the Dissenters' main pressure group, the Liberation Society. This was at its most active in the 1865 election, seeking a commitment to the abolition of church rates from Liberal candidates in return for active Nonconformist support at the polls. Significantly, and despite Sam Courtauld's residence in North Essex, there is no direct evidence for such a trade-off here. Indeed Courtauld's contribution to Western's candidature was minimal. He clearly regarded Western as a traditional Whig and not the type of advanced Liberal he would prefer to see contesting the seat. When written to by Gurdon Rebow for his support, he pointed out the likelihood of the elderly Thomas Western coming under the influence of his son, questioning whether Western's 'success now would be the greatest strength to us *hereafter* . . .'. He added as rebuke:

> 'For myself I have had no communication with the movers in this matter, nor with the electors more generally, that would warrant my taking at this time any step in the dark . . . by which . . . the Liberal electors . . . freedom of action might be . . . compromised.'[22]

It is true that Courtauld's nephew, George, served on the Liberal Central Committee (though not its inner circle) and his brother contributed £50 to the fund, but Samuel Courtauld's sole contribution of £25 needs to be set against the £2,500 he left to the Liberation Society whose Essex subscription, fattened by his contributions, was exceeded only by those of Lancashire, Yorkshire and Gloucestershire.[23]

Four key figures in Essex politics in 1865: John Gurdon Rebow, the Colchester candidate (top left);
John Stuck Barnes, the Liberal lawyer (top right); *Samuel Courtauld, the Nonconformist leader*
(bottom left); *William Warwick Hawkins, the Conservative leader* (bottom right).

Courtauld was right to deduce that Western's candidature had been foisted on North Essex by the Whig gentry, probably by Gurdon Rebow in consultation with the Whips' Office at Westminster. Certainly Rebow was on good terms with Henry Brand, the Liberal chief whip, securing £400 towards the electoral expenses of fighting North Essex.[24] Nor can it be accidental that Western received his baronetcy from a Liberal government in the summer of 1864. Even if no direct promises were made, it certainly strengthened the moral obligation upon him, not least because Western also harboured interests in the Lord Lieutenancy, a post rendered vacant by the long-anticipated death of Lord Maynard in May 1865.

Both Western and Rebow were well aware of the centrality of the Nonconformist vote. 'From what I can learn from Sir John Wood', wrote J. S. Barnes to Rebow, 'it is a *church* contest for *the Westerns*'.[25] Rebow, always more robust, urged on Wood the need to target wealthy Dissenters for campaign donations:

> '. . . of making instant application to those whose purses are full and are most interested in our success — I mean the Nonconformists and a few churchmen. I told Mr Courtauld Jr. that I thought they were much interested and I hoped his uncle would feel it was an occasion on which he might *shell out freely*.'[26]

There followed a check-list of names, all of which subsequently appeared in campaign donation lists for £25 or £50. For whatever reservations Sam Courtauld might have, the British two-party system tied the Dissenters' hands. They could not embrace the Tories for whom Establishment was a central belief; better a cautious Liberal than no Liberal at all. On this basis, in North Essex as elsewhere, the Liberal stand against church rates was a gateway into Radical politics, a useful bridge to both sides, the very sand and cement of Gladstonian Liberalism, as it was soon to become. However personally supportive they might be, neither Western nor Rebow need comment on Household Franchise or Secret Ballot, two Radical demands quite absent from the Liberal campaign in North Essex: the Nonconformist vote was already assured.

By contrast the Conservatives were compelled once more to cry 'Church and State' on an issue already appearing indefensible. The sight of dignified pillars of the community who happened to be Quakers, having their front door broken down, their finest furniture removed by bailiffs and sold at auction, largely to keep the parish church in repair, had long caused universal embarrassment. Samuel Courtauld's own campaign against Braintree's church rates had raised such precedents that prosecution of further cases seemed legally dubious. The Evangelical wing of the Church was already in sympathy with the Dissenters' case. It is significant that Sir Thomas Western had ten Anglican clergy on his Central Committee.

This left the Conservatives with the defence of agriculture as its main election 'cause', but here again they were undermined. Western's other firm commitment was to the repeal of the malt tax, a measure the Conservatives would have liked to make their own. Indeed, for being lukewarm over the malt tax, Gurdon Rebow's own brother, a Liberal, was to lose his West Norfolk seat in the same election.[27] The barley acreage in both Norfolk and Essex was, even at this date, quite as significant as that of wheat.

With an election campaign lasting over five months, both parties could hold public meetings in every corner of the North Essex constituency. The candidates' speeches were quite fully reported in the press and a content analysis gives some feel of the issues at stake. We have already mentioned the relative absence of 'personalities' in this campaign. It is also noticeable how little reference is made to local issues, except so far as the success of agriculture was a universal issue in North Essex. Beresford and du Cane attended rallies together and turned quickly to their main script. This usually involved criticism of the existing Liberal government and, while Palmerston was accorded some respect, Gladstone was targeted as the danger man waiting to unleash Radical forces lurking in the wings.

That said, it seems unlikely that, notwithstanding the issue of church rates, converts were made or the election won by arguments delivered in Essex newspapers or voices raised at public meetings. To understand why we need to turn to an analysis of voting behaviour.

4 — Voters and Voting Behaviour.

There are two essential reasons for Western's narrow election victory in 1865. The first was his ability to harness the Dissenters and with them to reap the urban, Radical vote. Second and more fundamental was the Registration Revision in North Essex in June 1864, one year before the contest. This was conducted on the Liberals' behalf by Thomas Roberts, Secretary to the Liberal Registration Association at Westminster, with the assistance of Thomas Steele.[28]

Founded in 1860, the Liberal Registration Association (L.R.A.) was the first body, other than the two political clubs, the Carlton and the Reform, to represent one of the two main parties nationally. It is significant that its task was voter registration. Contemporaries and modern commentators are all agreed on the extent to which this could swing an election result. In the case of North Essex, where there had not been a significantly contested election since 1847, there were, according to William Hawkins, only 1,332 out of the 4,904 voters on the completed 1864 electoral roll who had voted before. Understandably the annual Electoral Revision had ceased to be a major event. In 1863 Hawkins at his own expense got an agent to check about 100 of the parishes to the east of the constituency, leading to 269 additions to the Conservative electorate. Of course there was a cost. Rebow paid between £65 and £100 a year to have an eye kept on the Colchester register; Thomas Steele was paid £200 for the North Essex Registration of 1865; that of 1864 may have cost more. The outcome however was impressive: certainly a Liberal gain of 500 over the Conservatives; perhaps 1,000. (The imprecision lies in William Hawkins's statistic: the 3,577 who had not voted before. Many were only hoped-for Liberals.)[29]

This registration triumph was achieved by a host of legal devices, ruthlessly applied. Quibbles like the incorrect spelling of a road where a voter lived could disqualify him if objected to by the other side. Any such objection *required* the voter to appear in court. Facing the loss of a day's work (or pay), many voters were disfranchised by default rather than make an awkward journey across North Essex. In 1864 1,863 objections were registered in North Essex and 1,024 claims for new voters, compared with only 364 the year before.[30] Most went in the Liberal's favour. The result was a register which reflected more the Liberal's zeal than a correct list of eligible voters. Not only were significant numbers of resident Conservatives disfranchised: farmers, clergy, men of independent means, but legal niceties were stretched to include members of leading Liberal families who, in practice, did not live in the constituency at all. Of the 4,904 registered voters, 752 (15 per cent) did not live in the parish of their registration and many lived very far from North Essex. This could arise in several ways, relating to property rights, but there seems good cause to believe that such voters reflect the active hand of a registration agent, not least because their abstention rate (33 per cent) was infinitely higher than that of the resident voters. Thus, for example, nine members of the Western family secured votes, though only two lived in North Essex. Particularly interesting is a small army of out-voters at Witham, drawn from London and much of southern England, who voted 43 Liberal, 12 Conservative with 17 abstentions.[31]

It is of course harder to quantify the disinherited. Certainly it is worth noting how selective the traditional forty shilling freehold could be. In Witham, a town dominated by neither party, a contemporary directory shows how few tradesmen might be included. As to their voting behaviour and the popularity of splitting, more later.

Table 4.1 — 1865 Election: Witham, North Essex[32]

Trade	No. in Directory	No. with vote	Lib	Con	Split	Abs
Farmers	15	5	3	1	1	0
Inn/Pub Keepers	15	6	0	4	2	0
Bakers	9	4	1	1	2	0
Grocers	8	3	1	1	1	0
Boot/Shoe Makers	14	4	2	0	2	0
TOTAL	61	22	7	7	8	0

One of the most glaring examples of franchise shortfall is the Liberal stronghold of Braintree. Not only is there a complete absence of any Anglican clergy on the electoral roll, but of 24 farmers listed in a contemporary directory only six are enfranchised, and all but two voted for Western. This looks suspiciously like a registration culling.

The point has often been made that the 1832 Reform Act increased party-political commitment in the nation. The annual registration contest makes clear why: there was little point — for either side — in getting the names of the politically inert on the register. On the other hand, a presumed Liberal was not a certain Liberal: herein lay the function of the election campaign and herein lies the argument for a genuine floating vote to be won.

It is widely agreed by commentators that well into the late nineteenth century 'estates voted as a unit'; that Whig or Tory landlords expected (and secured) the support of their tenantry.[33] This was as much due to the feeling that an agricultural estate was a social institution, governed by traditional loyalty, as by the more negative view, much put about by Radicals, that landlords bluntly coerced. Was this true of North Essex and, if so, what sort of 'floating vote' did this leave?

No contemporary poll book for the North Essex election of 1865 is known to have survived. However the *Essex and West Suffolk Gazette* did publish a complete poll over four successive weekly editions, thus enabling us to see how every voter voted — or rather how the North Essex Conservative Party considered every voter voted, for the *Gazette* poll's figures differ from the official result. Since voting was based on the parish, a great deal of primary research would be needed to reconstruct entire estates, but a review of parishes known to have a political 'squire' supports the traditional explanation. It is interesting to note that the rule equally applied to an institutional owner like Guys Hospital:

Table 4.2 — Voting at 1865 Election, North Essex[34]

Parish	Liberal	Conservative	Landlord and Party
Kelvedon	32	2	Sir T. Western LIB
Rivenhall	14	4	Sir T. Western and C. Page Wood LIB
East Donyland	17	3	P. Havens LIB
Little Totham	9	1	Mrs Honeywood LIB
Alresford	0	7	W. W. Hawkins CON
Faulkbourne	0	7	Revd. W. Bullock CON
Birch	1	13	Charles G. Round CON
Layer-de-la-Haye	0	18	C. G. Round and T. White CON
Great Braxted	2	13	Charles du Cane CON
Great Clacton	3	28	Guys Hospital *et al.* CON

This list of course is selective — there are 235 parishes to choose from. Particularly in the rural north-west of the constituency, parish after parish brought in an overwhelming Conservative majority. Indeed with few exceptions agricultural Essex was predominantly Tory. Hence the importance to the Liberals of the towns and the coastal fishing communities at Brightlingsea and Wivenhoe (though not at Tollesbury, Mersea or St. Osyth). Colchester was a special case. Not only was it so much larger than any other North Essex community, but being a constituency itself, its county electorate was a less than typical cross-section, and its voting behaviour coloured by Gurdon Rebow's candidature. The overall urban picture was:

Table 4.3 — 1865 Election: North Essex 'towns'[35]

Town	Conservative	Liberal	Abstain	Split: Western/du Cane
Braintree	14	99	10	5
Bocking	14	50	6	3
Brightlingsea	23	71	13	4
Coggeshall	10	51	10	1
Halstead	20	108	16	3
Saffron Walden	50	63	17	2
Witham	25	30	7	12
Wivenhoe	9	32	9	6
Colchester	144	168	48	14
TOTAL				
(ex Colchester)	165	504	90	36

It is clear from this that Liberalism was strongest in Braintree, Bocking, Halstead and Coggeshall — Courtauld country. These were all towns with several Nonconformist chapels and a Radical tradition. An occupational breakdown (where known) of residential voting at Halstead shows the dominance of Liberalism:

Table 4.4 —. Known Occupational Voting at Halstead 1865[36]

Occupation	Conservative	Liberal	Split: Western/du Cane
Gent.(independent means)	4	6	1
Farmer	6	12	1
(Market) Gardener	0	4	0
Miller	0	4	0
Publican/Beerseller	3	7	0
Shopkeeper	0	7	0
Grocer	0	5	0
Baker	0	5	0
Butcher	0	2	0
Draper	1	1	0
Cabinet Maker	0	2	0
Plumber/Glazier	0	1	1
Farrier/Blacksmith	1	2	0
Others*	2	16	0
TOTAL	17	74	3

* 'Others' are a surgeon and clergyman voting Conservative and one each of the following voting Liberal: Carpenter, Wheelwright, Bank Manager, Silk Agent, Nonconformist Minister, Builder, Watch-maker, Straw Plait dealer, Auctioneer, Chemist, Ironmonger, Boot & Shoe Maker, Veterinary Surgeon, Maltster, Solicitor and Assistant Overseer of the Poor.

It is noticeable how, totally, tradesmen veer to the dominant political creed, while Conservative votes come almost solely from those of independent means and traditionally strong Conservative occupational groups.

Of course Nonconformist employers were as capable of coercion as agricultural landlords. To test for freedom of action, interest should focus on those voters who run counter to the majority in their parish. Several factors emerge: (i) that some are out-voters — they do not even live in that community; (ii) that many are of independent means and are therefore not directly under a landlord's bidding. This still leaves many individual examples which suggest — as a last resort — independence of action. Checking those few who split or voted Conservative at Halstead, Braintree or Bocking one finds gentlemen, farmers and publicans, traditional Tory voters, but more interest surrounds the Halstead pawnbroker, linen draper and farrier and a Braintree perfumer, the only four tradesmen to break from the Liberal phalanxes. John Causton, painter, plumber and glazier, one of only two Conservatives in Kelvedon, must surely have come under the gaze of Sutton Western who wrote:

> 'Wilson at Witham says he will plump for du Cane; now really this is too bad, as we get all our ironmongery from him and Sir T. W. Lennard and yourself have always employed him. Could you have a word with him . . .?'[37]

'Having a word' did the Westerns no good. Wilson still voted Conservative. Some two score farmers also voted Liberal in otherwise Conservative-dominated parishes. Some must have gone against a landlord's wish. The bottom line, of course, is that in England the ultimate political sanction — eviction — was rarely pursued. Coercion is a nasty word; better to say that tenants knew which side their bread was buttered.

'A personal canvas will have to be made in the summer', wrote Gurdon Rebow, 'either by Sir Thomas Western or his son. I of course will accompany them in my district — where they are least known.'[38] Two thoughts underpin this offer. Firstly, that to canvass on another gentleman's estate was bad form. Secondly, that Rebow himself was candidate for the Colchester seat.

The size of Western's clerical following has already been noted. Something more than church rates may lie behind the rector of Conservative-dominated Great Braxted voting Liberal under the nose of Charles du Cane, or the vicar of nearby Hatfield Peverel doing the same under the nose of his Tory patron. The vicar of Little Braxted did not vote at all. Nor did the vicars of Halstead or Kelvedon, but if they were both Tories, theirs was a tactical (as well as tactful) move. Abstentions indeed are probably a significant factor. In the case of out-voters this usually means they just did not get to Essex. In the case of others, it was a deliberately withheld vote. J. Yellowly Watson, a rare Tendring Hundred Liberal, regarded Conservative abstentions *on the day* as a major Liberal triumph in the stony Soken ground.[39]

5 — *Electioneering*

Elections then reflected a complex web of obligations, promises and conscience. There was everything to play for: how was this done?

'Because estates voted as a unit', Professor Hanham writes, 'county election-eering was a simple business. Once the register had been checked for errors and duplicate entries and a list of non-resident voters had been drawn up, little remained to be done.'[40] The 260 letters of the Page Wood archive do not support so determinist a view of electioneering. Rather they make it clear that no one regarded the election result as a foregone conclusion. Even before the Conservatives had sorted out their candidates, in December 1864 Rebow approached the Liberal Chief Whip, Brand, upon whom, at that date, the ultimate conduct of a general election fell. Failing to secure again the services of Roberts — whose place was clearly in London, Rebow came to a direct arrangement with Thomas Steele, his registration assistant, who had the added advantage of having family connections in North Essex. This upset Roberts, but to little effect, underlining what a passive role Westminster politics played at this stage in constituency affairs.[41] Even though they parted with £400 to finance the Agent's expenses (i.e. Steele and his district agents), neither the Chief Whip nor the L.R.A. sought to impose any policy, strategy or constraints on the constituency's actions. The North Essex Liberal campaign was run by an informal group made up of Gurdon Rebow, Page Wood and Sutton Western with the legal assistance and street wisdom of J. S. Barnes, the consent of Sir Thomas Western and the enthusiastic help of George de Horn Vaizey, who did some invaluable fund-raising and acted as Rebow's cypher.

Once in place, Steele proceeded to establish local committees in each electoral district while Wood and Rebow signed up experienced local agents — all friendly Liberal solicitors. Steele's initial task was to draw up a requisition of — hopefully — 2,000 signatures (a figure from the first thought to be impossible), requesting Western to contest the seat. The strategy behind this was twofold: firstly to tie as many natural Liberals as possible into a written commitment early on, and secondly to encourage the Conservatives to do a deal and split the seats, one each, avoiding a contest. Though this came to nothing, Steele saw that the circulation of requisition sheets also served as a crude initial canvass.

The full canvass came later and was clearly conducted with great thorough-ness. Steele purchased his own carriage to get about the country districts, spending weeks on end in one locality. His strategy of targeting men of standing and influence was both an acknowledgement of the power of deference and a recognition that votes could nonetheless be won. This extract from one of his numerous reports to Wood, nicely illustrates his methods:

> 'Yesterday I met Mr. Gent of Steeple Bumpstead, with whom I had a long interview. He said he could not see his way to desert his party, but . . . he had a very high opinion of Sir Thomas Western. He could not see there was any difference between him and the present Members.

I then pressed him closely with regard to his tenancy (knowing that many are disposed to go with us). He said he should not interfere with them and they were perfectly at liberty to vote as they thought proper and he should not feel in the least annoyed if they should vote for Sir Thomas . . . I think that if Sir Thomas could . . . write to him in acknowledgment of his willingness not to interfere with his tenants it would do good . . .'[42]

In the event there were 14 Liberal votes from Steeple Bumpstead (though not George Gent), a significant haul in a largely Conservative area. Of course a lot might happen between Steele's canvass in February and polling day in July. In March du Cane still lay under the shadow of his agent's revelations and one informed observer wrote:

'No one but Major Beresford would stand a chance against Sir Thomas Western and I am confident that very many will split their votes between these two candidates . . .'

In fact the reverse happened. That even a thorough canvass was not enough, is well illustrated by the comments of this district agent — albeit written to talk up the size of his fee:

'In 1847 we canvassed nearly all the parishes twice and some three times to keep the Liberals staunch against the threats of landowners, agents etc.'[43]

There is good evidence that on election day there were many surprises. After the main canvass in mid-June Steele expected Western to head the final poll by 'several hundreds', but admitted there were 673 doubtful or undecided voters. Although most of these were out-voters, this is not the traditional picture of a rural tenancy dragooned unthinkingly to the poll. Sutton Western was confident of retaining his Maldon seat: he did not. Major Beresford attributed his narrow defeat to voters in the Colchester District who had promised him their vote but deserted him. J. Yellowly Watson was told by Conservatives in the Tendring Hundred that they expected a majority of 300, but of 440 voters nearly 100 abstained, 106 voted for Western and only 236 for Beresford. All this suggests that, as in the late twentieth century, more voters could keep the parties guessing till the last moment than has sometimes been recognised.[44]   This is particularly relevant in trying to explain why Beresford (the Farmers' Friend) lost his seat. Western, after all, came second, not top of the poll, just squeezing ahead of the second Conservative. Why did Beresford, after all the fuss about his candidature, do so less well than his Conservative colleague? As the senior member, he would normally expect to gain the larger loyalty vote. Yet across the constituency 74 voters plumped for du Cane and 129 split their votes between du Cane and Western. It is true that this was offset by 13 plumps for Beresford and 16 splits between Beresford and Western, but these much smaller figures only highlight the case for the vote against Beresford being a personal rather than a party one.[45]

There is no clear geographical or occupational *locus* for this anti-Beresford vote — if we may so call it. It is scattered very thinly across the constituency: north, south, east, west and all voting groups. Two major factors could be at work: personal and party. Beresford could not exercise any economic sanction or persuasion on the electorate such as Radicals claimed resident landlords did. Western and du Cane could. This is well illustrated by the voting response of the Witham tradesmen. Witham, as we have seen, was fairly evenly divided between the two parties. It was also physically very close to Braxted Park and Felix Hall, the seats of Charles du Cane and Sir Thomas Western. The Westerns, after all, employed Wilson the ironmonger. Although splitting between Western and du Cane attracted only 2½ per cent of all voters, in Witham 12 out of the 76 voters did so, 17 per cent of the total (see Table 4.3. above). This is unique to the constituency and surely represents the wish of these tradesmen not to offend either great house. The occupations of the 12 splitters are: grocer, basketmaker, two shoemakers, innkeeper, builder, painter, carpenter, fishmonger/greengrocer, miller, baker and hairdresser.[46] As with their fellow-tradesmen at Halstead, customers had to be accommodated.

There is also an interesting general trend to the anti-Beresford vote. The shortfall between the two Conservative candidates, the percentage of votes by which du Cane exceeds Beresford, is largest, and notably so, in those voting districts with an overall Liberal majority and is lowest in the most dominant Conservative districts. This suggests that splitting between du Cane and Western, the commonest method of deserting Beresford, represents less of a personal statement against Beresford and more a concession to the dominant influence of Liberalism. This is an important distinction, as it reflects a phenomenon often noted by modern psephologists, that voters with less than a lifetime one-party commitment are swayed by a dominant political culture: floating voters float with the tide. The only exception to this general pattern is Saffron Walden where splitting is, uniquely, outweighed by plumping: 24 for du Cane, five for Beresford. Here, in a dominant Conservative district, perhaps a personal preference was truly at work.[47]

Beresford attributed his electoral defeat to voters in the Colchester district who deserted him and voted for Western and du Cane. This can be tested in a small way. Fourteen voters in Colchester split between Western and du Cane, four split between Western and Beresford, two plumped for du Cane and one for Beresford. Twelve of these can be traced also voting in the Colchester constituency where, by coincidence, a similar three-cornered contest occurred: a single Liberal (Gurdon Rebow) faced two Conservatives. Rebow owed his subsequent election, like Western, to splitters between himself and one of the Conservative candidates, usually Miller. A check through Colchester's voters shows 13 North Essex voters with 'unorthodox' Colchester voting patterns viz: 11 splitting between Rebow and Miller, one between Rebow and Papillon and one plumping for Miller. Analysing these 21 voters who voted in both constituencies and recorded less than a full party vote in at least one, produces these results:

Table 5.1 — Unorthodox North Essex or Colchester voters[48]

North Essex vote	Nos.	Colchester vote		
		Split	Liberal	Conservative
Western/Du Cane	8	3	3	2
Western/Beresford	2	1	1	0
Du Cane plump	1	0	0	1
Beresford plump	1	0	0	1

Colchester vote	Nos.	North Essex vote		
		Split	Liberal	Conservative
Rebow/Miller	11	3	3	5
Rebow/Papillon	1	1	0	0
Miller plump	1	0	0	1

N.B. Four voters appear in both lists since they split in both constituencies.

The following may be concluded from this small but perhaps representative sample. Some splitters may have split from lack of clear party preference — or for even-handedness. The four voters who split in both contests deserve credit for such consistency. Those who split in only one contest (14 voters) presumably were reflecting a candidate preference. If so, they are representative of the electorate as a whole, with the correct bias towards du Cane in North Essex and Miller in Colchester, both of whom headed their respective polls. In which case it is tempting to conclude that both parties contributed to this process — not just the Conservatives, as Beresford claimed. The 14 once-splitting voters voted in their other contest seven Liberal, seven Conservative.

Such statistical speculation should not be carried too far, but serves to remind us that despite the domination of general elections after 1832 by party political considerations, the ordinary voter still exercised a choice, a choice in which the candidate's merits, or perceived merits, might play a real part. This is particularly true of the 74 (presumed Conservatives) who plumped for du Cane, unwilling, apparently, to vote for Beresford on personal grounds. Nor should we forget that for many men of influence Western was not just the owner of wide acres but that:

> '. . . a more high-minded, honourable man and a more perfect type of English Gentleman does not exist.'[49]

These crucial personal qualities are again stressed in Rebow's confidential letter to Brand urging Western's suitability for the Lord Lieutenancy (see Appendix A).[50]

6 — *The Sinews of War*

The language of the Page Wood archive is littered with the imagery of the hunting field and military conflict — two activities in which county gentry were well versed. Understandably for an electoral contest there is a preoccupation with the search for money — 'the sinews of political war'.

The correspondence begins in November 1864 when Western agreed — reluctantly according to his son — to be the Liberal candidate on condition that the party leaders should sign a 'guarantee' undertaking to meet all electoral expenses over £1,000 and to submit a requisition inviting him to stand signed by 2,000 electors. The former limited his own expenses to £1,000; the latter, hopefully, gave him a reasonable prospect of success. Western's desirability as a candidate enabled him to exact such severe conditions. Certainly he was deeply conscious of maintaining his dignity and his standing. As a result his candidature was almost still-born. He required his 'guarantee' by 10 December and, even when the date was extended to 31 December, Sir John Wood's insistence that a campaign fund of £2,000 over and above Western's £1,000 should be 'guaranteed' proved quite beyond Rebow's list of promised donations.[51] Sutton Western became quite hysterical, pleading that

'. . . in this critical state we may yet escape disaster . . . no one can compute the ruin to our party if we now give up, having gone so far, and having led the Tories to believe we are in earnest.'[52]

George Courtauld and George Vaizey both refused to sign the guarantee, leaving Rebow to salvage what was probably his own campaign, signing an effective blank cheque against Western's election expenses. Much followed from this.[53]

Rebow's list of £25 and £50 subscriptions makes interesting reading. It is a mixture of old and new money. Mrs Honeywood of Marks Hall, Fuller Maitland of Stansted, Lord Dacre, Brand's brother and next Lord Lieutenant of Essex, and Wingfield Digby, neither of them Essex residents, Colonel Western, the candidate's brother, Gurdon Rebow, Sir John Page Wood, the Vaizeys, uncle and nephew, Chichester Fortescue, on behalf of Lady Waldegrave, Sir Thomas Lennard, the High Sheriff, and Wingfield Baker, the South Essex Liberal candidate, all represented traditional landed wealth. There was a clutch of Quaker brewers and bankers in Robert Hanbury, Charles and Sir Fowell Buxton and Gibson of Saffron Walden. Commerce and trade was represented by the Courtaulds, Bagshaw, the developer of Dovercourt, Gurteen, the clothing manufacturer of Haverhill and Wells and Perry, the Chelmsford brewers and merchants, all Dissenters, as were Joseph Hardcastle and John Stuck Barnes, both political lawyers. Given the limited number of Whig landowners to call on, the reluctance to raise any general subscription is striking. Vaizey raised about £75 in smallish donations at Halstead, but that was all.[54]

In the event, £3,000 proved quite inadequate. Steele's position as agent was often undermined by Rebow's deep suspicion of his spending tendencies. As Steele pointed out:

'. . . if this battle is to be won, money will have to be *spent freely*, at the same time not recklessly.'[55]

Subsn at Braintree — Saturday Decr 16th/64

Mr. Gurdon St. Inns.t	✓	£50 __	✓
J. Bagshawe	✓	50 __	✓
Pattison	✓	25:—	✓
Sir J. B. Wood	✓	25:—	✓
W. Horner	✓	25:—	✓
Dixon	•	25:—	✓
S. Courtauld	✓	25:—	✓
Savill	✓	25.	✓
Barnes		25.	✓
M Braintree 28 Do.	)	£ 275:—	
Mr.S.D. Vaizey	✓	50.—	✓
J.R. Vaizey	✓	50 __	✓
Gunteen	✓	50.—	✓
Col. Western	✓	50.—	✓
Mr. Honywood		100.—	✓
		£ 575:—	

John Gurdon Rebow's handwritten list of targeted contributors to the Liberal cause in 1865.

The months following the triumph at the polls in July are marked in the Page Wood archive by acrimonious efforts to balance the books. The full Liberal expenses exceeded £4,000. Steele's salary for working full-time from February to August was £365 (including a £50 bonus for winning) while 50 guineas (£52.50p.) were paid to each District Agent. Such sums however pale beside £550 expended at Saffron Walden and £700 at Colchester and Thorpe. Some of this was for 'refreshments', often for a meal on the day of the poll, such as some leading Liberals provided at their own expense for an army of Liberal supporters. There is no doubt that some expenses fell on public houses, though less than appears to have been normal in most borough constituencies.[56]

The meetings of the North Essex Election Liberal Finance Committee in August included several new faces: Mr Gurteen of Haverhill, Mr Smith of Pattiswick Hall, Mr Villiers Fowke, when it was learnt they might make financial contributions.[57] Gurdon Rebow went through the unsavoury process of asking the initial £25 and £50 subscribers for a second contribution — which was not always well received. Sutton Western thought of a few more names, speculating that

> 'Dixon might be able to get something more out of old Sam Courtauld and other rich men . . . but of course we must not descend too low . . .'[58]

The correspondence peters out in November 1865 with the Committee still almost £1,000 short, a sum for which Rebow was technically liable, but which, for the time being, Sir Thomas Western had met. As Barnes wrote reassuringly to Rebow:

> 'Mr. Sutton Western asked me how I supposed this amount might be raised. I told him . . . Sir Thomas must pay £500 and we must endeavour to obtain the balance. He seemed to fall in with this and . . . hinted Sir Thomas would not hold you personally to your guarantee, but the party. You must press Brand for £200 more . . .'[59]

The Finance Committee had another concern — that the Conservatives would present a petition against Western's election on grounds of electoral malpractice. For this reason many suspect bills were not paid until the requisite six month period passed in February 1866. By then Sir Charles Page Wood was dying. The archive includes his last letter, committing the election papers to Rebow. There was no Conservative petition.

Despite the traditional problems of paying the bills, it is hard to suggest on the basis of the 1865 contest that electioneering after 1832 cost any Essex family its fortune. Western had an annual rental of £13,000, Rebow of almost £10,000. It seems unlikely on the figures that either man spent more than £2,000 in 1865. Their real financial crisis came after 1876 with the catastrophic decline of agriculture.[60]

The 1865 North Essex victory was thus almost the last hurrah for Essex Whiggery and for three of its elder statesmen: Sir Thomas Western, aged 70, dignified but hesitant, depended on Wood, his sitting tenant at Rivenhall Place, for his election addresses, his speeches, his strategy. He lost his hard-won seat three years later in the general election of 1868, becoming soon afterwards Lord Lieutenant of Essex. Gurdon Rebow, aged 66, was made of sterner stuff, a no-nonsense, focused politician, without whom there might have been no Liberal challenge in 1865. The Revd. Sir Charles Page Wood, aged 69, emerges from these letters as the most attractive figure: witty, equable, respected and disinterested — there was nothing in it for him except duty to his party. He too died before the eclipse of Essex Whiggery. Charles du Cane became Governor of Tasmania in 1869. Of the 'coming men' Strutt had a distinguished scientific career ahead and Ruggles-Brise a seat in Parliament. Sutton Western never returned to the House; in 1883 the Western estate went into bankruptcy.

Appendix A

Letter of John Gurdon Rebow to Henry Brand, Chief Whip.

Honourable H Brand M.P.   **Private**
26 July 1865

I am just returned from the Treasury where I intercepted your letter to me of yesterday — singular enough I walked down St. James' Street on my way to the House with your brother[61] and we there had a conversation together on the subject of your letter & I can only repeat what I said to him that if he will accept the Ld. Lcy. of Essex & will appoint Western as his Vice Lt., I am sure it will give general satisfaction to the County. By both political parties Western is considered one of the leading residents in the Cy.[County], and by our side the chief of the Liberal Party both from personal character, social position, property & residence amongst us — Indeed I have no hesitation in saying that were he a Peer instead of only a Commoner no person of either political party in the Cy. wd. name any other person for a Liberal govt. to appoint to the Ld. Lietcy. Amongst the Commoners he stands second, if not first, in point of property. He has ever since Ld. W.'s death taken a leading part in Cy. business & indeed before he succeeded Ld. W.[62] He is thoroughly up to the business of the Cy. & is generally looked up to and respected by all Classes in the Cy. — I therefore confidently repeat to you what I stated to Dacre, that if the arrangement suggested be carried out, I am positive the appointment will give general satisfaction. I may add here in reference to property and status in the Cy, I consider Western quite equal to Ld. Braybrook's (in Essex) and much larger than Ld. Rayleigh's — Ld. Cowley's[63] is the largest (but said to be mortgaged up to the hilt), then Ld. Petre's — next W. Tufnell's (the leader of the Tory Party amongst the Commoners) then Western's. Furthermore Ld. P.[64] cannot have a stronger confirmation of his popularity than his winning the N.E. Election last week. No other man on our side of the question could have done it — Both sides have publicly borne witness to the fact.

Ever Yours,

J.G.R.

I shall remain in Eaton Squ. till the end of the week & will call again on Saturday, if I stay over that day.

This letter represents a salvage operation in the bid to secure the Lord Lieutenancy of Essex for Western. Five days after the election victory Rebow wrote to Wood from London, 'nothing positive on who is the new Ld. Lieutenant, but our new M.P. is favourite at the clubs . . .'. Later that day, Rebow learnt from Brand's letter that the post was to go to Lord Dacre (a Hertfordshire resident and Brand's brother), apparently because Lord Palmerston did not wish to see the office held by a Commoner. By securing the Vice-Lieutenancy for Western, Rebow ensured his success next time round. The letter is valuable for setting out that mix of property, status, competence and popularity that was expected of the post holder.

REFERENCES

This essay should be read in conjunction with my article 'Four Colchester Elections: Voting Behaviour in a Victorian Market Town' in K. Neale, ed., *An Essex Tribute*, 1987, pp.199–227.

1 The Revd. Sir John Page Wood was father to two celebrated Victorians. His son was General Sir Evelyn Wood, V.C. [see I. Robertson, 'Essex-born Victoria Cross Winners', in K. Neale, ed., *Essex Heritage*, 1992, pp.319–24]; his daughter, Katherine, as Kitty O'Shea, was involved in the celebrated divorce scandal with Charles Stuart Parnell, the Irish leader.

    The 1865 election papers are held by E.R.O. Accession C47: Rebow Papers, Box 5. I have listed individual letters by date. Thus 'Rebow to Wood 12.2.65' is a letter from Rebow to Wood dated 12 February 1865.

2 *Essex Standard* (*E.S.*) 26.8.1864; Steele to Wood 13.11.65.

3 See *Essex Telegraph* (*E.T.*) and *E.S.* 25.2.65 to 15.3.65.

4 *E.S.* 26.7.65.

5 H. J. Hanham, *Elections and Party Management: Politics in the time of Gladstone and Disraeli*, 1959, Part 1.

6 Calculated from the final poll in *Essex and West Suffolk Gazette* (*E.G.*) 28.7.65 to 11.8.65.

7 Sutton Western to Rebow 23.12.64.

8 Calculated from J. Bateman, *The Modern Domesday Book*, 1876. Three of the wealthiest were effectively ineligible: Mrs Honeywood, a widow, Lord Petre, a Catholic, and three-year-old Frances Maynard (the future Lady Warwick), a minor.

9 *E.S.* 17.3.65.

10 Sutton Western to Wood 8.2.65.

11 Beresford to Wood N.D. (prob. 13.2.65). For the relevance of King Ahaziah see 2 Kings 9.23.

12 *E.S.* 26.7.65.

13 *E.S.* and *E.T.* 25.2.65 to 15.3.65.

14 *E.S.* 31.3.65; Ambrose to Wood 31.3.65.

15 Sutton Western to Wood 29.8.65.

16 Calculated from White's Directory of 1863.

17 From a confidential report commissioned by the National Reform League: Howell Collection, Bishopsgate Institute, London.

18 E. J. T. Collins, 'Did Mid-Victorian Agriculture Fail?', *ReFRESH* 21, Autumn 1995.

19 Sutton Western to Wood 30.11.64.

20 *E.S.* and *E.T.* 14.2.65 to 15.3.65.

21 E.R.O., Rebow Papers, Box 5.

22 S. Courtauld to Rebow 19.12.64; For Courtauld's role in Nonconformist politics see D. C. Coleman, *Courtaulds: An Economic and Social History*, vol. 1, 1969, pp.217–22.

23 J. Vincent, *The Formation of the British Liberal Party*, Penguin Edition, 1972, p.105.

24 Rebow to Wood 28.12.64. Sir Henry Brand 1814–92 (later Viscount Hampdon and Lord Dacre) was a significant parliamentary figure: successively Parliamentary Secretary to the Treasury, Liberal Chief Whip and Speaker of the House of Commons.

25 Barnes to Rebow 16.11.65.

26 Rebow to Wood 12.12.64.

27 Rebow to Wood 26.7.65.

28 Vincent, *op. cit.*, pp.120–25.

29 *E.S.* 17.3.65; Rebow to Wood 14.5.65; Steele to Wood 13.11.65.

30 *E.S.* 9.9.64.

31 Calculations from 1865 poll in *E.G.* 28.7.65 to 11.8.65.

32 Calculations from 1865 *Gazette* poll and local directories.

33 Hanham, *op. cit.*, p.13.

34 Calculations from 1865 *Gazette* poll and local directories.

35 *Ibid.*

36 *Ibid.*

37 Sutton Western to Wood 13.4.65.

38 Rebow to Wood 2.1.65; On the question of the politically-motivated eviction of tenants in North Essex see Coleman, *op. cit.*, pp.221–22.

39 Calculations from 1865 *Gazette* poll; Watson to Wood 22.7.65.

40 Hanham, *op. cit.*, p.13.

41 Roberts to Rebow 27.1.65; Rebow to Vaizey 22.12.64.

42 Steele to Wood 28.2.65.

43 Thurgood to Wood 15.2.65.

44 Steele to Wood 11.6.65; *E.S.* 26.7.65; Watson to Wood 22.7.65.

45 Calculated from the *Essex and West Suffolk Gazette* poll. The official poll result gives a larger anti-Beresford vote.

46 Calculated from 1865 *Gazette* poll and local directories.

47 *Ibid.* On 'plumping' and 'splitting' see Phillips, *op. cit.*, pp.209–11.

48 Calculated from 1865 polls for Colchester and for North Essex. On the Colchester Election of 1865 see Phillips, *op.cit.*, pp.199–227.

49 Ambrose to Rebow 16.3.65.

50 Draft letter in Box 5, Rebow Papers.

51 See 15 letters between Rebow, Wood, Vaizey and Sutton Western.

52 Sutton Western to Rebow 23.12.64.

53 G. Courtauld to Wood 30.12.64; Vaizey to Rebow 30.12.64; Rebow to Wood 31.12.64.

54 See manuscript lists drawn up by Rebow in Box 5, Rebow Papers.

55 Steele to Wood 16.4.65.

56 The full Liberal expenses are hard to calculate. While only £3,946 was declared, a figure well over £4,000 is certain. See Rebow to Wood 22.8.65, 20.9.65, 22.9.65.; *E.S.* 6.10.65.

57 Steele to Wood 27.8.65.

58 Sutton Western to Rebow 29.8.65.

59 Barnes to Rebow 16.11.65.

60 Calculated from J. Bateman, *The Modern Domesday*, *op. cit.* The calculation presumes Rebow paid his election expenses at Colchester (£900) in full.

61 Brand's elder brother was the 22nd Lord Dacre.

62 Sir Thomas Western succeeded his cousin, Charles Callis Western, M.P., who was created a baron in 1833. The title became extinct on his death in 1844.
63 This interesting claim contradicts the 1871 'Modern Domesday'. The largest Essex landowner was Earl Cowper — did Rebow confuse the two names?
64 Lord Palmerston, the Prime Minister.

Family History in Essex Today

D. W. GRIMES

Having celebrated the 21st anniversary of its foundation in May 1995 the Essex Society for Family History looks forward with enthusiasm to the future.

As the largest voluntary society in Essex the society welcomes the continuous support of the national Public Record Office and the County Record Offices throughout the country who have responded magnificently to the interest shown by the large numbers of family historians who now form the largest group of researchers using their facilities. Within the county the Essex Society for Family History is proud of the close relations it enjoys with the Essex Record Office and the educational and publishing projects arising from this collaboration.

Previously thought of by many as an occupation for old gentlemen working in hushed solemnity, family history is a dynamic hobby for a wide range of people, and not only those whose life-styles have arisen from inheritance. Of course public interest is still aroused by reports of the lineage of long-established families both famous and infamous, but, by and large the great surge of interest experienced over the past 21 years has arisen from people who would not expect their ancestors to appear in history as taught.

Greater leisure time in pleasant surroundings plus the availability of birth, marriage and death records back to 1837 and the census returns unfolding under the hundred year rule may go some way to explain the change from latent to active interest. Thus in 1974 when John Rayment announced to the people of Essex that it was intended to form a county family history society he was surprised by the number of enthusiasts who attended the inaugural meeting and combined to give the Society a flying start by choosing him as the first Chairman.

John Rayment, later to become a Fellow of the Society of Genealogists, earned his daily bread as an engineer and whilst he had an engineer's concern for accuracy and precise documentation he was certainly no dry-as-dust researcher but was endowed with a deliciously wicked sense of humour. He was definitely of the new wave.

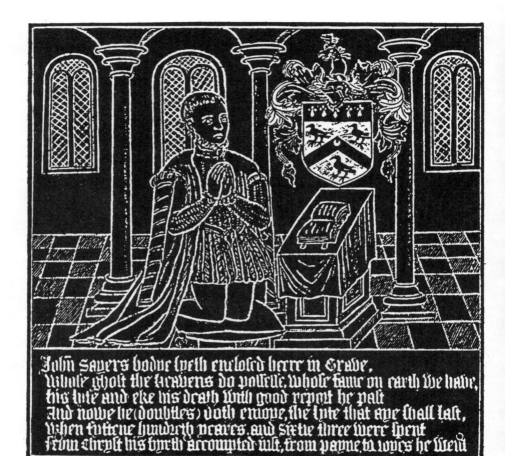

Brasses and other monumental inscriptions are a rich source of genealogical information and of considerable artistic interest. This, of John Sayer, 1563 is from St. Peter's, Colchester.

(Rubbing courtesy of H. Martin Stuchfield)

Open to all, the Essex Society for Family History soon brought together searchers from a wide range of occupations and disciplines all eager to learn and to use their personal skills to establish the Society as a social and knowledge centre for the family historian.

Generous assistance and guidance came from many distinguished lovers of all things Essex and helped push open the doors that were mostly already unlatched. Colonel Sir John Ruggles-Brise (then H.M. Lieutenant and Custos Rotulorum of the County of Essex), consented to become Patron, and the late Dr F. G. Emmison, President of the Society. Today, in 1995, our President is the avuncular L. D. Jarvis born in Stock but better known for his success in preserving the name of Middlesex.

John Rayment had not only launched the Essex Society but also the tradition of members freely giving their time to the aims he set out in the first issue of the magazine; 'to survey local sources of records, copy monumental inscriptions, transcribe parish registers, collect old documents and photographs, and generally finding out what's what and who's who, past and present'.

The new members went at their task with a great zest.

Supported by the encouragement of the late Dr Emmison and the ready assistance of his professionals at the Essex Record Office an excellent relationship soon developed between the Essex Record Office and the new Society whose members continue to spend many hours using the precious records. Goodness knows how these patient professionals really felt when confronted by the breed of hustling researchers used only to the rhythms of commerce and production who then invaded their world of scholarship and preservation largely bounded by legislation and local government finance. However, there is no doubt that the partnership has been a productive one, from the Essex marriage index compiled by Jack Baxter, to the recent joint publishing ventures and the joint promotion of the very successful course in Family History that was held in the Essex Record Office premises during 1994. The enthusiasm of Jack Baxter and his band of helpers knows no limits and he is now preparing an index of Essex burials whilst at the same time making a major contribution to the indexing of early Essex parish census records, the current joint venture between the Essex Record Office and the E.S.F.H.

Family history is of course chiefly concerned with the history of individuals and names provide the essential links for researchers. Lists of names are the raw material, starting with those gathered from the living memories of relatives and friends and then those found in the official and unofficial records of past times. Gossip and oral history is always with us and is not only diverting but can give a vivid insight into the way our forebears lived. As children people often get their first sense of the wider family through meeting the whole raft of aunts, uncles, nieces and cousins by the dozen, and then hold buried memories which can be prompted by children's curiosity or the interested inquiries of the family historian. In the past such knowledge of the family network and alliances could even be essential for survival during hard times. Women especially have an interest in

7

THE SOLDIER'S NEXT-OF-KIN NOW LIVING.

Any change becoming known is to be duly noted, with the date of such change.

Note.—No entry on this page has any legal effect as a Will.

Nearest degrees of relationship.		NAMES.	Latest known address to be given in full.
1st.	Wife.		
	Children.		
2nd.	Father.		
	Mother.		
3rd.	Brothers† and Sisters.		
	Nephews and nieces, if children of deceased brothers or sisters.		
4th.	Other relations. Uncle	C.G. Oxlee	Willow Villa, Oak Hollow (?), Wakes Hall E? Rd., Shoeburyness

Signature of Soldier: *J.C.A. Grimes*

Regimental number: 36760
Signature of Company, etc., Commander } *W.O. Angell ? Capt*
Date of Signature

† State whether brothers are younger or older.

6

SOLDIER'S NAME AND DESCRIPTION ON ATTESTATION.
(REGULAR FORCES).

Name: *John Arthur Grimes*
Enlisted at: *Shoeburyness*
in the County of: *Essex*
on the: *14th January 1912*
at the age of: *14* years *married*
for the: *RA (RGA)*
for *12* years in the Army and *—* years in the Reserve.
Born in the Parish of: *St. Andrews*
in or near the Town of: *Shoeburyness*
in the County of: *Essex*
Trade or calling: *None*
Last permanent residence:
Height: *4* feet *11* inches
Complexion: *Fresh*
Eyes: *Grey* Hair: *Brown*
Marks: *Nil*
* Religion: *Wesleyan*
† Signature of Soldier: *J.A. Grimes*

* This should be described under one of the following denominations, viz.,—"Church of England," "Presbyterian," "Wesleyan," "Baptist," or "Congregational," "other Protestant denomination" (name of denomination to be noted), "Roman Catholic, or "Jew."
† Whenever the soldier who cannot write makes his mark in acknowledgment of having received pay or allowances, &c., such mark is to be witnessed by the signature of a witness (other than the pay-serjeant).

Family archives will often provide detailed information, as does this page from a soldier's pay-book, not otherwise recoverable by research.

comparing their progress through the cycle of life with that of their relatives and friends and can frequently recall where 'Aunt Minnie's girl's son went to'. They can also confuse the paper researcher by their habit of returning to the family home for the birth of the first or even subsequent children and not being where it would be convenient to find them at that special time.

The preparation of lists and indexes is therefore the first essential step for any family historian, because in a sense if your name has not been recorded you do not exist and if your ancestors have not entered into records then the only proof that you have any is your existence. However, the purpose of the great mass of official records produced by officials of one body or another over the centuries has been to determine ownership, record spending, and punishments, or hateful as ever, to make an assesment of taxes due and paid.

Names there are bound to be but they need to be teased out of all the other information that the bureaucracy of the day strove to collect. Lists have been compiled from a great many sources and the beginner needs guidance to find the best sources if a lot of floundering about and duplication is to be avoided.

The keys to this problem are three. Firstly, the advice table which is always manned by an experienced member during the monthly meetings held at each of the five branches which meet in Chelmsford, Colchester, Saffron Walden, Southend and Harlow respectively on one afternoon or evening during the month. Secondly, the Branch bookstall which always has a large selection of booklets, maps and guides for sale at prices which do not plunder the pocket. Thirdly, the main printed and microfiche libraries of the Society. These libraries are held at the Chelmsford founding branch and are open to researchers during the Saturday of the Chelmsford meetings. The libraries hold not only such well known items as the International Genealogical Index published by the Church of Jesus Christ of Latter Day Saints but also copies of original research deposited by members, Society publications, and magazines published by other family history societies situated in the United Kingdom and overseas with whom the Society has an arrangement to exchange magazines. The library has grown from a modest start under the first librarian, Olwen Hall, to its present comprehensive coverage now in the care of Heather Bankowski and her team. Indeed the continual expansion of the holdings and usage is a credit to all involved.

Books, records and lists are then brought together in the production of the family tree enabling the detective work of cross indexing and the confirmation of each step back through the generations to be carried out. Assembling the genealogical jigsaw is a fascinating process abd it is not surprising that many remain hooked for life. Having satisfied their natural wish to discover their ancestry through the living memories of relatives and the record repositories, the family historian soon becomes aware that whilst the family tree shows the mechanics of descent something more is needed to make it come alive. Sometimes the memories of elderly relatives can chain back through parents and grandparents to events of 150 or more years ago and this with the aid of photographs, maps,

tithe records and books from the bookstalls or the postal book service enables
the bare bones of the family tree to be robed in the circumstances of their
own time.

In addition, the regular talks given at the branch meetings provide the
opportunity to marry a face to the name of the author of many of the books plus
the chance to seek the answer to some unsolved problem which even members of
long standing are likely to have tucked away. The talks are not only given by 'the
distinguished visiting expert' for the Society has many members who are walking
repositories of knowledge and are at the same time witty and entertaining
speakers. All those willing to share their knowledge with others are encouraged
to do so. Clayton Lewis and Geoffrey Howlett are amongst those who have
shared their specialist knowledge with delighted audiences. The monthly
meetings also enable members to compare the varied techniques used to record
the results of their researches including the latest ideas in moving from manual
methods to the use of computers.

Under the chairmanship of Colin Smith the E.S.F.H. Computer Group meets
at Chelmsford during the morning of the monthly meeting and has an active
programme which covers all aspects of the application of computers in the study
of family history and especially welcomes those who are considering the purchase
of a computer for their own use.

All members are kept abreast of these activities through the publication of the
Society's quarterly journal *The Essex Family Historian* which always contains
interesting reports from members. All succeeding editors have sought to emulate
the high professional standards set by Margaret Baker from the first issue in
1974 to no. 26 in 1982 and the current editions are a credit to the present editor
Mike Coombe and the Society's printers.

In the wider scheme of things Geoffrey Howlett organized on behalf of the
E.S.F.H. the indexing of the Essex parishes covered by the 1881 census as part of
the indexing of the complete 1881 census; a joint project of the Church of Jesus
Christ of Latter Day Saints, the Federation of Family History Societies and the
Public Record Office. Maureen Miller prepared the returns of members'
interests for inclusion in 'Big R' the Federation of Family History Societies project
for a national record of members' interests and Margaret Baker continues to use
her expertise in supervising the E.S.F.H. publications in microfiche format.

There is much still to be done and the E.S.F.H. always welcomes volunteers
upon whom the promotion and completion of projects depends, whilst being
keenly aware of the continuing assistance it receives from the E.R.O. The
E.S.F.H. offers a warm welcome and friendship and encourages all family
historians to carry the work forward, for great though the use of official records
has been to produce all kinds of lists and background knowledge there are
literally tonnes of records still awaiting analysis and family historians are well
placed to carry out the task and to make use of the results which are
produced.

Establishing the particular remains the essential step for family historians closely followed by the process of clothing the skeleton through the knowledge of how ancestors earned their daily bread and the general social milieu in which they lived. Enthusiasts such as Jack Baxter, Janette Scarborough, Michael Ginn, and Gwen Rawlingson whose idea of heaven is to extract a list of names from dusty manuscripts, or record burial headstones on a summer's day have helped many by placing their original research in the library but more is always welcome. Original research is augmented by a programme to publish under the E.S.F.H. imprint microfiche copies of Essex Directories, plus the recent purchase of the St. Catherine's House Birth, Marriage and Death Indexes which are held on behalf of the Society by John and Brenda Leach.

The E.S.F.H. and the Federation of Family History Societies, of which it was an early member, exists to provide a friendly social environment in which interested family historians can meet together to help one another in researching their families. Help for the voluntary organizers of groups is to be found in the publications and through the seminars organized by the Federation of Family History Societies based upon experience gathered over the past 21 years. Notable publications have included *Notes on the Recording of Monumental Inscriptions* written by the late John Rayment and later revised by Margaret Baker; *The Census and How to Use it* by the late John Boreham, and *How to Run a Family History Bookstall* by Mrs Pat Lewis.

Of course family history does not begin and end with those who join societies. Essex has a long history of people who prefer to be robustly independent and there are many who continue to do their own thing. All researchers, whether Society members or otherwise, are sure of a warm welcome at the Essex Record Office which is currently updating its procedures and thus improving access to the considerable and growing store of records held at the Chelmsford headquarters and at branch offices located in Southend and Colchester. Guidance in the use of the Diocesan, Essex County Council, and Essex Civil and Industrial records is generously given to the newest and experienced researcher alike. Further help is available from the network of Essex County Libraries who have responded to the upsurge of interest in local history and personalities by setting up local studies sections in most of their neighbourhood libraries.

The general public and Society members unable to attend one of the monthly meetings held at each of the branches of the Society meeting in Chelmsford, Colchester, Saffron Walden, Southend or Harlow can purchase the Society's publications and other books from the postal book service operated by yet another stalwart of the Society, Bob Henrys of Ingatestone.

To stimulate the interest of non-members the E.S.F.H. with the co-operation of the Essex Library Service places exhibitions in local libraries, and with the help of local newspapers publishes notices of future meetings, notices and reports of the proceedings. However the Society is the Essex focus of family historians with members living not only in Essex and throughout the U.K. but also in Canada, Australia, New Zealand and the U.S.A.

Janus, like the Society, looks both ways to a future provided with more and better lists compiled with and available through advancing technology, and to the past for greater knowledge and a sense of continuity.

Brickmaking in Essex

ADRIAN CORDER-BIRCH

THIS TREATISE which I present to a good friend and much respected resident of Essex is appropriate, as his home is one of the most interesting examples of Elizabethan brickwork in the county. Spains Hall was built about 1570, with later additions, all in brick, which blend in well with the original Tudor work. The seven gables, two large, five small, of the south-west elevation, make this one of the most visually attractive of sixteenth century mansions. Even the garden has some brick walls of *c.*1600; one with a large brick coping. Spains Hall is one of many large brick edifices in the county. This essay examines not only why the use of brick was so prolific in Essex, but also the history of the brickmaking industry and why it was carried out on a more extensive scale here than in many other counties of the British Isles.

As brick is the oldest manufactured building material, much of its history has, unfortunately, been lost in antiquity. The definition of brick is a moulded block of clay which is sun-dried or fired for use as a building material and was described by Dr Birch as:

> '. . . classed amongst the earlier inventions of the arts; and has descended, with various modifications, from the building of the Tower of Babel to the present day.'[1]

Brickmaking is one of the oldest crafts in the world with the earliest sun-dried mud bricks made in the Middle East over 10,000 years ago. However, it was the Romans who first introduced the craft to England well before the end of the first century A.D. They made tile-like bricks of various sizes, both oblong and square from 9in. × 9in. × 2in. to 24in. × 24in. × 2in. and floor bricks 6in. × 3in. × 1in. These large thin bricks have been found at all locations in Essex known to have had Roman settlements. They were fired in clamps (or possibly kilns), sites of which have been found in Essex, particularly around Colchester.

Unfortunately there is little evidence of Roman brick kilns compared with the large number of Roman pottery kilns which have been found. The likely explanation for this is that the majority of Roman bricks were fired in clamps and not kilns. Two possible sites for Roman brick clamps are near Serpentine Walk, Colchester and close to the church at West Mersea.[2] The main brickfields which

433

supplied the majority of tiles used in Roman Colchester lie to the west of Sheepen Farm.[3] Roman tile kilns were excavated at Lexden in 1970 and at Mount Bures in 1971. There were also tile kilns at Alphamstone, Braintree, Theydon Garnon and a group of kilns at Great Braxted. One of the best monuments from Roman Britain is the Balkerne Gate at Colchester which includes much Roman brick. The thickest known Roman brick recorded in Britain is from Chignall St. James which measures as much as 4 inches thick.[4]

Later builders, particularly during Saxon, Norman and Medieval periods, salvaged Roman bricks and tiles from the ruins of their buildings. They were re-used and can be found in no less than 106 Essex churches which is far more than any other county. Those of particular interest include Holy Trinity, Colchester; St. Peter-on-the-Wall, Bradwell; St. Mary the Virgin, Broomfield and St. Augustine of Canterbury, Birdbrook, where the Normans laid several courses of re-used Roman bricks in a herring-bone pattern in the north wall. Thin Roman bricks were incorporated into St. Botolph's Priory, Colchester, which was constructed during the late eleventh century.

It is not only ecclesiastical buildings in Essex that contain Roman brick but also walls such as those around Colchester, Bradwell and Great Chesterford, the latter now sadly demolished. In addition, the Norman keep at Colchester (the largest Norman keep in England) contains a large quantity of Roman brick, which has also been found on the castle mound at Ongar.

After the Roman period, brickmaking in this country lapsed until Essex and Suffolk pioneered in reviving the industry. One of, or possibly the earliest 'all English' brickwork in this country is to be found in the abbot's lodging and guest house at Little Coggeshall built about 1190 followed by the nearby St. Nicholas' Chapel, built about 1225 which contains brick dressings to the windows and brick quoins. These bricks were all made on the site.

Although 'Great Bricks' (large thin bricks e.g. 11in. × 12in. × 2in.) were used infrequently in Medieval England, examples can be found at the Waltham Abbey Gatehouse, built about 1370, where they were used as voussoirs.

'Red brick church towers remain the county's most impressive architectural feature . . .'[5] There are about 45 such churches in Essex which is far more than in any other county. There are also many churches with red brick chancels, chapels, porches, stair turrets, battlements, window mullions, quoins and even all brick churches such as East Horndon, Ingrave, North Fambridge, Theydon Mount, Woodham Walter, Wanstead, Shellow Bowells, Layer Marney and Chignal Smealy often called 'Brick' Smealy. The principal reason for the extensive use of brick in Essex was a combination of the lack of natural building stone and a considerable quantity of good brick earth stretching right across the county. Brick has since been used for its own merits, quality, strength (e.g. quoins and mullions) and decorative features. It was also relatively cheap compared with stone and more durable than wood. Some churches, including Layer Marney and Ingatestone, contain diaper work where the red brick is relieved by a pattern in dark grey, black or blue bricks. These grey, black or blue bricks were the result of firing with wood where the bricks came into direct contact with the wood fire and turned out a much darker colour than the other bricks. The use of coal for firing bricks was not readily available until transportation improved, initially by barge and later by rail.

It was not only Essex churches which were built in brick, but also large houses from the Medieval period to the present time. Those built in red brick (not all surviving) include:

Moynes Park, Steeple Bumpstead — fifteenth century with front built in 1580.

Faulkbourne Hall — a remarkable example of fifteenth century brickwork but the front was reconstructed in 1832.

Heron Hall, East Horndon — *c.*1460.

Nether Hall, Roydon — *c.*1470.

Horham Hall, Thaxted — built about 1505. It was owned by the Smijth family (who were ancestors of Colonel Sir John Ruggles-Brise) from 1617 until the death of Revd. Sir Edward Bowyer-Smijth, Bt., in 1850. He had altered and modernized the building in 1841.

St. Osyth Priory — very early sixteenth century.

Layer Marney Tower — 1520.

Quendon Hall — 1540.

Hill Hall, Theydon Mount — 1548 but was converted to a classical building between 1713 and 1719. It was once the home of Sir William Bowyer-Smith, M.P., an ancestor of Colonel Sir John Ruggles-Brise.

Gosfield Hall — *c.*1550 with later additions and alterations.

Ingatestone Hall — mid sixteenth century.

Leez Priory, Little Leighs — sixteenth century.

Spains Hall, Finchingfield — *c.*1570.

Old Thorndon Hall, West Horndon — late sixteenth century.

Marks Hall, near Coggeshall — built in red brick in the Tudor style about 1609 and sadly demolished shortly after the Second World War.

Dynes Hall, Great Maplestead — designed in 1689 being an early example of the Queen Anne style of architecture.

Belchamp Hall, Belchamp Walter — Queen Anne.

Mansion House, Hedingham Castle — 1719.

Hallingbury Place — *c.*1730.

Kelvedon Hall.

Colne Priory, Earls Colne — cased with brick about early eighteenth century.

New Thorndon Hall, West Horndon — 1764–70.

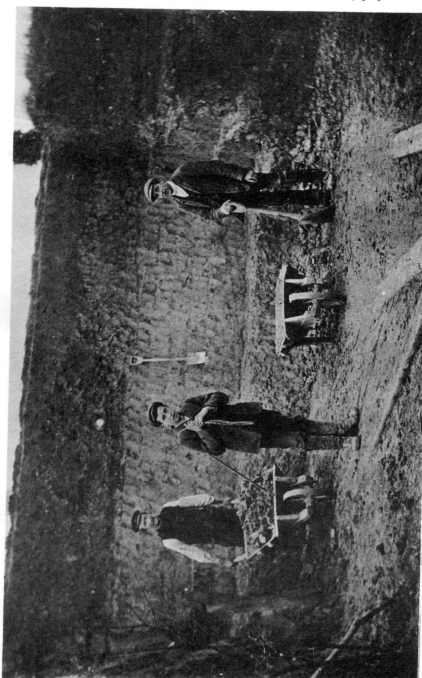

Digging clay, by hand, at Bulmer brickworks about 1910.

This is one of the last surviving brickworks in Essex where bricks are still made using the old traditional methods.

(Photograph courtesy of the late Harry and Lily Pinnissale)

Danbury Park — rebuilt 1832.

Stansted Hall, Stansted Mountfichet — 1875–76.

Berechurch Hall, near Colchester — built 1881–82 by Octavius Edward Coope, M.P., who was the maternal grandfather of Colonel Sir John Ruggles-Brise.

In addition there were a number of Essex houses built with white-brick including:

Braxted Park — mid seventeenth century.

Hylands, Chelmsford — 1738.

Stisted Hall — 1823.

Tendring Manor — 1824.

Terling Place.

Amongst other fine old brickwork in Essex is the early fifteenth century spiral stair in the Moot Hall at Maldon. One of the earliest and most splendid red brick bridges in the country, which was built in 1496, is at Hedingham Castle.

The bricks for these churches, houses and other buildings were made at or very close to the site where they were required. The owner or builder employed itinerant brickmakers to make the bricks for a particular building. The clay was dug on site, the bricks made, dried and fired, usually in an open clamp, and when sufficient were manufactured the brickmaker went to another site. The main reason for this was the poor transportation and roads or the cost of horse and cart. The sites used by early brickmakers can often be identified by ponds formed from the old clay pits and more commonly by field-names. In Essex almost every town and village has one or more field-names associated with brickmaking such as Brick Kiln Field, Brick Yard Piece, Clay Pit Meadow, Clamp Field and many other variations. In addition many road-names indicate the former existence of brickyards.

Some large estates had their own estate brickyard such as the Hedingham Castle Estate, Gosfield Hall, Marks Hall near Coggeshall, Mistley Hall, Boreham Hall and the Stansted and Birchanger Hall Estate Brick Works at Stansted Mountfitchet. These estate brickyards also sold bricks to the public as well as providing bricks for their estates. As late as 1937 the Easton Estate Brick Works were operating at Easton Lodge, Little Easton owned by Frances, Countess of Warwick.

It was not until the second half of the seventeenth century that some brick-yards became more permanent and kilns were erected. At about this time pug mills for mixing the clay were first introduced. By 1777 there were some thirteen brick kilns and a couple of tile kilns in Essex[6] This did not include sites where bricks were clamp fired or where there had been kilns which had fallen into disuse.

It is appropriate at this stage to define briefly how bricks were made and the difference between clamp and kiln firing.

Millbead Brickworks, Great Wakering.

Left to Right: *Tom Wiggins, Charles Wiggins, William Wiggins, Henry Barrel, George Adcock, George Wiggins, George Cox. The brickworks were owned by D. and C. Rutter who were brick and tile makers at Great Wakering by 1882. From 1894 Henry Juniper was their manager and by 1910 they were incorporated as D. and C. Rutter Limited in which name they continued until the First World War. The Wiggins family lived in 'Rutters Cottages', New Road, Great Wakering, which were built by Rutters for their workers.*

(Photograph, courtesy of Essex Re...

In the old traditional method bricks could only be made, dried and fired during the spring, summer and autumn when there was no risk of frost which would crack and break up a 'green' brick. During the winter months many men were laid off with no work, although a few were fortunate enough to find employment digging out clay (page 436) ready for the brick-making season. The clay was left in a heap to weather and when required the good clay, which was free from stones, was put through a pug-mill. Any clay which contained stones was either discarded or washed in a wash-mill amd later added to the other clay in the pug-mill. A pug-mill was a large stationary circular container with a central shaft, attached to which were a number of knives and as the shaft revolved, the knives rotated and cut and mixed the clay. Water was added to make the clay the correct consistency and the 'pug' as it then became known, was put on the brickmaker's table. On this table was a 'stock' board on top of which was a 'fillet' which formed the frog in the brick. The stock board kept the mould, a mere frame without top or bottom, in position. The mould was sanded or wetted, to prevent the pug adhering to the sides, and a warp of pug was then thrown by the brick-maker into the mould with some force to fill the corners. The surplus was then removed by pulling a wire or piece of wood across the top of the mould. The 'green' brick was then placed on a pallet board and onto a cradle barrow which held about 30 bricks (page 438). When the barrow was full it was wheeled away to the hacks (derived from 'hackstead' — a drying place for 'green' bricks). The hacks were rows of long low drying sheds consisting of a roof with no sides thus allowing the sun and wind to dry the bricks. After a few days the bricks were 'scintled', that is to say turned round so that the sun and wind could dry the other surfaces. When dry the bricks were put in kiln barrows and taken for firing. Whether fired in a clamp or kiln great care and skill was employed in stacking the dried bricks.

The clamp method of burning was widely used when brickmaking was carried out periodically and near to the building under construction. It saved the cost of constructing a kiln and had the advantage of firing a significantly larger quantity of bricks. The disadvantages were that there was more waste and pollution as the bricks were fired in the open. To build a clamp, a foundation layer of burnt bricks was laid on a piece of ground to provide an insulation from rising damp. The 'green' bricks were stacked above it and covered with combustible material, burnt bricks and earth. The clamp was then ignited by small fires started in special flues in the base. These in turn ignited the fuel mixed with the clay in the 'green' bricks. This process of burning often took several weeks before the clamp was allowed to burn itself out. Clamps were still in use in south Essex until the 1960s (page 440). These later clamps on permanent sites had specially constructed concrete bases.

From the late seventeenth century kilns became more common in Essex and were constructed with brick. Initially these kilns were 'up draught' kilns known as 'Suffolk' kilns which were square or rectangular in shape and had two chambers one above the other (page 440). The fire was in the lower chamber which contained

Hawkwell brickworks c.1955 *showing bricks having been fired in a clamp being removed for sale. The large cover in the background was mobile and could be wheeled along to cover the clamp. This brickworks was operated by the Staines family. Leslie Staines is standing on the clamp at the right and his father is standing behind the wheelbarrow on the left.*

(Photograph courtesy of Leslie Staines)

The Hedingham Brick and Tile works about 1895 showing bricks being loaded onto railway trucks on a siding from the Colne Valley and Halstead Railway. The kilns are 'up draught' kilns and the man on top of the kiln is John Corder (1863–1957) who was employed as burner there for over 50 years. His eldest son, Edward Corder, is on the left and the man with the bowler hat in the foreground is Daniel Cornish who was the manager of these brickworks for the proprietor, Mark Gentry.

(Photograph courtesy of the late Percy Corder)

The Sible Hedingham Red Brick Company Limited late 1940s showing Albert Redgewell, burner, firing the 'down draught' kilns. Some drying sheds are on the left and in the foreground newly fired bricks ready for delivery.

(Photograph courtesy of the late Albert Redgewell)

two to five fire holes or tunnels and the bricks were fired in the upper chamber hence the term 'up draught' meaning the bricks were fired with the heat rising. These kilns had one doorway and an open top. When loaded, the doorway was filled up with a few courses of old bricks which were temporarily daubed with clay paste or sand filling. The top was covered with layers of old bricks to protect the dried bricks below. The burners opened and closed the gaps between these old bricks to control the draught. This type of kiln was the most common in Essex and was in constant use in the majority of brickworks until the 1950s.

There were two other types of kilns to be found in Essex although not until the late nineteenth century and not so frequently. One was a 'down draught' kiln which was usually circular or 'beehive' shaped (although some were rectangular) with several furnaces around the outside (page 441). The heat rose to the centre and was drawn out through the bottom of the kiln along a tunnel and through a

The London Brick Company works at Great Bentley with Thorrington Creek in the foreground c.1910. The two Hoffmann kilns stand either side of the chimney with the drying sheds on the left. Some of the bricks made here were transported by barge via Flag Creek to the North Sea.
(Photograph courtesy of Alan Pryor)

tall chimney. The bricks were fired with the heat being drawn in a downwards direction hence a 'down draught' kiln. Three of these kilns were used at the Sible Hedingham Red Brick Company Limited and one is still in use at the Bulmer Brick and Tile Company Limited. In these 'down draught' kilns the bricks were fired more evenly than in the 'up draught' kilns The other kiln was a Hoffmann, named after its inventor, and was a continuous kiln divided up into several chambers in a circular or oval shape (page 442). Whilst some chambers were being fired others were being loaded or unloaded and the fire was directed around the kiln from chamber to chamber continuously. Although large and expensive to build these kilns were more economical to run as use could be made from surplus heat to dry bricks in adjoining chambers. There were two Hoffmann kilns at the London Brick Company works at Great Bentley, one at the Rayleigh Brick and Tile Works, one at the Harold Wood Brickworks and one at the W. H. Collier's works at Marks Tey, now all demolished. The present tunnel kiln at Marks Tey is now gas-fired and also makes use of surplus heat for drying as the bricks pass through the kiln on trucks.

As already indicated, bricks were fired with wood until transportation improved and coal became available in Essex. Wood firing a kiln containing up to 20,000 bricks took about a week compared with three or four days using coal and about double the weight in wood was required as compared with coal. Wood burning kilns required a larger flue to contain the bulkier fuel.

In April 1767, William Dennis, a Bocking brickmaker was sued by Jeremiah Scarf, a farmer of Gosfield, in the Exchequer Office of Pleas, London for the supply of 'kiln stuff' (loads of wood faggots and broom) for firing his kiln. Scarf supplied 13½ loads of kiln stuff comprising 60 faggots a load at 8s. 0d. and one load of broom at 10s. 0d. The Defendant brickmaker had made a payment on account and was sued for the balance. The Brief to Counsel for the Plaintiff is held in the Essex Record Office.[7]

As soon as the railways were constructed coal was delivered for firing the kilns. Acounts survive of the cost of coal delivered to William Corder of the Southey Green Brick, Tile and Pottery Works at Sible Hedingham in the 1860s. An example is:

'30th June, 1868 7 tons 12 cwt brights and carriage £6 17s. 9d.'

Among the Essex coal merchants were Thomas Moy Limited, R. A. Allen and Sons and Thomas Bradridge and Co. of which Edward Ruggles-Brise was a partner. In the 1930s the Essex Brick Co. Ltd. (formerly the Warley Brick and Tile Co. Ltd.) of Little Warley were using 3 cwt. of coal per 1,000 bricks in their three large Habla kilns of a nominal output each of 200,000 bricks weekly.[8] This coal consumption is very low compared with other Essex brickworks which were using about 8 cwt. per 1,000 bricks. In 1926 the brickworks of Beach and Son at Chelmsford successfully experimented with firing a 'down-draught' rectangular kiln, containing 38,000 bricks, with heavy oil.

To return to the history of brickmaking there was very little government control and until the late eighteenth century brickmakers and builders were usually left to their own devices. However in 1784 a brick tax was introduced which made two significant alterations; bricks became larger because the same tax was paid on a large brick as a small one and consequently larger bricks were made to avoid paying as much tax and tile-hung walls became popular since tiles escaped the tax. At this time ground floor walls of houses were usually built of brick with tiles being used for the walls of the first floor instead of bricks to avoid the tax. There are some houses in Bayley Street, Castle Hedingham where hanging tiles adorn the first floor.

The rate of duty in 1784 was 2s. 6d. a thousand on all bricks which increased to 4s. 0d. a thousand in 1794. However in 1803 tiles became taxed and bricks larger than 10in. × 3in. × 5in. paid double the tax. As a consequence the size settled down to 9in. × 4½in. × 3in. The rate in 1803 was 5s. 0d. for the smaller bricks, 10s. 0d. for the larger, 4s. 10d. for one thousand plain tiles and 12s. 10d. for one thousand pan or ridge tiles. In 1833 the duties on tiles were repealed and in 1835 the duty on bricks was raised to 5s. 10d. for a thousand common bricks. All taxes were abolished in 1850.

Within four years a Private Act of Parliament enabled Lord Petre 'To grant leases for making brick works'.[9]

When the brick tax was in existence there was an incentive to use stone where possible, but as there was very little stone available in Essex, there was a predominance of lathe and plaster and weather-boarding particularly among the smaller houses. Some bricks were used, for foundations and chimneys, but a complete brick house was the exception rather than the rule, unless expense was no object as with some larger houses. The use of brick increased slowly but steadily, parallel with growing prosperity and with consequent improvement in housing standards. The boom in brickmaking was created by the population explosion which followed the Industrial Revolution, the abolition of the brick tax and the construction of the railways to facilitate transportation. These factors led to an increase in established and extensive brick works with more permanent kilns and later, mechanized production processes.

The steady growth of the industry during the nineteenth century can be seen from the census records of persons engaged in brickmaking in Essex as follows:

1831	388
1871	860
1891	1207
1901	2136[10]

To the 1891 total of 1207 (which includes 2 females) must be added 26 for West Ham and 27 for Leyton.[11]

From about 1895 to 1905 between four and five hundred men were employed in the Hedinghams producing between ten and twelve million red facing bricks a year.[12] Of these nearly five million were manufactured by Mark Gentry whose Langthorne brickworks at Wethersfield Road, Sible Hedingham was one of the largest of its kind in the eastern counties.[13] The remainder were made by Thomas Moy Limited and William Rayner and Son at Castle Hedingham and Eli Cornish and William Corder at Sible Hedingham. Eli Cornish was proprietor of the Tortoise Brickworks and later the Hedingham Brick Company and made bricks for Colchester Town Hall and sixteen churches in north London. William Corder

The brickworks of W.H. Collier at Marks Tey about 1900.

This view shows three cradle barrows used for carrying 'green' bricks from the brickmaker's table to the backs. These barrows had special springs to minimize vibration. Some backs under which the bricks were dried can be seen in the background.

(Photograph courtesy of John Johnson)

was proprietor of the Southey Green Brick, Tile and Pottery Works at Sible Hedingham, the Potters Hall Brickworks at Great Yeldham and a brickworks off Park Hall Road, Gosfield.

Another major brickmaker in north Essex was William Collier at Marks Tey (page 445) whose works are still operating.

In south Essex there were also extensive brickworks particularly along the north bank of the river Thames. The population of South Shoebury increased from 158 in 1851 to 1080 in 1861 owing chiefly to the establishment of brickyards which employed over 400 hands making about 28 million bricks a year, mostly for London.[14] There were also a number of brickworks at Prittlewell, Great Wakering, Thorpe Bay, Rochford and Thundersley. Similarly, up river, there were more brickworks at Grays Thurrock and Tilbury.

An early brick and tile maker at Tilbury was author, Daniel Defoe (1661–1731), who established a brick and pantile works there in 1694. His tiles were reputed to be too porous to keep houses weatherproof. Dutch competition put him out of business and he is said to have lost £3,000 in the enterprise.[15]

Two hundred years later the industry was flourishing in nearby Grays Thurrock where the town was described as a scene of considerable traffic, especially in bricks and tiles of which large quantities were sent to London. A 200 foot long wooden pier, which was constructed in 1841 at a cost of £2,500, was later altered to serve as a wharf, where London and Gravesend steam vessels called several times a day.[16] It was not only from Grays Thurrock where bricks were transported by water but also from a number of other brickworks around the Essex coast and rivers. Messrs. Stockwell and Son of South Benfleet Brickfields had direct water carriage to Benfleet Creek.[17] The Hockley Brick, Tile and Pottery Works at Hullbridge near Hockley had an extensive frontage to the river Crouch giving facility for water carriage. When these works, which were owned by Alfred Hobman, were for sale in 1904 the advertisement included 'Jetty for barge loading' and 'cheap barge freights to London'.[18] D. and C. Rutter, brickmakers of Great Wakering (page 438) had their own fleet of sailing barges known as 'Rutters Pitch-piners'. They left, loaded with bricks, just before high tide to get maximum depth of water over the sand banks. They sailed out of Millhead and Potton Creeks, through Havengore (the bridge to Foulness not being built until 1926) and anchored off Southend pier for the flood tide to take them up to London.[19].

Further north, the London Brick Company works at Great Bentley transported bricks from Thorrington Creek and Flag Creek to the North Sea. Clifford White, a brickmaker at West Mersea also conveyed bricks by barge. On the Essex bank of the river Stour at Ballingdon were the large brickworks of Robert Allen and Sons who excavated the Ballingdon Cut to facilitate access to their works by barges from the river. The river Stour has been navigable since July, 1713, when the construction of fifteen locks and necessary clearance work was completed pursuant to the provisions of the River Stour Act, 1705. It therefore became one of the earliest rivers to be navigated and some of its early locks, barges and barge horses were accurately depicted in some of John Constable's well-known paintings. By 1817 there were 36 barges on the river of which three were owned by the Constable family of Dedham and six by Elliston Allen of Sudbury. In 1859 Allens were operating a fleet of 22 barges and by the end of the century were virtually in control of the navigation. Allens' brickworks at Ballingdon had commenced in 1812 and they later owned another brickworks at Bures Hamlet. At their peak they were employing about one hundred men in their brickworks. It was quite common for a small convoy of five or six river barges, loaded with bricks, to come down river and for their cargoes to be loaded by hand into one Thames barge at Mistley on the estuary of the river Stour. For the return journey the river barges carried coal for firing the kilns. During the eighteenth century coal was the principal cargo, carrying as much as 12,000 tons a year but in the nineteenth century the brick trade became very important. In the year ending April, 1864, nearly 3½ million bricks were carried along the river. Allens were makers of the well-known Suffolk white and red facing bricks and all kinds of ornamental bricks some of which were used in the construction of the Royal Albert Hall, South Kensington Museums and Liverpool Street Station. During the late nineteenth century the river traffic declined in favour of the railways but nevertheless the river was still used until the First World War to transport bricks, coal and other cargoes including malt, flour, maize, wheat, barley and oats.

When the railways were constructed throughout Essex immense numbers of bricks were required. A turnpike road bridge over a railway required 300,000 bricks and a railway tunnel 8,000 bricks for every yard of its length. Bricks were also required for station platforms, engine sheds and other railway buildings. The railways were very important customers of the brickmakers. Some railway contractors established their own brickworks along the routes of railways such as Thomas Brassey at Liston and William Munro at White Colne and Sible Hedingham.

The various railways throughout Essex derived considerable income from the carriage of bricks and many brickworks had sidings to nearby railways. The railway returns were a good indicator of the state of the brick trade. The weekly returns of the Colne Valley and Halstead Railway for 1897 reveal that it was a record year:

'. . . a large proportion of the increase being due to the development and extension of the brickmaking industry at Hedingham. . .'

The following year, railway chairman, W. Bailey Hawkins, stated in his half-yearly report:

'. . . that the brickworks traffic was going up by leaps and bounds. In 1887 the brick traffic from Hedingham was 5,000 tons a year and in 1898 it was 20,000 tons which was expected to double in a year or two . . .'[20]

By 1901 between 30 and 40 truck loads of bricks were despatched from Hedingham daily by rail and special 'brick' trains provided. The railway ordered 20 more waggons but they were not sufficient and the Directors had to consider if they could obtain more. The Great Eastern Railway had helped the Colne Valley and Halstead Railway as far as they could but they were also short of rolling stock.[21] For some years the railway had not been able to cope with the extent of the 'brick traffic' and therefore the Hedingham brickmakers supported the proposed construction of the Central Essex Light Railway from Ongar to Sible Hedingham which would have provided a more direct route to London.

In 1898 a public inquiry was held in Sible Hedingham into this and other proposed light railways for north Essex. All schemes were especially planned to include as many brickworks as possible along their routes. The Central Essex Light Railway was approved but it was not until 1914 that it was finally decided to commence construction but because of the First World War the building was initially deferred and later abandoned.[22] One Hedingham brickmaker who supported the proposed light railway was Mark Gentry who in giving evidence stated that he sold bricks all over England and even exported bricks to Ireland, Egypt and Africa.

Mark Gentry, who was Chairman of the Institute of Clayworkers in 1903, applied for several patents over the years for improvements in brickmaking processes, drying and burning bricks. Perhaps the most successful was his patent power sand-faced brick press which was manufactured by Thomas C. Fawcett of Leeds. Daniel Cornish of the Shenfield and Hutton brickworks (formerly of Sible Hedingham) (page 440) was in 1899 patentee of a tool to frog wire cut bricks. The Manor Brickworks Limited of Thundersley, for which Edward Corder was the manager, took out a patent on a new roofing tile in 1910. George Warren of Wickford had English and Canadian patents for his 'Perfected' kiln for best facing bricks and Arthur Brown, B.Sc., of Chelmsford, was very successful with his patent continuous kilns which were being erected in England, France and Belgium in 1905. In addition to Chelmsford, Brown also owned brickworks in Braintree, Boreham, Brentwood and Upminster. He lectured and was the author of a number of books and articles about brickmaking.

Throughout this century the industry in Essex has gradually declined. From mid 1904 there was a depression in the building industry leading to a number of brickworks closing down between 1906 and 1911 when prices became ruinously low. By 1914 the trade was improving with more demand for clay goods but unfortunately the shortage of men during the First World War led to the closure of more brickworks. There was a revival after the war but by the mid 1920s concern was expressed to the Government about the quantity of bricks being imported, even through Essex ports. From January to August, 1926, imports of bricks totalled 143,260,000 of which 391,000 were through Colchester, 287,000 Harwich and 120,581,000 London.[23] Throughout 1926 no less than 5,663,000 bricks were landed at Southend. The Southend-on-Sea Estates Co. Ltd. (who were associated with Milton Hall (Southend) Brick Co. Ltd.) kept a record of bricks landed at the Southend loading pier.[24]

The Second World War saw the closure of more brickworks due to loss of manpower and also to lighting restrictions. Those brickworks with 'up draught' kilns were forced to close for the duration of the war although 'down draught' kilns continued to be fired as they could be adequately covered to prevent enemy aircraft seeing the fires at night. Many brickworks re-opened in 1945–46 to meet the demand for bricks for rebuilding and new houses after the war. Several of these works closed down during the 1950s since when each decade has seen the closure of the remaining brickworks except for W. H. Collier Limited at Marks Tey (page 445) and the Bulmer Brick and Tile Company Limited (page 436) which both continue to make hand-made bricks. In addition Butterley Brick Limited still manufacture bricks at their Star Lane brickworks at Great Wakering.

It is sad to recall that the once flourishing brickmaking industry in Essex has almost disappeared. It was once a large employer and an important feature of many of our towns and villages where the only remaining signs of this once extensive industry are derelict sheds and kilns, overgrown clay pits and buildings constructed with 'Essex' bricks. The county should be justly proud of its large quantity of predominately red brick buildings, from various periods to the present day. Of these, Spains Hall, is one of the most outstanding.

REFERENCES

1 Dora Lunn, *Pottery in the making*, 1931, seventh ed., 1961, p.32.
2 H. Laver, 'Discovery of a supposed Roman Brick Kiln near Serpentine Walk, Colchester', *Transactions of the Essex Archaeological Society*, 1907, vol. X, p.325.
3 *V.C.H. Essex*, III, 1963, reprinted 1977, p.113.
4 G. Brodribb, *Roman Brick and Tile*, 1987, p.43.
5 W. Addison, 'The making of the Essex Landscape', *An Essex Tribute*, 1987, p.54.
6 *Chapman and André, Map of Essex*, 1777.
7 E.R.O., D/DO B 24/60.
8 *The British Clayworker*, August, 1937, p.147.
9 1854, 17, *Vic. C.33.* — William Bernard Petre, 12th Baron.
10 *V.C.H. Essex*, II, 1907, p.457.
11 *The British Clayworker*, November, 1893, p.165.
12 *Halstead Gazette*, 17 November, 1939, p.5.
13 *The Brickbuilder*, April, 1898, p.ii.
14 *Whites Directory of Essex*, 1863, pp.403–04.
15 Sir William Addison, *Essex Worthies*, 1973, p.57.
16 *Whites Directory of Essex*, 1863, p.581.

17 *The British Clayworker*, August, 1905, p.168.
18 *The British Clayworker*, July, 1904, p.136.
19 Information courtesy of Gwen Rawlingson.
20 *East Essex and Halstead Times*, 3 September, 1898.
21 A. Corder-Birch, 'The Hedingham Brick Industry and the Colne Valley and Halstead Railway', *Colne Valley Newsline*, No. 1, 1985.
22 A. Corder-Birch, 'Proposed Light Railways for North Essex', *Colne Valley Newsline*, No. 5, 1986.
23 *The British Clayworker*, October, 1926, pp.190–1.
24 *The British Clayworker*, July, 1927, p.114.

'Full of profitable thinges'

KENNETH NEALE

SINCE THE SUB-TITLING of this book relies on a quotation from John Norden's *Description of Essex* it is owed to his tradition and the readership to offer at least a brief account of the man and his work, as a postscript to this compilation of 'profitable thinges'.[1] The work of John Norden the elder, so far as it concerns Essex, is generally familiar to local historians and his famous *Description* of 1594 is frequently quoted for its informative and enjoyable text. Biographical knowledge of the cartographer and his family is inadequate and not always reliable. The importance of his role in the technical development of cartography is rarely acknowledged except among experts in that field. Stuart Mason, to whom I am indebted for advice on Essex cartography, is one such and his essay in this book and his other studies[2] put Norden and his art into an appropriate perspective. Primarily, Norden was in business as a professional map-maker, but the breadth of his versatile and enquiring mind has endowed county history with valuable insights into late sixteenth century Essex.

The man and his maps

John Norden was born in 1548 in the west country, probably Somerset, into what has been described as a 'genteel' family. Nothing is known of his childhood but he was admitted to Hart Hall at Oxford University as a Commoner in 1564. He graduated in 1568 and gained a master's degree in 1572. He turned to the legal profession as a career, but his deep interest in history and topography eventually prevailed. He associated with the celebrated antiquary William Camden and is said to have been encouraged by him to co-operate in the publication of a complete series of county histories. Certainly, by 1590 he was planning a range of county surveys for the use of travellers who at that time had no convenient maps.[3]

In 1593 he was authorized by the Privy Council to undertake comprehensive county surveys and the Lieutenants of the English counties were invited to facilitate his travel and work. Sadly, official support was limited to that and no financial resources were made available. Having, unlike Saxton, no patron, he

451

John Norden
(Photograph courtesy of *Essex Review*, vol. IX, pl.v)

became bitter and complaining about lack of support. However, the first, Middlesex, appeared in that year and was followed in 1594 by the description of Essex to which I shall come shortly. His county surveys, or 'chorographical descriptions' as he called them were published under the title *Speculum Britanniae*. That concerning Essex was printed by the Camden Society in 1840[4] having until then remained in its original manuscript form. Other manuscript county maps and surveys had been produced by Norden, for example Northamptonshire in 1591 and Hertfordshire in 1598, but most, like that of Essex, were not published for lack of finance., The maps he produced for William Camden's finest work, *Britannia*, were included, along with others by Christopher Saxton in the edition of 1607. This pioneering work was published in 13 editions between 1586–1800 and aimed, according to the Preface, to 'acquaint the World with the ancient State of Britain'.[5] It should be noted that John Speed, whose maps of 1610 were superior to those in *Britannia*, augmented the Essex map otherwise captioned as 'Described by John Norden'. Much of Norden's work has been lost but it is known that he produced maps and surveys of Surrey, Hampshire, Suffolk, Warwickshire, Norfolk, Kent, Cornwall, the Isle of Wight and the Channel Islands.[6]

'This simple discription'

In the surviving manuscript and printed versions of Norden's *Description of Essex* it is variously described by him. In that dedicated to the Earl of Essex as 'exact'; in that for Lord Burghley, a former Lieutenant of Essex, as 'this simple discription of Essex'. Four versions, presumably all deriving from a common but undiscovered draft are known. The extant papers are in the royal archives, at Hatfield House, the British Library and, the most detailed, at the Essex Record Office. The latter manuscript had lain, undiscovered, among the muniments of the Mildmay family in the Somerset Record Office until 1955 when it was transferred to Chelmsford. The family were strongly connected with Essex, in particular Marks at Romford.[7] The version dedicated by Norden to the Earl of Essex with a stilted and tedious address, in a style prevalent in such, was copied in manuscript by H. J. Ellis and presented to the Bournemouth Natural History Society by him in 1922. This was the British Library copy which is a folio edition.[8]

From the document at Chelmsford we may glean, through Norden's careful survey and logical presentation 'all necessarie particulars concerning the state and qualletie of the Countye of Essex'. These include, not only the general map of the county, but information about the towns, parishes, hamlets and great houses. There is an alphabetical table 'spedely to finde the same in the mappe'. The geography, industries and administrative arrangements are covered and there are useful references to delight the genealogists in 'An alphabeticall catalogue of the names of the noble men, gentlemen, and others of beste

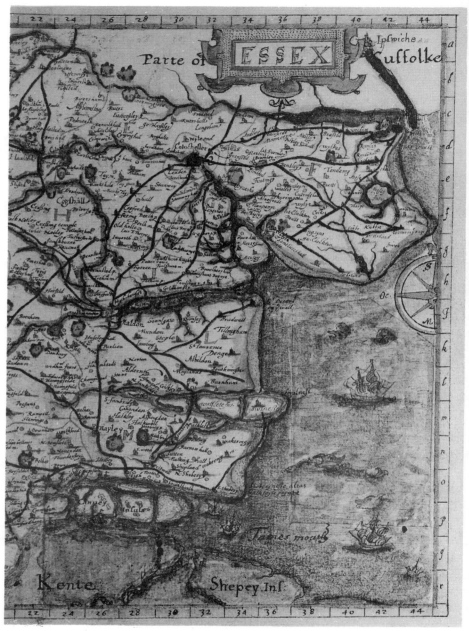

Part of Norden's map of Essex, 1594 (D/Dms P1).

accompte with there houses'. Among such we find 'Kempe Willm at Spaynes Hall' and 'Milbourne Jo' at Markes near Dunmow. In this 'simple' description is a wealth of information about Elizabethan Essex for which county historians are duly grateful.

'A lasting mark'

So far as the professional and technical aspects of map-drawing and topographical recording were concerned Norden's innovatory approaches left 'a lasting mark'.[9] He surveyed and recorded the landscapes of the English counties in which he worked in comprehensive dimensions and with intellectual discipline. His lapses into the florid prose habitually used by the antiquarians among his contemporaries and their subsequent followers can be excused for the pleasure it gives us in reading it. At the level of his technical expertise he was governed by what he found and faithfully set down.

He was the first English cartographer to employ conventional signs and symbols on maps to identify topographical features and to use a grid and grid-references on maps, techniques we now take for granted. This development is thought to have been derived from continental practice, he possibly having learned of this device from William Smith, a herald and topographer in Nuremberg.[10] Change, as always, and particularly in the matter of estate mapping was not universally welcomed. The opposition of farmers and their tenants to this in the latter part of the sixteenth century, when suspicion of the motives of the cartographers was aroused, was repudiated in Norden's *Surveyors' Dialogue*, 'very profitable for all men to peruse, but especially for Gentlemen, Farmers and Husbandmen'.[11] It was all part of the difficult struggle Norden had to establish the status of his profession and to attract patronage. He enjoyed little tangible encouragement from official sources or the Crown. The eminent patrons to whom he hopefully dedicated his work neglected him. However, he was busily employed but apparently poorly rewarded, as an estate surveyor after the accession of James I in 1603 and by 1617 he and his son were jointly surveyors to the Duchy of Cornwall. He seems to have lived at Hendon in Middlesex towards the end of his life 'in narrow circumstances'.[12] His industry and professionalism largely unrewarded, he died in poverty and obscurity in 1626.

But we, in publishing this book, may honour his work and his memory. The preambular remarks in his presentation to the Earl of Essex, nourish the virtues of the antiquarian tradition and we can rejoice in this:

'The knowledge of Antiquities is worthelie to be imbraced, for it reveyleth unto us what hath bene done by our moste ancient fathers, yet yeldeth accompte of time paste, and maketh us that now live partakers of the knowledge of things done from the beginning of the worlde. It reviveth, as it were, men that are dead. It stirreth up the foundations of ruynous and the olde decayed buildings. It findeth out the olde and ancient titles and names which cities townes castles etc. had loste. It showeth thinges past as if they were present.'[13]

I shall leave Norden with the last word in this volume of Essex essays for this extract from his *Description* evinces the spirit and dedication of this tribute to the county and John Ruggles-Brise:

'As touchinge the fertilitie of this shire thus I think that it may be called english Goshen the fatt of England, yeldinge infinite comodities excedinge as I take it any other shire in regard to the varietie of the good thinge(s) it yeldeth.'

REFERENCES

1   J. Norden, *Description of Essex*, 1594, E.R.O., D/DMs P1.
2   A. Stuart Mason, *Essex on the Map*, E.R.O., 1990.
3   R. A. Skelton, *Decorative Printed Maps of the 15th to 18th Centuries*, rev. ed., 1967, p.52.
4   J. Norden, *Speculum Britanniae Pars. Historical and Chorographical Description of the County of Essex*, *1594*, ed. H. Ellis, Camden Society, 1840.
5   B. Nurse, *The Antiquaries Journal*, vol. LXXIII, 1993, pp.158–9.
6   R. A. Skelton, *Decorative Printed Maps*, *op. cit.*, p.53.
7   F. G. Emmison and R. A. Skelton, ' "The Description of Essex" by John Norden, 1594', *Geographical Journal*, vol. CXXIII, part I, 1957, pp.37–41.
8   J. Norden, *Speculum Britanniae Pars*, E.R.O., T/A 299.
9   R. A. Skelton, *Decorative Printed Maps*, *op. cit.*, p.53.
10 R. A. Skelton, *Decorative Printed Maps*, *op. cit.*, p.52.
11 *The Art of the Map-Maker in Essex, 1566–1860*, E.R.O. Publications no. 4, 1947.
12 Sir Henry Ellis, ed., *Speculum Britanniae Pars*, *op. cit.*
13 J. Norden, E.R.O., T/A 299, *op. cit.*

Index

457